Film Review

1993-4

James Cameron-Wilson became a committed film buff when he moved to London at the age of seventeen. After a stint at the Webber Douglas Academy of Dramatic Art, he joined *What's On in London* and took over from F. Maurice Speed as cinema editor. He was also editor of *Showbiz* and commissioning editor of *Film Review* and *What's On*, and works as a consultant for several film reference books. He was a TV presenter and movie quizmaster for BSkyB, and is the author of *The Cinema of Robert De Niro*. He is now syndicated throughout England in *What's On*, and is a frequent presenter of the Radio 2 'Arts Programme'.

F. Maurice Speed began his working life as an apprentice on the *Harrow Observer*. From early on, his work reflected an interest in the cinema, and he calculates that he has now spent well over seven years watching films. He has contributed to many newspapers, journals and magazines in both Britain and America, and his books include the pre-war *Movie Cavalcade* and the later *Western Film and TV Annual*. His position as the grand old man of British film criticism was confirmed when the London Film Critics' Circle presented him in 1991 with a special award in recognition of his lifetime achievement and the 49 years over which he has now edited *Film Review*.

Film Review

1993-4
Including Video Releases

James Cameron-Wilson
and
F. Maurice Speed

Virgin

First published in Great Britain in 1993 by
VIRGIN BOOKS
an imprint of Virgin Publishing Ltd
332 Ladbroke Grove, London W10 5AH

Copyright © 1993 F. Maurice Speed and
James Cameron-Wilson

The moral right of the authors is asserted

*A catalogue record for this book is available
from the British Library*

ISBN 0 86369 792 5

Designed by Fred Price

Phototypeset by Intype Ltd, London

Printed in Great Britain by
Butler & Tanner Ltd, Frome and London

Contents

Introduction

F. Maurice Speed
*surveys the
cinematic year*

I find it perversely reassuring that, in spite of all the technical and other advances that have been made over the years, the film business still remains as crazy as ever. Sixty years ago I started paying weekly visits to the various British studios (so where have *they* all gone?), and I quickly learned that so-called 'normal' film business would send a logician into a nuthouse and a conventional accountant into permanent decline.

Where else but in Tinseltown would a writer get paid millions of dollars for an unremarkable story, only for millions more to go to a scriptwriter who probably changes it beyond recognition – and whose script is then passed to yet more scriptwriters for the final shooting script? And after all that the producer or director – or both – will probably have their say as well.

The folly doesn't end there, though. The next move is to sign up, for millions more, a bankable star, who may well give a no more than adequate performance. (And if you think I'm exaggerating, when did you last go to the movies?)

During the last few years we've heard a lot about new budget controls and that dreaded term 'rationalisation', but in reality it seems that the budget for each new blockbuster is even more inflated than its predecessor's. In fact Hollywood production costs rose by at least five per cent last year and look like exceeding that increase next year. The cost of the *average* film has now topped $30 million!

Of course, a few of these megabuck films have repaid their vast investment and been a financial success, but many, many more have been turkeys and lost fortunes for their makers. But as I say, moviemaking doesn't get any saner – or any safer for those who gamble on it.

Crazy too is the way that in order to keep to a movie's release date – possibly a fashionable and financially critical summer date – a multi-million dollar production can be hastily finished off. Movies which have been years in the making are often completed with all the rush and flurry of a daily newspaper. Peter Bart, a shrewd observer of Tinseltown, had this to say about the subject in a recent issue of *Variety*: 'One can almost hear a sadistic tour guide pointing out the sights: "Over there, folks, see the bleary sound mixers; they haven't slept in three weeks so they're screaming at their producer. Over there is a burnt-out film editor making eleventh-hour snips on a $70 million blockbuster, while his director pops aspirins and prays. Watch the distribution mavens sip Maslox while they shepherd grumpy exhibitors into hastily called screenings of films they'd expected to see months earlier. For a final thrill, take a look at the army mobilised to make middle-of-the-night deliveries of wet prints to edgy theatre managers." At the end of it all, any reasonable observer might ask "Is this the way to run a business?" Everyone out here would chorus "No", but they'll still be doing it the same way next spring!'

But the craziness maybe makes a kind of sense when you face the fact that moviemakers are tempting larger audiences than ever to see their films. in the UK alone, cinema admissions in 1992 increased to 102.5 million – the eighth year running when there has been an increase from the low point of 55 million in 1984. In the first quarter of 1993, admissions in the UK have shown a further rise of eleven per cent, and nearly 28 million tickets were sold in this period. (Interestingly, while several modestly budgeted British films – such as *Howards End* and *The Crying Game* – have drawn large audiences in the US and elsewhere, they haven't done comparably well in the UK.)

But the most significant news continues to be that from the video market. Quite simply, the UK video market is now (according to *Variety*) three times more profitable than the cinema business, with a staggering total value in 1992 of £900 million.

With figures like that, there's no disputing the continuing demand. And for all the craziness, excess, lapses of judgement and occasional downright failures from the studios and the stars, the fact remains – whether it's at home or in the cinema, we all love the movies.

Top Twenty Box-Office Hits

1 Basic Instinct
2 The Bodyguard
3 Lethal Weapon 3
4 Batman Returns
5 Home Alone 2: Lost in New York
6 Beauty and the Beast
7 Bram Stoker's Dracula
8 Wayne's World
9 Indecent Proposal
10 Sister Act
11 A Few Good Men
12 Alien 3
13 Beethoven
14 The Hand That Rocks the Cradle
15 The Jungle Book
16 Patriot Games
17 Unforgiven
18 Forever Young
19 Sommersby
20 Far and Away

Michael Douglas and Sharon Stone in Basic Instinct

Michael Keaton in Batman Returns

Whitney Houston and Kevin Costner in The Bodyguard

Mel Gibson and Danny Glover in Lethal Weapon 3

Macaulay Culkin in Home Alone 2: Lost in New York

Top Ten Box-Office Stars

STAR OF THE YEAR

Kevin Costner

2 Mel Gibson

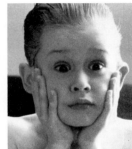

3 Michael Douglas

4 Macaulay Culkin

Without the aid of sex or a numeral in the title, Kevin Costner pulled in the crowds yet again, making *The Bodyguard* his eighth hit in six years. Of course the popularity of the film's No. 1 song 'I Will Always Love You' (courtesy of co-star Whitney Houston) helped the movie's high profile – but then Kevin's heard this before (remember last year's hit song from *Robin Hood*?). Mel Gibson, who previously held the fourth and fifth position in this chart (in 1989–90 and 1990–1, respectively), snatches second place due to the phenomenal success of *Lethal Weapon 3* and the surprisingly healthy gross of *Forever Young*. And, thanks to the continuing success of *Basic Instinct* in the second half of 1992, Michael Douglas moves up from last year's fourth place to this year's third, while Macaulay Culkin debuts on the list owing to his continued pulling power with *Home Alone 2: Lost in New York*. This year, near-misses include Jean-Claude Van Damme, Steven Seagal, Meryl Streep, Winona Ryder and Keanu Reeves.

5 Tom Cruise

6 Whoopi Goldberg

7 Demi Moore

8 Harrison Ford

9 Clint Eastwood

10 Richard Gere

Releases of the Year

In this section you will find details of all the films released in Great Britain from 1 July 1992 to the end of June 1993 – the period covered by all the reference features in the book.

The normal abbreviations operate as follows: Dir – for Director; Pro – for Producer; Assoc Pro – for Associate Producer; Ex Pro – for Executive Producer; Pro Ex – for Production Executive; Pro Sup – for Production Supervisor; Co-Pro – for Co-Producer; Pro Co-Ord – for Production Co-ordinator; Ph – for Photographer; Ed – for Editor; Art – for Art Director; Pro Des – for Production Designer; M – for Music; and a few others which will be obvious.

Abbreviations for the names of film companies are also pretty obvious when used, such as Fox for 20th Century-Fox, Rank for Rank Film Distributors, and UIP for Universal International Pictures. Where known, the actual production company is given first, the releasing company last.

When it comes to nationality of the film, you will find that this is noted wherever possible – those films without any mention of country of origin can usually be taken as being American – but in these days of increasing international co-productions between two, three or even four countries it is sometimes difficult to sort out where the premier credit is due.

Unless otherwise specified (i.e. black-and-white), it can be taken that the film is made in Technicolor or a similar process.

Censorship certificates: U represents films suitable for persons of any age; PG (Parental Guidance) represents films which some parents might consider unsuitable for their children; 12 or 15 means no persons under that age will be admitted; and films certified with an 18 (approximately the old 'X' certificate) means that nobody under that age will be admitted to the cinema while that film is showing. 'No cert' means that no certificate has been issued by the initial showing of the film but this does not mean that one will not subsequently be issued.

Films are reviewed by James Cameron-Wilson, with Charles Bacon, Jeremy Clarke, Marianne Gray, Karen Krizanovich, Frederick Deeps Malone and Simon Rose. Each review is followed by its writer's initials.

Some kind of hero: Bernie LaPlante (Dustin Hoffman) (left) at the scene of his greatest hour, in Stephen Frears's riveting Accidental Hero *(from Columbia Tri-Star)*

Accidental Hero

(US: *Hero*.) What if a miserable old sod did something heroic because he was in the right place at the right time? And what if a gracious, charming derelict took the credit for the deed? And what if the latter's charisma and subsequent media stardom made people want to be better because of it? And what if he was rewarded with a cheque for $1 million? Stephen Frears' genuinely funny and provocative satire tackles the media, humanity and the complexity of heroism with bold, entertaining strokes, while Chevy Chase's cynical asides (as a TV chief) dispel any notions of burgeoning corn. *Accidental Hero* is also a deeply moving story, as we gradually warm to Dustin Hoffman's insufferable anti-hero, a man so grumpy that nobody could believe him capable of chivalry. It is Andy Garcia's hypnotic imposter who makes a more palatable Lionheart for

public consumption, which throws into question our whole concept of good and evil and the marketability of truth. As Garcia admits, 'We're all heroes – if you catch us at the right moment.' [JC-W]

Cast: Dustin Hoffman (Bernie LaPlante), Geena Davis (Gale Gayley), Andy Garcia (John Bubber), Joan Cusack (Evelyn), Kevin J. O'Connor (Chucky), Maury Chaykin (Winston), Susie Cusack (Donna O'Day), James Madio (Joey LaPlante), Dan Healy (George Bush), Margery Jane Ross (Barbara Bush), Stephen Tobolowsky, Christian Clemenson, Tom Arnold, Warren Berlinger, Cady Huffman, Richard Riehle, Daniel Leroy Baldwin, Don S. Davis, Darrell Larson, Harry Northup, Lance Kinsey, Marita Geraghty, Vito D'Ambrosio, Darryl Davis, I. M. Hobson, James Callahan, Chevy Chase, Fisher Stevens, Edward Herrmann.
Dir: Stephen Frears. Pro: Laura Ziskin. Ex Pro: Joseph M. Caracciolo. Screenplay: David Webb Peoples; from a story by Peoples, Ziskin and Alvin Sargent. Ph: Oliver Stapleton. Ed: Mick Audsley. Pro Des: Dennis Gassner. M: George Fenton; 'Heart of a Hero' sung by Luther Vandross. Costumes: Richard Hornung. Sound: Jerry Ross. (Columbia Tri-Star.) Rel: 16 April 1993. 117 mins. Cert 15.

Alien 3

Take away the human interest and lived-in production design, slow down the pace and reduce the number of aliens to one, and you have one hell of a disappointing sequel. The bitch may be back, but she's lost her organic good looks – which no amount of drool can hide. First-time director David Fincher spent over $50 million on this 'intimate' thriller, encouraging his cast to overact (Brian Glover, as the head of the penal colony, is embarrassing), while shredding the narrative into an MTV promo. Only Elliot Goldenthal's moody, innovative score is exceptional. [JC-W]

Cast: Sigourney Weaver (Ellen Ripley), Charles S. Dutton (Dillon), Charles Dance (Clemens), Paul McGann (Golic), Brian Glover (Andrews), Ralph Brown (Aaron), Lance Henriksen (Bishop II), Danny Webb, Christopher John Fields, Holt McCallany, Chris Fairbank, Vincenzo Nicoli, Pete Postlethwaite, Clive Mantle, Peter Guinness, Philip Davis, Niall Buggy.
Dir: David Fincher. Pro: Gordon Carroll, David Giler and Walter Hill. Ex Pro: Ezra Swerdlow. Co-Pro: Sigourney Weaver. Screenplay: Giler, Hill and Larry Ferguson; based on a story by Vincent Ward, in turn

The bitch is back: Charles S. Dutton battles the iffy special effects in David Fincher's indifferent sequel, Alien 3 *(from Fox)*

based on characters created by Dan O'Bannon and Ronald Shusett. Ph: Alex Thomson. Ed: Terry Rawlings. Pro Des: Norman Reynolds. M: Elliot Goldenthal. Costumes: Bob Ringwood and David Perry. Visual Effects: Richard Edlund. Sound: Tony Dawe. (Brandywine–Fox.) Rel: 21 August 1992. 110 mins. Cert 18.

Alive

On Friday, 13 October 1972, an aeroplane carrying a Uruguayan rugby team crashed into the Andes. Out of 45 passengers and crew, 27 survived with bruises, bleeding, broken bones and difficulties adjusting to the high altitude. When no signs of rescue became apparent, the freezing, starving survivors were forced to do the unspeakable to stay alive – they ate their dead. An extraordinary story based on the non-fictional best-seller by Piers Paul Read, *Alive* is harrowing, to be sure, but never gratuitous, and is a hymn to the strength and spirit of man. Highlights include the plane crash itself, and the pathetic celebration of a birthday with a pack of ice crowned by a lit cigarette. To guarantee accuracy (down to the brand of chocolate they ate), real-life survivor Nando Parrado acted as technical advisor, and the film was shot in sequence while the cast submitted themselves to a medically supervised low-fat diet (the 'survivors' diet') – for four months. The story was previously filmed in 1976, in the exploitative Mexican feature *Survive!* [JC-W]

Cast: Ethan Hawke (Nando Parrado), Vincent Spano (Antonio Balbi), Josh Hamilton (Roberto Canessa), Bruce Ramsay (Carlitos Paez), John Haymes Newton (Tintin), David Kriegel (Gustavo Zerbino), Kevin Breznahan (Roy Harley), Sam Behrens (Javier Methol), Illeana Douglas (Lilliana Methol), Ele Keats (Susana Parrado), Jack Noseworthy, Christian Meoli, Jake Carpenter, Michael de Lorenzo, Jose Zuniga, Danny Nucci, Jerry Wasserman, Jan D'Arcy, John Malkovich (narrator).

Dir: Frank Marshall. Pro: Robert Watts

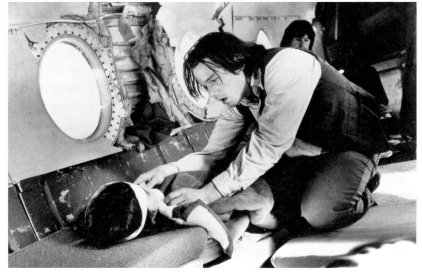

Staying Alive*: Susan Parrado and Ethan Hawke, as sister and brother, in the wreck of the notorious Fairchild F-227 (from UIP)*

Bridge over troubled water: the captivating Juliette Binoche in Leos Carax's stunning exercise in epic surrealism, Les Amants du Pont-Neuf *(from Artificial Eye)*

and Kathleen Kennedy. Co-Pro: Bruce Cohen. Screenplay: John Patrick Shanley; from the book by Piers Paul Read. Ph: Peter James. Ed: Michael Kahn and William Goldenberg. Pro Des: Norman Reynolds. M: James Newton Howard; 'Ave Maria' sung by Aaron Neville. Costumes: Jennifer Parsons. Sound: Eric Batut. (Paramount–UIP.) Rel: 30 April 1993. 126 mins. Cert 15.

Les Amants du Pont-Neuf – Lovers on the Pont-Neuf

Paris; 1991. Michèle (Juliette Binoche) is a beautiful 24-year-old painter slowly going blind. Alex (Denis Lavant) is a crabby vagrant living on the Pont-Neuf, which has been closed for repairs. Against the odds, the couple meet on the street and fall in love. As a piece of filmmaking, this is a remarkable picture, chock-a-block with magnificent set pieces, intercut with stark, *cinéma vérité* footage of the underbelly of Paris. At once a celebration of life and hope, the film is also a commanding picture of the anguish of love and commitment. Due to setbacks and an injury incurred by Lavant a week before shooting, *Les Amants* has become one of the most expensive French films ever made. After permission was granted to shoot on the Pont-Neuf, the bridge had to be reconstructed in a studio when the

film was delayed. The result is a spellbinding cross between the authentic and the surreal. [JC-W]

Cast: Juliette Binoche (Michèle), Denis Lavant (Alex), Klaus-Michael Gruber (Hans).
   Dir and Screenplay: Leos Carax. Pro: Christian Fechner. Ex Pro: Herve Truffaut and Albert Prevost. Ph: Jean-Yves Escoffier. Ed: Nelly Quettier. Art: Michel Vandestien. Costumes: Robert Nardone. Sound: Henri Morelle. (Films A2–Artificial Eye.) Rel: 11 September 1992. 125 mins. Cert 18.

Annabelle Partagée

Paris; today. Here we go again: another of those arty, rambling and pointless exercises in Gallic *cinéma vérité* and *amour fou*. This one is peppered with close-ups, off-centred shots and under-lit interiors to add to the pretension. Only notable in that it is the first 18 certificate film to show an ejaculating penis. [JC-W]

Cast: Delphine Zingg (Annabelle), Francois Marthouret (Richard), Jean-Claude Adelin (Luca).
   Dir: Francesca Comencini. No other credits available. (Gala.) Rel: 29 January 1993. 80 mins. Cert 18.

Army of Darkness

Third in the *Evil Dead* series, in which Ash (Bruce Campbell again) is transported back to 13th-century England to confront a legion of skeletons. Interestingly, the first *Evil Dead* was banned on video, the sequel was released with an 18 certificate, and this entry (subtitled *The Medieval Dead*) gets away with a 15. Although inventively yucky at times, the film's Pythonesque self-parody alleviates the horror, as do the loopy special effects

The medieval dead: Embeth Davidtz finds herself with a date from hell in Sam Raimi's outlandish Army of Darkness *(from Guild)*

and jokey dialogue (skeleton to Ash: 'I have a bone to pick with you'). N.B. Sam Raimi's original apocalyptic ending has been changed to the current, more up-beat one. [JC-W]

Cast: Bruce Campbell (Ash), Embeth Davidtz (Sheila), Marcus Gilbert (Arthur), Richard Grove (Duke Henry), Bridget Fonda (Linda), Ian Adercrombie, Michael Earl Reid, Timothy Patrick Quill, Patricia Tallman, Theodore Raimi, Don Campbell, Charlie Campbell, Harley Cokeliss, William Lustig, Ivan Raimi, Bernard Rose.
  Dir: Sam Raimi. Pro: Robert Tapert. Co-Pro: Bruce Campbell. Screenplay: Sam Raimi and Ivan Raimi. Ph: Bill Pope. Ed: Bob Murawski and R. O. C. Sandstorm. Pro Des: Tony Tremblay. M: Joseph LoDuca; 'March of the Dead' theme by Danny Elfman. Costumes: Ida Gearon. Sound: Alan Howarth. (Renaissance Pictures/Introvision Int–Guild.) Rel: 11 June 1993. 89 mins. Cert 15.

As You Like It

Modern-day, shoestring production of Shakespeare's romantic comedy, from the director of the exemplary *Little Dorrit* and *The Fool*. Using the empty, cavernous hallway of an old mansion as the court of Duke Frederick, and a

'No jewel like Rosalind'?: Emma Croft disguised as a boy in Christine Edzard's woefully misconceived As You Like It *(from Squirrel Films)*

Bad company: Phil Daniels and Stephen Rea discuss the problems of housing improvements in Les Blair's ticklish Bad Behaviour *(from First Independent)*

London wasteland for the Forest of Arden, the film's visual drabness is only topped by its verbal flatness. The acting is decidedly patchy, while Rosalind referring to her denims as doublet and hose is just plain daft. [JC-W]

Cast: James Fox (Jaques), Cyril Cusack (Adam), Andrew Tiernan (Orlando/Oliver), Celia Bannerman (Celia), Emma Croft (Rosalind), Griff Rhys Jones (Touchstone), Roger Hammond (Corin/Le Beau), Don Henderson (Duke Senior/Duke Frederick), Miriam Margolyes (Audrey), Ewen Bremner (Silvius), Valerie Gogan (Phebe), Cate Fowler, Arthur Kelly, Robin Meredith, John Tams, Bernard Padden, Tony Armatrading, Murray Melvin, Jonathan Cecil, Michael Mears.
  Dir and Ed: Christine Edzard. Ex Pro: Richard Goodwin. Screenplay: William Shakespeare. Ph: Robin Vidgeon. Pro Des: Sands Films. M: Michel Sanvoisin. Costumes: Barbara Sonnex and Marion Weise. Sound: Anthony Sprung. (George Reinhart/Sands Films/Aim Prods–Squirrel Films.) Rel: 9 October 1992. 114 mins. Cert U.

Bad Behaviour

Kentish Town, London; 1992. Ellie is going through a premature mid-life crisis; her husband, Gerry, is quietly falling for a young colleague, Sophie; and their friend, Howard Spink, is ripping them off. These are just three of the story strands running through this improvised, gently amusing comedy about domestic crisis in North London. But there are belly laughs, too, and more than a little sadness. [JC-W]

Cast: Stephen Rea (Gerry McAllister), Sinead Cusack (Ellie McAllister), Philip Jackson (Howard Spink), Clare Higgins (Jessica Kennedy), Phil Daniels (Roy and Ray Nunn), Mary Jo Randle (Winifred Turner), Saira Todd (Sophie Bevan), Amanda Boxer, Luke Blair, Joe Coles, Tamlin Howard, Emily Hill, Ian Flintoff, Kenneth Hadley.
  Dir: Les Blair. Pro: Sarah Curtis. Ex Pro: Sally Hibbin. Ph: Witold Stok. Ed: Martin Walsh. Pro Des: Jim Grant. M: John Altman. Costumes: Janty Yates. Sound: Bruce White. (Parallax Pictures/Channel 4/British Screen–First Independent.) Rel: 28 May 1993. 104 mins. Cert 15.

Bad Lieutenant

New York City; 1992. Arriving at the scene of the murder of two teenage girls, a police lieutenant casually discusses baseball with his colleagues. Shortly afterwards, he sits back naked watching a prostitute gag another from behind with a scarf. And later still, hefting his official badge, he pockets the $500 stolen from a late-night supermarket. Beyond these distractions, the bad lieutenant drinks heavily, snorts stolen cocaine, sexually humiliates young women and swears at his children. Abel Ferrara, described by actor Larry Fishburne as

Blessed by evil: Frankie Thorn and Harvey Keitel in Abel Ferrara's controversial, numbing Bad Lieutenant *(from Guild)*

'the poet gangster of the cinema', pads out his story with the brutal rape of a nun who forgives her attackers. It is her selfless act that proves to be the turning point in the lieutenant's descent into hell. Thanks to Harvey Keitel's committed performance, this is a grimly compelling character study with something to offend everyone. Needless to say, the film ran into censorship troubles in the States. [JC-W]

Cast: Harvey Keitel (the bad lieutenant), Frankie Thorn (the nun), Zoe Tamerlaine Lund (Zoe), Anthony Ruggiero (Lite), Paul Hipp (Jesus Christ), Victor Argo, Paul Calderone, Leonard Thomas, Robin Burrows, Victoria Bastel, Eddie Daniels, Bianca Bakija.

Dir: Abel Ferrara. Pro: Edward R. Pressman and Mary Kane. Ex Pro: Ronna B. Wallace and Patrick Wachsberger. Line Pro: Diana Phillips. Screenplay: Ferrara and Zoe Tamerlaine Lund. Ph: Ken Kelsch. Ed: Anthony Redman. Pro Des: Charles Lagola. M: Joe Delia. Costumes: David Sanaryn. (Odyssey/Live Entertainment–Guild.) Rel: 19 February 1993. 96 mins. Cert 18.

Batman Returns

Messy, bloated, undisciplined sequel to the 1989 phenomenon that made Jack Nicholson a very, very rich man. This time there's no Joker, Robin has been left on the cutting-room floor and it's up to the Caped Crusader, the Penguin and Catwoman to save the movie. Sadly, Danny DeVito's grotesque birdman lacks the sheer evil charisma of Nicholson, although Michelle Pfeiffer is a sharper romantic foil to Bruce Wayne that was Kim Basinger's Vicky Vale. The problem is, it is never satisfactorily explained why Michelle's bumbling Selina Kyle becomes Catwoman in the first place. And what has she got against Batman? A lack of logic dogs the film from the word go and the plot – when you can follow it – is virtually non-existent. The effects, too, are surprisingly humdrum (considering the film cost $80 million), while Michael Keaton does nothing to make his part more interesting (if anything, he transforms Bruce Wayne into an absolute dweeb). The film has also lost its sense of time, place and fantasy – witness Wayne's contemplation that he could become compared to Norman Bates and Ted Bundy. *They know about Bundy in Gotham City?* The biggest disappointment of the year. [JC-W]

Cast: Michael Keaton (Batman/Bruce Wayne), Danny DeVito (Penguin/Oswald Cobblepott), Michelle Pfeiffer (Catwoman/Selina Kyle), Christopher Walken (Max Schreck), Michael Gough (Alfred), Michael Murphy (Mayor), Cristi Conaway, Andrew Bryniarski, Pat Hingle, Vincent

Battier and battier: Michael Keaton as the Caped Crusader in Tim Burton's chaotic adult fantasy, Batman Returns *(from Warner)*

Schiavelli, Steve Witting, Jan Hooks, John Strong, Rick Zumwalt, Paul Reubens, Diane Salinger.

Dir: Tim Burton. Pro: Burton and Denise Di Novi. Ex Pro: Jon Peters, Peter Guber, Benjamin Melniker and Michael Uslan. Screenplay: Daniel Waters; from a story by Waters and Sam Hamm, based upon characters created by Bob Kane. Ph: Stefan Czapsky. Ed: Chris Lebenzon. Pro Des: Bo Welch. M: Danny Elfman; *Face to Face* sung by Siouxsie & The Banshees. Costumes: Bob Ringwood and Mary Vogt. Penguin Make-up and SFX: Stan Winston. Sound: Richard L. Anderson and David Stone. (Warner.) Rel: 10 July 1992. 127 mins. Cert 12.

Beauty and the Beast

Walt Disney's phenomenally successful animated version of Mme de Beaumont's famous story, *La Belle et la Bete*. The studio has cranked up the sentimentality a notch or two, added some glorious songs and brought in a team of *eight* writers to fine-tune the story. In this version Belle is a simple American girl living in a provincial French town where she is courted by Gaston, a brazen hunk with terrific

Never judge a book by its cover: Belle and her brute in Disney's resounding triumph, Beauty and the Beast

forearms. He's also terribly handsome, rude and conceited. Meanwhile, at a castle deep in the woods, a massive beast has captured Belle's father, and only releases him when she offers herself as hostage. The Beast has a terrible temper, but underneath his macho bravura he's a far more honest chap than Gaston. Belle is due to fall in love, so who will she choose? The animation, the camera moves, the background detail, the humour, the Oscar-winning music and, above all, the timeless message of the story all help to make this one of Disney's true instant classics. It is also the first cartoon ever to be nominated for an Academy Award as best film. [JC-W]

Voices: Paige O'Hara (Belle), Robby Benson (Beast), Richard White (Gaston), Jerry Orbach (Lumiere), David Ogden Stiers (Cogsworth/Narrator), Angela Lansbury (Mrs Potts), Bradley Michael Pierce (Chip, the teacup), Rex Everhart (Maurice), Jesse Corti (Le Fou), Hal Smith (Philippe), Jo Anne Worley (Wardrobe), Mary Kay Bergman (Bimbette).

Dir: Gary Trousdale and Kirk Wise. Pro: Don Hahn. Ex Pro: Howard Ashman. Animated Screenplay: Linda Wollverton. Ed: John Carnochan. Art: Brian McEntee. Songs: Ashman and Alan Menken. M: Menken. Sound: Michael Farrow and John Richards. (Walt Disney–Warner.) Rel: 9 October 1992. 85 mins. Cert U.

Love me, love my dog: Chris, in his first starring role, as Beethoven, *the canine answer to John Candy – from UIP*

Beethoven

First it was Tom Hanks, now Charles Grodin finds himself falling in love with a grotesque dog that he loathes. Beethoven is a photogenic, loyal, drooling, all-too-human 13-stone St Bernard who adopts the suburban Newton family. Father (Grodin) objects, but Mom and the children love him, and sentimentality will out. Naturally, Beethoven turns out to be a hero, but is dogged by Dean Jones's evil, ruthless vet. Artless, cute entertainment that younger children should love. Grodin works wonders with his limited material, upstaging Beethoven at every turn. [JC-W]

Cast: Charles Grodin (George Newton), Bonnie Hunt (Alice Newton), Dean Jones (Dr Varnick), Chris (Beethoven), Nicholle Tom (Ryce Newton), Christopher Castile (Ted Newton), Sarah Rose Karr (Emily Newton), David Duchovny (Brad), Patricia Heaton (Brie), Oliver Platt, Stanley Tucci, Laurel Cronin, O-Lan Jones, Nancy Fish, Robi Davidson, Chris Little.

Dir: Brian Levant. Pro: Joe Medjuck and Michael C. Gross. Ex Pro: Ivan Reitman. Screenplay: Edmond Dantes and Amy Holden Jones. Ph: Victor J. Kemper. Ed: Sheldon Kahn and William D. Gordean. Pro Des: Alex Tavoularis. M: Randy Edelman. Costumes: Gloria Gresham. Sound: Charles Wilborn. (Universal–UIP.) Rel: 24 July 1992. 87 mins. Cert U.

Scenes from a courtship: Pernilla August, Samuel Fröler and Björn Kjellman in Bille August's masterful The Best Intentions *(from Artificial Eye)*

Being at Home with Claude

Montreal; 1992. Dynamic, well-acted film version of René-Daniel Dubois' two-hander play, in which a street hustler confesses the murder of his lover to an elderly, uncomprehending police inspector. Although wordy, the film exudes a considerable cinematic power thanks to Jean Beaudin's motive interpretation. [CB]

Cast: Roy Dupuis (Yves), Jacques Godin (Inspector), Jean-François Pichette (Claude), Gaston Lepage, Hugo Dubé, Johanne-Marie Tremblay.

Dir and Screenplay: Jean Beaudin. Pro: Louise Gendron. Assoc Pro (NFB): Doris Girard. Ph: Thomas Vamos. Ed: André Corriveau. Art: François Séguin. M: Richard Grégoire. Costumes: Louise Jobin. Sound: Marcel Pothier. (Les Productions du Cerf/National Film Board of Canada–Out On a Limb.) Rel: 28 May 1993. 85 mins. Cert 18.

Best of the Best 2

The 1989 *Best of the Best* was so bad that it went straight to video, but it nevertheless did enough business to prompt the theatrical release of this flat, mundane sequel. The three karate champions of the original – played by Eric Roberts, Christopher Penn and Phillip Rhee – return to fight another day, but when Penn is killed in an illegal combat tournament, his buddies knuckle down to avenge his death. But who cares? [CB]

Cast: Eric Roberts (Alex Grady), Phillip Rhee (Tommy Lee), Edan Gross (Walter Grady), Ralph Moeller (Brakus), Christopher Penn (Travis Brickley), Sonny Landham (James), Wayne Newton (Weldon), Meg Foster (Sue), Nanah Khalsa, Simon Rhee, Myung Kue Kim, Mike Genovese, Claire Stansfield, Nicholas Worth, Rusty Meyers, Jonathan Strauss.

Dir: Robert Radler. Pro: Peter E. Strauss and Phillip Rhee. Co-Pro: Marlon Staggs and Deborah Scott. Ex Pro: Strauss and Frank Giustra. Screenplay: Max Strom and John Allen Nelson; based on characters created by Paul Levine. Ph: Fred Tammes. Ed: Bert Lovitt. Pro Des: Gary Frutkoff. M: David Michael Frank; num-bers performed by Raye Crusader, Public Nuisance, Jeff Steele, etc. Costumes: Mona May. Choreography: George Alexander. Sound: Steve Flick and John Dunn. (Picture Securities–Entertainment.) Rel: 9 April 1993. 100 mins. Cert 18.

The Best Intentions – Den Goda Viljan

Sweden; 1909–18. Henrik Bergman is a dour, shy theology student who meets his match when he falls in love with the spoilt, headstrong Anna Akerblom, daughter of an aristocratic family. The lovers' mothers both disapprove of the liaison, reflecting the rigid class system of Sweden at that time. Henrik and Anna are in fact the parents of the filmmaker Ingmar Bergman, who wrote this screenplay based on a smattering of facts, remembered anecdotes and fictitious amendments. The director, Bille August, describes his film as a 'psychological, spectacular epic about love's many complicated, subtle and poetic paths to human symbiosis'. Although a bit of a slog (it runs to three hours), many of the film's scenes linger in the memory and are masterfully executed by August, who won his second Palme d'Or for this, following on the 1989 prize for his *Pelle the Conqueror*. [JC-W]

Cast: Samuel Froler (Henrik Bergman), Pernilla August (Anna), Max Von Sydow (Johan Akerblom), Ghita Norby (Karin Akerblom), Lennart Hjulstrom (managing director Nordenson), Mona Malm (Alma Bergman), Lena Endre (Frida Strandberg), Bjorn Kjellman (Ernst Akerblom), Hans Alfredson (Reverend Gransjo), Anita Bjork (Queen Viktoria), Elias Ringquist (Petrus Farg), Keve Hjelm, Borje Ahlstedt, Lena T. Hansson.
  Dir: Bille August. Pro: Lars Bjalkeskog. Ex Pro: Ingrid Dahlberg. Screenplay: Ingmar Bergman. Ph: Jorgen Persson. Ed: Janus Billeskov Jansen. Pro Des: Anna Asp. M: Stefan Nilsson. Costumes: Ann-Mari Anttila. (Sveriges TV/SVT1 Drama/Film Four Int./ZDF/RAIDUE/La Sept/DR/YLE 2/NRK/RUV–Artificial Eye.) Rel: 3 July 1992. 180 mins. Cert 12.

Big Girls Don't Cry... They Get Even
See *Stepkids*.

Bitter Moon
An unrelenting study of emotional sadism, *Bitter Moon* is, by turns, repugnant, embarrassing and unintentionally hilarious. Re-exploring the claustrophobic, obsessive and carnal world of *Last Tango in Paris*, director-writer Roman Polanski has layered his sexual chronicle with a mini-series gloss and a fair amount of black humour. Most of the latter is at the expense of Hugh Grant, who plays the squirming, passive witness to a tale of extraordinary psychological cruelty. Set aboard a luxury liner headed for the Orient, the film stars a manic, wheelchair-bound Peter Coyote who regales his uncomfortable, frightfully English guest (Grant) with the story of his sado-masochist marriage. The film's ultimate downfall lies in the casting of Polanski's wife – the frequently naked Emmanuelle Seigner – in the central role of Coyote's (and Grant's) temptress. Mme Seigner is frankly not up to the dramatic demands of the film, while her weight gain – since her memorable appearance in Polanski's *Frantic* four years previously – is unfortunate. [JC-W]

Cast: Peter Coyote (Oscar), Emmanuelle Seigner (Mimi), Hugh Grant (Nigel), Kris-

tin Scott Thomas (Fiona), Victor Bannerjee (Mr Singh), Luca Vellani, Boris Bergman, Sophie Patel, Nathalie Galan, Jim-Adhi Limas, Olivia Brunaux, Charlene.
  Dir and Pro: Roman Polanski. Ex Pro: Robert Benmussa. Co-Pro: Alain Sarde. Screenplay: Polanski, Gerard Brach and John Brownjohn; based on the novel *Lunes de Fiel* by Pascal Bruckner. Ph: Tonino Delli Colli. Ed: Herve de Luze. Pro Des: Willy Holt and Gerard Viard. M: Vangelis. Costumes: Jackie Budin. Sound: Daniel Brisseau. (RP Prods/Timothy Burrill Prods/Canal Plus–Columbia Tri-Star.) Rel: 2 October 1992. 135 mins. Cert 18.

Blue Ice
There is a precarious thrill in watching actor-producer Michael Caine, now 59, running round London, clambering over roofs and leaping on to moving vehicles. Of course, with no allowances made in the script for his age, the man is far too old for this sort of thing – even if he *is* tastefully lit while bedding Sean Young. Still, Caine is an engaging presence on his old turf of 'sarf' London, playing a jazz-club owner and former hit man who gets into all sorts of trouble when

Sean Young and Michael's older: Ms Young and Mr Caine in an old-fashioned web of intrigue on the streets of the Big Smoke, in Blue Ice *(from Guild)*

he falls for a glacial American beauty (Ms Young). The familiarity of the plot-line is compensated for by some unusual location work and a humorous, literate script. [JC-W]

Cast: Michael Caine (Harry Anders), Sean Young (Stacy Mansdorf), Ian Holm (Sir Hector), Bobby Short (Buddy), Alun Armstrong (Detective Sgt Osgood), Jack Shepherd (Stevens), Alan MacNaughton (Lewis Mansdorf), Todd Boyce (Kyle Bellamy), Bob Hoskins (Sam Garcia), Sam Kelly, Philip Davis, Patricia Hayes, Peter Gordon, Oliver Haden, Roger Sloman, Dave Green, Charlie Watts.
  Dir: Russell Mulcahy. Pro: Martin Bregman and Michael Caine. Ex Pro: Gary Levinson. Co-Pro: Louis A. Stroller. Screenplay: Ron Hutchinson; based on a character created by Ted Allbeury. Ph: Denis Crossan. Ed: Seth Flaum. Pro Des: Grant Hicks. M: Michael Kamen. Costumes: Les Lansdown. Sound: Dave Weathers. (M & M Prods–Guild.) Rel: 9 October 1992. 105 mins. Cert 15.

Gospel truth: Tim Robbins as the ruthless, calculating Bob Roberts *(from Rank)*

Bob Roberts

Borrowing the mockumentary format of *This Is Spinal Tap*, actor-director-writer-songwriter-singer Tim Robbins sends up the political election circus of America with his teeth bared. Casting himself in the title role of a folk singer cum Wall Street multi-millionaire who campaigns to become governor of Pennsylvania, Robbins brings a new edge to his usually dull-witted persona and displays a formidable talent as filmmaker. Bob Roberts is an extreme right-winger who believes in making the individual rich ('we'll cut taxes, we'll cut spending'), in prayer, in the media and in more bombs. Roberts's campaign is a dirty one, as he slings accusations of alcoholism and sexual infidelity at his avuncular opponent (Gore Vidal, in a casting coup). The movie first examines the whiter-than-white media personality of the campaigner and, then, in a series of incidental revelations, exposes the dirt under the carpet. Shot for a mere $4 million, *Bob Roberts* boasts a string of star cameos and some uncanny parallels to the all-too-real US election of '92 (even though the screenplay was written five years earlier). [JC-W]

Cast: Tim Robbins (Bob Roberts), Giancarlo Esposito (Bugs Raplin), Ray Wise (Chet MacGregor), Brian Murray (Terry Manchester), Gore Vidal (Senator Brickley Paiste), Rebecca Jenkins (Delores Perrigrew), Alan Rickman (Lukas Hart III), Harry J. Lennix, John Ottavino, Robert Stanton, Anita Gillette, Jack Black, John Cusack, Peter Gallagher, Pamela Reed, Susan Sarandon, James Spader, David Strathairn, Fred Ward, Bob Balaban, Helen Hunt, Fisher Stevens.

Dir and Screenplay: Tim Robbins. Pro: Forrest Murray. Ex Pro: Ronna Wallace, Paul Webster and Tim Bevan. Ph: Jean Lepine. Ed: Lisa Churgin. Pro Des: Richard Hoover. M: David Robbins; songs by David and Tim Robbins. Costumes: Bridget Kelly. Sound: Marshall Grupp. (Polygram/Working Title/Barry Levinson/Mark Johnson/Live Entertainment–Rank.) Rel: 11 September 1992. 103 mins. Cert 15.

Body of Evidence

Portland, Oregon; 1992. Rebecca Carlson has been left $8 million in her late lover's will and is charged with using her body as a lethal weapon. It appears that the elderly, very rich Andrew Marsh had a heart condition and during his last hours alive was mounted, handcuffed and shown naughty videos. Rebecca tells her lawyer, 'They have taken something beautiful between two people and made it ugly,' while he tells the court, 'It's not a crime to be a great lay.' Some intentional self-mockery might have lent this preposterous 'erotic thriller' a modicum of camp status, but its clumsy attempts at *film noir* and fumbling scenes of sado-masochism

Security risque: Kevin Costner (backed by Whitney Houston) in the title role of Mick Jackson's savvy, entertaining The Bodyguard *(from Warner)*

lead only to embarrassment. Willem
Dafoe, as the lawyer, has never looked
more uncomfortable, while Madonna
as the body in question is no Sharon
Stone. [JC-W]

Cast: Madonna (Rebecca Carlson), Willem
Dafoe (Frank Dulaney), Joe Mantegna
(Robert Garrett), Anne Archer (Joanne
Braslow), Julianne Moore (Sharon
Dulaney), Jurgen Prochnow (Dr Alex
Paley), Frank Langella (Jeffrey Roston),
Michael Forest (Andrew Marsh), Lillian
Lehman (Judge Burnham), Charles Halla-
han, Mark Rolston, Richard Riehle, Aaron
Corcoran, John Chandler, Stan Shaw.
   Dir: Uli Edel. Pro: Dino De Laurentiis.
Ex Pro: Stephen Deutsch and Melinda
Jason. Screenplay: Brad Mirman. Ph: Doug
Milsome. Ed: Thom Noble. Pro Des: Vic-
toria Paul. M: Graeme Revell. Costumes:
Susan Becker. Sound: Keith A. Wester.
(Guild.) Rel: 16 April 1993. 100 mins.
Cert 18.

The Bodyguard

Whether you think of him as a samurai
in a suit or as a 'self-righteous son-
of-a-bitch', bodyguard Frank Farmer
knows his job – and his job is to save
people's lives. Normally, he doesn't do
'showbusiness', but he's never recovered from that 'Reagan thing', when
he wasn't there to save the president.
Spoilt movie star/singer Rachel
Marron is unaware of the dangers Out
There, and objects to Frank getting in
the way of her life. But she needs
Frank more than she realises . . . Written as a vehicle for Steve McQueen
more than fifteen years ago, *The Bodyguard* is a slick, punchy romantic thriller that delivers the goods. Costner,
with a McQueen buzz-cut, holds the
screen well, while Whitney Houston
in her film debut is never less than
watchable. And the climax at the
Academy Awards is a real pulse-
speeder. [JC-W]

Cast: Kevin Costner (Frank Farmer),
Whitney Houston (Rachel Marron), Gary
Kemp (Sy Spector), Bill Cobbs (Bill
Devaney), Ralph Waite (Herb Farmer),
Tomas Arana (Greg Portman), Michele
Lamar Richards (Nicki Marron), Mike
Starr (Tony), Christopher Birt (Henry),
DeVaughn Nixon (Fletcher), Gerry
Bamman (Ray Court), Debbie Reynolds
(herself), Joe Urla, Tony Pierce, Charles
Keating, Robert Wuhl, Chris Connelly,
Nathaniel Parker, Bert Remsen, David
Foster.
   Dir: Mick Jackson. Pro: Lawrence
Kasdan, Jim Wilson and Kevin Costner.
Screenplay: Kasdan. Ph: Andrew Dunn.

*Sex, Madonna and S & M: the body public
and Willem Dafoe in Uli Edel's daft and
delirious* Body of Evidence *(from Guild)*

Ed: Richard A. Harris and Donn Cambern.
Pro Des: Jeffrey Beecroft. M: Alan Silvestri;
numbers performed by Whitney Houston,
the S.O.U.L. S.Y.S.T.E.M., Kenny G, John
Doe, Lisa Stansfield, Curtis Stigers, Joe
Cocker, Aaron Neville, the Allman
Brothers, and the Left Banke. Costumes:
Susan Nininger. Sound: Richard Bryce
Goodman. (Tig–Warner.) Rel: 26 Decem-
ber 1992. 130 mins. Cert 15.

Boomerang

New York; 1992. In spite of Eddie
Murphy's widely reported prima
donna behaviour on this $42 million
film, the end result is a surprisingly
engrossing, slick romantic comedy,
thanks to an eventful, witty script and
some first-class supporting performances. Eddie is Marcus Graham, a
successful marketing executive and
irresistible Romeo, who will stoop to
any tactic to get his girl. When the
ruthless, tantalising Jacqueline (Robin
Givens) becomes his boss, she turns
the tables on him, using him, abusing
him and generally treating him like a
piece of meat (one night she even
brings him flowers, and leaves money
on his bedside table). Great soundtrack, great babes, great concept.
[JC-W]

Cast: Eddie Murphy (Marcus Graham),
Robin Givens (Jacqueline), Halle Berry
(Angela), David Alan Grier (Gerard
Jackson), Martin Lawrence (Tyler), Grace

*Romeo of conceit: Eddie Murphy with a not-
so-willing conquest, Halle Berry – in
Reginald Hudlin's sleek* Boomerang *(from
UIP)*

Smart moves: dimwit Melanie Griffith outclasses John Goodman at gin rummy in Luis Mandoki's agreeable remake of Born Yesterday *(from Buena Vista)*

Jones (Strangé), Geoffrey Holder (Nelson), Eartha Kitt (Lady Eloise), Chris Rock (Bony T), Tisha Campbell (Yvonne), Lela Rochon (Christie), John Witherspoon (Mr Jackson), Bebe Drake-Massey (Mrs Jackson), John Canada Terrell, Leonard Jackson, Melvin Van Peebles, Reginald Hudlin, Warrington Hudlin.
Dir: Reginald Hudlin. Pro: Brian Grazer and Warrington Hudlin. Ex Pro: Mark Lipsky. Assoc Pro: Ray Murphy Jr. Screenplay: Barry W. Blaustein and David Sheffield; from a story by Eddie Murphy. Ph: Woody Omens. Ed: Earl Watson. Pro Des: Jane Musky. M: Marcus Miller; numbers performed by Keith Washington, George Clinton, Boyz II Men, Kenny Vaughan, James Brown, PM Dawn, etc. Costumes: Francine Jamison-Tanchuck. Sound: Russell Williams. (Paramount/Brian Grazer/Imagine–UIP.) Rel: 30 October 1992. 116 mins. Cert 15.

Born Yesterday

On a visit to Washington DC, self-made millionaire Harry Brock is becoming acutely embarrassed by the spectacular ignorance of his live-in girlfriend, Billie Dawn, who worries about the masonry during the collapse of the Eastern Bloc. So Harry hires man-about-town Paul Verrall to give Billie a crash course in conversational

acumen – and subsequently discovers he's been living with somebody smarter than he'd ever imagined. An update of the hilarious Garson Kanin play (previously filmed in 1950), the story still holds good, although the reworked dialogue lacks the sparkle of the original. A fine cast works overtime to produce the goods, but the magic only really surfaces in the final act. [JC-W]

Cast: Melanie Griffith (Billie Dawn), John Goodman (Harry Brock), Don Johnson (Paul Verrall), Edward Herrmann (Ed Devery), Max Perlich (JJ), Michael Ensign, Benjamin C. Bradlee, Sally Quinn, William Frankfather, Fred Dalton Thompson, Celeste Yarnall, Nora Dunn, Meg Wittner, William Forward, Ted Raimi, Matthew Faison, Kate McGregor-Stewart, Drew Snyder, John Achorn, Ann Hearn.
Dir: Luis Mandoki. Pro: D. Constantine Conte. Ex Pro: Stratton Leopold. Screenplay: Douglas McGrath. Ph: Lajos Koltai. Ed: Lesley Walker. Pro Des: Lawrence G. Paull. M: George Fenton; numbers performed by Jackie Wilson, Dinah Washington, Stevie Wonder, and The Dave Clark Five. Costumes: Colleen Atwood; Gianni Versace, Paul Smith. Sound: Bobby Mackston. (Hollywood Pictures–Buena Vista.) Rel: 18 June 1993. 101 mins. Cert PG.

Boxing Helena

A deranged surgeon is so in love with Helena that he saws off her legs and arms and puts her in a box to keep her to himself. This preposterous – and

appallingly acted – notion gained some notoriety when first Madonna and then Kim Basinger walked off the project. Basinger was subsequently ordered to pay Main Line Pictures $8.9 million for breaking her 'oral contract' – she subsequently filed for bankruptcy. At least she didn't have this turkey hanging round her neck. [CB]

Cast: Sherilyn Fenn (Helena), Julian Sands (Nick Cavanaugh), Bill Paxton (Ray O'Malley), Kurtwood Smith (Dr Alan Harrison), Art Garfunkel (Dr Lawrence Augustine), Betsy Clark, Bryan Smith, Nicolette Scorsese, Carl Mazzocone Sr.
Dir and Screenplay: Jennifer Chambers Lynch (daughter of David Lynch); from a story by Philippe Caland. Pro: Caland and Carl Mazzocone. Ex Pro: James R. Schaeffer and Larry Sugar. Ph: Frank Byers. Ed: David Finfer. Art: Paul Huggins. M: Graeme Revell; numbers performed by Cab Calloway, Lenny Kravitz, Tears for Fears, Enigma, and Venice. Sound: Dane A. Davis. (Main Line Pictures–Entertainment.) Rel: 18 June 1993. 105 mins. Cert 18.

Braindead

It's hard to imagine that the director of the grotesque *Bad Taste* and *Meet the Feebles* could've topped himself, but Peter Jackson has done just that with this excessive homage to *Night of the Living Dead, The Texas Chain Saw Massacre, et al.* Set in 1957 in a quiet Wellington suburb, the film chronicles

Disarmed and dangerous: a typical scene from Peter Jackson's barf bout, Braindead *(from Rank)*

Young blood: Anthony Hopkins (right) crosses a victim (Sadie Frost) of the Count, in Francis Ford Coppola's impressive Bram Stoker's Dracula *(from Columbia Tri-Star)*

the ill-fated romance of a starry-eyed shopkeeper and her hapless boyfriend, who is kept on a leash by his widowed mother. When the latter is bitten by a Sumatran rat monkey, she turns into a putrefying zombie, hungry for human flesh, and the young couple's love becomes sorely tested. As all hell breaks loose, the back-yard special effects come into their own, each topping the last for comic and emetic effect. At first just plain outrageous, the film deteriorates into a numbing freak show, although Jackson's sick invention still manages to surprise (highlights include a hypodermic needle repeatedly plunged up a nostril, a baby in a blender and a farting, disembodied rectum). [JC-W]

Cast: Timothy Balme (Lionel Cosgrove), Diana Penalver (Paquita), Elizabeth Moody (Vera Elizabeth Cosgrove), Ian Watkin (Uncle Les), Brenda Kendall (Nurse McTavish), Stuart Devenie (Father McGruder), Jed Brophy, Elizabeth Brimilcombe, Stephen Papps, Murray Keane, Harry Sinclair, Peter Jackson, Jim Booth, Frances Walsh.
  Dir: Peter Jackson. Pro: Jim Booth. Screenplay: Jackson, Stephen Sinclair and Frances Walsh. Ph: Murray Milne. Ed:

Jamie Selkirk. Pro Des: Kenneth Leonard-Jones. M: Peter Dasent; theme from *The Archers* by Arthur Wood. Costumes: Chris Elliott. Gore FX: Bob McCarron. Sound: Mike Hedges and Sam Negri. (Wingut Films–Rank.) Rel: 14 May 1993. 104 mins. Cert 18.

Bram Stoker's Dracula

Transylvania, 1497/1897; London, 1897. By being faithful to the original text, setting the story in an historical context and infusing it all with inspired state-of-the-art filmmaking, Francis Ford Coppola has managed to create a fresh, exhilarating look at a very familiar story. Gary Oldman makes a surprisingly dashing Vlad the Impaler, and is equally at home as the ancient, smirking Count condemned to centuries of emotional torment. He is a monster, yes, but has never been more sympathetically drawn, while the human beings in his way are no more than a bunch of nincompoops. Most surprising of all, this Dracula (or, as he would have it, 'Drarkhoola') is a romantic fool with a wicked sense of humour. An operatic, surreal feast for strong-stomached lovers of Grand Guignol. [JC-W]

Cast: Gary Oldman (Count Dracula/Vlad the Impaler), Winona Ryder (Mina Murray/Elisabeta), Anthony Hopkins (Professor Abraham Van Helsing), Keanu

Reeves (Jonathan Harker), Richard E. Grant (Dr Jack Seward), Cary Elwes (Lord Arthur Holmwood), Bill Campbell (Quincey P. Morris), Sadie Frost (Lucy Westenra), Tom Waits (R. M. Renfield), Monica Bellucci, Michaela Bercu, Florina Kendrick, Jay Robinson, I. M. Hobson, Laurie Franks.
  Dir: Francis Ford Coppola. Pro: Coppola, Fred Fuchs and Charles Mulvehill. Ex Pro: Michael Apted and Robert O'Connor. Screenplay and Co-Pro: James V. Hart; based on the novel by Bram Stoker. Ph: Michael Ballhaus. Ed: Nicholas C. Smith, Glen Scantlebury and Anne Goursaud. Pro Des: Thomas Sanders. M: Wojciech Kilar; *Love Song for a Vampire* performed by Annie Lennox. Costumes: Eiko Ishioka. Visual Effects: Roman Coppola. Sound: Leslie Shatz. (American Zoetrope/Osiris–Columbia TriStar.) Rel: 29 January 1993. 127 mins. Cert 18.

A Bright Summer Day

An impressive window on another world. Very long Taiwanese film which gives a clear and detailed picture of life in Taiwan in the 1960s. The main protagonist is a dogged student who refuses to compromise his moral standards. All based on director/writer Edward Yang's memories of his own youth. Very relevant to the Western world today, with the problems of unemployment, immigration (in his case from China) and religion. A long haul but patience is rewarded in this case. [FDM]

Prom night: Luke Perry and Kristy Swanson find true romance amongst the vampires in Fox's Buffy the Vampire Slayer

Cast: Zhang Guozhu (father), Elaine Jin (mother), Zang Zhen (the student), Zhang Han (older brother), Wang Juan (older sister), Lisa Yang (Ming).
Dir: Edward Yang. Pro: Yu Welyan. Ex Pro: Zhan Hongzhi. Screenplay: Yang, Yan Hongya, Shunqing and Lai Mintang. Ph: Zhang Huigong and Li Longyu. Ed: Chen

Psychiatry meets clairvoyance: Jeff Daniels and Demi Moore confront their feelings in Terry Hughes's utterly delightful The Butcher's Wife *(from Blue Dolphin)*

Bowen. Sound: Do Duzhi. Pro Des: Yu Weiyan Yang. (Jane Balfour Films–Yang and His Gang Filmmakers–ICA.) Rel: 12 March 1993. 237 mins. No cert.

Buffy the Vampire Slayer
Southern California; The Lite Years. Trendy take on the vampire movie, about an undisciplined, vacuous (and very pretty) cheerleader who discovers that her real destiny is to annihilate vampires. Like, *really*. Taking its cue from *Heathers* and *Pretty in Pink*, and cross-fertilising it with *The Lost Boys*, this hip teen comedy is too broad by

half, while the vampires overact dreadfully. It would've been a much classier, funnier movie if everybody had played it straight. However, there are some great lines, while highlights include Luke Perry shaving his sideburns and vampiric sidekick Paul Ruebens (replacing Joan Chen) dying more in irritation than agony. [JC-W]

Cast: Kristy Swanson (Buffy), Donald Sutherland (Merrick), Paul Reubens (Amilyn), Rutger Hauer (Lothos), Luke Perry (Pike), Michele Abrams (Jennifer), Hilary Swank (Kimberly), Paris Vaughan (Nicole), David Arquette (Benny), Randall Batinkoff (Jeffrey), Stephen Root (Garry Murray), Andrew Lowery, Sasha Jenson, Candy Clark, Natasha Gregson Wagner, Mark DeCarlo, Tom Janes, James Paradise, David Sherrill, Liz Smith, Paul M. Lane, J. C. Cole.
Dir: Fran Rubel Kuzui. Pro: Kaz Kuzui and Howard Rosenman. Ex Pro: Sandy Gallin, Carol Baum and Fran Rubel Kuzui. Screenplay: Joss Whedon. Ph: James Hayman. Ed: Camilla Toniolo and Jill Savitt. Pro Des: Lawrence Miller. M: Carter Burwell; numbers performed by C & C Music Factory, Matthew Sweet, the Cult, Ozzy Osbourne, Susannah Hoffs, etc. Costumes: Marie France. Sound: Steve Aaron. (Sandollar/Kuzui Enterprises–Fox.) Rel: 23 October 1992. 94 mins. Cert 12.

The Butcher's Wife
What promises to be a rather awful piece of whimsy, with Demi Moore gravely miscast as a Southern inno-

cent, recovers from its sticky opening to blossom into a delightful, magical romantic-comedy. Thanks is due to a smart, well thought-out script, brisk direction from Britain's Terry Hughes and a great turn by Jeff Daniels as an incredulous psychiatrist falling in love against his better professional instincts. Ms Moore, replacing Meg Ryan at the eleventh hour, plays a North Carolina clairvoyant who follows her dreams and intuition and marries an overweight butcher from New York. Once installed in her new home, Demi starts changing the lives of those around her with flashes of inspired advice, while her own marriage flounders. A feel-good entertainment spiced up by a stand-out supporting cast, particularly Mary Steenburgen and Margaret Colin. [JC-W]

Cast: Demi Moore (Marina), Jeff Daniels (Dr Alex Tremor), George Dzundza (Leo), Frances McDormand (Grace), Margaret Colin (Robyn), Mary Steenburgen (Stella), Max Perlich (Eugene), Miriam Margolyes, Helen Hanft, Christopher Durang, Diane Salinger.
  Dir: Terry Hughes. Pro: Wallis Nicita and Lauren Lloyd. Ex Pro: Arne Schmidt. Screenplay: Ezra Litwik and Marjorie Schwartz. Ph: Frank Tidy. Ed: Donn Cambern. Pro Des: Charles Rosen. M: Michael Gore; numbers performed by Julia Fordham, Banderos, Bessie Smith, Ray Charles, Angel, Mary Steenburgen. Costumes: Theodora Van Runkle. (Paramount–Blue Dolphin.) Rel: 3 July 1992. 104 mins. Cert 12.

California Man

(US: *Encino Man.*) Disney jumps on the *Wayne's World* bandwagon with this feeble comedy about a caveman who chills out with two likeable dweebs at Encino High. The caveman, Link, fits surprisingly well into the teen routine of being cool, while the morons around him behave like Neanderthals. Some social statement is wasted here as the film aims for the cheapest laughs and lowest common denominator, complete with an incessant heavy metal soundtrack and silly sound effects (*BOINGGG!*). For severely undemanding audiences. [JC-W]

Cast: Sean Astin (Dave Morgan), Brendan Fraser (Linkovitch Chomofsky 'Link'), Megan Ward (Robyn Sweeney), Mariette Hartley (Mrs Morgan), Richard Masur (Mr Morgan), Pauly Shore (Stoney Brown), Robin Tunney (Ella), Michael DeLuise (Matt Wilson), Patrick Van Horn, Dalton James, Rick Ducommun, Jonathan Quan, Ellen Blain, Esther Scott, Steven Elkins.
  Dir: Les Mayfield. Pro: George Zaloom. Ex Pro: Hilton Green. Screenplay: Shawn Schepps; from a story by Zaloom and Schepps. Ph: Robert Brinkmann. Ed: Eric Sears. Pro Des: James Allen. M: J. Peter Robinson; numbers performed by PM Dawn, the Edgar Winter Group, Right Said Fred, Cheap Trick, Queen, the Smithereens, Crystal Waters, Tone Loc, Alice Cooper, the Jesus and Mary Chain, Brad Fiedel, etc. Costumes: Marie France. Sound: Robert Allan Wald. (Hollywood Pictures–Warner.) Rel: 25 September 1992. 88 mins. Cert PG.

Candyman

Helen Lyle is researching her thesis on 'Graffiti Art and Urban Despair' at the University of Illinois, Chicago. Six

In the jaws of hell: Virginia Madsen goes prospecting for a good story in Bernard Rose's rather scary Candyman *(from Rank)*

blocks away, in a crumbling neighbourhood, the locals live in fear of a serial killer called Candyman. The legend goes that if you say his name five times in front of the mirror he will appear – and then kill you. Foolhardy Helen attempts to get to the bottom of the myth . . . The British-born Bernard Rose has already exhibited his knack for building suspense (with *Paperhouse*) and here ladles it on by the tubful. Photography, music and particularly the special effects all add to the disquiet. Easily one of the year's most potent horror films. [JC-W]

Cast: Virginia Madsen (Helen Lyle), Tony Todd (Candyman), Xander Berkeley

The right Charlie: Robert Downey Jr, superb in the title role of Richard Attenborough's Chaplin *(from Guild)*

(Trevor Lyle), Kasi Lemmons (Bernadette Walsh), DeJuan Guy (Jake), Vanessa Williams (Anne-Marie McCoy), Marianna Elliott (Clara), Ted Raimi (Billy), Gilbert Lewis (Det. Frank Valento), John Rensenhouse, Carolyn Lowery, Michael Culkin, Baxter Harris.

Dir and Screenplay: Bernard Rose; based on the short story *The Forbidden* by Clive Barker. Pro: Steve Golin, Sigurjon Sighvatsson and Alan Poul. Ex Pro: Barker. Ph: Anthony B. Richmond. Ed: Daniel Rae. Pro Des: Jane Stewart. M: Philip Glass. Costumes: Leonard Pollack. Sound: Reinhard Stergar. (PolyGram/Propaganda–Rank.) Rel: 19 March 1993. 99 mins. Cert 18.

Carry On Columbus

King Ferdinand (Leslie Phillips), turning to his wife, questions her passionate belief in Columbus: 'What makes you think he's up to it?' Queen Isabella (June Whitfield), eking out her reply, answers, 'Because . . . I've . . . seen . . . his . . . testimonials . . .' Oh, they don't tell 'em like they used to. Not counting the omnibus feature *That's Carry On*, this painful entry marks the 30th instalment (and, all sentiment aside, *please* let it be the last) in the cheap and cheerful comic series that began in 1958. A few crumbs of the old Carry On team have been resurrected to support members of the Comic Strip, while Jim Dale stars (without apparent embarrassment) as the Italian explorer. Only Maureen Lipman survives with her dignity intact in this cheap, crude amateur pantomime. [JC-W]

Cast: Jim Dale (Chris Columbus), Bernard Cribbins (Mort), Maureen Lipman (Countess Esmeralda), Peter Richardson (Bart Columbus), Alexei Sayle (Achmed), Leslie Phillips (King Ferdinand), Julian Clary (Lovely Diego), Sara Crowe (Fatima), James Faulkner (Torquemada), Rebecca Lacey (Chiquita), June Whitfield (Queen Isabella), Rik Mayall, Charles Fleischer, Larry Miller, Nigel Planer, Holly Aird, Keith Allen, Harold Berens, Martin Clunes, Allan Corduner, Jack Douglas, Peter Gilmore, Peter Gordeno, Don Henderson, Philip Herbert, Burt Kwouk, Chris Langham, Daniel Peacock, Jon Pertwee, Tony Slattery, Sara Stockbridge, Richard Wilson.

Dir: Gerald Thomas. Pro: John Goldstone. Ex Pro: Peter Rogers. Screenplay: Dave Freeman. Ph: Alan Hume. Ed: Chris Blunden. Pro Des: Harry Pottle. M: John Du Prez. Costumes: Phoebe De Gaye. Sound: Chris Munro. (Island World/Comedy House–UIP.) Rel: 2 October 1992. 91 mins. Cert PG.

Chaplin

There is plenty to admire and applaud in Richard Attenborough's long-awaited, much-delayed screen biography, but ultimately the film is too ambitious for its own good. From a screenplay by the novelist William Boyd, scenarist William Goldman, film director Bryan Forbes and playwright Tom Stoppard (uncredited), *Chaplin* attempts to capture *the life* more than the man, complete with a conveyor belt of wives, mistresses, female co-stars, *et al*, decorating the screen. But ultimately it is a downbeat tale, and unfolds in great melancholy wads, detailing the poverty, the workhouse, the madness of Chaplin's mother, the early days in vaudeville, the first trip to America, the meeting with Mack Sennett and then the downhill path to world celebrity (professional jealousies, personal exploitation, artistic disillusionment, destructive workaholism, *et al*). Robert Downey Jr, one of the most dynamic actors of his generation, seems swamped by the sheer size of the film and by the demands of his English accent, but, physically, is an uncanny facsimile. Better served are Kevin Kline, playing Douglas Fairbanks, and Moira Kelly, as Chaplin's fourth – and last – wife, Oona. The make-up is superb. [JC-W]

Cast: Robert Downey Jr (Charles Spencer Chaplin), Dan Aykroyd (Mack Sennett), Geraldine Chaplin (Hannah Chaplin), Kevin Dunn (J. Edgar Hoover), Anthony Hopkins (George Hayden), Milla Jovovich

(Mildred Harris), Moira Kelly (Hetty Kelly/Oona O'Neill Chaplin), Kevin Kline (Douglas Fairbanks), Diane Lane (Paulette Goddard), Penelope Ann Miller (Edna Purviance), Paul Rhys (Sydney Chaplin), John Thaw (Fred Karno), Marisa Tomei (Mabel Normand), Nancy Travis (Joan Barry), James Woods (Joseph Scott), Deborah Maria Moore (Lita Grey Chaplin), Hugh Downer (Charlie, aged five), Nicholas Gatt (Charlie, aged 9), Tom Bradford (Charlie, aged 14), Bill Paterson, Bryan Coleman, P. H. Moriarty, Brian Lipson, Gerald Sim, Malcolm Terris, David Duchovny, Benjamin Whitrow, Robert Stephens, Tim Chaplin, Vicki Frederick, John Standing.

Dir: Richard Attenborough. Pro: Attenborough and Mario Kassar. Co-Pro: Terence Clegg. Screenplay: William Boyd, Bryan Forbes, William Goldman, and (uncredited) Tom Stoppard; from a story by Diana Hawkins. Ph: Sven Nykvist. Ed: Anne V. Coates. Pro Des: Stuart Craig. M: John Barry. Costumes: John Mollo and Ellen Mirojnick. Sound: Jonathan Bates. (Carolco/RCS/Canal Plus/VOF/Japanese Satellite Broadcasting–Guild.) Rel: 18 December 1992. 144 mins. Cert 12.

Christopher Columbus: The Discovery

From the director of five James Bond films, the producers of *Superman* and the author of *The Godfather* comes the swashbuckling, soap-operatic story of a Genoese ladies' man who knew his tailwinds. Franco-Greek unknown George Corraface (who took over from Timothy Dalton at the eleventh hour) injects dash and innumerable cheesy grins into his role as the explorer, while a most improbable cast (Tom Selleck as the king of Spain?!) grapple with their accents and some horrendous dialogue ('Oh Lord, why have you forsaken me?'). Too awful to be true. (See also *1492* and *Carry On Columbus*.) [JC-W]

Cast: Marlon Brando (Torquemada), Tom Selleck (King Ferdinand), George Corraface (Cristobal Colon), Rachel Ward (Queen Isabella), Robert Davi (Martin Pinzon), Catherine Zeta Jones (Beatriz), Oliver Cotton (Harana), Benicio Del Toro, Mathieu Carriere, Manuel De Blas, Glyn Grain, Peter Guinness, Nigel Terry, Steven Hartley, Hugo Blick, Christopher Chaplin, Michael Gothard, Clive Arrindell, Nicholas Selby, John Grillo, Branscombe Richmond, Tailinh Forest Flower, Genevieve Allenbury, Georgi Fisher.

Dir: John Glen. Pro: Ilya Salkind. Ex Pro: Jane Chaplin. Co-Pro: Bob Simmonds. Screenplay: John Briley, Cary Bates and Mario Puzo; based on Puzo's story. Ph: Alec Mills; Arthur Wooster. Ed: Matthew Glen. Pro Des: Gil Parrondo. M: Cliff Eidelman. Costumes: John Bloomfield. Sound: Peter J. Devlin. (Alexander and Ilya Salkind–Rank.) Rel: 11 September 1992. 121 mins. Cert PG.

City of Joy

A rich, engrossing portrait of Calcutta as seen through the eyes of a young American doctor who has lost his way. Patrick Swayze, in a controversial casting choice, top-bills as Max Lowe,

The adventures of Cristobal Colon: the Santa Maria *sets sail for 'India' in the Salkinds' rollicking, catastrophic* Christopher Columbus: The Discovery *(from Rank)*

originally a minor character in Dominique Lapierre's best-selling novel, beefed up here to give the film a stronger Western perspective. However, the picture's true focus is Hasari

Art Malik (right) threatens prostitute Suneeta Sengupta in Roland Joffe's engrossing look at Calcutta life, in City of Joy *(from Warner)*

Michael Rooker (right) *finds himself caught between a Rocky and a hard place in Renny Harlin's giddy, slam-bang* Cliffhanger *(Guild) – with Sylvester Stallone*

Pal (Om Puri), a Bengali peasant who has lost his farm to famine and the money-lenders. Moving his wife and three children to Calcutta to find work, Hasari is shocked by the city's poverty, dishonesty and crime, not to mention its resident beggars, lepers and corrupt policemen. As Max and Hasari come to befriend and understand each other, so the true character of this fascinating, nightmarish metropolis comes to life. Director Roland Joffé (*The Killing Fields, The Mission*) met enormous local opposition when he proposed to film on actual locations (for starters, two native assistant directors were framed for murder and the set was firebombed), but persevered under seemingly insurmountable odds to produce a picture of enormous humanity, texture and emotional power. [JC-W]

Cast: Patrick Swayze (Max Lowe), Pauline Collins (Joan Bethel), Om Puri (Hasari Pal), Art Malik (Ashoka), Shabana Azmi (Kamla Pal), Ayesha Dharker (Amrita Pal), Suneeta Sengupta (Poomina), Shyaman-and Jalan (Godfather/Ghatak), Santu Chowdhury, Imran Badsah Khan, Nabil Shaban, Debtosh Ghosh, Mansi Upadhyay, Chetna Jalan, Sam Wanamaker.

Dir: Roland Joffé. Pro: Jake Eberts and Joffé. Co-Pro: Iain Smith. Screenplay: Mark Medoff. Ph: Peter Biziou. Ed: Gerry Hambling. Pro Des: Roy Walker. M: Ennio Morricone. Costumes: Judy Moorcroft. Sound: Daniel Brisseau. (Lightmotive-Warner.) Rel: 2 October 1992. 135 mins. Cert 12.

Cliffhanger

For sheer excitement, awe-inspiring stunts, spectacular scenery and the 'how the hell did they do that?' factor, *Cliffhanger* is in a class of its own. But this potentially class-A action thriller is incapacitated by a formulaic plot, crass improbabilities (the opening set-up is risible in its unfeasibility) and cod acting. Bad guy John Lithgow, who's experienced at chewing the scenery, here maniacally attempts to compete with the Italian Alps (where this very expensive – $70 million – epic was shot). [JC-W]

Cast: Sylvester Stallone (Gabe Walker), John Lithgow (Eric Qualen), Michael Rooker (Hal Tucker), Janine Turner (Jessie Deighan), Rex Linn (Travers), Caroline Goodall (Kristel), Leon (Kynette), Craig Fairbrass (Delmar), Michelle Joyner (Sarah), Ralph Waite (Frank), Paul Winfield, Gregory Scott Cummins, Denis Forest, Max Perlich, Trey Brownell, Bruce McGill.
Dir: Renny Harlin. Pro: Harlin and Alan Marshall. Ex Pro: Mario Kassar. Screenplay: Michael France and Sylvester Stallone; from a story by France, based on a premise by John Long. Ph: Alex Thomson. Ed: Frank J. Urioste. Pro Des: John Vallone. M: Trevor Jones; 'Do You Need Some?' performed by Mind Bomb. Costumes: Ellen Mirojnick. Sound: Wylie Stateman and Gregg Baxter. (Carolco/Canal Plus/Pioneer/RCS Video–Guild.) Rel: 25 June 1993. 112 mins. Cert 15.

Close to Eden

(US: *A Stranger Among Us.*) Sidney Lumet continues his love affair with New York by exploring the secluded Hasidic community. Melanie Griffith is an improbable, tough-talking trig-

The Rebbe and the shiksa: Eric Thal and Melanie Griffith in Sidney Lumet's well-intentioned Close to Eden *(from Rank)*

ger-happy Brooklyn cop who is asked to find a missing Hasidic diamond cutter. Clashing abrasively with the Jews' gentle, devout culture, Griffith goes undercover and starts making eyes at the future Rebbe (i.e. spiritual leader). At first the documentary-like attention to the Hasidic way of life is fascinating, but it's quickly undermined by a trite whodunnit and romance. *Witness* this ain't – it's more like *V. I. Warshawski* meets *Yentl*. Oy, vey. [JC-W]

Cast: Melanie Griffith (Emily Eden), John Pankow (Levine), Tracy Pollan (Mara), Lee Richardson (Rebbe), Mia Sara (Leah), Jamey Sheridan (Nick), Eric Thal (Ariel), Jake Weber, David Margulies, James Gandolfini, Chris Collins, Burtt Harris.
   Dir: Sidney Lumet. Pro: Steve Golin, Sigurjon Sighvatsson and Howard Rosenman. Line Pro: Burtt Harris. Co-Pro: Susan Tarr and Robert J. Avrech. Screenplay: Avrech. Ph: Andrzej Bartkowiak. Ed: Andrew Mondshein. Pro Des: Philip Rosenberg. M: Jerry Bock. Costumes: Gary Jones and Ann Roth. Sound: Chris Newman. (Polygram/Propaganda Films/Sandollar/Isis–Rank.) Rel: 11 June 1993. 109 mins. Cert 15.

Un Coeur en Hiver – A Heart in Winter

Paris; 1992. Stephane and Maxime have been friends since their days at the music conservatory. They are now

The food of love: the alluring Emmanuelle Béart finds herself strung along by two men in Claude Sautet's elegant Un Coeur en Hiver *(from Artificial Eye)*. Brigitte Catillon looks on

'partners' in the making, selling and repair of violins and both are experts at what they do. Maxime is the handsome, jet-setting deal-maker, Stephane the quiet, reserved artist creating violins with the skill of a master. For Maxime, music is the food of love and life, but for Stephane it is his only love. However, when Maxime leaves his wife for the beautiful, talented violinist Camille, Stephane embarks on an invisible seduction of the same woman. Or does he? Claude Sautet's twelfth feature in 42 years, this is an intellectually and aesthetically seductive film, although, ultimately, it is no more than an eloquently devised vignette. It is nevertheless a fascinating insight into the rarefied world of music, taking much delight in exploring the minutiae of violin-making (apparently, it takes a whole month and 80 pieces to construct one instrument). Also, the acting is uniformly commendable, while the always watchable Emmanuelle Béart devoted 18 months to mastering the violin. [JC-W]

Cast: Daniel Auteuil (Stephane), Emmanuelle Béart (Camille), André Dussollier (Maxime), Elisabeth Bourgine (Helene), Brigitte Catillon (Regine), Maurice Garrel (Lachaume), Myriam Boyer (Madame Amet), Stanislas Carre de Malberg (Brice), Jean-Luc Bideau (Ostende).
   Dir: Claude Sautet. Pro: Jean-Louis Livi and Philippe Carcassonne. Screenplay: Sautet, Jacques Fieschi and Jerome Tonnerre. Ph: Yves Rouve. Ed: Jacqueline Thiedot. Art: Christian Marti. M: Philippe Sarde; Maurice Ravel, Gabriel Faure. Costumes: Corinne Jorry. Sound: Pierre

Domestic blitz: Kevin Kline and Mary Elizabeth Mastrantonio find themselves the victims of a con artist in Alan J. Pakula's disappointing Consenting Adults *(from Buena Vista)*

Lenoir. (Film Par Film/Cinea/Orly Film/Canal Plus/etc–Artificial Eye.) Rel: 23 April 1993. 105 mins. Cert 12.

Consenting Adults

Richard and Priscilla Parker have been married for fourteen years, are the parents of a bright and gifted child and live in a comfortable housing complex in the suburbs of Atlanta. Outwardly, their world seems perfect. Then the Otises, a vibrant, attractive and extremely rich couple, move in next door. They could make a husband and wife jealous . . . Exploring the undercurrent of yuppie complacency, envy and greed, Matthew Chapman's screenplay would seem to have hit a gold streak in cinematic neurosis. But Chapman's characters are so one-dimensional, his structure so episodic and the premise so preposterous, that there's little to grip on to in this slick, superficial thriller. Worse still, Kevin Kline sleepwalks through his role as the trusting, tempted and ultimately manipulated Richard, while the plot boasts more holes than a championship golf course. [JC-W]

Cast: Kevin Kline (Richard Parker), Mary Elizabeth Mastrantonio (Priscilla Parker), Kevin Spacey (Eddy Otis), Rebecca Miller (Kay Otis), Forest Whitaker (David Duttonville), E. G. Marshall (George Gordon), Kimberly McCullough (Lori Parker), Billie Neal, Benjamin Hendrickson, Lonnie Smith, Joe Mulherin, Ginny Parker, Rick Hinkle, Edward Seamon.

Ever seen a dream walking? Gabriel Byrne has, in Ralph Bakshi's self-consciously hip, absolutely unbearable Cool World *(from Blue Dolphin)*

Dir: Alan J. Pakula. Pro: Pakula and David Permut. Ex Pro: Pieter Jan Brugge. Co-Pro: Katie Jacobs. Screenplay: Matthew Chapman. Ph: Stephen Goldblatt. Ed: Sam O'Steen. Pro Des: Carol Spier. M: Michael Small; numbers performed by Q Rose and Kevin Spacey. Costumes: Gary Jones and

Tough witness: Ralph Wilcox, Burt Reynolds and Holland Taylor interrogate eight-year-old Norman D. Golden II in Henry Winkler's lamentable Cop and a Half *(from UIP)*

Ann Roth. Sound: Ron Bochar. (Hollywood Pictures–Buena Vista.) Rel: 5 March 1993. 99 mins. Cert 15.

Cool World

Ralph Bakshi, creator of the notorious X-rated cartoons *Fritz the Cat* and *Heavy Traffic*, ventures into *Roger Rabbit* territory with this promising tale of a cartoon nymphomaniac ('Holli would, if she could . . .') who wants to experience sex in the real world. Gabriel Byrne is the jaded underground cartoonist who finds himself transported into his own ani-

mated nightmare, where he falls for the charms of Holli. Sounds great, but it's actually excrutiating. The live-action/animation sequences are nothing to write home about (*Roger Rabbit* spoiled us), the script is bland and the film is witless, charmless and ugly. [JC-W]

Cast: Kim Basinger (Holli Would), Gabriel Byrne (Jack Deebs), Brad Pitt (Frank Harris), Michele Abrams (Jennifer Malley), Deidre O'Connell (Isabelle Malley), Carrie Hamilton (comic-store cashier), Frank Sinatra Jr (himself).
Dir: Ralph Bakshi. Pro: Frank Mancuso Jr. Assoc Pro: Vikki Williams. Screenplay: Michael Grais and Mark Victor. Ph: John A. Alonzo. Ed: Steve Mirkovich and Annamaria Szanto. Pro Des: Michael Corenblith. M: Mark Isham. Costumes: Malissa Daniel. Conceptual design: Barry Jackson. Sound: James Thornton. (Paramount–Blue Dolphin.) Rel: 18 December 1992. 102 mins. Cert 12.

Cop and a Half

As the sole witness to a murder, 8-year-old crimebuster wannabe Devon Butler (Norman D. Golden II: can't act) trades information for a day on the force. Tough Florida cop Nick McKenna (Burt Reynolds) is not amused, but a man's gotta do what a man's gotta do. An excruciatingly witless and cloying action comedy, this was originally earmarked for a vehicle for Macaulay Culkin – but the wise child turned it down. Pity Burt Reynolds. [JC-W]

Cast: Burt Reynolds (Nick McKenna), Ray Sharkey (Vinnie Fountain), Ruby Dee (Rachel), Norman D. Golden II (Devon Butler), Holland Taylor (Officer Rubio), Sammy Hernandez, Rocky Giordani, Frank Sivero, Marc Macaulay, Tom McCleister, Ralph Wilcox, Carmine Genovese, Paul Vroom, Andrew Reynolds.
Dir: Henry Winkler. Pro: Paul Maslansky. Ex Pro: Tova Laiter. Screenplay: Arne Olsen. Ph: Bill Butler. Ed: Daniel Hanley and Roger Tweten. Pro Des: Maria Caso. M: Alan Silvestri. Costumes: Lillian Pan. Sound: Joe Foglia. (Imagine Films/Universal–UIP.) Rel: 28 May 1993. 97 mins. Cert PG.

Cousin Bobby

Oscar-winning director Jonathan Demme (*The Silence of the Lambs*) was asked to make a personal documentary as part of a 'collective series'. For his subject, the filmmaker chose his

Guilt and obsession: Stephen Rea and Miranda Richardson as IRA volunteers in Neil Jordan's tantalising The Crying Game *(from Mayfair Entertainment)*

long-lost older cousin, the Rev. Robert Castle, now a charismatic, pioneering Episcopalian minister in Harlem. The result is not so much a documentary as a slapdash home movie, complete with shaky camera work (surprising, considering that Demme had the celebrated Ernest Dickerson on board as cinematographer). [JC-W]

Dir: Jonathan Demme. Pro: Edward Saxon. Assoc Pro: Valerie Thomas and Lucas Platt. Ph: Ernest Dickerson, Craig Haagensen, Tony Jannelli, Jacek Laskus and Declan Quinn. Ed: David Greenwald. Ph: Ernest Dickerson, Craig Haagensen, Tony Jannelli, Jacek Laskus and Declan Quinn. M: Anton Sanko. Sound: Judy Karp, J. T. Takagi and Pam Yates. (Tesauro–Electric.) Rel: 4 September 1992. 70 mins. Cert PG.

Crush

An enigmatic American woman arrives in a small New Zealand town

and irreversibly transforms the lives of three people – a female journalist, a jaded novelist and the latter's socially backward 15-year-old daughter. A theme with enormous opportunities is largely wasted in this flat, styleless thriller, which just begs for a touch of weirdness or, at the very least, a hint of tension. [JC-W]

Cast: Marcia Gay Harden (Lane), Donogh Rees (Christina), Caitlin Bossley (Angela Iseman), William Zappa (Colin Iseman), Peter Smith, Jon Brazier, Geoffrey Southern, Shirley Wilson.
   Dir: Alison Maclean. Pro: Bridget Ikin. Assoc Pro: Trevor Haysom. Screenplay: Maclean and Anne Kennedy. Ph: Dion Beebe. Ed: John Gilbert. Pro Des: Meryl Cronin. M: JPS Experience. Costumes: Ngila Dickenson. Sound: Robert Allen. (Hibiscus Films/New Zealand Film Commission/Avalon/NFU Studios/NZ On Air/ The Sundance Institute/Movie Partners– Metro Tartan.) Rel: 19 March 1993. 96 mins. Cert 15.

The Crying Game

South Armagh/London; 1992. A black British soldier is kidnapped by the IRA and is held hostage in a derelict green-

house. The man's captor, an easy-going, altruistic 'volunteer', falls under the soldier's spell and becomes obsessed by him – and his wife. Written and directed by Neil Jordan, *The Crying Game* is an intriguing, surprising piece of storytelling, ingeniously realised and convincingly played. Whitaker, a controversial choice for the role of the soldier (the actor was born in Texas and raised in Los Angeles), copes well with his English accent, but is no better than the rest of an excellent cast. Jordan's seventh – and best – film. [JC-W]

Cast: Stephen Rea (Fergus), Miranda Richardson (Jude), Forest Whitaker (Jody), Jim Broadbent (Col), Ralph Brown (Dave), Adrian Dunbar (Maguire), Jaye Davidson (Dil), Breffini McKenna, Tony Slattery, Shar Campbell, Brian Coleman.
   Dir and Screenplay: Neil Jordan. Pro: Stephen Woolley. Ex Pro: Nik Powell. Co-Pro: Elizabeth Karlsen. Assoc Pro: Paul Cowan. Ph: Ian Wilson. Ed: Kant Pan. Pro Des: Jim Clay. M: Anne Dudley; numbers performed by Percy Sledge, Mungo Jerry, Pet Shop Boys, Kate Robbins, the Blue Jays, Lyle Lovett, etc. Costumes: Sandy Powell. Sound: Colin Nicolson. (Palace/

Breaking the ice: Coach Roy Dotrice (centre) *advises his skating stars D. B. Sweeney and Moira Kelly in Paul Michael Glaser's skilfully engineered* The Cutting Edge *(from UIP)*

Channel Four/Euro-trustees/Nippon Film/British Screen–Mayfair Entertainment.) Rel: 30 October 1992. 112 mins. Cert 18.

Cup Final – Gemar Gavia

Inspired by a number of true stories that surfaced during the Israeli invasion of Lebanon in June of 1982, *Cup Final* is a war film, not a sporting epic. However, it is the love of football – in particular interest in that year's World Cup in Spain – that unites the humanity of the men forced to go to war by their respective governments. A brave, compassionate and occasionally very funny anti-war film shot for a mere $800,000. You have to admire it. [CB]

Cast: Moshe Ivgi (Cohen), Muhamad Bacri (Ziad), Salim Dau (Mussa), Basam Zuamut, Yussef Abu Warda, Suheil Haddad.
   Dir: Eran Riklis. Pro: Michael Sharfshtein. Screenplay: Eyal Halfon; based on an idea by Riklis. Ph: Amnon Salomon. Ed:

Anat Lubarsky. Art: Arie Weiss. M: Raviv Gazit. Costumes: Zemira Hershkovitz. Sound: Shabtai Sarig and Tami Shir. (Local Prods/Israeli Broadcasting Authority–Gala.) Rel: 14 May 1993. 109 mins. Cert 15.

The Cutting Edge

A young figure-skating prima donna is unable to find a perfect partner, dismissing eight talented hopefuls in two months. In a last-ditch attempt, her Russian coach hires a former ice-hockey star to fill the gap. He is a good ol' boy from the wrong patch of Minnesota, she is a spoilt bitch from moneyed gentry. What on earth will happen? As predictable and clichéd as a Mills & Boon romance, *The Cutting Edge* is so skilfully executed and acted, that it succeeds in spite of itself. Newcomer Moira Kelly (*Billy Bathgate*) is particularly fetching as the athletic, temperamental beauty, and is well matched by the throwaway charm of D. B. Sweeney as her Petruchio. Amazingly, Ms Kelly couldn't skate *at all* before signing up for the film: her ease on the ice is attributable to the

expert tutelage of Robin Cousins. [JC-W]

Cast: D. B. Sweeney (Doug Dorsey), Moira Kelly (Kate Moseley), Roy Dotrice (Anton Pamchenko), Terry O'Quinn (Jack Moseley), Dwier Brown (Hale), Chris Benson (Walter Dorsey), Kevin Peeks, Barry Flatman, Rachelle Ottley, Steve Sears, Judy Blumberg and Robin Cousins (commentators).
   Dir: Paul Michael Glaser. Pro: Ted Field, Karen Murphy and Robert W. Cort. Co-Pro: Dean O'Brien and Cynthia Sherman. Screenplay: Tony Gilroy. Ph: Elliot Davis. Ed: Michael E. Polakow. Pro Des: David Gropman. M: Patrick Williams; numbers performed by Nia Peeples, Chris Isaak, Black Box, Arrow, Malcolm McLaren, Rosemary Butler, Yello, Joe Cocker, etc. Costumes: William Ivey Long. Choreography: Robin Cousins. Sound: David Lee. (Interscope Communications/MGM–UIP.) Rel: 28 August 1992. 101 mins. Cert PG.

Dakota Road

Off-beat, bittersweet comedy-drama set in the picturesque Fenland of East Anglia. There, amidst the isolated, endless flat farmland, nine characters interact to create some refreshing, striking black comedy, their respective sexual desires remaining unfulfilled. Making his film debut, writer-director Nick Ward is a talent to be watched, with a telling eye for the underplayed scene. Acting, music, photography and editing are all top-notch. The first feature to be made under The British Film Partnership, a scheme set up to encourage native finance of low-budget British films. [JC-W]

Cast: Amelda Brown (Maud Cross), Jason Carter (Raif Benson), Charlotte Chatton (Jen Cross), Alan Howard (Alan Brandon), Rachel Scott (Amy Cross), Matthew Scurfield (Bernard Cross), Liz Smith (Joan Benson), David Warrilow (Douglas Stonea), Alexis Denisof (pilot), David Bamber (man on train).
   Dir and Screenplay: Nick Ward. Pro: Donna Grey. Ex Pro: Sarah Radclyffe. Ph: Ian Wilson. Ed: William Diver. Pro Des and Costumes: Careen Hertzog. M: Paul Stacey. Sound: Simon Okin. (Film Four/British Screen/Working Title–Mayfair Entertainment.) Rel: 17 July 1992. 88 mins. No cert.

Damage

'Remember, damaged people are dangerous,' warns *femme fatale* Juliette Binoche; 'they know they can survive.'

Sexual politics: Juliette Binoche and Jeremy Irons push the envelope of passion in Louis Malle's detached Damage *(from Entertainment)*

To his discredit, MP Jeremy Irons ignores this advice and carries on an affair with his son's fiancée, a beautiful antiques dealer with a mysterious past. Adapted by David Hare from Josephine Hart's novel, this is a studied, calculating erotic drama, in which scenario and attention to detail take priority over character. But the film's greatest weakness lies in the casting of Mlle Binoche in the central role of the temptress, who provides neither sufficient mystery nor enough fatal attraction to spark the story's credibility. However, Miranda Richardson as Irons's wife is superb. [JC-W]

Cast: Jeremy Irons (Stephen Fleming), Juliette Binoche (Anna Barton), Miranda Richardson (Ingrid Fleming), Rupert Graves (Martyn Fleming), Leslie Caron (Elizabeth Prideaux), Ian Bannen (Edward Lloyd), Gemma Clarke (Sally Fleming), Peter Stormare, Julian Fellowes, Roger Llewellyn, Susan Engel, Jeff Nuttall, Tony

Doyle, Benjamin Whitrow, David Thewlis, Simon Hardy.

Dir and Pro: Louis Malle. Co-Pro: Vincent Malle and Simon Relph. Screenplay: David Hare. Ph: Peter Biziou. Ed: John Bloom. Pro Des: Brian Morris. M: Zbigniew Preisner. Costumes: Milena Canonero. Sound: Jean-Claude Laureux. (NEF/SKREBA/Le Studio Canal Plus/Channel 4/European Co-Production Fund–Entertainment.) Rel: 5 February 1993. 111 mins. Cert 18.

Danzon

Mexico City; 1991. Julia, a single mother, and her elegant, mysterious partner, Carmelo, have been dancing together twice a week for the last ten years, winning several competitions into the bargain. Then suddenly Carmelo disappears, and Julia goes after him, in spite of knowing nothing about the man . . . A colourful, imaginatively filmed odyssey, with the ever-popular Maria Rojo again giving a performance to die for. For the record, *danzon* is the name of a 'refined, intricate ballroom dance'. [CB]

Cast: Maria Rojo (Julia), Carmen Salinas

(Doria Ti), Margarita Isabel (Silvia), Tito Vasconcelos (Susy), Blanca Buerra (La Colorada), Victor Carpinteiro, Cheli Godinez, Daniel Rergis.

Dir: Maria Novaro. Pro: Jorge Sanchez. Ex Pro: Dulce Kuri. Screenplay: Maria and

The beat goes on: the irrepressible Maria Rojo (right) partners Daniel Rergis in Maria Novaro's exploration of the feminine psyche, Danzon *(from Metro)*

A pain in the neck? Meryl Streep discovers she has her head screwed on the wrong way in Robert Zemeckis's dark, daring Death Becomes Her *(from UIP)*

I talk to the animals: crazy Miranda Otto in the Feature Film Co's dotty Daydream Believer

Beatriz Novaro. Ph: Rodrigo Garcia. Ed: Maria Novaro and Nelson Rodriguez. Art: Marisa Pecanins and Norberto Sanchez. M: Various. Sound: Nerio Barberis. (Mexican Film Institute/Macondo Cine Video/FFCC/TVE/Tabasco Films/Gobierno del Estado de Veracruz–Metro.) Rel: 14 September 1992. 96 mins. No cert.

Daydream Believer

Why Martin Kemp decided to headline this disaster is a question only his agent can answer. A contemporary romantic comedy revolving around a megastar horse breeder and an irritatingly daffy girl who talks to horses, this independent Australian feature fails on all counts. Horse lovers and Spandau Ballet fans should stay away in droves: even the Monkees' title song doesn't help. [KK]

Cast: Miranda Otto (Nell), Martin Kemp (Digby), Anne Looby (Margot), Alister Smart (Ron), Gia Carides (Wendy), Bruce Venables, Katie Edwards, Russell Kiefel, Kerry Walker, Keith Robinson.
Dir: Kathy Mueller. Pro: Ben Gannon. Screenplay: Saturday Rosenberg. Ph: Andrew Lesnie. Ed: Robert Gibson. Pro

Des: Roger Ford. M: Todd Hunter and Johanna Pigott. Sound: Guntis Sics. (Feature Film Co.) Rel: 7 August 1992. 88 mins. Cert 15.

Death Becomes Her

1978–2029; Beverly Hills. Best buddies Meryl Streep and Goldie Hawn star as a couple of age- and beauty-obsessed 'friends' who fight over the affections of a meek plastic surgeon (Bruce Willis). Fuelled by years of mounting hatred, these Beverly Hills sirens will go to *any* lengths to get what they want – be it men, fame or eternal youth. Not since Danny DeVito's *The War of the Roses* has Hollywood produced such a sick black comedy, a surreal Gothic rollercoaster ride of bile and special effects. Robert Zemeckis, who made his actors age significantly in *Back to the Future* and then played with animation in *Who Framed Roger Rabbit*, here combines both to devastating effect. The special effects are *so* real, that they are often stomach-churning (Goldie, weighing in at an extra 200 pounds, has to be seen to be believed). A truly daring, original and

Snookered again: Gregory Sierra (left) takes a cue in Bill Duke's hip thriller Deep Cover *(from First Independent).* Jeff Goldblum and Larry Fishburne (far right) *look on*

spectacular farce – with something important to say, to boot. [JC-W]

Cast: Meryl Streep (Madeline Ashton), Bruce Willis (Ernest Menville), Goldie Hawn (Helen Sharp), Isabella Rossellini (Lisle Von Rhuman), Ian Ogilvy (Chagall), Adam Storke, Nancy Fish, Alaina Reed Hall, Michelle Johnson, Mary Ellen Trainor, John Ingle, Anya Longwell, Jonathan Silverman, Carrie Yazel, Ron Stein (Elvis), Bonnie Cahoon (Greta Garbo), Stephanie Anderson (Marilyn Monroe), Bob Swain (Andy Warhol), Eric Clark (James Dean), Dave Brock (Jim Morrison), Susan Kellerman, Sydney Pollack, Michael Caine.
Dir: Robert Zemeckis. Pro: Zemeckis and Steve Starkey. Co-Pro: Joan Bradshaw. Screenplay: Martin Donovan and David Koepp. Ph: Dean Cundey. Ed: Arthur Schmidt. Pro Des: Rick Carter. M: Alan Silvestri. Costumes: Joanna Johnston. Visual Effects: Ken Ralston. Make-up: Dick Smith. Sound: William B. Kaplan. (Universal–UIP.) Rel: 4 December 1992. 103 mins. Cert PG.

Deep Cover

Los Angeles; 1991. Larry Fishburne, a long-established character actor in such films as *Apocalypse Now, Class Action* and *Boyz N The Hood*, makes a powerful leading man in this stylish drugs drama. Fishburne is Russell Stevens Jr, a product of ghetto life who is determined 'to make a difference'. Joining the police force, he goes under-cover as a drug dealer, a job he finds infinitely easier than law enforcement . . . A provocative soundtrack, muscular direction and a wry turn from Jeff Goldblum as Fishburne's drug-dealing partner make this a gripping, witty thriller with a conscience. [JC-W]

Cast: Larry Fishburne (Russell Stevens Jr/ John Q. Hull), Jeff Goldblum (David Jason), Gregory Sierra (Fritz Barbosa), Clarence Williams II ('Reverend' Taft), Charles Martin Smith (Jerry Carver), Victoria Dillard (Betty McCutcheon), Sydney Lassick (Gopher), Roger Guenveur Smith (Eddie), Kamala Lopez (Belinda), Arthur Mendoza (Gallegos), Glynn Turman (Russell Stevens Sr), Rene Assa (Guzman), Julio Oscar Mechoso, Alex Colon, Erik Kilpatrick, Shannon McPherson, Yvette Heyden, Harry Frazier, Donald Bishop,

John Shepherd, Paunita Nichols, Tyrone Townsend.
Dir: Bill Duke. Pro: Pierre David. Ex Pro: David Streit. Co-Pro: Henry Bean and Deborah Moore. Screenplay: Bean and Michael Tolkin; from a story by Tolkin. Ph: Bojan Bazelli. Ed: John Carter. Pro Des: Pam Warner. M: Michel Colombier; numbers performed by Dr Dre, Shabba Ranks, the Deele, Calloway, Po', Broke & Lonely?, Ko-Kane, Emmage, Jewell, etc. Costumes: Arline Burks-Gant. Sound: Tony Smyles. (New Line Cinema–First Independent.) Rel: 22 January 1993. 105 mins. Cert 18.

Desperate

The first feature (in black-and-white) by Rico Martinez; a black comedy about the efforts of wannabe stars Toy and Tan-yah to achieve some sort of stardom, with unfortunate results. [FDM]

Cast: Kimberli Ghee and Elvis Christ etc. (Cinematheque/Strand Releasing.) Rel: 7 October 1992. 90 mins. No cert.

Diggstown

See *Midnight Sting*.

A black heart for the White House: Eddie Murphy swindles his way into politics in Jonathan Lynn's rather obvious The Distinguished Gentleman *(from Buena Vista)*

The Distinguished Gentleman

Florida conman and mimic Thomas Jefferson Johnson tricks his way into Congress for the money and finds a conscience. A perfect vehicle for Eddie Murphy, in which the comedian puts on funny voices, makes utter idiots of white authority figures and falls for a pale-skinned beauty (who puts him on the road to integrity). Very broad, very predictable, very familiar. [JC-W]

Cast: Eddie Murphy (Thomas Jefferson Johnson), Lane Smith (Dick Dodge), Sheryl Lee Ralph (Miss Loretta), Joe Don Baker (Olaf Andersen), Victoria Rowell (Celia Kirby), Grant Shaud (Arthur Reinhardt), Charles S. Dutton (Elijah Hawkins), Victor Rivers (Armando), Sonny Jim Gaines (Van Dyke), Noble Willingham (Zeke Bridges), Daniel Benzali ('Skeeter' Warburton), James Garner (Jeff Johnson), Doris Grau (Hattie Rifkin), Chi, Gary Frank, Cynthia Harris, Susan Forristal, Autumn Winters, Frances Foster, Sarah Carson, John Doolittle, Tom Finnegan, Marty Kaplan, Daniel Petrie Jr, J. D. Williams.
    Dir: Jonathan Lynn. Pro: Leonard Goldberg and Michael Peyser. Ex Pro: Marty Kaplan. Screenplay: Kaplan; from a story by Kaplan and Jonathan Reynolds. Ph: Gabriel Beristain. Ed: Tony Lombardo and

Barry B. Leirer. Pro Des: Leslie Dilley. M: Randy Edelman. Costumes: Francine Jamison-Tanchuck. Sound: Russell Williams II. (Hollywood Pictures–Buena Vista.) Rel: 26 March 1993. 112 mins. Cert 15.

Don't Move, Die and Rise Again – Zamri Oumi Voskresni

Soviet Asia; 1946. Stark, almost documentary-like recollection of life in a mining town as experienced by a 12-year-old boy and girl. While the locals consist of poor miners, Japanese POWs, drunks, prostitutes, thieves, murderers and simpletons, Valerka and Galia manage to glean some moments of happiness in a depressed,

hopeless world. Filmmaking at its most direct – unglamorised, unstylised and unembellished, filmed in low-grade black-and-white. A.k.a. *Freeze – Die – Come To Life.* [JC-W]

Cast: Pavel Nazarov (Valerka), Dinara Droukarova (Galia), Eléna Popova (Nina, Valerka's mother).
    Dir and Screenplay: Vitali Kanévski. Ph: Vladimir Bryliakov. Pro Des: Youri Pachigorev. M: Sergei Banevitch. Sound: Akaana Strouguina. (Lenfilm Studio–Artificial Eye.) Rel: 1 October 1992. 105 mins.

Dracula

See *Bram Stoker's Dracula.*

Dust Devil

The Namib desert, Namibia; 1990. A charismatic loner hitchhikes to the neighbourhood of Bethany to collect the fingers and souls of beautiful women so that he can return, revitalised, to a world beyond ours. Sluggish and self-important attempt to bring an edge of gravity to the slasher genre by introducing mythological undertones with a Sergio Leone sensibility. Unfortunately, director Richard Stanley (*Hardware*) fails to endow his film with suspense, drive or even logic. [CB]

Cast: Robert Burke (Hitch), Chelsea Field (Wendy Robinson), Zakes Mokae (Ben Mukurob), John Matshikiza (Joe Niemand), Marianne Sagebrecht (Dr Leidzinger), William Hootkins (Capt.

Showing it how it was: Dinara Droukarova and Pavel Nazarov in Vitali Kanevski's grim, straightforward Don't Move, Die and Rise Again *(from Artificial Eye)*

Beyman), Rufus Swart, Andre Odendaal, Russell Copely, Terri Norton.

Dir and Screenplay: Richard Stanley. Pro: JoAnne Sellar. Ex Pro: Nik Powell and Stephen Woolley. Ph: Steve Chivers. Ed: Derek Trigg. Pro Des: Joseph Bennett. M: Simon Boswell. Costumes: Michelle Clapton. Sound: Robin Harris. (Palace/ Film Four Int./British Screen/ Miramax–Polygram.) Rel: 16 April 1993. 105 mins. Cert 18.

Electric Moon

Deep in the rainforest of central India, an impoverished Maharajah and his younger brother and sister run an exclusive lodge for western tourists. Promising an exotic vacation of Oriental hospitality and rare wildlife, the royal trio shortchange their guests at every opportunity. The resident tiger is stuffed (its flinching tail operated by a hidden winch), the exotic birdcalls played over a loudspeaker and the stories of former derring-do entirely made-up. The possibilities here for incisive parody are endless, but the filmmakers have unwisely opted for a more gentle, satirical approach, while the actors (except for the always reliable Roshan Seth) are not up to the material. [JC-W]

Cast: Roshan Seth (Ranveer Singh), Naseeruddin Shah (Goswami), Leela Naidu ('Socks'), Gerson Da Cunha ('Bubbles'), Raghubir Yadav (Boltoo), Alice Spivak, Frances Helm, James Fleet, Francesca Brill, Gareth Forwood, Surendra Rajan, Malcolm Jamieson, Barbara Lott.

Dir and Ed: Pradip Krishen. Pro: Sundeep Singh Bedi. Screenplay and Pro Des: Arundhati Roy. Ph: Giles Nuttgens. M: Simeon Venkov. Sound: Robert Taylor. (Grapevine Media/Channel 4/Times TV–Film 4/Winstone.) Rel: 4 December 1992. 103 mins. Cert 15.

Elenya

Rural Wales; 1940. Elenya is a 12-year-old girl who feels ostracised by the small community in which she lives. She has never met her Italian mother, her father has signed up to fight the Germans and her Aunt Maggie, bitter and hard, cannot love her. In need of even a glint of affection, Elenya finds her salvation in the form of Franz, a wounded German airman she discovers in the woods. He can be her father, her friend, maybe even more . . . An Anglo-Welsh-German co-production predominantly filmed

Ill-met: Juliette Binoche and Ralph Fiennes as the tragic lovers of Emily Bronte's Wuthering Heights *(from UIP)*

in Luxembourg (both in Welsh and English) on a budget of £700,000, *Elenya* is a remarkable filmmaking achievement. Pascale Delafouge Jones in the title role is extraordinary. [CB]

Cast: Sue Jones Davies (Maggie), Klaus Behrendt (Franz), Pascale Delafouge Jones (Elenya), Margaret John (old Elenya), Iago Wynn Jones (Sidney), Pauline Yates (voice-over), Edward Elwyn Jones, Seiriol Tomos, Llio Millward, Catrin Llwyd.

Dir and Screenplay: Steve Gough. Pro: Heidi Ulmke. Ex Pro: Ben Gibson, Michael Smeaton and Dafydd Huw Williams. Ph: Patrick Duval. Ed: Alan Smithee. Pro Des: Hayden Pearce. M: Simon Fisher Turner. Costumes: Aideen Morgan. Sound: Simon Happ. (Frankfurter Film-produktion/BFI/S4C/ZDF–BFI.) Rel: 11 December 1992. 88 mins. Cert PG.

Emily Brontë's Wuthering Heights

1775–1802; the Yorkshire moors. Ryuichi Sakamoto's stirring theme tune, Mike Southon's haunting photography and Juliette Binoche's to-die-for beauty cannot salvage this (fifth) plodding screen interpretation of Emily Brontë's only novel. Hailed as one of the greatest love stories of all

Foreign affair: the remarkable Pascale Delafouge Jones in Steve Gough's Elenya *(from BFI)*

Standing up: Michael Douglas (with Barbara Hershey) fighting for his rights in Joel Schumacher's ruthlessly entertaining Falling Down *(from Warner)*

time, and plotted out to the bitter end, here Catherine and Heathcliff have five minutes of bliss and then an hour and a half of emotional torment (in William Wyler's classic 1939 version they wisely stopped at chapter 17). A real downer. [JC-W]

Cast: Juliette Binoche (Cathy Linton/Catherine Earnshaw), Ralph Fiennes (Heathcliff), Janet McTeer (Ellen Dean), Sophie Ward (Isabella Linton), Simon Shepherd (Edgar Linton), Jeremy Northam (Hindley Earnshaw), Jason Riddington (Hareton Earnshaw), Paul Geoffrey (Mr Lockwood), John Woodvine (Thomas Earnshaw), Sinead O'Connor (Emily Brontë), Simon Ward, Robert Demeger, Janine Wood, Trevor Cooper, Jonathan Firth.

Dir: Peter Kosminsky. Pro: Mary Selway. Ex Pro and 2nd Unit Dir: Simon Bosanquet. Screenplay: Anne Devlin. Ph: Mike Southon. Ed: Tony Lawson. Pro Des: Brian Morris. M: Ryuichi Sakamoto. Costumes: James Acheson. Sound: Peter Glossop. (Paramount–UIP.) Rel: 16 October 1992. 108 mins. Cert U.

Encino Man
See *California Man.*

The End of the Golden Weather
New Zealand; the 1930s. Self-consciously whimsical rites-of-passage saga based on the autobiographical play by Bruce Mason. Geoff, an imaginative and solitary 12-year-old boy, who dreams of being a writer, befriends the village idiot, Firpo, and becomes obsessed with helping him realise his own dream – to win the Olympic Games. [CB]

Cast: Stephen Fulford (Geoff Crome), Stephen Papps (Firpo), Paul Gittins (Dad), Gabrielle Hammond (Mum), David Taylor (Ted), Alison Bruce (Kass), Greg Johnson, Ray Henwood, Bill Johnson, Alice Fraser.

Dir: Ian Mune. Pro: Mune and Christina Milligan. Ex Pro: Don Reynolds. Screenplay: Mune and Bruce Mason. Ph: Alun Bollinger. Ed: Michael Horton. Pro Des: Ron Highfield. M: Stephen McCurdy. Costumes: Barbara Darragh. (South Pacific Pictures Ltd–Blue Dolphin.) Rel: 5 February 1993. 103 mins. Cert PG.

Falling Down
On a broiling hot day in Los Angeles, stuck in the middle of a traffic jam, a motorist snaps. It's a sick world out there and, he decides, he's no longer going to take any more bull from anybody. In short, he does what most of us wish we had the guts to do: he fights back. While attempting to get change for a 'phone call from a convenience store, he is told he must buy something first. But he cannot find anything cheap enough that will leave him change for the call. So he pays what he believes to be a reasonable price for a Coke, picks up a baseball bat and trashes the joint. And so he goes on, until he's past the point of no return . . . On the same day, a cop is trying to stay alive on his last day on the job. He's to retire to Lake Havasu in Arizona with a wife who drives him nuts. Still, it's got to be better than life in Los Angeles. Hasn't it? Director Joel Schumacher skilfully weaves these two stories of two men facing an extraordinary day in the city with a powerful narrative thrust, showering his dark vision with broad flecks of humour. A superbly made, very black comedy-thriller, *Falling Down* panders to our most basic instincts, but the lesson is for us to enjoy the film as a cathartic experience, and not to imitate the hero's vigilantism (seductive as the latter course may seem). An extremely dangerous and entertaining film, exceptionally well acted by a top-notch cast. [JC-W]

Cast: Michael Douglas (William 'D-FENS' Foster), Robert Duvall (Det. Martin Prendergast), Barbara Hershey (Elizabeth Foster), Rachel Ticotin (Sandra), Frederic Forrest (surplus store owner), Tuesday Weld (Mrs Prendergast), Lois Smith (Mrs Foster), Michael Paul Chan (Mr Lee), Raymond J. Barry (Captain Yardley), Karina Arroyave (Angie), Dedee Pfeiffer (Sheila, Whammyburgeress), Joey Hope Singer, Ebbe Roe Smith, D. W. Moffett, Steve Park, Kimberly Scott, James Keane, Agustin Rodriguez, Eddie Frias, Irene Olga Lopez, Benjamin Mouton, John Fleck, Brent Hinkley, Vondie Curtis-Hall, Mark Frank, Peter Radon, Spencer Rochfort, Carole Ita White, Jack Kehoe, Valentino D. Harrison, Jack Betts, Al Mancini, John Diehl, Amy Morton.

Dir: Joel Schumacher. Pro: Arnold Kopelson, Herschel Weingrod and Timothy Harris. Ex Pro: Arnon Milchan. Screenplay: Ebbe Roe Smith. Ph: Andrzej Bartkowiak. Ed: Paul Hirsch. Pro Des: Barbara Ling. M: James Newton Howard; numbers performed by David Rose & His Orchestra, Fu-Schnickens, Luisa Maria Guell, and Arabella. Costumes: Marlene Stewart. Sound: David MacMillan. (Studio Canal Plus/Regency Enterprises/Alcor Films–Warner.) Rel: 4 June 1993. 112 mins. Cert 18.

Far and Away

1892–3; Western Ireland/Boston/Oklahoma. Epic romantic drama following the fortunes of a brash, illiterate Irish farmhand and a stifled, moneyed Irish woman – thrown together on a quest to find land in the New World. Although married in real life, Tom Cruise and Nicole Kidman generate little human chemistry, leaving the grandiose sweep of Ron Howard's direction to carry the emotion. Technically, the film is a supreme achievement (filmed in Panavision Super 70mm), while its narrative canvas of tempestuous love, landed gentry and the struggle for land solicits affectionate comparisons with *Gone With the Wind*. [JC-W]

Cast: Tom Cruise (Joseph Donnelly), Nicole Kidman (Shannon Christie), Thomas Gibson (Stephen), Robert Prosky (Daniel Christie), Barbara Babcock (Nora Christie), Colm Meaney (Kelly), Michelle Johnson (Grace), Barry McGovern (McGuire), Cyril Cusack, Eileen Pollock, Douglas Gillison, Wayne Grace, Niall Toibin, Jared Harris, Steven O'Donnell, Mark Mulholland, P. J. Brady, J. G. Devlin, Todd Hallowell, Clint Howard, Rance Howard.

Dir: Ron Howard. Pro: Howard and

Romance of the strawberry tart and the rough diamond: Nicole Kidman and Tom Cruise in Ron Howard's affectionate, sweeping love story, Far and Away *(from UIP)*

Brian Grazer. Ex Pro: Todd Hallowell. Co-Pro: Bob Dolman and Larry DeWaay. Screenplay: Dolman; from a story by Dolman and Howard. Ph: Mikael Salomon. Ed: Michael Hill and Daniel Hanley. Pro Des: Jack T. Collis and Allan Cameron. M: John Williams; *Book of Days* performed by Enya. Costumes: Joanna Johnston. Sound: Ivan Sharrock. (Imagine/Universal–UIP.) Rel: 31 July 1992. 140 mins. Cert 12.

FernGully The Last Rain Forest

'Aren't you a bit old, Crysta, to still believe in humans?' asks Crysta's father, a corpulent tree fairy living deep in the jungle paradise of Fern-

Joy to the world: Fox's entertaining, magical FernGully . . . The Last Rain Forest, *a film for all the family – with a message as big as the Amazon itself*

For unit, corps, God and country: Col Jack Nicholson bends the rules in Rob Reiner's gripping A Few Good Men *(from Columbia Tri-Star)*

Gully. And thus the stage is set for a topical, magical, funny, beautiful, moving and frightening animated fantasy that knocks the socks off Disney. An ambitious Danish-Canadian-British-Korean-Thai co-production, *FernGully* is a cartoon that succeeds in reaching a multi-faceted audience comprising children, adults and environmentalists. Crysta, a spirited, adolescent fairy in the Tinkerbell mould, befriends a high-octane, wise-cracking bat, and together they tumble on to the human threat to their Eden. The humans are coming, and their apocalyptic machines are devouring the forest. Worse still, a malevolent force is released by the destruction, which takes over the machines headed straight for FernGully. But, as the wise, matronly Magi Lune points out, it only takes one seed to unleash the magic of creation. An instant

children's classic with a powerful message for adults, *FernGully* should delight, entertain and appeal for years to come. Also, the music, sound and art-work are all well above average, fortified by a strong cast of well-known voices. [JC-W]

Voices: Tim Curry (Hexxus), Samantha Mathis (Crysta), Christian Slater (Pips), Jonathan Ward (Zak), Robin Williams (Batty Koda), Grace Zabriskie (Magi Lune), Geoffrey Blake (Ralph), Cheech Marin (Stump), Tommy Chong (Root), Tone-Loc (The Goanna), Robert Pastorelli, Townsend Coleman, Brian Cummings, Kathleen Freeman, Pamela Segall.
  Dir: Bill Kroyer. Pro: Wayne Young and Peter Faiman. Co-Pro: Jim Cox, Brian Rosen and Richard Harper. Ex Pro: Ted Field and Robert W. Cort. Screenplay: Cox; based on the stories of *FernGully* by Diana Young. Ed: Gillian Hutshing. Art: Susan Kroyer. M: Alan Silvestri; numbers performed by Johnny Clegg, Robin Williams, Tone-Loc, Tim Curry, Raffi, Sheena Easton, Ladysmith Black Mambazo, Elton John, etc. Sound: Jon Johnson, Hari Ryatt and Bruce Stubblefield. (FAI Films/Youngheart Prods–Fox.) Rel: 7 August 1992. 75 mins. Cert U.

A Few Good Men
Washington DC; 1992. In the words of his superior officer, Lt Daniel Kaffee is 'a fast food, slick-ass' Navy lawyer, or, to be really nasty, 'a used car salesman and an ambulance-chaser with rank'. Still, Kaffee has won 44 cases in nine months, even if he hasn't seen the inside of a courtroom. But his latest clients, two Marines accused of murder, will not accept his offer of a 'five-minute plea bargain' and six months in jail. Of course, Kaffee doesn't give a toss what they will or won't accept . . . Based on the Broadway play by Aaron Sorkin, *A Few Good Men* is an eloquent, lusty entertainment, all of it funny, moving, articulate and largely predictable. Still, there are *some* surprises, and Jack Nicholson has never been more watchable as the reptilian, charismatic and frightening Colonel Jessep. [JC-W]

Cast: Tom Cruise (Lt J. G. Daniel Kaffee), Jack Nicholson (Col Nathan R. Jessep), Demi Moore (Lt-Cdr JoAnne Galloway), Kevin Bacon (Capt Jack Ross), Kiefer Sutherland (Lt Jonathan Kendrick), Kevin Pollack (Lt Sam Weinberg), James Marshall (Pfc Louden Downey), J. T. Walsh (Lt Col Matthew Markinson), J. A. Preston (Judge Randolph), Wolfgang Bodison (Lance Cpl Harold W. Dawson), Christopher Guest, Matt Craven, Xander Berkeley, John M. Jackson, Noah Wyle, Cuba Gooding Jr, Lawrence Lowe, Matthew Saks, Harry Caesar, David Bowe, Maud Winchester.

Dir: Rob Reiner. Pro: Reiner, David Brown and Andrew Scheinman. Ex Pro: William Gilmore and Rachel Pfeffer. Screenplay: Aaron Sorkin; based on his play. Ph: Robert Richardson. Ed: Robert Leighton. Pro Des: J. Michael Riva. M: Marc Shaiman; numbers performed by Willie Mae Thornton, Patty Loveless, Jimmy Cotton, and UB40. Costumes: Gloria Gresham. Sound: Bob Eber. (Castle Rock Entertainment–Columbia Tri-Star.) Rel: 1 January 1993. 138 mins. Cert 15.

Fire in the Sky

On 5 November 1975, six Arizona loggers encountered a brilliant incandescence in the woods. One of them, Travis Walton, got out of a pick-up truck to take a closer look and was zapped by a bolt of blue light. Believing him dead, his colleagues fled for their lives, leaving Walton's body behind. Suspected of murder, the men took a lie detector test and were eventually exonerated. Amazing, but true. So says Travis Walton, on whose sensational (and best-selling) account this film is based. Some good actors invest their stock characters with presence, but the scenario oozes contrivance. Travis himself is portrayed as a whiter-than-white good ol' boy, while the authorities' cynicism is predictably one-sided. Still, the climatic sci-fi sequence is inventively and chillingly done, courtesy of Industrial Light & Magic. [JC-W]

Cast: D. B. Sweeney (Travis Walton), Robert Patrick (Mike Rogers), Craig Sheffer (Allan Dallis), Peter Berg (David Whitlock), James Garner (Sheriff Frank Watters), Henry Thomas (Greg Hayes), Bradley Gregg (Bobby Cogdill), Kathleen Wilhoite (Katie Rogers), Georgia Emelin (Dana Rogers), Tom McGranahan Sr (Dr Wilson), Noble Willingham, Scott Macdonald, Travis Walton.

Dir: Robert Lieberman. Pro: Joe Wizan and Todd Black. Ex Pro: Wolfgang Glattes. Co-Pro: Tracy Tormé and Robert Strauss. Screenplay: Tormé. Ph: Bill Pope. Ed: Steve Mirkovich. Pro Des: Laurence Bennett. M: Mark Isham; numbers performed by Freddy Fender, Johnny Winter, Danea Mitchell, The Doobie Brothers, and The Neville Brothers. Costumes: Joe I.

Gross encounters: Julia Ariola and Georgia Emelin comfort a confused and terrified D. B. Sweeney in Robert Lieberman's Fire in the Sky *(from UIP)*

Tompkins. Sound: Henry Garfield. (Paramount–UIP.) Rel: 18 June 1993. 109 mins. Cert 15.

Folks!

Chicago/Florida; 1992. If your idea of high comedy is Alzheimer's disease, senile dementia, suicide, premature deafness, crushed testicles, countless pratfalls, obnoxious children and broken families, then you'll love this. Tom Selleck, *sans* moustache, is Jon Aldrich, a wealthy, well-liked stockbroker with a beautiful, loving wife and two gorgeous kids. Watch and guffaw as his life disintegrates when his gaga parents and waspish sister move in. Wearing a cloak of black comedy, *Folks!* is actually witless slapstick, dripping in cheap sentimentality. Excruciating. [JC-W]

Cast: Tom Selleck (Jon Aldrich), Don Ameche (Harry Aldrich), Anne Jackson (Mildred Aldrich), Christine Ebersole (Arlene Aldrich), Wendy Crewson (Audrey Aldrich), Michael Murphy (Ed), Robert Pastorelli, Kevin Timothy Chevalia, Margaret Murphy, Joseph Miller, T. J. Parish, John McCormack, George O, Jerry Hotchkiss, Juan Ramirez, Gerald Owens.

Dir: Ted Kotcheff. Pro: Victor Drai and Malcolm R. Harding. Ex Pro: Mario and Vittorio Cecchi Gori. Screenplay: Robert Klane. Ph: Larry Pizer. Ed: Joan E. Chapman. Pro Des: William J. Creber. M: Michel Colombier. Costumes: Jay Hurley. Sound: Scott D. Smith. (Penta Pictures–First Independent.) Rel: 5 February 1993. 109 mins. Cert PG.

Parents from hell: Dom Ameche and Anne Jackson wreak havoc in Ted Kotcheff's unendurable Folks! *(from First Independent)*

Young at heart: Isabel Glasser and Mel Gibson in happier times in Steve Miner's unashamedly romantic Forever Young *(from Warner)*

Forever Young

1939/1992; California. Test pilot Daniel McCormick was fit, happy and in love. He had the job of his dreams – flying B-52s – and the woman of his heart, childhood valentine Helen. But he couldn't find the courage to say, 'Will you marry me?' When Helen is struck down in a car accident, Daniel volunteers to be a guinea pig in his best friend's test in cryogenic preservation – and is frozen for a year. The war interrupts the secret experiment, and the still-mourning Daniel wakes up 50 years later – in 1992! *Forever Young* is corny, improbable and sentimental, but if you're prepared to share its vision, underneath you will find a smart, inventive and extremely well-written ode to life, love and hope. Mel Gibson is at his charismatic best as the gung-ho romantic, while Jamie Lee Curtis delivers a sassy turn as the single mother who has the hots for him. Their scenes together are magic and touching and subtly illustrate the chasm between a 1939 man and a 1992 woman. Previously known as *The Rest of Daniel*. [JC-W]

Cast: Mel Gibson (Daniel McCormick), Elijah Wood (Nat), Isabel Glasser (Helen), George Wendt (Harry Finley), Jamie Lee Curtis (Claire), Joe Morton (Dr Cameron), Nicolas Surovy (John), Robert Hy Gorman (Felix), Veronica Lauren (Alice), Eric Pierpoint (Fred), David Marshall Grant, Millie Slavin, Michael Goorjian, Art LaFleur, Karla Tamburrelli.

Dir: Steve Miner. Pro: Bruce Davey. Ex Pro: Edward S. Feldman and Jeffrey Abrams. Screenplay: Abrams. Ph: Russell Boyd. Ed: Jon Poll. Pro Des: Gregg Fonseca. M: Jerry Goldsmith; 'The Very Thought of You' sung by Billie Holiday. Costumes: Aggie Guerard Rodgers. Make-up: Dick Smith. Sound: Jim Tanenbaum. (Icon–Warner.) Rel: 26 March 1993. 102 mins. Cert PG.

1492: Conquest of Paradise

Ridley Scott's enthralling, spectacular

Into the unknown: Gerard Depardieu lands in the West Indies in Ridley Scott's stunning vision of history, 1492: Conquest of Paradise *(from Guild)*

and excessively violent story of Christopher Columbus is as spellbinding and authentic as the Salkinds' movie is cod and trite (see *Christopher Columbus*). Running at two and a half hours, this is an epic portrayal of the man and the times he lived in, showing the stake burnings of the Spanish Inquisition, the sacking of Granada, the financing of the trip to discover a new route to India (which cost the equivalent of two royal banquets), the voyage across the Atlantic, the confrontation with the American Indians, the ill-fated attempt to set up a colony in Haiti and Columbus's ultimate disgrace and downfall. As a history lesson, this is a powerful, unforgettable achievement, but Gerard Depardieu's Columbus lacks the charisma and diction to carry off the role. Also, the film attempts too much history yet not enough detail to make this the masterpiece it so nearly was. [JC-W]

Cast: Gerard Depardieu (Christopher Columbus), Armand Assante (Sanchez), Sigourney Weaver (Queen Isabel), Angela Molina (Beatrix), Michael Wincott (Adrian de Moxica), Tcheky Karyo (Martin Alonzo Pinzon), Kevin Dunn (Captain Mendez), Loren Dean, Fernando Rey, Frank Langella, Mark Margolis, Kario Salem, Billy Sullivan, Steven Waddington.

Dir: Ridley Scott. Pro: Scott and Alain Goldman. Ex Pro: Mimi Polk Sotela and Iain Smith. Screenplay: Roselyne Bosch. Ph: Adrian Biddle. Ed: William Anderson and Francoise Bonnot. Pro Des: Norris Spencer. M: Vangelis. Costumes: Charles Knode and Barbara Rutter. Sound: Pierre Gamet. (Percy Main/Legende/Cyrk–Guild.) Rel: 23 October 1992. 150 mins. Cert 15.

Frauds

Australia; the 1960s/1992. In his second film lead, Phil Collins attempts – with mixed success – to throw off his nice guy image. As an insurance investigator with a passion for game-playing and nasty practical jokes, he makes life hell for a married couple, blackmailing them over a false claim. An uneasy mix of comedy and thrills marred by heavy-handed direction, *Frauds* provides some fascination in a final confrontation reminiscent of a campy TV episode of *The Avengers* or *Batman*. [SR]

Cast: Phil Collins (Roland Copping), Hugo Weaving (Jonathan), Josephine Byrnes (Beth), Peter Mochrie (Michael Allen),

Helen O'Connor, Rebel Russell, Nicholas Hammond, Vincent Ball.

Dir and Screenplay: Stephen Elliott. Pro: Andrena Finlay and Stuart Quin. Ex Pro: Rebel Penfold-Russell. Ph: Geoff Burton. Ed: Frans Vandenburg. Pro Des: Brian Thomson. M: Guy Gross. Costumes: Fiona Spence. Sound: Ross Linton. (Latent Image–First Independent.) Rel: 4 June 1993. 94 mins. Cert 15.

Freddie as F.R.0.7

This animated feature is more than your average fairy tale. One-time prince Freddie becomes a top French secret agent – despite being a large frog – and the only one who can stop an evil mastermind from stealing Britain's tourist attractions. However, it takes more than splendid animation and snappy tunes to save this cute story from the doldrums. Take the kids and a book. [KK]

Voices: Ben Kingsley (Freddie), Jenny Agutter (Daffers), Brian Blessed (El Supremo), Nigel Hawthorne (Brigadier G), Michael Hordern (King), Phyllis Logan (Nessie), Jonathan Pryce (Trilby), Prunella Scales (Queen), Billie Whitelaw (Messina), John Sessions (Scotty), David Ashton, Victor Maddern, Bruce Purchase.

Genesis of a villain: Phil Collins turns nasty in Stephan Elliott's Frauds *(from First Independent)*

It takes a frog (a.k.a. Prince Frederic) to rescue the United Kingdom in this overly familiar fantasy, Freddie as F.R.0.7. *(from Rank)*

Women without men: Fairuza Balk looking for love in Allison Anders's poignant, touching Gas Food Lodging *(from Mainline)*

Power play: Al Pacino as the unscrupulous Ricky Roma in James Foley's powerful adaptation of David Mamet's Glengarry Glen Ross *(from Rank)*

Johnson. Sound: John Bateman. (Hollywood Road Films–Rank.) Rel: 14 August 1992. 91 mins. Cert U.

Dir: Jon Acevski. Pro: Acevski and Norman Priggen. Screenplay: Acevski and David Ashton. Ph: Rex Neville. Ed: Alex Rayment and Mick Manning. Art: Paul Shardlow. M: David Dundas and Rick Wentworth; lyrics: Don Black, Acevski and Ashton; songs performed by George Benson & Patti Austin, Grace Jones, Barbara Dickson, Boy George, Asia, and Holly

Gas Food Lodging

Laramie, New Mexico; 1991. Although based on the novel *Don't Look and It Won't Hurt* by Richard Peck, this bittersweet drama smacks of autobiography way beyond its literary source. The story of a single mother and her two teenage daughters growing up in a desert trailer park, the book was adapted by debuting filmmaker Allison Anders to fit her own experience. Anders herself grew up without a father and, following a trip to England, became a single mother at 18. Ione Skye, who plays the rebellious Trudi, never even met her father, the folk singer Donovan. It all helps. The writing, acting and atmosphere are all so real that you can believe in these people and cry along with them. Fairuza Balk (an erstwhile Dorothy in *Return to Oz*) is particularly impressive as the adolescent narrator, but it is for Anders's tart, truthful and funny screenplay that we must be truly thankful. [JC-W]

Cast: Brooke Adams (Nora), Ione Skye (Trudi), Fairuza Balk (Shade), James Brolin (John Evans), Robert Knepper (Dank), David Landsbury (Hamlet Humphrey), Jacob Vargas (Javier), Donovan Leitch (Darius), Chris Mulkey (Raymond), Adam Biesk (Brett), Leigh Hamilton (Kim), Nina Belanger (Elvia Rivero), Laurie O'Brien, Julie Condra, Diane Behrens, J. Mascis, Tiffany Anders, Cathryn Balk.
   Dir and Screenplay: Allison Anders. Pro: Daniel Hassid, Seth M. Willenson and William Ewart. Ex Pro: Carl-Jan Colpaert and Christoph Henkel. Ph: Dean Lent. Ed: Tracy S. Granger. Pro Des: Jane Ann Stewart. M: J. Mascis; numbers performed by Japan, Nick Cave, Mark Fosson, the Velvet Monkeys, Victoria Williams, etc. Sound: Clifford (Kip) Gynn. (Cineville Inc.–Mainline.) Rel: 2 October 1992. 102 mins. Cert 15.

Glengarry Glen Ross

In a sleazy real-estate office in Chicago a quartet of salesmen are given a career incentive. First prize is a Cadillac Eldorado; second, a set of steak knives; and third and fourth, unemployment. Adapted by David Mamet from his own hard-hitting play, this is

a workmanlike translation and a plat-form for some spectacular bravura acting. Al Pacino, a Mamet regular, comes off best as the alternately silver-tongued and gutter-mouthed hustler with an unethical modus operandi, while Alec Baldwin delivers a powerful cameo as a brutal company spokes-man. Never rising above its theatrical origins, this is nonetheless a compel-ling look at the cut-throat arena of pro-fessional oneupmanship, based on Mamet's own experiences in real estate. [JC-W]

Cast: Al Pacino (Ricky Roma), Jack Lemmon (Shelley 'The Machine' Levene), Alec Baldwin (Blake), Ed Harris (Dave Moss), Alan Arkin (George Aaronow), Kevin Spacey (John Williamson), Jonathan Pryce (James Lingk), Bruce Altman, Jude Ciccolella, Paul Butler.
  Dir: James Foley. Pro: Stanley R. Zupnik and Jerry Tokofsky. Ex Pro: Joseph Carac-ciolo. Screenplay: David Mamet; based on his play. Ph: Juan Ruiz Anchia. Ed: Howard Smith. Pro Des: Jane Musky. M: James Newton Howard; *Blue Skies* performed by Al Jarreau; *Prelude to a Kiss* by the Bill Holman Orchestra. Costumes: Jane Green-wood. Sound: Danny Michael. (Zupnik

Hog wild: Bill Murray and marmot in Harold Ramis's ingenious comedy Groundhog Day *(from Columbia Tri-Star)*

Enterprises–Rank.) Rel: 30 October 1992. 100 mins. Cert 15.

Groundhog Day

Phil Connors (Bill Murray) is an ego-centric, cynical weatherman sent to the small town of Punxsutawney, west-ern Pennsylvania, to cover the annual Groundhog Day festival on 2 February – which, myth has it, will determine the weather for the next six weeks. Connors is dreading the outing and is making the worst of it, when the day keeps repeating itself. Trapped inside 2 February, Connors soon discovers that he can do what he likes, and will always wake up again intact – *the same day*. A fascinating concept, this, which is well exploited, as Connors quickly makes the most of the 'previous' day's experience, to both bad and good ends. However, Bill Murray has played this smug bastard once too often, and, again, is inevitably redeemed through the goodwill of a seasonal festival (remember *Scrooged*?). Still, there are plenty of enjoyable moments, not least the scenes in which Connors gleans information from women to use on their next 'first date'. [JC-W]

Cast: Bill Murray (Phil Connors), Andie MacDowell (Rita Hanson), Chris Elliott (Larry), Stephen Tobolowsky (Ned Ryerson), Brian Doyle-Murray (Buster

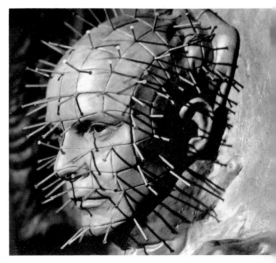

Hell is a face mistaken for a pincushion: Doug Bradley as the master of mayhem in Anthony Hickox's unnerving Hellraiser III – Hell On Earth *(from Arrow Films)*

Greene), Marita Geraghty (Nancy Taylor), Angela Paton (Mrs Lancaster), Rick Duc-ommun, Rick Overton, Robin Duke, Carol Bivins, Willie Garson, Ken Hudson Campbell, Les Podwell, Rod Sell, John Watson Jr, Peggy Roeder, Harold Ramis, David Pasquesi, Sandy Maschmeyer, Michael Shannon.
  Dir: Harold Ramis. Pro: Ramis and Trevor Albert. Ex Pro: C. O. Erickson. Screenplay: Ramis and Danny Rubin. Ph: John Bailey. Ed: Pembroke J. Herring. Pro Des: David Nichols. M: George Fenton; numbers performed by Delbert McClin-ton, Sonny & Cher, Ray Charles, Nat King Cole, etc. Costumes: Jennifer Butler. Sound: George H. Anderson. (Columbia Tri-Star.) Rel: 7 May 1993. 101 mins. Cert PG.

Hellraiser III – Hell on Earth

Wildly unpleasant sequel in which the demonic, debonair Pinhead moves to New York stuck inside a sculpture made up of tortured souls (a weird piece of masonry that would make H. R. Giger proud). All Pinhead needs is a bit more flesh and blood to return to his former glory. The extremely leggy and lovely Terry Farrell is the strong-willed TV reporter who tries to send him back to hell. Stylish, inven-tive, terminally sick. [JC-W]

Cast: Terry Farrell (Joey Summerskill), Doug Bradley (Pinhead/Elliott Spencer), Paula Marshall (Terri), Kevin Bernhardt (J. P. Monroe), Ken Carpenter (Doc/ Camerahead), Lawrence Mortoff, Aimee Leigh, Brent Bolthouse, Anthony Hickox, Shanna, Clayton Hill.

Labouring the point: Jack Nicholson as Danny DeVito's Hoffa *(from Guild)*

Dir: Anthony Hickox. Pro: Lawrence Mortorff. Ex Pro: Clive Barker. Screenplay: Peter Atkins; from a story by Atkins and Tony Randel, based on characters created by Clive Barker. Ph: Gerry Lively. Ed: Chris Cibelli. Pro Des: Steve Hardie. M: Randy Miller and Christopher Young. Costumes: Leonard Pollack. Sound: Kim Ornitz. (Fifth Avenue Ent./Nostradamus Pics–Arrow Films.) Rel: 19 February 1993. 93 mins. Cert 18.

Hero
See *Accidental Hero.*

Hoffa
James Riddle Hoffa, the unscrupulous leader of America's Teamsters union, was described by Robert F. Kennedy as 'the second most powerful man in America'. He was also suspected of bribery, tax evasion, embezzling pension funds, murder and even conspiring in the assassination of John F. Kennedy. He also plotted with the Mafia, and in 1967 was jailed for mail

fraud and jury tampering. Danny DeVito's plodding, flat biographical feature paints Hoffa as a flawed, crusading saint, and misses the point. Jack Nicholson, unrecognisable behind impressive make-up, fails to exude any charisma in the title role, while DeVito is omnipresent and intrusive as his fictitious sidekick Bobby Ciaro. Surprisingly, David Mamet's script is confusingly structured, with few dramatic payoffs, while DeVito's direction lacks the style the film so badly needs. There are a few directorial flourishes, but this is no *Godfather* or *The Untouchables.* However, the supporting cast is excellent, particularly Armand Assante's self-possessed, deadly mob boss, and Kevin Anderson as a flustered Bob Kennedy. For the record, Nicholson directed DeVito in the 1978 western *Goin' South.* [JC-W]

Cast: Jack Nicholson (James Riddle Hoffa), Danny DeVito (Bobby Ciaro), Armand Assante (Carol D'Allesandro), J. T. Walsh (Frank Fitzsimmons), Robert Prosky (Billy Flynn), John C. Reilly (Peter Connelly), Kevin Anderson (Robert F. Kennedy), Natalija Nogulich (Josephine Hoffa), Frank Whaley, John P. Ryan, Nicholas Pryor, Paul Guilfoyle, Karen Young, Cliff Gorman, Tom Finnegan, Jennifer Nicholson, William Cameron.

Dir: Danny DeVito. Pro: DeVito, Edward R. Pressman and Caldecot Chubb. Ex Pro: Joseph Isgro. Screenplay: David Mamet. Ph: Stephen H. Burum. Ed: Lynzee Klingman and Ronald Roose. Pro Des: Ida Random. M: David Newman. Costumes: Deborah L. Scott. Sound: Thomas D. Causey. (Jersey Films/Fox–Guild.) Rel: 19 March 1993. 140 mins. Cert 15.

Home Alone 2: Lost in New York
In spite of that tearful reunion at the end of *Home Alone,* Mr and Mrs McCallister forget Kevin on their next Christmas vacation – to rainy Miami. This time they leave him at the airport, and Kevin boards the wrong plane – to the Big Apple. Repeating the formula of the first, phenomenally successful film, producer/writer John Hughes has created a hugely enjoyable, frequently ingenious entertainment. Again, Kevin relishes the prospect of spending Christmas on his own, again the villainous Harry and Marv conspire to ruin it, and again Kevin unleashes a rein of terror at their

Home & away: Kevin McCallister (Macaulay Culkin) befriends a character straight out of Mary Poppins *(Brenda Fricker) in the only successful Christopher Columbus film of 1992 –* Home Alone 2: Lost in New York *(from Fox)*

expense. He also befriends another lonely old soul who initially scares the living daylights out of him. And again Kevin learns that he mustn't judge a book by its cover. Sentimental, funny and violent (even more so this time around), *Home Alone 2* is formulaic escapism that works. [JC-W]

Cast: Macaulay Culkin (Kevin McCallister), Joe Pesci (Harry), Daniel Stern (Marv), Catherine O'Hara (Kate McCallister), John Heard (Peter McCallister), Tim Curry (Mr Hector, the concierge), Brenda Fricker (pigeon lady), Eddie Bracken (Mr Duncan), Devin Ratray (Buzz McCallister), Gerry Bamman (Uncle Frank), Dana Ivey (Hester Stone, the desk clerk), Rob Schneider (Cedric, the bellman), Ally Sheedy (New York ticket agent), Hillary Wolf, Maureen Elisabeth Shay, Michael C. Maronna, Terrie Snell, Jedidiah Cohen, Senta Moses, Daiana Campeanu, Kieran Culkin, Anna Slotky, Leigh Zimmerman, Ralph Foody, Clare Hoak, Bob Eubanks, Rip Taylor, Jaye P.

Morgan, Jimmie Walker, Rod Sell, Ron Canada, Cedric Young, Donald Trump.

Dir: Chris Columbus. Pro and Screenplay: John Hughes. Ex Pro: Mark Radcliffe, Duncan Henderson and Richard Vane. Ph: Julio Macat. Ed: Raja Gosnell. Pro Des: Sandy Veneziano. M: John Williams; numbers performed by Darlene Love, Andy Williams, Johnny Mathis, etc. Costumes: Jay Hurley. Sound: Jim Alexander. (Fox.) Rel: 11 December 1992. 119 mins. Cert PG.

Honey, I Blew Up the Kid

Vista Del Mar, suburban Nevada; 1992. Predictably icky sequel to the 1989 hit *Honey, I Shrunk the Kids*, with 'wacky' absent-minded professor Wayne Szalinski repeating his mistakes

It's not the size that counts: the tot totters over Las Vegas in Disney's tiresome Honey, I Blew Up the Kid

Can't help falling in love: Nicolas Cage (centre) disguised as Elvis (aren't they all?) in Andrew Bergman's most enjoyable Honeymoon in Vegas *(from First Independent)*

as an irresponsible parent. This time, thanks to 'a surge of electro-magnetic flux', he turns his 2-year-old into a 114-foot toddler. Thin jokes, predictable villains, unimpressive sight gags and iffy special effects fail to dampen the deeply disturbing message of the film: big isn't necessarily better. The only remotely credible thing in this mess is the giant baby. [JC-W]

Cast: Rick Moranis (Wayne Szalinski), Marcia Strassman (Diane Szalinski), Robert Oliveri (Nick Szalinski), Daniel and Joshua Shalikar (Adam Szalinski), Lloyd Bridges (Clifford Sterling), John Shea (Hendrickson), Keri Russell (Mandy), Ron Canada (Marshall Brooks), Amy O'Neill (Amy Szalinski), Michael Milhoan, Gregory Sierra, Leslie Neale, Julia Sweeney, Linda Carlson, Ken Tobey.
　Dir: Randal Kleiser. Pro: Dawn Steel and Edward S. Feldman. Ex Pro: Albert Band and Stuart Gordon. Screenplay: Thom Eberhardt, Peter Elbling and Garry Goodrow; based on characters created by Gordon, Brian Yuzna and Ed Naha. Ph: John Hora. Ed: Michael A. Stevenson and Harry Hitner. Pro Des: Leslie Dilley. M: Bruce Broughton. Costumes: Tom Bronson. (Walt Disney–Buena Vista.) Rel: 5 February 1993. 90 mins. Cert U.

Honeymoon in Vegas

New York/Las Vegas/Hawaii. Mrs Singer's dying wish is that her son Jack should never marry. Four years later Jack is having trouble hanging on to his adoring girlfriend, Betsy, who

Domestic subterfuge: vagrants Laurel Cronin and Richard B. Shull (left) masquerade as Goldie Hawn's parents while Steve Martin looks on – in Frank Oz's inventive Housesitter *(from UIP)*

offers an ultimatum: commitment or separation. Finally, Jack suggests a weekend wedding in Vegas – in spite of disturbing dreams of his mother. In Nevada, smarmy big-timer gambler Tommy Korman is stunned by Betsy's resemblance to his dead wife, and sets up a poker game to win her from Jack. This is a madcap, old-fashioned comedy with a crazy veneer and a rather sweet centre. Nicolas Cage, in his *Raising Arizona* mode, makes a suitably appealing oaf out of Jack, but James Caan in the straight role of Korman tries too hard for laughs: the supporting cast steals them all. [JC-W]

Cast: James Caan (Tommy Korman), Nicolas Cage (Jack Singer), Sarah Jessica Parker (Betsy Nolan/Donna), Pat Morita (Mahi), Johnny Williams (Johnny Sandwich), John Capodice (Sally Molars), Robert Costanzo (Sidney Tomashefsky), Anne Bancroft (Bea Singer), Peter Boyle (Chief Orman), Keone Young (Eddie Wong), Burton Gilliam, Brent Hinkley, Dean Hallo, Seymour Cassel, Earnie Shavers, Tony Shalhoub.
　Dir and Screenplay: Andrew Bergman. Pro: Mike Lobell. Ex Pro: Neil Machlis. Ph: William A. Fraker. Ed: Barry Malkin. Pro Des: William A. Elliott. M: David Newman; songs performed by Bruce Springsteen, Jeff Beck, Amy Grant, Bryan Ferry, Billy Joel, Willie Nelson, John Mellencamp, Dwight Yoakam, Elvis Presley, Peter Boyle, etc. Costumes: Julie Weiss. Sound: David MacMillan. (Castle Rock/

Dirty laundry: Mia Farrow and Judy Davis discuss their private lives in Woody Allen's acutely unsettling Husbands and Wives *(from Columbia Tri-Star)*

New Line Cinema–First Independent.) Rel: 26 February 1993. 96 mins. Cert 12.

The Hours and the Times

Cinema curio department! Black-and-white *cinéma vérité*, financed, written, directed and produced by Christopher Munch – and made in *four days*! – which *imagines* what may have happened during a holiday Beatle John Lennon and manager Brian Epstein uneasily took together in 1963, when Epstein possibly hoped to seduce Lennon but failed. Audacious, interesting in some ways, but of limited appeal. It won awards at the Berlin and Sundance Film Festivals. [FDM]

Cast: David Angus (Epstein), Ian Hart (Lennon), Stephanie Pack, Robin Mac-Donald.

Dir, Pro, Screenplay, Ed: Christopher Munch. Ph: Munch and Juan Carlos Valls. (Antarctic Pictures–ICA.) Rel: 18 September 1992. 60 mins. No cert.

Housesitter

It was the perfect marriage – until the husband showed up. Gwen is a pathological liar ('the Ernest Hemingway of bullshit') who turns out to be a one-night stand from hell for Boston architect Newton Davis. Without his knowledge, Gwen moves into his dream house, befriends his parents – *and becomes his wife*. Newton, however, intends to sell the house and marry his childhood sweetheart. Balancing their 'in-house' relationship on a bed of lies, Gwen and Newton invent their own memories and struggle to free themselves from the nightmare they have created. Steve Martin mugs a little *too* much, Goldie Hawn is a little *too* old (replacing Meg Ryan, 17 years her junior), and the film is a trifle on the slushy side, but for the most part this is a sweet nightmare. [JC-W]

Cast: Steve Martin (Newton Davis), Goldie Hawn (Gwen), Dana Delany (Becky), Julie Harris (Edna Davis), Donald Moffat (George Davis), Peter MacNicol (Marty), Richard B. Shull (Ralph), Laurel Cronin (Mary), Roy Cooper (Moseby), Christopher Durang (Rev. Lipton), Hey-

wood Hale Broun, Cherry Jones, Vasek Simek, Suzanne Whang.

Dir: Frank Oz. Pro: Brian Grazer. Ex Pro: Bernie Williams. Assoc Pro: Karen Kehela and Michelle Wright. Screenplay: Mark Stein and Grazer. Ph: John A. Alonzo. Ed: John Jympson. Pro Des: Ida Random. M: Miles Goodman. Costumes: Betsy Cox. Sound: Martin Raymond Bolger. (Imagine/Universal–UIP.) Rel: 11 September 1992. 102 mins. Cert PG.

Husbands and Wives

It is hard – nay, *impossible* – to view Woody Allen's thirteenth movie with Mia Farrow without superimposing his troubled private life. Woody plays Gabe, a writer who is married to Judy, played by Mia Farrow. Judy wants a baby, Gabe doesn't. Judy is afraid that Gabe isn't telling her everything. He isn't: he's falling in love with a 21-year-old student, who's *actually* played by an 18-year-old Juliette Lewis. In real life, Woody claims that his lover Soon-Yi Previn (Mia's adopted daughter) is 21, while others suggest she is nearer 18 . . . Watching *Husbands and Wives* is a disturbing experi-

Down among the eunuchs: James Wilby in a dramatic moment from Jamil Dehlavi's fascinating Immaculate Conception *(from Feature Film Co.)*

Cultural exchange: Maria Schrader and Dani Levy, the stars, writers and director of the quirky little black comedy, I Was on Mars *(from Metro Tartan)*

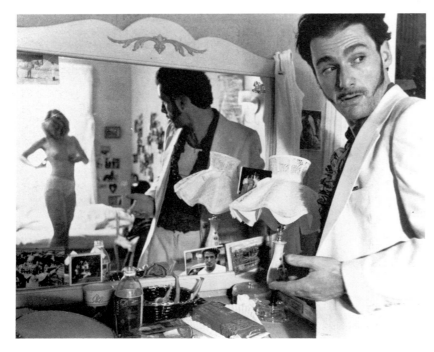

prise. And surprise is a prerequisite ingredient of cinema. [JC-W]

Cast: Woody Allen (Gabe Roth), Judy Davis (Sally), Mia Farrow (Judy Roth), Juliette Lewis (Rain), Liam Neeson (Michael), Sydney Pollack (Jack), Lysette Anthony (Sam), Jeffrey Kurland (Interviewer/Narrator), Bruce Jay Friedman, Cristi Conaway, Benno Schmidt, Ron Rifkin, Blythe Danner, Caroline Aaron, Nora Ephron, Ira Wheeler.

Dir and Screenplay: Woody Allen. Pro: Robert Greenhut. Ex Pro: Jack Rollins and Charles H. Joffe. Ph: Carlo Di Palma. Ed: Susan E. Morse. Pro Des: Santo Loquasto. M: Mahler, Cole Porter, Irving Berlin, Jerome Kern & Oscar Hammerstein III, etc. Costumes: Jeffrey Kurland. Sound: Frank Graziadei. (Tri-Star–Columbia Tri-Star.) Rel: 23 October 1992. 107 mins. Cert 15.

I Was on Mars

Unable to speak English, a young Polish woman, Silva, arrives in the city of her dreams – New York. At first staying in the best hotels and taking extravagant taxi rides, Silva soon finds her finances depleted and her innocence taken advantage of ... An unflattering character study both of a stubborn, ridiculous woman and of the city that disappoints her, this German homage to Jim Jarmusch starts off promisingly but fails to keep the attention. [JC-W]

Cast: Maria Schrader (Silva), Dani Levy (Alio), Mario Giacalone (Nic), Antonia Rey (La Mama), Penny Arcade a.k.a. Susana Ventura (coffee shop waitress), Lisa Langford, Ben Berman, Cyndi Coyne.

Dir: Dani Levy. Line Pro: Ted Hope and James Schamus. Ex Pro: Gudrun Ruzick-ová-Steiner, Rolf Schmid and Janet Jacobson. Screenplay: Levy and Maria Schrader. Ph: Carl F. Koschnick. Ed: Susann Lahaye. Pro Des: Dan Oullette. M: Niki Reiser. Costumes: Arndt Wiegering. Sound: Chris Logan. (Balthazar Pictures/Berlin Film Board, etc–Metro Tartan.) Rel: 21 May 1993. 86 mins. Cert 15.

Immaculate Conception

Alistair, a British representative of the World Wildlife Organisation, and Hannah, his Jewish-American wife, work and live in Karachi and are longing for a baby. In desperation, they attend a holy shrine, where they are invited to stay for three nights to conceive their child. Run by cross-dressed eunuchs, the shrine gives Alistair the creeps and he has good reason to dis-

ence. Its stench of authenticity is further magnified by a documentary approach that Woody shoves down our throats with manic camera work that eventually produces a feeling of seasickness. As usual, his writing is brilliant, the performances exemplary, but he's made this film so many times before that there is no element of sur-

trust it . . . This film, shot in the heat of the Gulf War crisis, is a fascinating, suspenseful and topical insight into the ancient, mystical culture of Pakistan, where Jackie Collins is devoured and Salmon Rushdie condemned. Directed by the Pakistani Jamil Dehlavi, who now lives in England. [JC-W]

Cast: James Wilby (Alistair), Melissa Leo (Hannah), Shabana Azmi (Samira), Zia Mohyeddin (Shehzada), James Cossins (Godfrey), Shreeram Lagoo (Dadaji), Ronny Jhutti (Kamal), Tim Choate (David Schwartz), Bhaskar, Bill Bailey, Zafar Hameed.

Dir, Pro and Screenplay: Jamil Dehlavi. Ph: Nic Knowland. Ed: Chris Barnes. Pro Des: Mike Porter. M: Richard Harvey. Costumes: Jane Moxon. Sound: John Poyner. (Feature Film Co.) Rel: 11 September 1992. 120 mins. Cert 15.

In the Soup

New York; 1992. Highly idiosyncratic, low-budget black-and-white comedy about an impoverished would-be filmmaker who befriends a lively gangster willing to finance his first feature (*Unconditional Surrender*). A series of promising vignettes fails to gather any momentum, ultimately leading to tedium. The film was apparently inspired by the director's real liaison with an art-loving hood who became his first 'producer'. [JC-W]

Cast: Seymour Cassel (Joe), Steve Buscemi (Adolpho Rollo), Jennifer Beals (Angelica), Pat Moya (Dang), Will Patton (Skippy), Stanley Tucci (Gregoire), Sully Boyer, Steven Randazzo, Francesco Messina, Jim Jarmusch, Carol Kane, Rockets Redglare, Elizabeth Bracco, Debi Mazar.

Dir: Alexandre Rockwell. Pro: Jim Stark and Hank Blumenthal. Ex Pro: Ryuichi Suzuki. Screenplay: Rockwell and Tim Kissel. Ph: Phil Parmet. Ed: Dana Congdon. Pro Des: Mark Friedberg. M: Mader. Costumes: Elizabeth Bracco. Sound: Pavel Wdowczak. (Will Alliance Co/Pandora Film/Why Not Prods/Odessa/Alta/Mikado–NFT/Theatrical Experience.) Rel: 14 May 1993. 93 mins. Cert 15.

Indecent Proposal

Robert Redford, still looking great at 55, is in Gatsby mode as a suave, charming, but emotionally distanced billionaire who offers Demi Moore $1 million to spend the night with him. Together with her husband of seven years, Woody Harrelson, Demi is des-

Sleeping with the enemy: Demi Moore considers an offer she can't refuse – from Robert Redford – in Adrian Lyne's intriguing Indecent Proposal *(from UIP)*

titute, desperate and decidedly suspicious of Redford's offer. His proposition proves to be not so much a carrot dangled in front of the despondent couple as a live grenade dropped between them. Initially repulsed by the offer, neither Demi nor Woody can stop thinking about it. After all, they argue, both had slept with others before they were married,

Celluloid croutons: Steve Buscemi and Seymour Cassel in Alexandre Rockwell's episodic In the Soup *(from NFT/Theatrical Experience)*

Orient excess: Vincent Perez in the epic, meandering and Oscar-winning Indochine *(from Electric)*

and this would only be one night that could solve all their problems – and set them up for a lifetime. Redford, on first consideration, might seem unlikely casting as a man in need of a one-night stand, but he is perfect as the charismatic counterpoint to Harrelson's passionate, down-to-earth and sensitive Everyman. Director Adrian Lyne (*Fatal Attraction*, *9½ Weeks*) pushes the emotional buttons skilfully and never labours a point, bringing class and style to this high-concept confection. [JC-W]

Cast: Robert Redford (John Gage), Demi Moore (Diana Murphy), Woody Harrelson (David Murphy), Oliver Platt (Jeremy), Seymour Cassel (Mr Shackleford), Billy Bob Thornton, Rip Taylor, Billy Connolly, Joel Brooks, Danny Zorn, Kevin West, Sheena Easton, Herbie Hancock.
　Dir: Adrian Lyne. Pro: Sherry Lansing. Ex Pro: Tom Schulman and Alex Gartner. Co-Pro: Michael Tadross. Screenplay: Amy Holden Jones; based on the novel by Jack Engelhard. Ph: Howard Atherton. Ed: Joe

Hutshing. Pro Des: Mel Bourne. M: John Barry; numbers performed by Sade, Ray Charles, David Bowie, Little Feat, The Pretenders, Lisa Stansfield, Sheena Easton, Herbie Hancock, etc. Costumes: Bobbie Read, Bernie Pollack and Beatrix Aruna Pasztor. Sound: Keith Wester. (Paramount–UIP.) Rel: 14 May 1993. 117 mins. Cert 15.

Indochine

1930–54; Indo-China. Catherine Deneuve, in familiar glacial mode, plays the rich, aloof owner of a 6,000 hectare rubber plantation. Her only love is Camille, the 16-year-old Vietnamese girl she has adopted, an innocent spirit spoilt by the wealth and attention of her guardian. The arrival of a handsome French officer transforms both their uneventful lives, and coincides with the deep-felt passion and resentment rising in the Indo-Chinese people. A lush, sweeping romantic drama set at a turbulent time in French history, *Indochine* takes a while to get going, but is always surprising and never resorts to cliché. A stronger directorial style would have made it a film of some distinction, but

nevertheless it won the 1992 Oscar for Best Foreign Film. [JC-W]

Cast: Catherine Deneuve (Elaine Devries), Vincent Perez (Jean-Baptiste LeGuen), Linh Dan Pham (Camille), Jean Yanne (Guy Asselin), Dominique Blanc (Yvette), Henri Marteau (Emile), Trinh Van Thinh (Madam Minh Tam), Carlo Brandt, Gerard Lartigau, Hubert Saint-Macary, Andrzej Seweryn, Mai Chau, Jean-Baptiste Huynh, Eric Nguyen, Nhu Quynh.
　Dir: Régis Wargnier. Pro: Eric Heumann. Ex Pro: Alain Blemondo and Gerard Crosnier. Screenplay: Wargnier, Erik Orsenna, Louis Gardel and Catherine Cohen. Ph: François Catonné. Ed: Geneviève Winding. Pro Des: Jacques Bufnoir. M: Patrick Doyle; songs sung by Dominique Blanc. Costumes: Gabriella Pescucci and Pierre-Yves Gayraud. Sound: Guillaume Sciama. (Paradis Films and Général D'Images/Bac Films/Orly Films/Ciné Cinq–Electric.) Rel: 26 March 1993. 150 mins. Cert 12.

Innocent Blood

Pittsburgh; 1992. John Landis, who put the joke into horror with his ground-breaking *An American Werewolf in London*, returns to the giggle-and-shudder genre with this comic

In a comic vein: Anne Parillaud gets to grips with Robert Loggia in John Landis's outrageous Innocent Blood *(from Warner)*

vampire horror film crossed with a Mafia crime melo. Anne Parillaud (of *Nikita*) plays a lonely, hungry vampire from out of town who's in the mood for some Italian, and sees the Mafia gang war as the perfect feeding ground. But then lonely undercover cop Anthony LaPaglia gets in her way. Yes, this is a love story to boot. Landis, who loves to slip from one genre to the next, enjoys himself immensely with this entertaining, wildly uneven hotchpotch, piling in-joke on to in-joke and relishing the gruesome special effects. Favourite scene: the all-powerful vampire Parillaud seducing LaPaglia after supplying him with condoms. Even vampires need safe sex. [JC-W]

Cast: Anne Parillaud (Marie), Robert Loggia (Salvatore 'The Shark' Macelli), Anthony LaPaglia (Joe Gennaro), Don Rickles (Emmanuel Bergman), David Proval (Lenny), Chazz Palminteri (Tony), Leo Burmester (Flinton), Angela Bassett (US attorney Sinclair), Luis Guzman (Morales), Elaine Kagan (Frannie Bergman), Rocco Sisto, Tony Sirico, Tony Lip, Kim Coates, Marshall Bell, Rohn Thomas, Tom Savini, Christopher Lee, Peter Cushing, Dan Quayle, Frank Oz, Bela Lugosi, Michael Ritchie, Sam Raimi, Dario Argento, Alfred Hitchcock, Robert Walker, Linnea Quigley, Michael Wolk, Rick Avery.
  Dir: John Landis. Pro: Lee Rich and Leslie Belzberg. Ex Pro: Jonathan Sheinberg. Screenplay: Michael Wolk. Ph: Mac Ahlberg. Ed: Dale Beldin. Pro Des: Richard Sawyer. M: Ira Newborn; numbers performed by Jackie Wilson, Frank Sinatra, Sturm & Twang, Prince & The New Power Generation, and Rhythm Syndicate. Costumes: Deborah Nadoolman. Sound: Joseph Geisinger. Make-up FX: Steve Johnson. (Warner.) Rel: 25 June 1993. 113 mins. Cert 15.

Into the West

Dublin; 1992. A magnificent white horse turns up at an urban encampment of 'travelling people', where it is immediately adopted by an 8-year-old

You can take a white horse anywhere: the charismatic Tir Na nOg is given supper by Ciaran Fitzgerald in Mike Newell's wondrous Into the West *(from Entertainment)*

All in the family: Robert J. Steinmiller Jr, Miko Hughes and Danny DeVito cling to their dreams in Marshall Herskowitz's poignant Jack the Bear *(from Fox)*

entertainment that manages to cover a number of bases. From the screenwriter of *Awakenings*. [JC-W]

Cast: Danny DeVito (John Leary), Robert J. Steinmiller Jr (Jack Leary), Miko Hughes (Dylan Leary), Gary Sinise (Norman Strick), Andrea Marcovicci (Elizabeth Leary), Julia Louis-Dreyfus (Peggy Etinger), Justin Mosley Spink (Dexter Mitchell), Christopher Lawford (Vince Buccini), Art LaFleur, Stefan Gierasch, Erica Yohn, Bert Remsen, Carl Gabriel Yorke, Lee Garlington, Lorinne Vozoff, Jessica Steinmiller.

Dir: Marshall Herskovitz. Pro: Bruce Gilbert. Ex Pro: Ron Yerxa. Screenplay: Steven Zaillian; based on the novel by Dan McCall. Ph: Fred Murphy. Ed: Steven Rosenblum. Pro Des: Lilly Kilvert. M: James Horner; numbers performed by The Youngbloods, Little Feat, Glenn Miller and His Orchestra, Percy Sledge, Spencer Davis Group, Jefferson Airplane, Country Joe & The Fish, Blind Faith, The Band, and Rick Nelson. Costumes: Deborah L. Scott. Sound: Jeff Wexler. (American Filmworks/Lucky Dog–Fox.) Rel: 28 May 1993. 99 mins. Cert 12.

boy, Ossie Riley. The attraction seems to be mutual, as Ossie appears to 'have the gift'. However, when the boy invites the horse – christened Tir na nOg (which sounds something like 'Turnin' Oak') – into his small tower-block apartment, the authorities intervene and Tir na nOg is 'sold' to a horse stud owner. So Ossie and his 12-year-old brother, Tito, kidnap the horse and ride out west . . . Skilfully blending local mythology with gritty realism and a sense of adventure, *Into the West* is a rich, authentic look at the life of Ireland's 'travellers' (a nomadic people with Celtic roots) and is also a children's film that should appeal to all ages. The real magic in this naturalistic tale of poverty and authoritarian oppression springs from the children's own imagination. Imaginatively filmed, superbly photographed and beautifully scored. [JC-W]

Cast: Gabriel Byrne (Papa Riley), Ellen Barkin (Kathleen), Ciarán Fitzgerald (Ossie Riley), Ruaidhrí Conroy (Tito Riley), David Kelly (grandfather), Colm Meaney (Barreller), John Kavanagh (Noel Hartnett), Brendan Gleeson (Inspector Bolger), Jim Norton (Superintendent O'Mara), Anita Reeves, Ray McBride, Dave Duffy, Phelim Drew, Sean Madden, Tony Rohr, Gladys Sheehan.

Dir: Mike Newell. Pro: Jonathan Cavendish and Tim Palmer. Ex Pro: James Mitchell. Co-Pro: Jane Doolan. Screenplay: Jim Sheridan; based on a story by Michael Pearce. Ph: Tom Sigel. Ed: Peter Boyle. Pro Des: Jamie Leonard. Costumes: Consolata Boyle. Sound: Peter Lindsay. (Majestic Films/Miramax/Film Four Int/Newcomm/Little Bird/Parallel Films/British Screen–Entertainment.) Rel: 11 December 1992. 102 mins. Cert PG.

Jack the Bear

He's no monster. In fact, he's the 12-year-old son of John Leary, the 'Monster of Ceremonies' of a late, late night horror-movie TV show. When (in 1972) Jack's mother is killed in a car accident, the Leary family – John, Jack and Jack's 3-year-old brother, Dylan – relocate to a seemingly quiet neighbourhood in Oakland, California. There, the Leary children discover that monsters really do exist . . . The film, bathed in a nostalgic autumnal glow, defies categorisation as it wafts from horror comedy to pre-teen romance to domestic drama, weaving a dreamlike spell over its audience. A very unusual, touching and charming

Jamon, Jamon

A stylised, rough-and-ready homage to the Spanish and their obsession for food and sex. Six characters converge in a story of seduction, machismo and ham, as the beautiful gamine Silvia discovers she is pregnant by the no-good Jose Luis. The latter's mother disapproves of the liaison, and hires a local stud to lure the poor girl away, leading to no end of complications. Lurching from black comedy to Greek tragedy, the film never misses an allusion to ham and humping and challenges the sex comedies of Pedro Almodovar for its sheer eccentricity and crudeness. [JC-W]

Cast: Penelope Cruz (Silvia), Anna Galiena (Carmen), Javier Bardem (Raul), Stefania Sandrelli (Conchita), Juan Diego (Manuel), Jordi Molla (Jose Luis), Tomas Penco (Raul's friend).

Dir: Bigas Luna. Screenplay: Luna, Cuca Canals and Quim Monzo. Ex Pro: Andres Vicente Gomez; Ph: J. L. Alcaine. Ed: Pablo Del Amo. Pro Des: Ricardo Albarran. M: Nicola Piovanni. Costumes: Neus Olivella. Sound: Miguel Rejas. (Lolafilms SA–Metro Tartan.) Rel: 4 June 1993. 93 mins. Cert 18.

Jersey Girl

Toby is a working-class New Jersey nursery schoolteacher who dreams of

Goyl talk: Jami Gertz and Molly Price talk men and romance in David Burton Morris's winning Jersey Girl *(from Entertainment)*

dating a handsome millionaire. When she meets Mr Right after accidentally forcing his Mercedes off the road, she refuses to let him go. Of course, she's just a poor girl with outsize ambitions and earrings, while he's a fashion plate with style, looks and power. But does he have *everything*? A predictable rip-off of *Pretty Woman*, this is nonetheless an enjoyable, workmanlike fairytale with some great costume design. [JC-W]

Cast: Jami Gertz (Toby Mastellone), Dylan McDermott (Sal Tomei), Molly Price (Cookie), Aida Turturro (Angie), Star Jasper (Dot), Sheryl Lee (Tara), Joseph Bologna (Bennie Mastellone), Philip Casnoff (Mitchell), Pat Collins (Gabe), Page Johnson (Maitre D').

Dir: David Burton Morris. Pro: David Madden, Nicole Seguin and Staffan Ahrenberg. Ex Pro: Ted Field and Robert W. Cort. Screenplay: Gina Wendkos. Ph: Ron Fortunato. Ed: Norman Hollyn. Pro Des: Lester Cohen. M: Misha Segal; numbers performed by May May, David Hallyday, The Beaver Brown Band, Tag. Costumes: Claudia Brown; Verri. Sound: Mark Weingarten. (Electric Pictures/Interscope Communications–Entertainment.) Rel: 21 August 1992. 95 mins. Cert 15.

Juice

The Hood is Harlem, and The Boyz are turning against themselves. Raw, hard-hitting suburban drama from Spike Lee's cinematographer Ernest R. Dickerson. Dickerson, who dreamed up the story of four Afro-Americans growing up in New York, co-scripted the screenplay with Gerard Brown, and then spent six years trying to finance it. Shot for a mere $3.6 million, the film finally grossed over $8m in its opening weekend in the States. The direction, photography and particularly the rap/R & B/hip-hop soundtrack are all top-notch. [JC-W]

Cast includes: Omar Epps (Quincy 'Q' Powell), Khalil Kain (Raheem), Jermaine Hopkins (Steel), Tupac Shakur (Roland Bishop), Cindy Herron (Yolanda), Vincent Laresca (Radames), Samuel L. Jackson

A rage in Harlem: Khalil Kain, Omar Epps, Tupac Shakur and Jermaine Hopkins in Ernest Dickerson's hard-hitting Juice *(from Electric)*

Dino-might: an exciting scene from Steven Spielberg's box-office-trampling Jurassic Park *(from UIP)*

(Trip), Queen Latifah, Tretch, K. Force, Eric & Parrish, Special Ed, DJ Scratch, Kid Capri, Rich E. Rich, Plaz-tic Man, Bones Malone, Ralph McDaniel, DJ Red Alert, Fab Five Freddie, Ed Lover & Dr Dre.

Dir: Ernest R. Dickerson. Pro: David Heyman, Neal H. Moritz and Peter Frankfurt. Screenplay: Dickerson and Gerard Brown. Ph: Larry Banks. Ed: Sam Pollard and Brunilda Torres. Pro Des: Lester Cohen, M: Hank Shocklee and The Bomb Squad. (Island World–Electric.) Rel: 28 August 1992. 92 mins. Cert 15.

Jurassic Park

By extracting the blood from a prehistoric mosquito preserved in amber, scientists discover the DNA of dinosaurs bitten 65 million years ago. Then, by copying the DNA (or genetic code) and placing it in the cell of a frog, they are able to hatch a dinosaur embryo in laboratory conditions. Dotty Scottish billionaire John Hammond (Richard Attenborough) capitalises on the idea by masterminding an epic theme park populated by brachiosauruses, triceratops, a tyrannosaurus rex and whathaveyou. Before revealing his secret to the public, Hammond invites a palaeontologist (Sam Neill), a palaeobotanist (Laura Dern), a mathematician (Jeff Goldblum) and a financier (Martin Ferrero) to his unique zoo of a bygone era. Big mistake . . . Drawing from a budget of $60 million, Spielberg and Industrial Light & Magic produce the goods and then some, creating an astonishing range of gentle, intelligent and ferocious creatures that move, breathe and attack like the real thing. Unfortunately, the prehistoric cast is introduced too soon for full dramatic effect, while the human characters are less convincing. Still, *Jurassic Park* is an exhilarating and often intensely frightening experience that should outlast the next millennium. Interestingly, the week that the film opened in the US (on 11 June 1993), scientists successfully isolated genetic material from an extinct weevil dating from 120 to 130 million years ago, providing the sort of publicity that not even Spielberg could afford to buy. [JC-W]

Cast: Sam Neill (Dr Alan Grant), Laura Dern (Ellie Sattler), Jeff Goldblum (Ian Malcolm), Richard Attenborough (John Hammond), Bob Peck (Robert Muldoon), Martin Ferrero (Donald Gennaro), Joseph Mazzello (Tim Murphy), Ariana Richards (Alexis Murphy), Samuel L. Jackson (Arnold), Wayne Knight (Dennis Nedry), Richard Kiley (tour voice), B. D. Wong, Jerry Molen, Miguel Sandoval, Cameron Thor, Dean Cundey.

Dir: Steven Spielberg. Pro: Kathleen Kennedy and Gerald R. Molen. Screenplay: Michael Crichton and David Koepp; based on the novel by Crichton. Ph: Dean Cundey. Ed: Michael Kahn. Pro Des: Rick Carter. M: John Williams. Sound: Ron Judkins. Live Action Dinosaurs: Stan Winston. (Universal/Amblin–UIP.) Rel: 16 July 1993. 126 mins. Cert PG.

What a drag: Adrian Pasdar and Julie Walters explore their sexual idiosyncrasies in Christopher Monger's homely Just Like a Woman *(from Rank). Anyone for home-made scones and lipstick?*

Just Like a Woman

Claims that one in 20 men has an urge to dress up in women's clothing. Based on Monica Jay's book *Geraldine*, itself inspired by her romance with a transvestite, this is a jokey, occasionally semi-serious look at the world of crossdressing. It is also – incongruously – the melodramatic story of how Gerald T. Tilson, an American merchant banker and transvestite in London, gets his revenge in the world of high finance. The quieter moments work best, with Julie Walters quite moving (and more restrained than usual) as the woman who accepts Gerald for what he is. [JC-W]

Cast: Julie Walters (Monica), Adrian Pasdar (Gerald T. Tilson), Paul Freeman (Miles Millichamp), Gordon Kennedy (C. J. McKenzie), Togo Igawa (Akira Watanabe), Mark Hadfield (Dennis), Susan Wooldridge, Ian Redford, Shelley Thompson, Jill Spurrier, Corey Cowper, Joseph Bennett, Brooke, Eve Bland, Jeff Nuttall, David Hunt, Tim Stern, Rohan McCullough.

Dir: Christopher Monger. Pro and Screenplay: Nick Evans. Ex Pro: Archie Tait, Fred Turner and Nick Elliott. Ph: Alan Hume. Ed: Nicolas Gaster. Pro Des: John Box. M: Michael Storey; numbers performed by Doris Day, The Thompson Twins, Elvis Presley, Duke Ellington, Eurythmics and Aretha Franklin. Costumes: Suzy Peters. Sound: John Poyner. (LWT/British Screen/Zenith–Rank.) Rel: 25 September 1992. 106 mins. Cert 15.

The King's Whore

By the very nature of its three-year delay and polylingual cast, this suggests all the potential of a co-production clinker, but in fact it's a handsomely mounted, extremely well-acted drama. Timothy Dalton stars as a 17th-century Italian king obsessed by the wife of his chamberlain. His highness, the court, the church and even the chamberlain himself pressurise the wife to give in to the king's demands. Eventually, she capitulates, but only at a terrible price . . . A French-Austrian-British-Italian co-production. [CB]

Cast: Timothy Dalton (King Vittorio Amadeo), Valeria Golino (Jeanne de Luynes), Stéphane Freiss (Count di Verua), Eleanor David (Queen), Robin Renucci, Feodor Chaliapin, Margaret Tyzack, Paul Crauchet.

Dir: Axel Corti. Pro: Maurice Bernart, Wieland Schulz-Keil and Paolo Zaccaria. Screenplay: Corti, Daniel Vigne and Frederic Raphael; based on the novel *Jeanne, putain du roi* by Jacques Tournier. Ph: Gernot Roll. Ed: Joelle Van Effenterre. Pro Des: Francesco Frigeri. M: Gabriel Yared. Costumes: Carlo Diappi. Sound: Michele Boehm. (ASC/FR3 Film/Cinema é Cinema/Umbrella Productions–Premiere.) Rel: 16 April 1993. 93 mins. Cert 15.

Check mate: Christopher Lambert as the enigmatic anti-hero of Knight Moves *(from Columbia Tri-Star)*

Knight Moves

A number of neat ideas are tossed into the casserole of this psychological thriller set in the world of international chess. Christopher Lambert is Peter Sanderson, an arrogant, self-obsessed champion with an enigmatic past. When a series of beautiful blonde corpses turns up in the small Pacific Northwest town hosting a grandmaster tournament, suspicion falls on Sanderson. It is then up to him to clear his name as the deadly, parallel game of cat-and-mouse reaches its checkmate. Some suspense is built up by the Swiss director Carl Schenkel, but the porous script ultimately defeats the film's logic. [JC-W]

Cast: Christopher Lambert (Peter Sanderson), Diane Lane (Kathy Sheppard), Tom Skerritt (Frank Sedman), Daniel Baldwin (Andy Wagner), Ferdinand Mayne (Jeremy Edmonds), Katherine Isobel (Erica Sanderson), Charles Bailey-Gates (David Willerman), Arthur Brauss (Viktor Yurilivich), Rehli O'Byrne (Debi Rutledge), Blu Mankuma (Steve Nolan), Rebecca Toolan (Mayor), Walter Marsh, Sam Malkin, Elizabeth Baldwin, Elizabeth Barclay.
   Dir: Carl Schenkel. Pro: Ziad El Khoury and Jean-Luc Defait. Ex Pro: Christopher Lambert and Brad Mirman. Screenplay: Mirman. Ph: Dietrich Lohmann. Ed: Norbert Jerzner. Pro Des: Graeme Murray. M: Anne Dudley. Costumes: Deborah Everton and Trish Keating. Sound: Ralph Parker (Lamb Bear Entertainment/Ink Slinger–Columbia Tri-Star.) Rel: 4 September 1992. 116 mins. Cert 18.

L.627 – Law 627

Bertrand Tavernier, whose son is a reformed heroin addict, turns his camera on the crumbling back streets of Paris as he follows the day-to-day routine of an ill-equipped narcotics squad. Harshly criticised for its uncompromising portrayal of police procedure and brutality and, indeed, for its racism (the drug dealers are predominantly African or Arabic), *L.627* tells it as it is, which makes for disheartening viewing. Discarding plot in favour of a docudrama feel, the film is relentlessly long, disturbing and convincing. [JC-W]

Cast: Didier Bezace (Lucien 'Lulu' Marguet), Charlotte Kady (Marie), Philippe Torreton (Tonio), Jean-Paul Comart (Dodo), Lara Guirao (Cecile), Cecile Garcia (Katy), Nils Tavernier, Jean-Roger Milo, Jean-Claude Calon, Francis Girard, Alain Sarde.
   Dir: Bertrand Tavernier. Ex Pro: Frederic Bourboulon. Co-Pro: Alain Sarde. Screenplay: Michel Alexandre. Ph: Alain Choquart. Ed: Ariane Boeglin. Pro Des: Guy-Claude Francois. Costumes: Jacqueline Moreau. Sound: Michel Desrois. (Little Bear–Artificial Eye.) Rel: 8 January 1993. 145 mins. Cert 15.

Labyrinth of Passion

Yet another 'discovery' of an early Pedro Almodovar work, which would have been best left forgotten. Made in 1982, this crude, overly complex farce exhibits another gallery of perverted characters who show up in a story about a nymphomaniac called Sexilia

A law unto themselves: Didier Bezace and Nils Tavernier question a suspect in Bertrand Tavernier's no-holds-barred L.627 *(from Artificial Eye)*

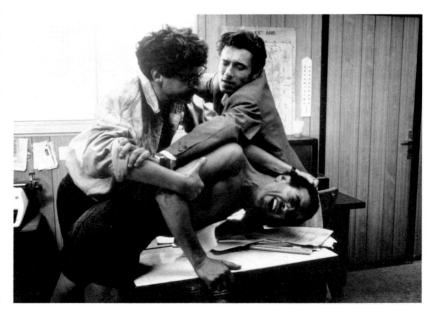

and her bisexual lover, Riza Niro, heir to the throne of a fictitious Islamic country. Almodovar, like an immature schoolboy, has obvious glee thumbing his nose at incest, drugs, transvestism, sexual abuse and potent laxatives, entirely for the artless sake of being smutty. Very tiresome. [CB]

Cast: Cecilia Roth (Sexilia), Imanol Arias (Riza Niro), Helga Line (Toraya), Marta Fernandez-Muro (Queti), Fernando Vivanco (Doctor de la Pena), Antonio Banderas (Sadeq), Ofelia Angelica, Angel Alcazar, Concha Gregori, Cristina Sanchez Pascual, Fany McNamara.
 Dir and Screenplay: Pedro Almodovar. Ph: Angel Luis Fernandez. Ed: Jose Salcedo. Art: Virginia Rubio. Sound: Martin Muller. (Alphaville–Metro.) Rel: 1 January 1993. 100 mins. Cert 18.

The Last Days of Chez Nous
Sydney, Australia; 1991. Gillian Armstrong directs this unusual and intimate family drama about the uncertainties of love within a colourfully eccentric family. Lisa Harrow in the wife-and-mother role plays Beth, a novelist, whose relationship with her French husband (Bruno Ganz) is starting to sag with emotional fatigue. Ground rules change when her sister Vicki flies back from Europe and daughter Annie readies to peel off from the mould. With a deeply textured script, this is Armstrong back on her best form, very at home on her own territory with this attractive and alluring story. [MG]

Cast: Lisa Harrow (Beth), Bruno Ganz (JP), Kerry Fox (Vicki), Miranda Otto (Annie), Kiri Paramore (Tim), Bill Hunter (Beth's father), Lex Marinos, Mickey Camilleri, Lynne Murphy, Claire Haywood, Leanne Bundy.
 Dir: Gillian Armstrong. Pro: Jan Chapman. Screenplay: Helen Garner. Ph: Geoffrey Simpson. Ed: Nicholas Beauman. Pro Des: Janet Patterson. M: Paul Grabowsky. Costumes: Janet Patterson. Sound: Ben Osmo. (Australian Film Commission/Australian Broadcasting Corporating/Australian Film Finance/Beyond Films–Metro Tartan.) Rel: 19 February 1993. 97 mins. Cert 15.

The Last of the Mohicans
North America; 1757. Picturesque, action-packed and bloody version of James Fenimore Cooper's classic tale of the frontiersman Hawkeye, raised

Daniel Day-Lewis as an imposing Hawkeye in Michael Mann's painstaking re-creation of James Fenimore Cooper's The Last of the Mohicans *(from Warner)*

by the Mohicans and reluctantly assisting the British against the bloodthirsty Huron Indians. Initially hard to follow, the film comes into its own as an action adventure and love story when Hawkeye falls for Cora Munro, the daughter of an English colonel. Bypassing the novel's more racist elements, *Mohicans* concentrates on the historical detail to its detriment, spreading confusion where it should have brought enlightenment. To underline its political correctness, the film has cast the celebrated Indian activist Russel Means in the title role. [JC-W]

Cast: Daniel Day-Lewis (Nathaniel Bumppo, 'Hawkeye'), Madeleine Stowe (Cora Munro), Russell Means (Chingachgook), Eric Schweig (Uncas), Jodhi May (Alice Munro), Steven Waddington (Duncan Heyward), Wes Studi (Magua), Maurice Roeves (Colonel Munro), Patrice Chereau (General Montcalm), Justin M. Rice (James

Women with balls: Lori Petty bats for the opposition, while big sister Geena Davis (below left) attempts to catch her out – in Penny Marshall's baseball hit, A League of Their Own *(from Columbia)*

Cameron), Edward Blatchford, Terry Kinney, Tracey Ellis, Pete Postlethwaite, Colm Meaney, Malcolm Storry, David Schofield, Dylan Baker, Jared Harris. Dir: Michael Mann. Pro: Mann and Hunt Lowry. Ex Pro: James G. Robinson. Screenplay: Mann and Christopher Crowe; based on the novel by James Fenimore Cooper and screenplay by Philip Dunne, adapted by John L. Balderston, Paul Perez and Daniel Moore. Ph: Dante Spinotti. Ed: Dov Hoenig and Arthur Schmidt. Pro Des: Wolf Kroeger. M: Trevor Jones, Randy Edelman and Daniel Lanois; *I Will Find You* performed by Clannad. Costumes: Elsa

Zamparelli. Sound: Simon Kaye. (Morgan Creek–Warner.) Rel: 6 November 1992. 112 mins. Cert 12.

A League of Their Own

1943–5; the ballparks of the USA. Described as *Steel Magnolias* meets *Bull Durham*, this is more like *The Bad News Bears* meets *Cocoon*. Based on real events, the film follows the growth of women's baseball in the war years when the men were off slugging Hitler. Focusing on the competition between two unlikely sisters – the tall, sinewy Dottie Hinson (Geena Davis) and the short, spunky Kit Keller (Lori Petty) – the dramatic comedy opens out into a sentimental history lesson, complete with newsreel footage and sepia-tinged photography. Bookended by a beautiful, tall geriatric version of Dottie

(played by Lynn Cartwright, but dubbed by Ms Davis) recalling those golden years, the film is at its best in its exposition of character, with star turns from Madonna as a streetwise nymphomaniac and Tom Hanks as an overweight, burnt-out, has-been baseball legend saddled with managing the all-girl Rockford Peaches. [JC-W]

Cast: Tom Hanks (Jimmy Dugan), Geena Davis (Dorothy 'Dottie' Hinson), Madonna (Mae 'All the Way Mae' Mordabito), Lori Petty (Kit Keller), Jon Lovitz (Ernie 'Cappy' Capadino), David Strathairn (Ira Lowenstein), Garry Marshall (Walter Harvey), Bill Pullman (Bob Hinson), Rosie O'Donnell (Doris Murphy), Megan Cavanagh (Marla Hooch), Tracy Reiner (Betty 'Spaghetti' Horn), Bitty Schram (Evelyn Gardner), Ann Cusack (Shirley Baker), Eddie Jones (Dave Hooch), Lynn Cartwright (older Dottie), Kathleen Butler (older Kit), Ann Elizabeth Ramsey, Freddie Simpson, Renee Coleman, Robin Knight, Patti Pelton, Kelli Simpkins, Neezer Tarleton, Connie Pounds-Taylor, Kathleen Marshall, Justin Scheller, Alan Wilder, Janet Jones, Joe Krowka, Harry Shearer, Ellie Weingardt, Douglas Blakeslee, Joseph Slotnick, Rae Allen, Eddie Mekka, Joette Hodgen, Eunice Anderson, Patricia Wilson.

Dir and Ex Pro: Penny Marshall. Pro: Robert Greenhut and Elliott Abbott. Screenplay: Lowell Ganz and Babaloo Mandel; from a story by Kim Wilson and Kelly Candalee. Ph: Miroslav Ondricek. Ed: George Bowers. Pro Des: Bill Groom. M: Hans Zimmer; numbers performed by Madonna, Carole King, Billy Joel, James Taylor, Art Garfunkel, The Manhattan Transfer, Doc's Rhythm Cats, the Rockford Peaches. Costumes: Cynthia Flynt. Sound: Les Lazarowitz. (Parkway–Columbia.) Rel: 18 September 1992. 124 mins. Cert PG.

Leap of Faith

Steve Martin, in his most dramatic role to date, plays an evangelist who, with the help of song, technology and eavesdroppers, can convince an audience that God speaks through him. Usually he preys on rich folk, but when his ministerial cavalcade breaks down in a poor Kansas backwater he has 'no choice' but to exploit the people there. His show is spectacular and full of state-of-the-art trickery, and for less than the price of a Broadway show he can bring his audience hope and entertainment (while lining his own pocket). And why not? The fact that this film flopped in the States is due, no doubt, to Martin's unremittingly unpleasant character, but it's a brave departure for the actor, even though he still plays the wild and crazy guy on stage. The film itself is often quite moving and thought-provoking, and a real eye-opener to the technique of fake evangelists. [JC-W]

Cast: Steve Martin (Jonas Nightengale), Debra Winger (Jane Larson), Lolita Davidovich (Marva Carpenter), Liam Neeson (Sheriff Will Braverman), Lukas Haas (Boyd Carpenter), Meat Loaf (Hoover), Philip Seymour Hoffman, M. C. Gainey, La Chanze, Delores Hall, John Toles-Bey, Albertina Walker, Ricky Dillard, Phyllis Somerville, Grover Washington.

Dir: Richard Pearce. Pro: Michael Manheim and David V. Picker. Ex Pro: Ralph S. Singleton. Screenplay: Janus Cercone. Ph: Matthew F. Leonetti. Ed: Don Zimmerman, Mark Warner and John F. Burnett. Pro Des: Patrizia Von Brandenstein. M: Cliff Eidelman; songs performed by Don Henley, Meat Loaf, Angels of Mercy, Wynonna, Lyle Lovett, Patti LaBelle, etc. Costumes: Theadora Van Runkle. Sound: Petur Hliddal. (Paramount–UIP.) Rel: 9 April 1993. 107 mins. Cert PG.

Léolo

Set in a squalid tenement block in the Mile End neighbourhood of East Montreal, *Léolo* is arguably the most exotic and visually fertile film ever to emerge from Canada. Distancing himself from his grotesque and largely insane family, young Leo Lauzan changes his name to Léolo Lozone and concocts a vivid interior world in which he imagines he was conceived by an accident with an Italian tomato. 'Italy,' he says in his colourful voice-over, 'is too beautiful to be inhabited by Italians alone.' What follows is a provocative, lyrical, challenging, overlong and brilliant exploration of unbridled fantasy, drawn largely from the director's own childhood imaginings. Disturbing and unforgettable. [JC-W]

Cast: Maxime Collin (Léolo), Ginette Reno (mother), Julien Guiomar (grandfather), Pierre Bourgault (the 'word tamer'), Giuditta del Vecchio (Bianca), Yves Montmarquette (Fernand), Roland Blouin (father), Geneviève Samson (Rita), Marie-Hélène Montpetit (Nanette), Alex Nadeau (Fernand, aged 16), Gilbert Sicotte (narration), Denys Arcand, Germain Houde, Lorne Brass, Francis Saint-Onge.

Tales from the bathroom: Maxime Collin contemplates his family in Jean-Claude Lauzon's startlingly personal Léolo *(from Metro)*

The devil in disguise: Steve Martin as evangelist Jonas Nightengale in Richard Pearce's provocative Leap of Faith *(from UIP)*

Abbott & Costello or James Bond? Rene Russo and Mel Gibson mix romance with thrills in Richard Donner's Lethal Weapon 3 *(from Warner)*

Dir and Screenplay: Jean-Claude Lauzon. Pro: Lyse Lafontaine and Aimée Danis. Ex Pro: Danis and Claudette Viau. Line Pro: Léon G. Arcand. Ph: Guy Dufaux. Ed: Michel Arcand. Art: François Séguin. M: Tom Waits, Sister Marie Keyrouz, The Tallis Scholars, Gilbert Becaud, The Rolling Stones, K. Khatchaturian, Bangal, etc. Costumes: François Barbeau. Sound: Marcel Pothier (Productions du Verseau/Flach Film/Le Studio Canal Plus–Metro.) Rel: 14 May 1993. 107 mins. Cert 18.

Leon the Pig Farmer

A North London Jewish estate agent discovers that he is the product of artificial insemination, his real father being a Yorkshire pig farmer. With a budget of just £150,000, the filmmakers have worked wonders, persuading the actors and technicians to defer payment. However, although there are plenty of laughs – particularly from Brian Glover as the pigman trying to speak Yiddish – the film's unevenness still betrays its creators' inexperience. With more money behind them, the directing-producing team of Vadim Jean and Gary Sinyor promises much for the future. [SR]

Cast: Mark Frankel (Leon Geller), Janet Suzman (Judith Geller), Brian Glover (Brian Chadwick), Connie Booth (Yvonne Chadwick), David De Keyser (Sidney Geller), Maryam D'Abo (Madeleine), Gina Bellman (Lisa), Vincenzo Ricotta, John Woodvine, Jean Anderson, Annette Crosbie, Stephen Greif, Burt Kwouk, Sean Pertwee, Barry Stanton, Bernard Bresslaw.
Dir and Pro: Gary Sinyor and Vadim Jean. Ex Pro: Paul Brooks. Co-Ex Pro: David Altschuler, Howard Kitchner and Steven Margolis. Assoc Pro: Simon Scotland. Screenplay: Sinyor and Michael Normand. Ph: Gordon Hickie. Ed: Ewa J. Lind. Pro Des: Simon Hicks. M: John Murphy and David Hughes. Sound: Danny Hambrook. (Electric.) Rel: 26 February 1993. 102 mins. Cert 15.

Lethal Weapon 3

One week before Murtaugh's retirement, the squabbling pair of LA detectives team up with an Internal Affairs cop to crack a stolen guns case. The twist here is that the new cop is a woman (the leggy, angular Rene Russo) and the firearms are police property – and their bullets ('cop-killers') capable of piercing steel. The English Stuart Wilson makes a convincing American heavy (although not as hissable as most), while Danny Glover, as Murtaugh, looks younger than he did in the first film. Mel Gibson (sporting an unlikely ponytail for a patrolman), builds on the comedy he injected into the previous sequel, and with the return of the fast-talking Joe Pesci as their sidekick, the film often resembles an extended Three Stooges sketch. The stunts are untoppable (entire office blocks are demolished, a housing development is burned to the ground), the pace relentless and the violence more cartoonish than ever. Budgeted at $40 million, this instalment outgrossed its predecessors, clocking up $100m in its first three weeks in the US alone. [JC-W]

Cast: Mel Gibson (Martin Riggs), Danny Glover (Roger Murtaugh), Joe Pesci (Leo

Getz), Rene Russo (Lorna Cole), Stuart Wilson (Jack Travis), Steve Kahan (Capt. Murphy), Darlene Love (Trish Murtaugh), Traci Wolfe (Rianne Murtaugh), Damon Hines (Nick Murtaugh), Ebonie Smith (Carrie Murtaugh), Gregory Millar (Tyrone), Delores Hall (Delores), Nick Chinlund, Jason Meshover-Iorg, Alan Scarfe, Mary Ellen Trainor, Mark Pellegrino, John Cenatiempo, Andrew Hill Newman, Lauren Shuler-Donner, Stephen T. Kay.

Dir: Richard Donner. Pro: Donner and Joel Silver. Co-Pro: Steve Perry and Jenny Lew Tugend. Screenplay: Jeffrey Boam and Robert Mark Kamen; based on characters created by Shane Black. Ph: Jan De Bont. Ed: Robert Brown and Battle Davis. Pro Des: James Spencer. M: Michael Kamen, Eric Clapton and David Sanborn; numbers performed by Clapton, Sting, Elton John, Boyz II Men, and Cypress Hill. Sound: Thomas Causey. (Silver Pictures–Warner.) Rel: 14 August 1992. 118 mins. Cert 15.

The Living End

Self-labelled 'an irresponsible movie', this is the defiant, stubbornly perverse story of two HIV-positive gay men on a journey of sodomy and murder across America. Knowing that their time is limited, Luke and John seek to find the freedom that they have been hitherto denied. For all its public posturing, the film does contain some humour and even an element of romance beneath its pachydermic surface, but

is still guilty of wallowing in self-pity. Previously known as – if you'll forgive our French – *Fuck the World*. [CB]

Cast: Mike Dytri (Luke), Craig Gilmore (Jon), Mark Finch (Doctor), Mary Woronov (Daisy), Johanna Went (Fern), Darcy Marta (Darcy), Scot Goetz, Bretton Vail, Nicole Dillenberg, Paul Bartel.

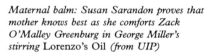

Maternal balm: Susan Sarandon proves that mother knows best as she comforts Zack O'Malley Greenburg in George Miller's stirring Lorenzo's Oil *(from UIP)*

Dir, Screenplay, Ph and Ed: Gregg Araki. Pro: Marcus Hu and Jon Gerrans. Ex Pro: Evelyn Hu, John Jost, Henry Rosenthal and Mike Thomas. Assoc Pro: Andrea Sperling. M: Cole Coonce. Sound: George Lockwood. (Mainline.) Rel: 12 February 1993. 84 mins. Cert 18.

Lorenzo's Oil

Pittsburgh/Washington DC/East Africa; 1983–92. Lorenzo is a happy, stable 5-year-old who is diagnosed as having adrenoleukodystrophy (ALD), a rare disease that destroys the nervous system and for which, in 1984, there was no known cure. All that the doctors can say for certain was that the life expectancy of ALD patients was 24 months and that fits, dementia, deafness and blindness preceded death. But Lorenzo's parents, the obstinate Michaela and her crusading Italian husband Augusto, are not prepared to sit idly by while their son

Dead end: Craig Gilmore and Mike Dytri taunt their director, Gregg Araki (centre), on the set of The Living End *(from Mainline)*

dies. Even if the medical establishment doesn't know it, there *must* be a cure – somewhere, somehow. A true story, *Lorenzo's Oil* doesn't flinch from showing the awful effects of the disease, nor does it soft pedal the complex medical jargon. Consequently, the film is both a fascinating medical detective story and a moving tribute to the determination of two people to save their child. As the mother, Susan Sarandon is particularly believable, but Nick Nolte's Italian accent takes some getting used to. In real life, Michaela and Augusto agreed to let George Miller (himself a former doctor) film their story, as he alone wanted to concentrate on the child, not the parents. Sadly, the young actor chosen to portray Lorenzo was far from cooperative, forcing Miller to bypass many of his scenes, ultimately leaving an emotional vacuum at the film's centre. Consequently, *Lorenzo's Oil* is the story not of a child's struggle, but of parental devotion. [JC-W]

Cast: Nick Nolte (Augusto Odone), Susan Sarandon (Michaela Odone), Peter Ustinov (Professor Nikolais), Zack O'Malley Greenburg (Lorenzo Michael Murphy Odone), Kathleen Wilhoite (Deirdre Murphy), Gerry Bamman (Doctor Judalon), Margo Martindale (Wendy Gimble), James Rebhorn (Ellard Muscatine),

Ill-at-sleaze: Sean Young at the mercy of Patrick Bergin in Lizzie Borden's Love Crimes *(from Rank)*

The hot mama and the damp squib: Victoria Abril and Jorge Sanz in Vicente Aranda's steamy true-life offering, Lovers *(from Mainline)*

Ann Hearn (Loretta Muscatine), Maduka Steady (Omouri), Jennifer Dundas (Nurse Nancy Jo), Don Suddaby (himself), Mary Wakio, Colin Ward, La Tanya Richardson, William Cameron.
 Dir: George Miller. Pro: Miller and Doug Mitchell. Ex Pro: Arnold Burk. Screenplay: Miller and Nick Enright. Ph: John Seale. Ed: Richard Francis-Bruce and Marcus D'Arcy. Pro Des: Kristi Zea. M: Verdi, Sviridov, Mahler, Barber, Bellini, Marcello, Donizetti, Elgar and Mozart. Costumes: Colleen Atwood. Sound: Ben Osmo. (Universal/Kennedy Miller–UIP.) Rel: 26 February 1993. 135 mins. Cert 12.

Love Crimes

What aspires to be an erotic thriller is neither titillating nor suspenseful. Sean Young is an unconvincing assistant DA from Atlanta on the trail of a charismatic rapist posing as a photographer. A superficial, misogynistic film that fails to expose the complex allure of sado-masochism. [JC-W]

Cast: Sean Young (Dana Greenaway), Patrick Bergin (David Hanover), Arnetia Walker (Marie Johnson), James Read (Stanton Gray), Ron Orbach (Det. Eugene Tully), Fern Dorsey, Tina Hightower, Donna Biscoe, Bob Hannah.
 Dir: Lizzie Borden. Pro: Borden and Rudy Langlais. Ex Pro: Forrest Murray. Screenplay: Allan Moyle and Laurie Frank. Ph: Jack N. Green. Ed: Nicholas C. Smith and Mike Jackson. Pro Des: Armin Ganz. M: Graeme Revell. Sound: Brit Warner. (Sovereign Pictures/Miramax–Rank.) Rel: 5 March 1993. 85 mins. Cert 18.

Lovers – Amantes

Madrid; the 1950s. Atmospheric, erotic, but somewhat ponderous film based on a true story. Paco, a young Adonis engaged to the beautiful, virginal Trini, enjoys a steamy affair with his landlady, Luisa, a recent widow. Both women vie for his affections but, thanks to Jorge Sanz's vacant, utterly charmless performance as Paco, it's hard to see why. However, Victoria Abril as Luisa – employing a silk handkerchief as a kinky new sex aid – was voted best actress at the 1991 Berlin Film Festival. [JC-W]

Cast: Victoria Abril (Luisa), Jorge Sanz (Paco), Maribel Verdu (Trini).
 Dir: Vicente Aranda. Pro: Pedro Costa-Muste. Screenplay: Aranda, Alvaro Del Amo and Carlos Perez Merinero. Ph: Jose Luis Alcaine. Ed: Tersa Font. Art: Josep Rosell. M: Jose Nieto. Costumes: Nereida Bonmati. Sound: Miguel Angel Polo. (Pedro Costa PCSA/TVE–Mainline.) Rel: 21 August 1992. 103 mins. Cert 18.

Madame Bovary

Ludicrous screen adaptation of Gustave Flaubert's notorious masterpiece, the story of a woman with romantic ideals rebelling against the mediocrity of her time. Condemned in 1857 for its candid portrait of adultery, this *Madame Bovary* will offend for its risible compression of plot. The novel's power was due to its uncompromising look at France in the 19th century, which shaped the fate of Emma Bovary. Here, the period is used purely as decorative background (and is flatly photographed, at that), while the plot gallops frantically to its conclusion. [JC-W]

X-cessive: Denzel Washington struggles manfully to hold the screen for 202 minutes in Spike Lee's self-indulgent Malcolm X *(from Guild)*

Period pains: Isabelle Huppert as Madame Bovary, *stifled by nineteenth-century France (from Arrow)*

Cast: Isabelle Huppert (Emma Bovary), Jean-Francois Balmer (Charles Bovary), Christophe Malavoy (Rodolphe Boulanger), Jean Yanne (Monsieur Homais, the pharmacist), Lucas Belvaux (Leon Dupuis), Sabeline Campo (Felicite), Marie Mergey (Mother Bovary), Francois Perier (narrator), Florent Gibassier, Jean-Claude Bouillaud, Yves Verhoeven, Etienne Draber, Gilette Barbier.

Dir and Screenplay: Claude Chabrol. Pro: Marin Karmitz. Ph: Jean Rabier. Ed: Monique Fardoulis. Set Design: Michele Abbe. M: Matthieu Chabrol. Costumes: Corinne Jorry. Sound: Maurice Gilbert. (MK2/CED/FR3–Arrow.) Rel: 28 May 1993. 140 mins. Cert PG.

Malcolm X

Before the opening credits have finished, director Spike Lee has burned the American flag and shown footage of the Rodney King video (the controversial amateur film in which LA police beat a black motorist), while Malcolm Little's incendiary words boom out, 'We are not Americans, we are victims of America . . .' At first glance, *Malcolm X* looks set to be another opportunity for Lee to court fame and controversy, but after the

opening, this biography of the black nationalist leader is surprisingly tame and frequently boring. The facts are fascinating: the son of a Baptist minister, Malcolm turned to a life of crime, drugs and women. In prison for burglary, he converted to Islam, and on release became an outspoken and eloquent opponent of white America, advocating violence in self-defence. However, as Lee drags his story out to over 202 minutes, he dulls the ironies of Malcolm's life. Had a brave editor carved an hour out of the film, it would have been a far more dynamic piece. However, Denzel Washington in the title role is superb. [JC-W]

Cast: Denzel Washington (Malcolm 'X' Little), Angela Bassett (Betty Shabazz), Albert Hall (Baines), Al Freeman Jr (Elijah Muhammed), Delroy Lindo (West Indian Archie), Spike Lee (Shorty), Theresa Randle (Laura), Kate Vernon (Sophia), Lonette McKee (Louise Little), Tommy Hollis (Earl Little), James McDaniel (Brother Earl), Ernest Thomas (Sidney), Jean LaMarre, O. L. Duke, Larry McCoy, Maurice Sneed, Debi Mazar, James E. Gaines, Joe Seneca, Giancarlo Esposito, Leonard Thomas, David Patrick Kelly, Shirley Stoler, Lennis Washington, Karen

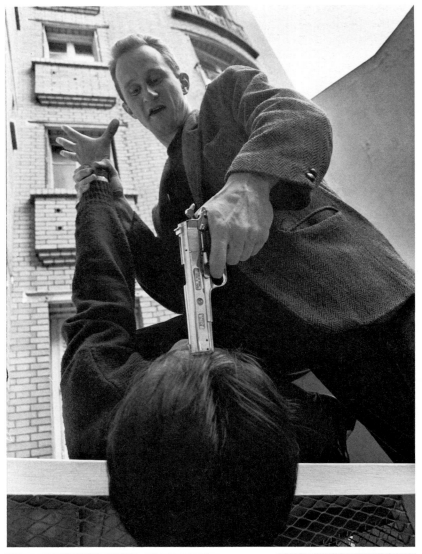

Death for a laugh: Benoit Poelvoorde flexes his piece in the darkly humorous, disturbing Man Bites Dog *(from Metro/Tartan)*

Allen, Peter Boyle, Vincent D'Onofrio, William Kunstler, Christopher Plummer, Bobby Seale, Craig Wasson, Matt Dillon, John Sayles, Martin Donovan, Al Sharpton, Ossie Davis, Nick Turturro.

Dir: Spike Lee. Pro: Lee and Marvin Worth. Co-Pro: Monty Ross, John Kilik and Preston Holmes. Screenplay: Lee and Arnold Perl; based on Alex Haley's *The Autobiography of Malcolm X*. Ph: Ernest Dickerson. Ed: Barry Alexander Brown. Pro Des: Wynn Thomas. M: Terence Blanchard. Costumes: Ruth E. Carter. Historical Consultant: Paul Lee. Sound: Rolf Pardula and Skip Lievsay. (Largo Int/40 Acres & a Mule Filmworks–Guild.) Rel: 5 March 1993. 202 mins. Cert 15.

Man Bites Dog

Ben is a gawky, endearing and cheerful man who regularly writes poetry for love and habitually kills for cash. His life story is being recorded by a small documentary crew who, at first stunned by the frivolity of his acts of murder, eventually become co-conspirators. Like *This Is Spinal Tap* and *Bob Roberts*, the film is presented in documentary form, and is the promising first feature from Belgian film graduates Remy Belvaux, Andre Bonzel and Benoit Poelvoorde (the last-named also playing Ben). Initially, *Man Bites Dog* plays for black laughs, soliciting our complicity as voyeurs, but then turns our shame on us. Ultimately, it's an old trick given a new twist, and leaves a very nasty taste in the mouth. But, the directors insist, the film is as much about the documentary filmmaking process as it is about killing. (The Belgian title translates as *It Happens In Your Neighbourhood*.) [JC-W]

Cast: Benoit Poelvoorde (Ben), Jacqueline Poelvoorde-Pappaert, Nelly Pappaert, Jenny Drye, Malou Madou, Willy Vandenbroeck, Rachel Deman, Valerie Parent, Remy Belvaux, Andre Bonzel.

Dir and Pro: Remy Belvaux, Andre Bonzel and Benoit Poelvoorde. Screenplay: Belvaux, Bonzel, Poelvoorde and Vincent Tavier; based on an idea by Belvaux. Ph:

Air of the dog: Jack Nicholson makes a point to Vilas, in Bob Rafelson's would-be comedy Man Trouble *(from First Independent)*

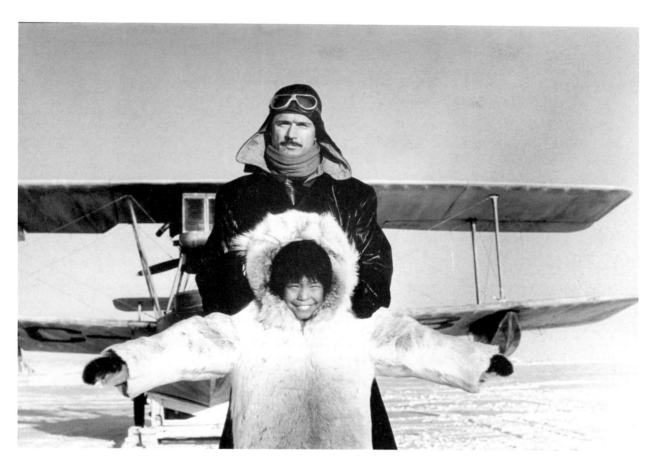

Emotional cartography: Young Avik (Robert Joamie) and the mapmaker (Patrick Bergin) in Vincent Ward's sweeping Map of the Human Heart *(from Rank)*

Bonzel. Ed: Belvaux and Eric Dardill. M: Jean-Marc Chenut. Sound: Tavier and Alain Oppezzi. (Les Artistes Anonymes–Metro/Tartan.) Rel: 15 January 1993. 95 mins. Cert 18.

Man Trouble

Los Angeles; 1992. The refined, exalted arena of opera and the sleazy, dingy world of attack-dog training collide in the unlikely romance of concert soprano Joan Spruance and compulsive liar and flirt Harry Bliss. Ellen Barkin is suitably attractive and dizzy as the singer plagued by an unseen aggressor; but Jack Nicholson's dishevelled lecher, although initially charming, soon grows tiresome. Ultimately, this is a heavy-handed stab at black screwball comedy, although there are some nice character turns from an impressive supporting cast. Co-produced and scripted by Carole Eastman, who wrote the screenplays

for *The Shooting, Five Easy Pieces* and *The Fortune*, all starring Nicholson. [JC-W]

Cast: Jack Nicholson (Harry Bliss/Eugene Earl Axline), Ellen Barkin (Joan Spruance), Harry Dean Stanton (Redmond Layls), Beverly D'Angelo (Andy Ellerman), Michael McKean (Eddy Revere), Veronica Cartwright (Helen Dextra), David Clennon (Lewie Duart), John Kapelos (Det. Melvenos), Lauren Tom (Adele 'Iwo Jima' Bliss), Betty Carvalho (Socorro), Saul Rubinek, Viveka Davis, Paul Mazursky, Mark J. Goodman, Robin Greer, Sandy Ignon, Rebecca Broussard, Mary Robin Redd.
    Dir: Bob Rafelson. Pro: Bruce Gilbert and Carole Eastman. Ex Pro: Vittorio Cecchi Gori. Co-Ex Pro: Gianni Nunnari. Screenplay: Eastman. Ph: Stephen H. Burum. Ed: William Steinkamp. Pro Des: Mel Bourne. M: Georges Delerue; Bach, Sting. Costumes: Judy Ruskin. Sound: David Ronne. (Penta/American Filmworks/Budding Grove–First Independent.) Rel: 15 January 1992. 99 mins. Cert 15.

Map of the Human Heart

The Arctic/Canada/England/Germany; 1929–65. Visually impressive, dramatically unconvincing saga of an

Eskimo half-breed who leaves his remote, Arctic community to find the woman of his dreams. Along the way he is dazzled by the technology and inhumanity of the white man, culminating in the blanket bombing of Dresden – which, for Arik, is the ultimate act of human savagery. Vincent Ward, who brought us the visionary, award-winning *The Navigator*, is fascinated by the effect of the modern world on sheltered, backward peoples, and here expands his theme, weaving in otherworldly threads of fate and coincidence. [JC-W]

Cast: Patrick Bergin (Walter Russell), Anne Parillaud (Albertine), Jason Scott Lee (Avik), John Cusack (mapmaker), Jeanne Moreau (Sister Banville), Ben Mendelsohn (Farmboy), Robert Joamie (young Avik), Annie Galipeau (young Albertine), Clotilde Courau, Jerry Snell, Jayko Pitseolak, Reepah Arreak, Harry Hill, Anik Matern, Charlotte Coleman.
    Dir: Vincent Ward. Pro: Ward and Tim Bevan. Co-Pro: Tim White. Ex Pro: Harvey and Bob Weinstein, and Graham Bradstreet. Screenplay: Ward and Louis Nowra. Ph: Eduardo Serra. Ed: John Scott. Pro Des: John Beard. M: Gabriel Yared.

A conspiracy of bad luck: Wayne Bowman and Saeed Jafrey in Srinivas Krishna's compassionate, absurdist comic-drama, Masala *(from Metro)*

Costumes: Renee April. Sound: Andrew Plain. (Polygram/Working Title/Les Films Ariane/Sunrise Films–Rank.) Rel: 4 June 1993. 109 mins. Cert 15.

Gross antics: Mant takes Cathy Moriarty hostage in Joe Dante's Matinee *(from Guild)*

Masala

Tagged a Canadian *My Beautiful Laundrette*, this is actually a far broader, crazier and more whimsical film, a surreal pastiche of the Hindu epic crossed with *Rebel Without a Cause*. Set in the Indian community of Toronto, *Masala* features Saeed Jaffrey in three different roles – as a wealthy businessman, a poor post office worker and a camp Lord Krishna, who is summoned by the hero's grandmother on the remote control of her VCR. Debuting Indian director Srinivas Krishna (now a Canadian resident) stars as the disenchanted Krishna, a drug-dealing malcontent recovering from the demise of his parents, obliterated in a plane crash. A spirited, brave and startling screen original, taking its cue from mainstream Bombay cinema, modern Indian literature and magic-realist fiction. [CB]

Cast: Srinivas Krishna (Krishna), Saeed Jaffrey (Lallu Bhai Solanki/Hariprassad Tikkoo/Lord Krishna), Sakina Jaffrey (Rita Tikkoo), Zohra Segal (Grandma Tikkoo), Herj Singh Johal (Anil Solanki), Madhuri Bhatia, Ronica Sajnani, Les Porter.
  Dir and Screenplay: Srinivas Krishna. Pro: Krishna and Camelia Freiberg. Ph: Paul Sarossy. M: Leslie Winton. Sound: Ross Redfern. (Metro.) Rel: 7 August 1992. 110 mins. Cert 18.

Matinee

Florida; 1962. Schlock horror director Lawrence Woolsey plans to test his latest picture – *Mant!* ('Half Man, Half Ant, All Terror!') – in Key West, to capitalise on the mounting panic surrounding the Cuban missile crisis. An affectionate homage to the films of William Castle and Vincent Price and a satire of coming-of-age pictures, *Matinee* is neither one thing nor the other. Director Joe Dante's parody of hormonally unbalanced teenagers is repetitive and heavy-handed, while the B-movie spoofing is only intermittently funny. Of course, the real horror is the Cold War looming on the horizon. [JC-W]

Cast: John Goodman (Lawrence Woolsey), Cathy Moriarty (Ruth Corday/Carole), Simon Fenton (Gene Loomis), Omri Katz (Stan), Kellie Martin (Sherry), Lisa Jakub (Sandra), Jesse Lee (Dennis Loomis), James Villemaire (Harvey Starkweather), Robert Picardo (Howard Dartmouth), Jesse White (Mr Spector), Lucinda Jenney (Anne Loomis), David Clennon, Lucy Butler, Dick Miller, John Sayles, Belinda Balaski, Charlie Haas, Naomi Watts, Mary

Moriarty, William Schallert, Robert Cornthwaite, Kevin McCarthy.

Dir: Joe Dante. Pro: Michael Finnell. Co-Pro: Pat Kehoe. Screenplay: Charlie Haas; from a story by Jerico Haas. Ph: John Hora. Ed: Marshall Harvey. Pro Des: Steven Legler. M: Jerry Goldsmith; numbers performed by The Tokens, The Challengers, The Angels, Shelly Fabares, Little Eva, Gene Pitney, Skeeter Davis, and The Platters. Costumes: Isis Mussenden. Sound: Howard Warren. (Universal–Guild.) Rel: 18 June 1993. 99 mins. Cert PG.

Mediterraneo

The Aegean Sea; 1941–5. A donkey and a ragbag of nervous men representing the Italian army occupy a remote, virtually deserted island in the Mediterranean. Shortly after their arrival, the soldiers' radio transmitter is irreparably damaged and a few hours after that a volley of enemy fire destroys their battleship. Frightened and homesick, the men are stranded and cut off from the outside world. They are in Paradise. Dedicated 'to all those who are running away', *Mediterraneo* is a film of delightful vignettes, complete with luscious photography, dulcet Greek music and amusing caricatures. But ultimately it is a slight affair which goes nowhere, and, understandably, was a controversial choice for the Oscars' 1991 Best Foreign Film statuette, which it won over such distinguished entries as *Raise the Red Lantern* and *The Ox*. [JC-W]

Cast: Diego Abatantuono (Sgt Nicola Lo Russo), Claudio Bigagli (Lt Montini), Giuseppe Cederna (Farina), Claudio Bisio (Noventa), Gigio Alberti (Strazzabosco), Vanna Barba (Vasilissa), Luigi Montini (Pope), Ugo Conti, Memo Dini, Vasco Mirondolo, Irene Grazioli, Antonio Catania.

Dir: Gabriele Salvatores. Pro: Gianni Minervini, Mario Cecchi Gori and Vittorio Cecchi Gori. Screenplay: Vincenzo Monteleone. Ph: Italo Pettriccione. Ed: Nino Baragali. Art: Thalia Istikopoulos. M: Giancarlo Bigazzi. (Mayfair Entertainment.) Rel: 30 April 1993. 90 mins. Cert 15.

A Midnight Clear

1944, the Ardennes Forest, France. A depleted squad of young, ill-prepared American soldiers find themselves holed up in a picturesque 17th-

In the line of fire: Gary Sinise suffers a breakdown as Ethan Hawke looks on – in Keith Gordon's intelligent and moving A Midnight Clear *(from Rank)*

century chateau on the edge of a snowy mountainside. Headed by the callow 19-year-old William Knott ('Won't' to his friends), the men wait for signs of the enemy. However, when the Germans do turn up, their offensive is far from expected. These, too, are bewildered men – some of them merely boys – who want the war to be over. An earnest, sensitive adaptation of William Wharton's novel, *A Midnight Clear* is a most unusual and tender war film that relies less on blood and guts than on the development of compassion through character. Beautifully filmed in Park City, Utah, the popular ski resort doubling for North-Eastern France. [JC-W]

Paradise in war: Vanna Barba and Giuseppe Cederna enjoy the peace and quiet of World War II in Gabriele Salvatores's Oscar-winning Mediterraneo *(from Mayfair Entertainment)*

Boxing clever: James Woods and Louis Gossett Jr plan the ultimate scam in Michael Ritchie's engrossing Midnight Sting *(from UIP)*

The producer as backer: producer Robert De Niro plays a producer of sorts in the decidedly uneven Mistress *(from Arrow)*

Dir and Screenplay: Keith Gordon. Pro: Dale Pollock and Bill Borden. Ex Pro: Army Bernstein, Tom Rosenberg and Marc Abraham. Ph: Tom Richmond. Ed: Donald Brochu. Pro Des: David Nichols. M: Mark Isham. Costumes: Barbara Tfank. Sound: John 'Earl' Stein. (Sovereign–Rank.) Rel: 5 March 1993. 108 mins. Cert 15.

Midnight Sting

(US: *Diggstown*.) 'The difference between a hustler and a good conman is that a good conman doesn't have to get out of town as fast as he can.' Thus reasons ace conman James Woods, fresh out of prison, who hangs around town to carry out an audacious sting. He bets crooked businessman and gambler Bruce Dern $100,000 that his old friend Louis Gossett Jr can knock out any ten men Dern cares to name – in the space of 24 hours. He may just be insane... Refreshingly straightforward, unpretentious yet colourful B-movie, with a smart turn from James Woods as the lizard who refuses to sweat. [JC-W]

Cast: Ethan Hawke (Will Knott), Kevin Dillon (Mel Avakian), Frank Whaley ('Father' Mundy), Peter Berg (Bud Miller), Gary Sinise ('Mother' Wilkins), Arye Gross (Stan Shutzer), John C. McGinley (Major Griffin), Larry Joshua (Lt Ware), Rachel Griffin (Janice), Curt Lowens, Tim Shoemaker.

Cast: James Woods (Gabriel Caine), Louis Gossett Jr ('Honey' Roy Palmer), Bruce Dern (John Gillon), Oliver Platt (Fitz), Heather Graham (Emily Forrester), Randall 'Tex' Cobb (Wolf Forrester), Thomas Wilson Brown (Robby Gillon), Marshall Bell (Warden Bates), Cyndi James Gossett (Mary Palmer), Duane Davis, Willie Green, Orestes Matacena, Kim Robillard, John Short, Michael McGrady, Roger Hewlett, Rocky Pepeli.
Dir: Michael Ritchie. Pro: Robert Schaffel. Co-Pro: Youssef Vahabzadeh. Screenplay: Steven McKay; based on the novel *The Diggstown Ringers* by Leonard Wise. Ph: Gerry Fisher. Ed: Don Zimmerman. Pro Des: Steve Hendrickson. M: James Newton Howard. Costumes: Wayne A. Finkelman. Sound: Kim Harris Ornitz. (MGM/Eclectic Films–UIP.) Rel: 22 January 1993. 97 mins. Cert 15.

Mistress

Hollywood; 1992. Yet another look at the soul-destroying process of compromising artistic integrity in order to finance a movie. This time Marvin Landisman, director of instructional videos, can only realise his achingly personal project – *The Darkness and the Light* – by casting the three backers' girlfriends. Complications ensue. At its worst, *Mistress* is a poor man's *The Player*, and is at its most acutely embarrassing when aiming for satire. However, in its more serious moments (particularly in the scene in which Marvin has to choose between his wife and his dream), the film comes into its own. Produced by Robert De Niro. [JC-W]

Cast: Robert Wuhl (Marvin Landisman), Danny Aiello (Carmine Rasso), Robert De Niro (Evan Wright), Martin Landau (Jack Roth), Eli Wallach (George Lieberhof), Jace Alexander (Stuart Stratland Jr), Sheryl Lee Ralph (Beverly), Laurie Metcalfe (Rachel Landisman), Tuesday Knight (Peggy), Jean Smart (Patricia), Vasek C. Sinek (Hans), Christopher Walken (Warren Zell), Ernest Borgnine (himself).
   Dir: Barry Primus. Pro: Meir Teper and Robert De Niro. Ex Pro: Ruth Charney. Screenplay: Primus and Jonathan F. Lawton. Ph: Sven Kirsten. Ed: Steven Weisberg. Pro Des: Phil Peters. M: Galt MacDermott. Costumes: Susan Nininger. Sound: Jacob Goldstein. (Tribeca–Arrow.) Rel: 14 May 1993. 105 mins. Cert 15.

Mo' Money

Chicago; today. Offensive, morally reprehensible shambles that resembles an extended TV sketch tacked on to a tired plot. Damon Wayans (the black stand-up comic of TV's *In Living*

Street crud: Marlon Wayans as ace conman Seymour Stewart in his brother Damon's noisy, formulaic Mo' Money *(from Columbia)*

Color) stars in his own screenplay about a conman who gets unwittingly involved in an even bigger credit card scam. There's the predictable romance with the unattainable beauty (who's really good at heart), the by-the-numbers villain and your routine vehicular carnage. Without any likeable characters to root for – and some ill-placed gratuitous violence – *Mo' Money* is a cinematic migraine. [JC-W]

Cast: Damon Wayans (Johnny Stewart), Stacey Dash (Amber Evans), Joe Santos (Lt Raymond Walsh), John Diehl (Keith Heading), Harry J. Lennix (Tom Dilton), Marlon Wayans (Seymour Stewart), Mark Beltzman (Chris Fields), Almayvonne (Charlotte), Gordon McClure (Rev Pimp Daddy), Quincy Wong, Kevin Casey, Larry Brandenburg, Garfield, Evan Lionel Smith, Richard Hamilton, John Allen, Will Zahrn, Ted Topolski, James Spinks.
   Dir: Peter Macdonald. Pro: Michael Rachmil. Ex Pro: Damon Wayans and Eric L. Gold. Co-Pro: Carl Craig. Screenplay: Wayans. Ph: Don Burgess. Ed: Hubert C.

Holiday heroics: Marie Gillain grows up in Mauritius, in Gerard Lauzier's delightful Mon Père Ce Héros *(from Gala)*

de La Bouillerie. Pro Des: William Arnold. M: Jay Gruska; numbers performed by Jimmy Jam, Terry Lewis, Ralph Tresvant, Damon Wayans, Krush, Public Enemy, Luther Vandross, Janet Jackson, Big Daddy Kane, Lo-Key?, Color Me Badd, Little Richard, etc. Costumes: Michelle Cole. Sound: Russell Williams II. (Wife N' Kids– Columbia Tri-Star.) Rel: 18 December 1992. 90 mins. Cert 15.

Mon Père, Ce Héros – My Father the Hero

Taking his 14-year-old daughter on holiday to Mauritius, André discovers that little Veronique has blossomed into an attractive young woman. At first reluctant to recognise her blatant womanhood and sex appeal, he gradu-

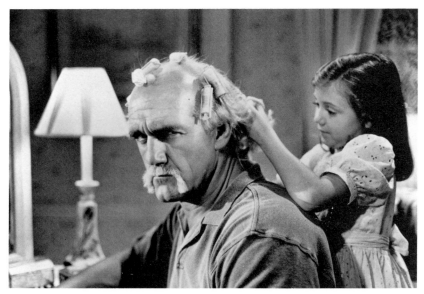

*Would you trust this man with your tutu?
Hulk Hogan is cared for by Madeline Zima
in* Mr Nanny *(from Entertainment)*

*Joking apart: Jerry Lewis and Billy Crystal
swap wisecracks in Crystal's navel-gazing*
Mr Saturday Night *(from First
Independent)*

sings the closing number, *I'm Fine*. A
most pleasing, unconventional bittersweet comedy. [JC-W]

Cast: Gerard Depardieu (André), Marie
Gillain (Veronique), Patrick Mille
(Benjamin), Catherine Jacob (Christelle),
Charlotte De Turckheim, Jean-Francois
Rangasamy, Nicolas Sobrido, Yan Brian,
Franck-Olivier Bonnet, Harriet Batchelor,
Eric Berger, Gerard Herold.
  Dir and Screenplay: Gerard Lauzier.
Pro: Jean-Louis Livi. Ph: Patrick Blossier.
Ed: Georges Klotz. Pro Des: Christian
Marti. M: Francois Bernheim. Costumes:
Gil Noir. Sound: Pierre Gamet. (Film Par
Film/DD Prods/Orly Films/Paravision Int/
TF-1 Films/Canal Plus–Gala.) Rel: 30
October 1992. 103 mins. Cert PG.

Mr Nanny

The peroxide wrestler plays bodyguard
to two ultra-spoiled brats. Lacking the
sophistication, subtlety or satire of
Hulk Hogan's previous underrated
outing, *Suburban Commando*, you
know the film's got problems when
even Hulk clad in a purple tutu and
leotard cannot get a giggle. In the right
hands, Hogan could be a wonderful
antidote to Schwarzenegger, Van
Damme, Seagal and the rest, even
though he does give us the worst imi-
tation of a person asleep for many
years. [SR]

Cast: Terry 'Hulk' Hogan (Sean
Armstrong), Sherman Hemsley (Burt
Wilson), Austin Pendelton (Alex Mason
Sr), Robert Gorman (Alex Mason Jr),
Madeline Zima (Kate Mason), Afa Anoia
'Alfa' (himself), Raymond O'Connor,
Mother Love, David Johansen, Brutus
Beefcake.
  Dir: Michael Gottlieb. Pro: Bob Engel-
man. Ex Pro: Benni Korzen and Michael
Harpster. Screenplay: Gottlieb and Edward
Rugoff. Ph: Peter Stein. Ed: Earl Ghaffari
and Michael Ripps. Pro Des: Don De Fina.
M: David Johansen and Brian Koonin;
Tchaikovsky, Mozart; numbers performed
by Buster Pointdexter, Doghouse, Hulk
Hogan, Madeline Zima, Rigor Mortis, etc.
Costumes: Marianna Astreom-De Fina.
Sound: Ben Wilkins. (Entertainment
Film–Entertainment.) Rel: 2 April 1993.
84 mins. Cert PG.

Mr Saturday Night

Buried under latex, Billy Crystal plays
a 73-year-old Jewish comedian nobody
remembers any more. Playing old
people's homes and promoting the joys
of unromantic products on TV, Buddy

ally enters into the spirit of her fraudu-
lent courtship of a handsome young
man. Keeping his traditional scene-
stealing to a minimum, Gerard Depardieu is quietly affecting as the
bemused father, and reveals a gift for
underplayed comedy. His snowballing
amazement at his daughter's increasing sexuality is a joy to behold. He also

Young Jr dreams of the good old days when he held an audience in the palm of his hand. Crystal first created Young on his 1982 TV special *A Comic's Line*, reintroduced him on *Saturday Night Live* and now, nine years later, brings him to the big screen in collaboration with Lowell Ganz and Babaloo Mandel (who scripted Crystal's *City Slickers*). There are some memorable moments (Young's audition for a Hollywood film, the farewell speech at his mother's funeral), but the story is neither strong enough, nor Young's character sympathetic enough, to give the film momentum or appeal. True, the one-liners are frequently amusing, but a film cannot exist on jokes alone. [JC-W]

Cast: Billy Crystal (Buddy Young Jr), David Paymer (Stan Yankelman), Julie Warner (Elaine), Helen Hunt (Annie), Ron Silver (Larry Meyerson), Mary Mara (Susan), Jerry Orbach (Phil Gussman), Sage Allen (Mom), Jason Marsden (Abie: Buddy Young aged 15), Michael Weiner (Stan aged 18), Will Jordan (Ed Sullivan), Larry Gelman, Kay Freeman, Irving Wasserman, Phil Forman, Jackie Gayle, Marc Shaiman, Jerry Lewis, Adam Goldberg, Lindsay Crystal, Lowell Ganz, Babaloo Mandel, Steven Kravitz.
  Dir and Pro: Billy Crystal. Ex Pro: Lowell Ganz and Babaloo Mandel. Screenplay: Crystal, Ganz and Mandel. Ph: Don Peterman. Ed: Kent Beyda. Pro Des: Albert Brenner. M: Marc Shaiman. Costumes: Ruth Myers. Sound: Jeff Wexler. (Castle Rock–First Independent.) Rel: 23 April 1993. 119 mins. Cert 15.

The Muppet Christmas Carol
Following in the screen footsteps of Sir Seymour Hicks, Reginald Owen, Alastair Sim, Albert Finney, George C. Scott and Bill Murray, Michael Caine makes a suitably dour impact as Ebenezer Scrooge. Only in this instance the rest of the cast conspire to upstage him and, in the form of Kermit, Miss Piggy and Gonzo, almost do. Paul Williams's songs are only so-so, and Caine's singing is of the William Shatner variety, while the mood of the film is a little dark for younger audiences. Still, there's fun to be had, and plenty of laughs. Directed by Brian Henson, son of Muppets' creator Jim Henson. [CB]

Cast: Michael Caine (Scrooge), Kermit the Frog (Bob Cratchit), Miss Piggy (Emily

Together for the first time: Kermit and Michael Caine cause friction in Brian Henson's The Muppet Christmas Carol

Cratchit), The Great Gonzo (Charles Dickens), Rizzo the Rat, Fozzie Bear, Steven Mackintosh, Meredith Braun, Robin Weaver, Donald Austen. Muppet performers: Dave Goelz, Steve Whitmire, Jerry Nelson, David Rudman, and Frank Oz.
  Dir: Brian Henson. Pro: Henson and Martin Baker. Ex Pro: Frank Oz. Co-Pro and Screenplay: Jerry Juhl. Ph: John Fenner. Ed: Michael Jablow. Pro Des: Val Strazovec. M: Miles Goodman. Songs: Paul Williams. Costumes: Polly Smith. Choreography: Pat Garrett. Sound: Bobby Mackston. (Walt Disney/Jim Henson Prods–Buena Vista.) Rel: 18 December 1992. 86 mins. Cert U.

My Cousin Vinny
Wahzoo City, Alabama; 1992. Refreshingly polished, well-constructed and efficiently acted comedy about two college kids accidentally imprisoned for a murder they didn't commit. Their only hope is Vinny La Guardia Gambini, a streetwise, foul-mouthed lawyer relation from Brooklyn. The problem is that Vinny took six years to pass his bar exam and has never tackled a case before. Thanks to a vacuum-packed script by Dale Launer (*Ruthless People*, *Dirty Rotten*

Down by law: Joe Pesci dresses up for a dressing down in Jonathan Lynn's genuinely amusing My Cousin Vinny *(from Fox)*

Scoundrels), fluid direction from Jonathan Lynn (*Nuns on the Run*) and some dexterous acting, this is a very funny, engaging comedy. Marisa Tomei as Vinny's spirited girlfriend is a genuine delight. [JC-W]

Cast: Joe Pesci (Vinny Gambini), Ralph Macchio (Bill Gambini), Marisa Tomei (Mona Lisa Vito), Mitchell Whitfield (Stan Rothenstein), Fred Gwynne (Judge Chamberlain Haller), Lane Smith (Jim Trotter III), Austin Pendleton, Bruce McGill, Maury Chaykin, Pauline Meyers, Raynor Scheine, James Rebhorn, Chris Ellis.
 Dir: Jonathan Lynn. Pro: Dale Launer and Paul Schiff. Screenplay: Launer. Ph: Peter Deming. Ed: Tony Lombardo. Pro Des: Victoria Paul. M: Randy Edelman; numbers performed by the Fabulous Thunderbirds, Jimmie Rodgers, Connie Francis, Jesse Harnell, etc. Costumes: Carol Wood. Sound: Robert Anderson Jr. (Fox.) Rel: 17 July 1992. 119 mins. Cert 15.

My Father Is Coming

New York's East Village; 1991. Cheerfully promiscuous comedy about a German waitress in New York who misleads her father into believing that she is married and is leading a successful career as an actress. When he turns up unexpectedly, she is forced to act out an elaborate charade, employing the resources of her sexually unique friends and colleagues. A refreshingly bawdy, ironic and rather sweet film, shot on a minuscule budget of £120,000. [CB]

Cast: Alfred Edel (Hans), Shelley Kastner (Vicky), Annie Sprinkle (Annie), Mary Lou Graulau (Lisa), David Bronstein (Ben), Michael Massee (Joe), Fakir Musafar (Fakir), Mario de Colombia, Dominique Gaspar, Flora Gaspar, Israel Marti, Bruce Benderson.
 Dir and Pro: Monika Treut. Screenplay: Treut, Bruce Benderson and Sarah Schulman. Ph: Elfi Mikesch. Ed: Steve Brown.

Finty Williams, daughter of Michael Williams and Judi Dench, plays the young heroine in Timothy Forder's leaden version of Dickens's The Mystery of Edwin Drood *(from Mayfair Entertainment)*

Art: Robin Ford. M: David Van Tieghem. Sound: Neil Danziger and Julie Wilde. (Bluehorse Films, Inc.–Out On a Limb.) Rel: 25 September 1992. 82 mins. Cert 18.

The Mystery of Edwin Drood

Cloisterham, Kent; 1870. It is a novel conceit to film an unfinished literary masterpiece, and writer-director Timothy Forder has failed to meet the challenge. Basically, he's employed a dry BBC2 style to record the novel's existing first half, and then slapped on a Hollywood ending that is more John Carpenter than Charles Dickens. There are some nice moments, particularly the comic delineations of minor characters (nicely played by a hardy cast, most notably Barry Evans, Glyn Houston, Andrew Sachs and Ken Wynne), but otherwise it's a hard slog, not helped by the drama-school acting from the juveniles. It's enough to put anybody off Dickens. Filmed in Rochester, Kent. [JC-W]

Cast: Robert Powell (John Jasper), Finty Williams (Rosa Bud), Jonathan Phillips (Edwin Drood), Rupert Rainsford (Neville Landless), Michelle Evans (Helena Landless), Gemma Craven (Miss Twinkleton), Barry Evans (Bazzard), Ronald Fraser (Dean), Glyn Houston (Grewgious), Freddie Jones (Sapsea), Leonard Kirby (Deputy), Rosemary Leach (Mrs Tope), Nanette Newman (Mrs Crisparkle), Peter Pacy (Rev. Septimus Crisparkle), Andrew Sachs (Durdles), Marc Sinden (Honeythunder), Kate Williams (old woman), Ken Wynne (Tope).
   Dir and Screenplay: Timothy Forder. Pro: Keith Hayley. Ex Pro: Mary Swindale. Ph: Martin McGrath. Ed: Sue Alhadeff. Pro Des: Edward Thomas. M: Kick Production. Costumes: Justine Luxton. Sound: Peter Corley. (Bevanfield Films/First Standard Media–Mayfair Entertainment.) Rel: 30 April 1993. 112 mins. Cert 12.

National Lampoon's Loaded Weapon I

Less a spoof of *Lethal Weapon* than a rip-off of *Airplane!*, *The Naked Gun* and *Hot Shots!* Emilio Estevez, with his face so straight it's flat, is the maverick cop with the blow-dried hair and a penchant for dogs who's teamed up with family man Samuel L. Jackson, on the verge of retirement. Together, the mismatched duo encounter *dramatis personae* from *The Silence of the*

'Read all about it!': The News Boys *go on strike in Disney's brave attempt at resurrecting the musical*

Lambs (F. Murray Abraham as Anthony Hopkins), *Basic Instinct* (Kathy Ireland as a braindead Sharon Stone) and *Lethal Weapons 2* and *3* (Jon Lovitz in the Joe Pesci part, originally conceived for Lovitz in the first place!). But parodying other movies is no substitute for wit, while this film's terminal lack of comic flair and timing adds to the tedium. A veritable graveyard for disembodied gags. [JC-W]

Cast: Emilio Estevez (Jack Colt), Samuel L. Jackson (Wes Lugar), Jon Lovitz (Becker), Tim Curry (Jigsaw), Kathy Ireland (Destiny Demeanor), Frank McRae (Captain Doyle), William Shatner (General Mortors), Whoopi Goldberg (Billie York), Lance Kinsey, Bill Nunn, Dr Joyce Brothers, Robert Willis, Vito Scotti, James Doohan, Richard Moll, F. Murray Abraham, Charlie Sheen, Denis Leary, Michael Castner, Corey Feldman, Phil Hartman, J. T. Walsh, Erik Estrada, Larry Wilcox, Paul Gleason, Allyce Beasley, Ric Ducommun, Charles Napier, Charles Cyphers, Danielle Nicolet, Beverly Johnson, Phillip Tan, Bruce Willis.
   Dir: Gene Quintano. Pro: Suzanne Todd and David Willis. Ex Pro: Michel Roy, Howard Klein and Erwin Stoff. Screenplay:

Quintano and Don Holley; from a 'story' by Holley and Tori Tellem. Ph: Peter Dening. Ed: Christopher Greenbury. Pro Des: Jaymes Hinkle. M: Robert Folk; songs performed by Denis Leary, Freddie Mercury and Queen. Costumes: Jacki Arthur. Sound: Marty Bolger and John Coffey. (New Line–Guild.) Rel: 30 April 1993. 83 mins. Cert PG.

The News Boys

(US: *Newsies*.) If for nothing else, this must go down in the annals of history as the bravest film of '92. Based on the newspaperboys' strike of 1899 in New York, this is a full-scale musical that takes its cue from *Oliver!*, *West Side Story*, *Annie* and any number of other get-up-and-go singalongs. Britain's Christian Bale (*Empire of the Sun*, *Treasure Island*) affects a pronounced Noo Yoyk accent as the street urchin who rebels when crusty old Joe Pulitzer (Robert Duvall enjoying himself) puts up the wholesale price of *The New York World*. Director/choreographer Kenny Ortega's rousingly clichéd songfest has it all: music, romance, slapstick, courage, a few decent villains, a good story and above all some splendid dance sequences. The songs stink (and are sung very badly), but *The News Boys* still makes it as one of the more irresistible stinkers of the year. [JC-W]

Night work: Robert De Niro and Jessica Lange plot out their dreams in Irwin Winkler's gritty drama Night and the City *(from First Independent)*

Cast: Christian Bale (Jack Kelly), Bill Pullman (Bryan Denton), Ann-Margret (Medda Larkson), Robert Duvall (Joseph Pulitzer), David Moscow (David Jacobs), Luke Edwards (Les Jacobs), Marty Belafsky (Crutchy), Ele Keats (Sarah Jacobs), David James Alexander (Teddy Roosevelt), Michael Lerner (Weasel), Kevin Tighe (Snyder), Max Casella, Aaron Lohr, Trey Parker, Gabriel Damon, Joseph Conrad, Jeffrey DeMunn, Deborra-Lee Furness, Marc Lawrence, Charles Cioffi.

Dir: Kenny Ortega. Pro: Michael Finnell. Screenplay: Bob Tzudiker and Noni White. Ph: Andrew Laszlo. Ed: William Reynolds. Pro Des: William Sandell. M: Alan Menken; lyrics: Jack Feldman. Costumes: May Routh. Choreography: Ortega and Peggy Holmes. Sound: David Kelson. (Walt Disney–Warner.) Rel: 14 August 1992. 122 mins. Cert PG.

Newsies
See *The News Boys.*

Night and the City

Manhattan; 1992. *'You* don't even trust you!' screams an exasperated Jessica Lange at Robert De Niro. De Niro, in high-octane mood, plays Harry Fabian, a double-dealing legal hustler, whose massive turnover of impoverished clients makes him a living – sort of. Then he decides to realise his dream to become a boxing promoter. But raising the money for the first event proves to be a colossal headache – even for Harry Fabian. In spite of a live-wire script by Richard Price (*Sea of Love, The Color of Money*) and a pedigree soundtrack (see music credits), neither can salvage this downbeat, deeply depressing tale of betrayal and cheap human values. Based on the 1950 film of the same name, which starred Richard Widmark as a London hustler who takes on the wrestling world. Beautifully done, but why remake it? [JC-W]

Cast: Robert De Niro (Harry Fabian), Jessica Lange (Helen Nasseros), Cliff Gorman (Phil Nasseros), Alan King (Ira 'Boom Boom' Grossman), Jack Warden (Al Grossman), Eli Wallach (Peck), Pedro Sanchez (Cuda Sanchez), Anthony Canarozzi (Emmet Gorgon), Margo Winkler (judge), Richard Price (doctor), Barry Primus, Gene Kirkwood, Byron Utley, Maurice Shrog, Regis Philbin, Joy Philbin.

Dir: Irwin Winkler. Pro: Winkler and Jane Rosenthal. Ex Pro: Harry J. Utland and Mary Jane Utland. Screenplay: Richard Price. Ph: Tak Fujimoto, Ed: David Brenner. Pro Des: Peter Larkin. M: James Newton Howard; numbers performed by Smokey Robinson & the Miracles, Aretha Franklin, the Red Hot Chili Peppers, etc. Costumes: Richard Bruno. Sound: Tod Maitland. (Mario & Vittorio Cecchi Gori and Silvio Berlusconi/Penta Entertainment/Tribeca–First Independent.) Rel: 22 January 1993. 105 mins. Cert 15.

Night of the Living Dead
A group of squabbling Americans find themselves trapped in a farmhouse as they are besieged by the undead. Pointless remake of the 1968 black-and-white classic, which fails to top the two sequels of the original for atmosphere, wit or even acting ability. [JC-W]

Baby, you can ride my cab: Winona Ryder and Armin Mueller-Stahl as taxi drivers from very different backgrounds – in Jim Jarmusch's magical, gritty Night on Earth *(from Electric)*

Cast: Tony Todd (Ben), Patricia Tallman (Barbara), Tom Towles (Harry Cooper), McKee Anderson (Helen), William Butler (Tom), Kate Finneran (Judy Rose), Bill Mosley, Heather Mazur, David Butler, Zachary Mott, William Cameron.
Dir: Tom Savini. Pro: John A. Russo and Russ Streiner. Ex Pro: Menahem Golan and George A. Romero. Co-Ex Pro: Ami Artzi. Screenplay: Romero; based upon his own screenplay *Night of the Living Dead*, co-written with John A. Russo. Ph: Frank Prinzi. Ed: Tom Dubensky. Pro Des: Cletus R. Anderson. M: Paul McCollough. Costumes: Barbara Anderson. Make-up: John Vulich and Everett Burrell. Sound: Felipe Borrero. (Tartan Films–Blue Dolphin.) Rel: 2 April 1993. 96 mins. Cert 18.

Night on Earth

Jim Jarmusch, who displayed his singular sense of humour with *Stranger Than Paradise, Down by Law* and

Mystery Train, is on top form with this ingenious quintet of stories, all of which take place in an urban taxi cab. 'I want *my* films to be about the things that *other* directors take out of theirs,' Jarmusch explains, and, indeed, some of the best things in *Night on Earth* take place in the background. Originally titled *LosAngelesNewYorkParis-RomeHelsinki*, the movie starts at seven minutes past the hour in five cities at the same time and introduces us to a variety of characters at cross-cultural purposes with one another. An acquired taste, maybe, but a delicious, unusual bouquet for the converted, mixing outrageous black humour with moments of incredible tenderness and sweetness. Winona Ryder, Armin Mueller-Stahl, Isaach De Bankolé, Roberto Benigni and Matti Pellonpaa play the five cab drivers. [JC-W]

Cast: *Los Angeles*: Winona Ryder (Corky), Gena Rowlands (Victoria Snelling). *New York*: Giancarlo Esposito (Yo Yo), Armin Mueller-Stahl (Helmut Grokenberger), Rosie Perez (Angela). *Paris*: Isaach De Bankolé (Ivory Coast cab driver), Béatrice Dalle (blind passenger). *Rome*: Roberto Benigni (cab driver), Paolo Bonacelli

(priest). *Helsinki*: Matti Pellonpää (cab driver), Tomi Salmela (Aki), Kari Väänänen, Saku Kuosmanen.
Dir, Pro and Screenplay: Jim Jarmusch. Ex Pro: Jim Stark. Co-Pro: Demetra J. MacBride. Co-Ex Pro: Masahiro Inbe and Noboru Takayama. Ph: Frederick Elmes. Ed: Jay Rabinowitz. M: Tom Waits. Sound: Drew Kunin. (JVC/Victor Gorp/Victor Musical Industries/Pyramide/Le Studio Canal Plus/Pandora Film/Channel 4/Locus Solus–Electric.) Rel: 31 July 1992. 120 mins. Cert 15.

Noises Off

Des Moines/Cleveland/Miami/New York. 'Theatre', intones stage director Michael Caine, 'is all about sardines and doors.' At least, that is the case with the hit London sex farce *Nothing On*, now on its disastrous pre-Broadway leg. The film, based on Michael Frayn's phenomenally successful play, itself a play-within-a-play, had long been avoided by filmmakers. Now Peter Bogdanovich, who demonstrated his ability with farce on the hilarious, vastly underrated *They All Laughed* (1981), returns to the genre with some

The show must go on: Carol Burnett, Michael Caine, Marilu Henner, Denholm Elliott, Nicollette Sheridan and Julie Hagerty in Peter Bogdanovich's celluloid take on theatrical farce – Noises Off (from Touchstone Pictures and Amblin Entertainment – all rights reserved)

Romantic action man: Jean-Claude Van Damme reveals his tender side with Rosanna Arquette in Robert Harmon's Nowhere to Run (from Columbia Tri-Star)

guts and an unfailing eye for the material. *Noises Off* is ideal theatrical material, but is also an estimable insight into the workings of farce, and is given tremendous life support here by some superlative camerawork and adroit editing. The cast, too, is mouth-watering, with surprisingly effective turns from Marilu Henner, Christopher Reeve and Nicollette Sheridan. Although the play has been American-ised, all the American actors play their on-stage roles with English accents, which must be worth the price of admission alone. [JC-W]

Cast: Carol Burnett (Dotty Otley/Mrs Clackett), Michael Caine (Lloyd Fellowes), Denholm Elliott (Selsdon Mowbray), Julie Hagerty (Poppy Taylor), Marilu Henner (Belinda Blair/Flavia Brent), Mark Linn-Baker (Tim Allgood), Christopher Reeve (Frederick Dallas/Philip Brent), John Ritter (Garry Lejeune/Roger Tramplemain), Nicollette Sheridan (Brooke Ashton/Vicki), J. Christopher Sullivan, Kimberly Neville, Bronson Dudley.

Dir: Peter Bogdanovich. Pro: Frank Marshall. Ex Pro: Bogdanovich and Kathleen Kennedy. Screenplay: Marty Kaplan. Ph: Tim Suhrstedt. Ed: Lisa Day. Pro Des: Norman Newberry. M: Phil Marshall. Costumes: Betsy Cox. Sound: James E. Webb. (Touchstone/Amblin–Warner.) Rel: 24 July 1992. 104 mins. Cert 15.

Nowhere to Run

California; 1993. An escaped convict hides out on a farm and ends up protecting the property's widow from evil land developers (while male-bonding with her son). Upgrading his image as a martial arts side of beef, Jean-Claude Van Damme for once plays a character deeper than scar tissue. What's more, he's working from a script by Joe Eszterhas (*Music Box, Betrayed*) and opposite Rosanna Arquette. However, you can take a horse to the water, but you can't make him act ... [JC-W]

Cast: Jean-Claude Van Damme (Sam Gillen), Rosanna Arquette (Clydie), Kieran Culkin (Mookie), Ted Levine (Mr Dunston), Joss Ackland (Franklin Hale), Tiffany Taubman (Bree), Edward Blatchford (Lonnie), Anthony Starke (Billy), Leonard Termo, James Greene, Stephen Wesley Bridgewater, Luana Anders, Stanley White.
Dir: Robert Harmon. Pro: Craig Baumgarten and Gary Adelson. Ex Pro: Michael Rachmil. Screenplay: Joe Eszterhas, Leslie Bohem and Randy Feldman; from a story by Eszterhas and the late Richard Marquand. Ph: David Gribble. Ed: Zach Staenberg and Mark Helfrich. Pro Des: Dennis Washington. M: Mark

John Malkovich as Lennie in Gary Sinise's affecting screen version of John Steinbeck's classic Of Mice and Men *(from UIP)*

Isham; numbers performed by Clint Black, Charlie Mitchell, and Damn Yankees. Costumes: Gamila Mariana Fahkry. Sound: Fred J. Brown. (Columbia Tri-Star.) Rel: 21 May 1993. 94 mins. Cert 15.

Of Mice and Men
California; the Depression. Third film adaptation of John Steinbeck's classic 1937 novel, starring, produced and directed by Gary Sinise, founder of Chicago's Steppenwolf Theatre Company. Fears that this may be a stagebound production (Steppenwolf performed it in 1980) are allayed by Horton Foote's original screen adaptation and Kenneth MacMillan's handsome, burnished photography. John Malkovich (a tad too theatrical) re-creates his stage role as Lennie Small, the gentle, simple-minded giant, while Ray Walston is heartbreaking as the old man who dreams of a corner of land he can call his own. A moving piece of Americana. [JC-W]

Cast: John Malkovich (Lennie Small), Gary Sinise (George Milton), Ray Walston (Candy), Casey Siemaszko (Curley), Sherilyn Fenn (Curley's wife), John Terry (Slim), Richard Riehle (Carlson), Alexis

Senility's a bitch: Jeanne Moreau and Michel Serrault bicker their way through Laurent Heynemann's The Old Lady Who Walked in the Sea *(from Gala)*

Arquette (Whitt), Joe Morton (Crooks), Noble Willingham (the Boss).
Dir: Gary Sinise. Pro: Russ Smith and Sinise. Ex Pro: Alan C. Blomquist. Screenplay: Horton Foote. Ph: Kenneth MacMillan. Ed: Robert L. Sinise. Pro Des: David Gropman. M: Mark Isham. Costumes: Shay Cunliffe. Sound: David Brownlow. (MGM–UIP.) Rel: 27 November 1992. 111 mins. Cert PG.

The Old Lady Who Walked in the Sea – La Vieille Qui Marchait dans la Mer
If you get a kick out of old people hurling crude insults at each other, then this one is for you. Jeanne Moreau and Michel Serrault play a couple of grouchy, bickering con artists living out their last days in such sunny climes as Guadeloupe and the Riviera. Then Lady M (Moreau) takes a fancy to a young buck, Lambert (Luc Thullier), and trains him to execute their more taxing tasks – like stealing a diamond diadem at an Indian gala. But Serrault has a bad feeling about their new accomplice ... A black comedy with a romantic twist, *The Old Lady* ... starts off promisingly, but its unlikeable characters and stunted plot – not to mention the ripe dialogue – ultimately become tiresome. [JC-W]

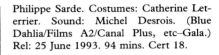

Childhood lost: Faye Gatteau and Emmanuel Morozof in Agnieszka Holland's haunting Olivier Olivier *(from Gala)*

High calibre: Bill Paxton stars as the gung-ho Arkansas sheriff Dale 'Hurricane' Dixon in Carl Franklin's spellbinding One False Move *(from Metro Tartan)*

Philippe Sarde. Costumes: Catherine Leterrier. Sound: Michel Desrois. (Blue Dahlia/Films A2/Canal Plus, etc–Gala.) Rel: 25 June 1993. 94 mins. Cert 18.

Olivier Olivier

Olivier, a 9-year-old French boy, and his older sister, Nadine, imagine aliens descending in the wheatfields of their small rural community. While Olivier enjoys the doting ministrations of his mother, Nadine practises her telekinetic skills. Theirs is an almost idyllic childhood until, one day, Olivier vanishes without trace. Nothing is quite what it seems in this arresting French parable, in which the tensions of domestic friction collide with benign magic-realism. From the director of *Europa, Europa.* [JC-W]

Cast: Francois Cluzet (Serge), Brigitte Rouan (Elisabeth), Jean-Francois Stevenin (Druot), Gregoire Colin (Olivier), Marina Golovine (Nadine), Frederic Quiring (Marcel), Faye Gatteau, Emmanuel Morozof.
Dir: Agnieszka Holland. Pro: Marie-Laure Reyre. Co-Pro: Christian Ferry. Screenplay: Holland, Yves Lapointe and Regis Debray. Ph: Bernard Zitzermann. Ed: Isabelle Lorente. Pro Des: Helene Bourgy. M: Zbigniew Preisner. Sound: Pierre Befve. (Oliane Prods/Film A-2–Gala.) Rel: 12 February 1993. 105 mins. Cert 15.

Cast: Jeanne Moreau (Lady M), Michel Serrault (Pompilius), Luc Thuillier (Lambert), Geraldine Danon (Noemie), Jean Bouchaud, Marie-Dominique Aumont, Mattia Sbragia.
Dir: Laurent Heynemann. Pro: Gerard Jourd'hui. Screenplay: Dominique Roulet and Heynemann; from the novel by San Antonio. Ph: Robert Alazraki. Ed: Jacques Comets. Pro Des: Valerie Grall. M:

One False Move

A black man, a white man and a mulatto woman steal a stash of cocaine in South Central Los Angeles and leave behind a litter of corpses. A black cop and a white cop pursue them – all the way to Star City, Arkansas, a quiet backwater presided over by a callow young sheriff spoon-fed on TV cop shows . . . Shot on a minuscule budget by first-time black director Carl Franklin (a former actor), *One False Move* grips from the start. A dog barking on the soundtrack, a deserted street, locked doors – little details that set up a foreboding atmosphere with remarkable economy. And then almost instantly comes the carnage: a young black woman is sprinkled with lighter fuel, another is repeatedly punched in the face, a man is suffocated with a plastic bag. The violence is not so much gory or graphic as brutally casual, accelerating the heartbeat and maintaining the tension on cruise control until the final reel. Franklin subtly

A Woolf in men's clothing: Tilda Swinton as the young man adopted by Her Majesty Queen Elizabeth I (Quentin Crisp) in Sally Potter's industrious film version of Virginia Woolf's timeless novel Orlando *(from Electric)*

builds the reality of his six characters through perceptive dialogue, injecting humanity, humour and history into their tortured souls. While exploring familiar territory – the road movie, *film noir* – Franklin has created a contemporary human drama that surprises, shocks and touches unlike anything Hollywood could ever produce. [JC-W]

Cast: Bill Paxton (Dale 'Hurricane' Dixon), Cynda Williams (Fantasia/Lila), Billy Bob Thornton (Ray Malcolm), Michael Beach (Pluto), Earl Billings (McFeely), Jim Metzler (Dud Cole), Kevin Hunter (Ronnie), John Mahon (Chief Jenkins), Natalie Canerday, Robert Ginnaven, Robert Anthony Bell, Phyllis Kirklin, Meredith 'Jeta' Donovan, James D. Bridges, Phyllis Sutton, Duncan Rouleau, Layne Beamer, Mea Combs, Rocky Giordani, Walter Norman.
    Dir: Carl Franklin. Pro: Jesse Beaton and Ben Myron. Ex Pro: Miles A. Copeland

III, Paul Colichman and Harold Welb. Screenplay: Billy Bob Thornton and Tom Epperson. Ph: James L. Carter. Ed: Carole Kravetz. Pro Des: Gary T. New. M: Peter Haycock and Derek Holt. Costumes: Ron Leamon. Sound: Ken Segal. (Metro Tartan.) Rel: 9 April 1993. 106 mins. Cert 18.

Orlando

1600–1992; England/Central Asia. Intellectually ambitious film version of Virginia Woolf's most popular novel, in which an Elizabethan aristocrat attempts to find true happiness over a period of 400 years. Backed up by unusual locations, spectacular costumes and, above all, some bizarre casting choices (Quentin Crisp as Queen Elizabeth I, the writer Heathcote Williams as a grubby poet), the film is full of surprises, and is beautifully transcribed from Woolf's original. However, Tilda Swinton, in the title role, lacks the charisma to hold the piece together, while the fractured narrative becomes increasingly irritating. For connoisseurs of the unconventional. Filmed in St Petersburg, Uzbekhistan and England. [JC-W]

Cast: Tilda Swinton (Orlando), Billy Zane (Shelmerdine), Lothaire Bluteau (the Khan), John Wood (Archduke Harry), Charlotte Valandrey (Sasha), Heathcote Williams (Nick Greene), Quentin Crisp (Queen Elizabeth I), Dudley Sutton (King James I), Jessica Swinton (Orlando's daughter), Thom Hoffman, Anna Healy, Sara Mair-Thomas, Anna Farnworth, Mary MacLeod, Barbara Hicks, Jerome Willis, John Bott, Peter Eyre, Ned Sherrin, Roger Hammond, Lol Coxhill, Jimmy Somerville, John Grillo.
    Dir: and Screenplay: Sally Potter. Pro: Christopher Sheppard. Ph: Alexei Rodionov. Ed: Herve Schneid. Pro Des: Ben Van Os and Jan Roelfs. M: Potter and David Motion. Costumes: Sandy Powell. (Adventure Pictures/Lenfilm/Mikado Film/ Rio/Sigma Filmproductions/British Screen– Electric.) Rel: 12 March 1993. 92 mins. Cert PG.

The Ox – Oxen

1868; Sweden. Based on a true story, *The Ox* is a heartbreaking tale of a young couple forced to compromise their beliefs in order to survive a time of terrible famine and poverty. Unfolding its narrative in simple, bold strokes and utilising a minimum of words, *The*

Rough justice: Stellan Skarsgard and Ewa Froling in Sven Nykvist's heart-rending The Ox *(from Artificial Eye)*

Hijack hijinks: Wesley Snipes and Bruce Payne struggle with their testosterone levels, in Kevin Hooks's gripping Passenger 57 *(from Warner)*

Cast: Max Von Sydow (the vicar), Ewa Fröling (Elfrida Roos), Stellan Skarsgard (Helga Wilhelm Roos), Erland Josephson (Silver), Liv Ullmann (Maria), Lennart Hjulstrom (Svenning Gustevsson), Bjorn Granath (Flyckt), Rikard Wolff, Helge Jordal, Jaqui Safra.

Dir: Sven Nykvist. Pro: Jean Doumanian. Ex Pro: Jaqui Safra. Co-Ex Pro: Klas Olofson. Screenplay: Nykvist and Lasse Summanen. Ph: Nykvist. Ed: Summanen. Pro Des: Peter Hoimark. Costumes: Inger Pehrsson. Sound: Bo Persson. (Sweetland Films–Artificial Eye.) Rel: 9 April 1993. 92 mins. Cert 12.

Paris Is Burning

This Paris is a gay dance hall in Harlem where the clientele attend balls where they try to outshine each other in the magnificence of their apparel, competing for prizes and hoping to satisfy their dreams. Producer Jennie Livingstone takes us into a bizarre world in her well-made documentary. Made on a shoestring and showing considerable talent. Winner of the 1991 Sundance Festival Grand Jury Prize for Best Documentary. [FDM]

Dir: Jennie Livingstone. Pro: Livingstone and Barry Swimar. Ph: Paul Gibson and Maryse Alberti. (Off White Productions–ICA.) Rel: 9 April 1993. 78 mins. No cert.

Passenger 57

Charles Rane, an English aristocrat, is hunky, intelligent and fearless. He's also the world's most dangerous terrorist and is being flown to prison in Los Angeles by jumbo jet. Bad move. Still, by *sheer coincidence*, also on board the aircraft is security expert John Cutter. Cutter is hunky, intelligent and fearless. He's also the world's leading anti-terrorist authority and a dab hand at martial arts. OK, so there's little that's wildly original about this manipulative, gratuitously violent action-thriller – and maybe too much coincidence for airtight credibility. Still, it's slick, entertaining and well crafted, with a nice line in disaster-site dialogue. It's also a smart move to feature a black hero, although an English villain is now bordering on cliché. [JC-W]

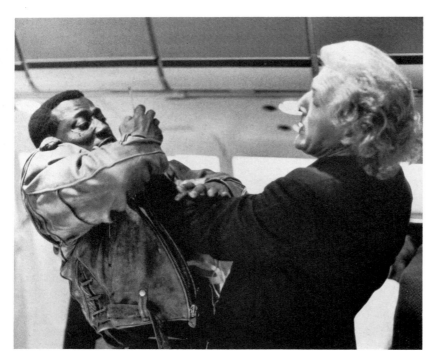

Ox is a commendable exercise in cinematic economy, relying on the power of the actors' faces for dramatic effect. Directed by Sven Nykvist, Ingmar Bergman's cinematographer for 30 years, the film is beautifully shot in the remote district of Smaland, the filmmaker's homeland. [JC-W]

Cast: Wesley Snipes (John Cutter), Bruce Payne (Charles Rane), Tom Sizemore (Sly Delvecchio), Alex Datcher (Marti Slayton), Robert Hooks (Dwight Henderson), Elizabeth Hurley (Sabrina Ritchie), Michael

Horse (Forget), Ernie Lively (Chief Biggs), Bruce Greenwood, Marc Macaulay, Duchess Tomasello, Cameron Roberts, James Short, Lori Bedford, Lou Bedford, Lesa Thurman, Frank Causey, Gary Rorman.

Dir: Kevin Hooks. Pro: Lee Rich, Dan Paulson and Dylan Sellers. Ex Pro: Jonathan Sheinberg. Co-Pro: Robert J. Anderson. Screenplay: David Loughery and Dan Gordon; from a story by Gordon and Stewart Raffill. Ph: Mark Irwin. Ed: Richard Nord. Pro Des: Jaymes Hinkle. M: Stanley Clarke; Stevie Wonder's *Too High* performed by Norman Brown. Costumes: Brad Loman. Sound: Robert G. Henderson. (Warner.) Rel: 21 May 1993. 84 mins. Cert 15.

Patriot Games

Cutting back on the hardware utilised on *The Hunt for Red October*, this highly competent, big-budget sequel (price tag: $42.5 million) concentrates on Jack Ryan's defence of his wife and child against a ruthless IRA killer bent on revenge. Ryan (Harrison Ford, replacing Alec Baldwin) is holidaying in London with his wife and daughter when he witnesses a terrorist attack on a member of the royal family. Intervening, Ryan foils the assassination and kills one of the terrorists, the kid brother of IRA man Sean Miller (Sean Bean). Miller swears revenge and follows Ryan to America. A nail-biting thriller bursting with suspense, *Patriot Games* concentrates on Ryan as family man, now retired from the CIA and teaching history. Skilfully directed by Australia's Phillip Noyce (*Dead Calm*), the film is full of unexpected touches and makes the most of its varied locations. It is also the first feature permitted to shoot at CIA headquarters in Langley, Virginia. [JC-W]

Cast: Harrison Ford (Jack Ryan), Anne Archer (Cathy Ryan), Patrick Bergin (Kevin O'Donnell), Sean Bean (Sean Miller), Thora Birch (Sally Ryan), James Fox (Lord Holmes), James Earl Jones (Admiral Greer), Richard Harris (Paddy O'Neill), Samuel L. Jackson (Robby Jackson), Polly Walker (Annette), J. E. Freeman (Marty Cantor), Alex Norton (Dennis Cooley), Hugh Fraser (Watkins), David Threlfall, Alun Armstrong, Berlinda Tolbert, Hugh Ross, Gerald Sim, Pip Torrens, Thomas Russell, Jonathan Ryan, Andrew Connolly, Karl Hayden, Claire Oberman, Tom Watt, Ellen Geer, John Lafayette, Duke Moosekian, Theodore Raimi, Debora Weston, Bob Gunton.

Dir: Phillip Noyce. Pro: Mace Neufeld and Robert Rehme. Ex Pro: Charles H. Maguire. Screenplay: W. Peter Iliff and

Family at war: Thora Birch, Anne Archer and Harrison Ford jump for cover in Phillip Noyce's finger-gnawing Patriot Games *(from UIP)*

Donald Stewart; based on the novel by Tom Clancy. Ph: Donald McAlpine. Ed: Neil Travis. Pro Des: Joseph Nemec III. M: James Horner; 'Harry's Game' performed by Clannad. Costumes: Norma Moriceau. Sound: Jack Solomon. (Paramount–UIP.) Rel: 25 September 1992. 116 mins. Cert 15.

Pepi, Luci, Bom and All the Other Girls – Pepi, Luci, Bom y Otras Chicas del Monton

Pedro Almodovar's very first feature, a raw, undisciplined, vulgar and episodic

look at the friendship between three remarkably different women. Filmed in 1980 in the punk milieu of Madrid, the film concentrates on the bizarre path of vengeance taken by Luci, who was raped by her policeman husband. Rape is only one of the sexual 'pleasures' Almodovar sticks his nose in, dredging up every known carnal

Cry freedom: Stephen Dorff attains a small victory in John G. Avildsen's epic, hard-hitting The Power of One *(from Warner)*

perversion. Look out for the penis-size competition and the new line of dolls that menstruate. If only it wasn't so unremittingly tedious. [CB]

Cast: Carmen Maura (Pepi), Eva Siva (Luci), Olvida 'Alaska' Gara (Bom), Felix Rotaeta (policeman), Concha Gregori, Kitty Mamber, Cecilia Roth, Julieta Serrano, Agustin Almodovar.
   Dir: Pedro Almodovar. Ex Pro: Pepon Coromina and Felix Rotaeta. Screenplay: Almodovar and Uge Cuesta. Ph: Paco Femenia. Ed: Pepe Salcedo. Costumes: Manuela Camacho. Sound: Miguel Polo. (Metro.) Rel: 10 July 1992. 89 mins. Cert 18.

Peter's Friends

Six friends from university meet up ten years later for a reunion at the stately manor of Lord Peter Malton. Peter and Maggie are still single, Roger and Mary have married each other, Sarah continues her career as a nymphomaniac and brings her latest lover, the crass Brian, while would-be dramatist Andrew has sold out to Hollywood and married a brash American actress. Over three days, the eight characters humour and insult each other as poor Peter attempts to rally a spirit of *bonhomie*. Best summarised as an English *Big Chill*, Kenneth Branagh's third film as director is the funniest, slickest British comedy since *A Fish Called Wanda*. A witty, insightful script from Rita Rudner and Martin Bergman is brought to vivid life by a superb cast, while Branagh's crisp direction never labours the humour nor patronises the film's more serious themes. [JC-W]

Cast: Kenneth Branagh (Andrew), Alphonsia Emmanuel (Sarah), Stephen Fry (Lord Peter Malton), Hugh Laurie (Roger), Phyllida Law (Vera), Rita Rudner (Carol Benson), Tony Slattery (Brian), Imelda Staunton (Mary), Emma Thompson (Maggie), Alex Lowe, Richard Briers, Edward Jewesbury, Hetta Charnley.
   Dir and Pro: Kenneth Branagh. Ex Pro: Stephen Evans. Line Pro: David Parfitt. Ph:

Peter's problems: Stephen Fry and Emma Thompson put a brave face on a calamitous weekend in the country – in Kenneth Branagh's hilarious Peter's Friends *(from Entertainment)*

Roger Lanser. Ed: Andrew Marcus. Pro Des: Tim Harvey. M: Numbers performed by Tears For Fears, Nina Simone, Queen, Cyndi Lauper, Bruce Springsteen, Pretenders, Tina Turner, Eric Clapton, Pasadenas, Michael Nesmith, and Dalry Braithwaite. Costumes: Susan Coates and Stephanie Collie. Sound: David Crozier. (Samuel Goldwyn/Renaissance Films–Entertainment.) Rel: 13 November 1992. 102 mins. Cert 15.

The Power of One

Sweeping, glossy adaptation of Bryce Courtenay's best-selling semi-autobiographical novel about an English boy, PK, growing up in South Africa and fighting apartheid. Despised by the Afrikaners, PK learns to stand up for himself and respect his fellow man thanks to the friendship of two elderly men, one black and one white. Photographed with an eye for the tourist industry and superbly over-scored, the film manages to be disturbing, thought-provoking and even engrossing at times, but too often resembles a mini-series or 'a good read' to genuinely engage our emotions. [JC-W]

Cast: Stephen Dorff (PK, aged 18), Armin Mueller-Stahl (Doc), John Gielgud (Headmaster St John), Morgan Freeman (Geel Piet), Guy Witcher (PK, aged 7), Simon Fenton (PK, aged 12), Fay Masterson (Maria Marais), Marius Weyers (Professor Daniel Marais), Nomadlozi Kubheka, Tracy Brooks Swope, Robbie Bulloch, Winston Ntshona, Dominic Walker, Alois Moyo, Ian Roberts, Daniel Craig, Faith Edwards, Christien Anholt.
   Dir and Ed: John G. Avildsen. Pro: Arnon Milchan. Ex Pro: Steven Reuther, Graham Burke and Greg Coote. Screenplay: Robert Mark Kamen. Ph: Dean Semler. Pro Des: Roger Hall. M: Hans Zimmer; songs by Johnny Clegg. Costumes: Tom Rand. Sound: Clive Winter. (Regency Enterprises/Le Studio Canal +/ Alcor Films/Village Roadshow–Warner.) Rel: 4 September 1992. 125 mins. Cert 12.

Prague

Alexander Novak, a gauche young Scot, visits Prague to find newsreel footage of his grandparents – shortly before they 'vanished' in 1941. While exploring his Czech origins, Alexander puts down a few roots of his own as he becomes involved with members of the archive library staff. A gently endearing comedy-drama that seduces

It started with a kiss: Alan Cumming greets his Czech destination in Ian Sellar's offbeat Prague *(from Winstone)*

the eye and teases the mind, but fails to fully engage the emotions. [JC-W]

Cast: Alan Cumming (Alexander Novak), Sandrine Bonnaire (Elena), Bruno Ganz (Josef), Raphael Meis, Hana Gregorova, Petr Jakl, Luba Skorepova, Zdena Keclikova, Ladislav Brothanek.
   Dir and Screenplay: Ian Sellar. Pro: Christopher Young. Co-Pro: Claudie Ossard. Assoc Pro: David Brown. Ph: Darius Khondji. Ed: John Bloom. Pro Des: Jiri Matolin. M: Jonathan Dove. Costumes: Evelyne Francois Correard. Sound: Colin Nicholson. (Constellation/UGC/Hachette Premiere–Winstone.) Rel: 23 October 1992. 88 mins. Cert 12.

The Princess and the Goblin

Very basic children's cartoon, about a button-nosed princess and a snub-nosed miner's lad who unite to thwart a plot by goblins to overthrow the throne. Threadbare sound design and too many jarring close-ups conspire to eliminate any magic the story may have had. For undiscerning children only. Based on the celebrated children's novel by George MacDonald (originally serialised 1870–1), which was much admired at the time by C. S. Lewis and G. K. Chesterton

Rik Mayall in one of his more unlikely guises, in the limp The Princess and the Goblin *(from Entertainment)*

The naked city: Joe Pesci (with camera) brings art to the underbelly of New York, in Howard Franklin's distinctive The Public Eye *(from UIP)*

and later served as the inspiration for Tolkien's *The Hobbit*. [JC-W]

Voices: Joss Ackland (King Papa), Claire Bloom (great-great-great-grandmother Irene), Sally Ann Marsh (Princess Irene), Rik Mayall (Froglip), Peggy Mount (Goblin Queen), Peter Murray (Curdie), Mollie Sugden (Lootie), Roy Kinnear, Victor Spinetti, Frank Rozelaar Green, William Hootkins, Maxine Howe.
    Dir: Jozef Gemes. Pro and Screenplay: Robin Lyons. Ex Pro: Steve Walsh and Marietta Dardai. Ph: Arpad Lessecry, Gyorgy Verga, Ede Pagner, Nick Smith,

Pete Turner, Steve Turner and Andreas Klawsz. Ed: Magda Hap. M: Istvan Lerch. Sound: Imre Andras Nyerges, John Griffiths and Clive Pendry. (Siriol Prods/Pannonia Film/S4C Wales/NHK Enterprises–Entertainment.) Rel: 18 December 1992. 78 mins. Cert U.

The Public Eye

New York; 1942. Leon Bernstein doesn't take sides, he takes pictures. Using 'Life as it happens' as his motto, 'Bernzy' is a freelance tabloid photographer with the cunning of a rat and the eye of an artist. He can get to the scene of a crime faster than anyone, and if the picture is good enough, can demand more than the standard 'three bucks a corpse'. For

Bernzy, photography is his life, and that leaves no room for security, comfort or women. One day, he would like to present his startling, vivid pictures in a book to 'capture the public eye'. Inspired by an exhibition of tabloid photography at New York's International Center of Photography, *The Public Eye* was scripted nine years ago by its director, Howard Franklin (*Quick Change*), who bided his time to bring the film he wanted to the screen. The result is a touching, funny, unusual and superbly crafted character study. [JC-W]

Cast: Joe Pesci (Leon 'Bernzy' Bernstein), Barbara Hershey (Kay Levitz), Stanley Tucci (Salvator Minetto), Jerry Adler (Arthur Nabler), Jared Harris (Danny the Doorman), Richard Foronjy (Farinelli), Dominic Chianese (Marc-Anthony Spoleto), Richard Riehle, Del Close, Kevin Dorsey, Gerry Becker, Bob Gunton, Patricia Healy, Al Mancini, Nick Tate, Shay Duffin.
    Dir and Screenplay: Howard Franklin. Pro: Sue Baden-Powell. Ex Pro: Robert Zemeckis. Ph: Peter Suschitzky. Ed: Evan Lottman. Pro Des: Marcia Hinds-Johnson. M: Mark Isham. Costumes: Jane Robinson. Sound: Stephan Von Hase-Mihalik. (Universal–UIP.) Rel: 5 February 1993. 99 mins. Cert 15.

The Quince Tree Sun – El Sol Del Membrillo

Madrid; September-December, 1990. A gently obsessive film about a gently obsessive man, Victor Erice's third picture in twenty years observes the realist painter Antonio Lopez attempting to paint a quince tree. The 'quince tree sun', like Britain's Indian summer, produces a special light which the artist is obsessed with capturing, but his technical perfectionism constantly obstructs his objective. By turns fascinating, mesmerising and incredibly boring, *The Quince Tree Sun* attempts to bridge the gap between film and painting, and narrative and reality. But is it art? You *really* have to be in the mood to appreciate this one. [JC-W]

With: Antonio Lopez, Maria Moreno, Enrique Gran, Jose Carrtero, Maria Lopez, Carmen Lopez, Elisa Ruiz, Fan Xiao Ming, etc.
    Dir: Victor Erice. Ex Pro: Maria Moreno. Assoc Pro: Angel Amigo. Ph: Javier Aguirresarobe and Angel Luis Fernandez. Ed: Juan Ignacio San Mateo. M: Pascal Gaigne. Sound: Eduardo Fernan-

The art of perfectionism: an arboriphilic Antonio Lopez in Victor Erice's diligent The Quince Tree Sun *(from Artificial Eye)*

dez. (Euskal Media/Igeldo Zine Produkzioak–Artificial Eye.) Rel: 2 April 1993. 139 mins. Cert U.

Raising Cain

Northern California; 1992. After the debacle of *The Bonfire of the Vanities*, Brian De Palma returns to what he does best: the suspense thriller. Pitted with false alarms, dream sequences and sudden acts of violence, *Raising Cain* is pure De Palma, complete with his fondness for prowling camera work and fish-eye lenses. Unfortunately, the script is too stupid for words and John Lithgow, last of the great hams, goes way over the top and out of the picture. Not to spoil the corkscrew plot, the film involves a fanatical child psychologist, a failing marriage and a lethal dose of schizophrenia. The film's cliffhanging climax – a melodramatic tribute to Hitchcock – will keep you laughing for days. [JC-W]

Cast: John Lithgow (Carter/Cain/Dr Nix/Josh/Margo), Lolita Davidovich (Jenny Nix), Steven Bauer (Jack Dante), Frances Sternhagen (Dr Waldheim), Gregg Henry (Lt Terri), Tom Bower (Sgt Cally), Mel Harris (Sara), Teri Austin (Karen), Gabrielle Carteris (Nan), Barton Heyman, Amanda Pombo, Kathleen Callan.

Dir and Screenplay: Brian De Palma. Pro: Gale Anne Hurd. Co-Pro: Michael R. Joyce. Ph: Stephen H. Burum. Ed: Paul Hirsch, Bonnie Koehler and Robert Dalva. Pro Des: Doug Kraner. M: Pino Donaggio. Costumes: Bobbie Read. Sound: Nelson Stoll. (Pacific Western/Universal–UIP.) Rel: 8 January 1993. 92 mins. Cert 15.

Rapid Fire

The Far East/Los Angeles/Chicago. Action-packed martial arts thriller with the accent on violence and lines like 'Think positive. He's got you by the balls. So cut off his hands.' Brandon Lee, the late son of Bruce, is still haunted by the death of his father in Tiananmen Square and abhors violence. Only after he has been shot at by the heroin-dealing baddies and set

'Let me out of this movie!': Lolita Davidovich cries for help in Brian De Palma's ludicrous Raising Cain *(from UIP)*

High jinks: Brandon Lee runs up the bodycount in Dwight H. Little's fast-moving Rapid Fire *(from Fox)*

Mixed blessings: Kimberly Cullum and Mimi Rogers pray for deliverance in Michael Tolkin's intriguing The Rapture *(from Electric)*

up by the police does he put up his dukes and kick the hell out of Chicago. In spite of some classy fight choreography (c/o Mr Lee), snappy dialogue and decent performances, *Rapid Fire* is let down by a story that fizzles out in the last act. [JC-W]

Cast: Brandon Lee (Jake Lo), Powers Boothe (Mace Ryan), Nick Mancuso (Antonio Serrano), Raymond J. Barry (Agent Stuart), Kate Hodge (Karla Withers), Tzi Ma (Kinman Tau), Tony Longo (Brunner Gazzi), Michael Paul Chan, Dustin Nguyen, Brigitta Stenberg, Basil Wallace, Al Leong, Francois Chau, Quentin O'Brien.
　Dir: Dwight H. Little. Pro: Robert Lawrence. Ex Pro: Gerald Olson and John Fasano. Screenplay: Alan McElroy; from his and Cindy Cirile's story. Ph: Ric Waite. Ed: Gib Jaffe. Pro Des: Ron Foreman. M: Christopher Young; numbers performed by Hardline. Costumes: Erica Edell Phillips. Sound: Rob Janiger. (Fox.) Rel: 20 November 1992. 95 mins. Cert 18.

The Rapture

Intriguing little film about a decadent LA woman, Sharon, who grows tired of her endless sexual encounters and kinky foursomes with her lover, Vic. Instead, she turns to the Bible, fuelled by enigmatic talk of 'The Dream', 'The Pearl' and 'The Boy' uttered all around her. Soon Sharon is trying to spread the Word herself and is prepared to test her love of God. The film has been praised both for its passionate attack on born-again Christianity and for its religious convictions. Whichever way you look at it, you have to admire the film for its straight face – and daring. Unless of course it's just hedging its bets. [JC-W]

Cast: Mimi Rogers (Sharon), David Duchovny (Randy), Patrick Bauchau (Vic), Kimberly Cullum (Mary), Will Patton (Sheriff Foster Maddison), James Le Gros (Tommy), Dick Anthony Williams, Carole Davis, De Vaughn Nixon, Marvin Elkins, Douglas Roberts.
　Dir and Screenplay: Michael Tolkin. Pro: Nick Wechsler, Nancy Tenenbaum and Karen Koch. Ex Pro: Laurie Parker. Ph: Bojan Bazelli. Ed: Suzanne Fenn. Pro Des: Robin Standefer. M: Thomas Newman. Costumes: Michael A. Jackson. Sound: David Kelson. (New Line–Electric.) Rel: 3 July 1992. 102 mins. Cert 18.

Reservoir Dogs

Powerful, strikingly original comedy-drama that separates the men from the boys. Opening in a contemporary Los Angeles restaurant, the film introduces us to its eight main characters as they crack (extremely) dirty jokes and discuss the content of old songs. Cutting forward in time, the film pieces together the lead-up to a recent jewel

Dog eat dog: Michael Madsen, Harvey Keitel, Tim Roth and director Quentin Tarantino on a killing spree, in Rank's chilling Reservoir Dogs

heist with flashbacks devoted to each character. There are surprises galore, and the violence and language is as strong as it gets, but there's plenty of humour, too. The performances are all first-rate, with co-producer Harvey Keitel heading the macho cast, while London-born Tim Roth makes a thoroughly convincing Yank. But the true honours go to scriptwriter and first-time director Quentin Tarantino, who presents a film of remarkable economy and style. Maybe the best independent American film of the year. [JC-W]

Cast: Harvey Keitel (Mr White/Larry), Michael Madsen (Mr Blonde/Vic), Christopher Penn (Nice Guy Eddie), Steve Buscemi (Mr Pink), Lawrence Tierney (Joe Cabot), Tim Roth (Mr Orange/Freddy), Kirk Baltz (Marvin Nash), Eddie Bunker (Mr Blue), Quentin Tarantino (Mr Brown), Steven Wright (K-Billy DJ), Randy Brooks, Rich Turner, Michael Sottile.

Dir and Screenplay: Quentin Tarantino. Pro: Lawrence Bender. Ex Pro: Richard N. Gladstein, Ronna B. Wallace and Monte Hellman. Co-Pro: Harvey Keitel. Ph: Andrzej Sekula. Ed: Sally Menks. Pro Des: David Wasco. M: Numbers performed by George Baker Selection, Stealer's Wheel, Joe Tex, Harry Nilsson, Bedlam, etc. Costumes: Betsy Heimann. Sound: Ken Segal. (Manifesto/Live America Inc–Rank.) Rel: 8 January 1992. 100 mins. Cert 18.

Rich in Love

South Carolina; 1992. Another dysfunctional Southern family wrestles to keep our attention as Momma leaves for no apparent reason and her daughters struggle to find their sexual identity. An extraordinary cast (Albert Finney appears to be impersonating W. C. Fields) looks ill at ease (except for Suzy Amis, who gives a luminous performance), while the slushy score stops and starts predictably on cue. Lethargic, aimless and rather gauche. From the director, producers, screenwriter, cinematographer and editor of *Driving Miss Daisy*. [JC-W]

Cast: Albert Finney (Warren Odom), Jill Clayburgh (Helen Odom), Kathryn Erbe (Lucille Odom), Kyle MacLachlan (Billy McQueen), Piper Laurie (Vera Delmarge), Ethan Hawke (Wayne Frobiness), Suzy Amis (Rae Odom), Alfre Woodard, J. Leon Pridgen II, David Hager, Ramona Ward, Wayne Dehart, D. L. Anderson.

Dir: Bruce Beresford. Pro: Richard D. Zanuck and Lili Fini Zanuck. Co-Pro: David Brown. Screenplay: Alfred Uhry; from the novel by Josephine Humphreys.

Carolina on their mind: Kathryn Erbe and Jill Clayburgh find themselves and each other in Bruce Beresford's dreary Rich in Love *(from UIP)*

Zen and the art of fly-fishing: Tom Skerritt shows his sons (Vann Gravage, Joseph Gordan-Levitt) how, in Robert Redford's aesthetic A River Runs Through It *(from Guild)*

Ph: Peter James. Ed: Mark Warner. Pro Des: John Stoddart. M: Georges Delerue; numbers performed by Billie Holiday, Lonnie Hamilton & The Diplomats, Suzanne Benson, Anita O'Day, and The Graces. Costumes: Colleen Kelsall. Sound: Hank Garfield. (MGM–UIP.) Rel: 7 May 1993. 105 mins. Cert PG.

A River Runs Through It

Missoula, Montana; 1910–35. 'Eventually,' intones Robert Redford's laid-back voice-over, 'all things merge – and a river runs through it.' There is much poetic posturing in this immensely tasteful adaptation of Norman Maclean's autobiographical novel, the story of a Presbyterian minister, his two sons and, above all, the art of Zen and fly-fishing. And they say fishing is dull. N.B. No fish were killed or injured during the production of this film. [JC-W]

Cast: Craig Sheffer (Norman Maclean), Brad Pitt (Paul Maclean), Tom Skerritt (Reverend Maclean), Brenda Blethyn (Mrs Maclean), Emily Lloyd (Jessie Burns), Edie McClurg (Mrs Burns), Stephen Shellen (Neal Burns), Nicole Burdette (Mabel), Vann Gravage, Susan Traylor, Michael Cudlitz, Joseph Gordon-Levitt, MacIntyre Dixon, William Hootkins, Rex Kendall, Jack Kroll, Prudence Johnson.

Dir: Robert Redford. Pro: Redford and Patrick Markey. Ex Pro: Jake Eberts. Screenplay: Richard Friedenberg. Ph: Philippe Rousselot. Ed: Lynzee Klingman and Robert Estrin. Pro Des: Jon Hutman. M: Mark Isham. Costumes: Bernie Pollack and Kathy O'Rear. Sound: Hans Roland. (Allied Filmmakers–Guild.) Rel: 19 February 1993. 124 mins. Cert PG.

Romper Stomper

Raw, frightening look at a gang of neo-Nazi skinheads who take up arms (and knives, baseball bats, etc) against the growing Vietnamese community in Melbourne. The film, which was designed to shock and open our eyes to the growing racial intolerance in Australia, succeeded in its objective, attracting phenomenal controversy Down Under. However, by failing to condemn its central protagonist (powerfully played by Russell Crowe), the film does prompt doubts about its moral gravity. Civilised audiences will be sickened by it, lager louts will be inspired, and intellectuals mesmerised. Very disturbing. [CB]

Cast: Russell Crowe (Hando), Daniel Pollock (Davey), Jacqueline McKenzie (Gabe), Alex Scott (Martin), Leigh Russell (Sonny Jim), Daniel Wyllie, Eric Mueck, Frank Magree, Christopher McLean.

Dir and Screenplay: Geoffrey Wright. Pro: Daniel Scharf and Ian Pringle. Assoc Pro: Phil Jones. Ph: Ron Hagen. Ed: Bill Murphy. Pro Des: Steve Jones-Evans. M: John Clifford White. Costumes: Anna Borghesi. Sound: Frank Lipson. (Seon Films/Australian Film Commission/Film Victoria–Medusa.) Rel: 26 February 1993. 94 mins. Cert 18.

Ruby Cairo

Dreary romantic comedy-thriller starring Andie MacDowell as a poor American wife who embarks on an adventurous mission to unravel the true identity of her late husband, a

Travels with Andie: Andie MacDowell with Liam Neeson in the enchantingly old-fashioned tripe Ruby Cairo *(from Entertainment)*

Machiavellian LA pilot. Clues to his double life lead MacDowell to Mexico, Berlin, Athens, Egypt and Liam Neeson. Simple-minded tosh. [CB]

Cast: Andie MacDowell (Bessie Faro), Liam Neeson (Fergus Lamb), Viggo Mortensen (Johnny Faro), Jack Thompson (Ed), Amy Van Nostrand, Pedro Gonzalez-Gonzalez, Lucy Rodriquez, Jeff Corey.
 Dir: Graeme Clifford. Pro: Lloyd Phillips. Line Pro: David Nicols. Ex Pro: Haruki Kadokawa. Screenplay: Robert Dillon and Michael Thomas. Ph: Laszlo Kovacs. Ed: Caroline Biggerstaff. Pro Des: Richard Sylbert. M: John Barry; 'You Belong To Me' sung by Patsy Cline. Costumes: Rudy Dillon. (Entertainment.) Rel: 30 April 1993. 100 mins. Cert 15.

Sarafina!

Based on the hit South African and Broadway show, *Sarafina!* is that rare cinematic animal – a musical that doesn't feel staged. The music, by Mbongeni Ngema and Hugh Masekela, feels such a part of the way of life of the people of Soweto, that it permeates and lifts the action rather than stopping it. The story centres on Sarafina, a beautiful, spirited schoolgirl who opposes the injustice of white emergency rule. Through the wisdom and strength of her history teacher (beautifully played by Whoopi Goldberg), Sarafina learns to fight the children's war without guns. While the production numbers are stunningly choreographed to uplifting songs, they do not intrude on the numbing reality of Botha's war on the blacks. Indeed, the film opens with the horrific statement that 8000 schoolchildren have been imprisoned and 750 murdered, before gearing up to its message of hope and celebration of life. Young Leleti Khumalo, in the title role, gives the film a magical emotional charge, and is backed up all the way by a production that is both daring and accomplished. [JC-W]

Cast: Whoopi Goldberg (Mary Masombuka), Miriam Makeba (Angelina), Leleti

Soweto sings!: Leleti Khumalo leads the dance in Darrell James Roodt's invigorating Sarafina! *(from Warner)*

The fragrance of life: Al Pacino dances Gabrielle Anwar off her feet in Martin Brest's colourful Scent of a Woman *(from UIP)*

Khumalo (Sarafina), John Kani (school principal), Mbongeni Ngema (Sabela), Dumisani Dlamini (Crocodile), Sipho Kunene (Guitar), Tertius Meintjes (Lt Bloem), Robert Whitehead (interrogator), Somizi 'Whacko' Mhlongo, Nhlanhla Ngema, Faca Kulu, Wendy Mseleku, Mary Twala, James Mthoba.
    Dir: Darrell James Roodt. Pro: Anant Singh and (for the BBC) David M. Thompson. Ex Pro: Kirk D'Amico and Sudhir Pragjee. Screenplay: William Nicholson and Mbongeni Ngema. Ph: Mark Vicente. Ed: Peter Hollywood and Sarah Thomas. Pro Des: David Barkham. M: Stanley Myers. M and lyrics: Ngema; additional songs: Hugh Masekela. Choreography: Ngema and Michael Peters. Sound: Henry Prentice. (Distant Horizon/ Ideal Films/Videovision Enterprises/Les Films Ariane/VPI/BBC–Warner.) Rel: 15 January 1993. 115 mins. Cert. 15.

Savage Nights – Les Nuits Fauves

Unable to find a star actor willing to play the HIV-positive hero of his autobiographical film, writer-director Cyril Collard took on the role himself. Exuding an easy, self-effacing charm, Collard displays the looks of a matinee idol, making the reprehensible behaviour of his character all the harder to condemn. Collard plays Jean, a 30-year-old film cameraman who drives too fast, drinks too much, snorts coke and gropes anonymous men under the bridges of the Seine. When he discovers that he is HIV-positive, he doesn't tell his girlfriend, the 17-year-old Laura, and continues his sexual adventures elsewhere. And even when he does inform Laura and his boyfriend – the sado-masochistic Samy – they both insist on unprotected sex with him. This is a hard story to like, told with an abrasive, in-your-face style, but knowing that the actor on the screen is the real thing makes it compulsive viewing. *Les Nuits Fauves* was an enormous success in France (where there are 500 per cent more AIDS cases than in Britain), but three days before it picked up the César (the French Oscar) for best film, Collard was dead. [JC-W]

Cast: Cyril Collard (Jean), Romane Bohringer (Laura), Carlos Lopez (Samy), Rene-Marc Bini (Marc), Maria Schneider (Noria), Corine Blue, Claude Winter, Clementine Celarie, Laura Favali, Jean-Jacques Jauffret.
    Dir: Cyril Collard. Pro: Nella Banfi. Ex Pro: Jean-Frederic Samie. Screenplay: Collard and Jacques Fieschi; from Collard's novel. Ph: Manuel Teran. Ed: Lise Beaulieu. Art: Jacky Macchi and Katja Kosenina. M: Numbers performed by Collard, INXS, Dave Stewart, The Pogues, New Model Army, Damia, Rene-Marc Bini, etc. Costumes: Regine Arniaud. Sound: Michel Brethez and Dominique Hennequin. (Banfilm Ter/La Sept Cinema/Erre Prods/ SNC/Canal Plus–Artificial Eye.) Rel: 18 June 1993. 126 mins. Cert 18.

Scent of a Woman

Charlie Simms (Chris O'Donnell) is on scholarship to the hallowed halls of Baird School in New Hampshire. An outsider, he is patronised by his colleagues but refuses to snitch on them, even when the school's principal threatens him with expulsion. Such integrity is not the stuff of Lt-Colonel Frank Slade (Al Pacino), a blind old warhorse whom Charlie is forced to babysit for extra pocket money ($300). But Slade is no baby, and takes Charlie on a luxurious, eventful trip to New York where the bull elephant and the timid fawn learn from each other. Nudging sentimentality and flirting with corn, this misleadingly titled would-be soap opera is rescued by its fine acting (although Pacino's gung-ho performance is a tad OTT) and is spiced with fine moments. The sterling screenplay is by Bo Goldman (*One*

Flew Over the Cuckoo's Nest, Melvin and Howard), and is based on the 1974 Italian film of the same name. [JC-W]

Cast: Al Pacino (Lt-Col Frank Slade), Chris O'Donnell (Charlie Simms), James Rebhorn (Mr Trask), Gabrielle Anwar (Donna), Philip S. Hoffman (George Willis Jr), Richard Venture (WR Slade), Nicholas Sadler (Harry), Gene Canfield (Manny), Frances Conroy (Christine Downes), Ron Eldard (Officer Gore), Sally Murphy (Karen Rossi), Baxter Harris (George Willis Sr), Leonard Gaines (Freddie Bisco), Bradley Whitford, Rochelle Oliver, Margaret Eginton, David Lansbury.

Dir and Pro: Martin Brest. Ex Pro: Ronald L. Schwary. Screenplay: Bo Goldman. Ph: Donald E. Thorin. Ed: William Steinkamp, Michael Tronick and Harvey Rosenstock. Pro Des: Angelo Graham. M: Thomas Newman; *Evangeline* sung by Emmylou Harris. Costumes: Aude Bronson-Howard. Sound: Danny Michael. (City Lights Films/Universal–UIP.) Rel: 12 March 1993. 156 mins. Cert 15.

Schtonk!

Frenetic German farce based on the hoax surrounding the Hitler diaries. The facts of the case being so bizarre in themselves, the broad approach of Helmut Dietl's comedy seems entirely unnecessary. An historical curio. [JC-W]

Cast: Götz George (Hermann Willie), Uwe Ochsenknecht (Fritz Knobel), Christiane Hörbiger (Freya von Hepp), Dagmar Manzel (Biggi), Veronica Ferres (Martha), Rolf Hoppe, Rosemarie Fendel, Karl Schönböck, Harald Juhnke, Ulrich Mühe,

Ham and scam: master-forger Uwe Ochsenknecht seeks inspiration from Veronica Ferres, in Helmut Dietl's frenetic Schtonk! *(from Artificial Eye)*

Martin Benrath, Hermann Lause, Hark Bohm.

Dir: Helmut Dietl. Pro: Dietl and Gunter Rohrbach. Screenplay: Dietl and Ulrich Limmer. Ph: Xaver Schwarzenberger. Ed: Tanja Schmidbauer. Art: Götz Weidner and Benedikt Herforth. M: Konstantin Wecker. Costumes: Bernd Stockinger and Barbara Ehret. Sound: Chris Price. (Bavarian Film/WDR–Artificial Eye.) Rel: 22 January 1993. 111 mins. Cert 15.

Secret Friends

A man on a train to London loses his memory and cannot separate his sexual fantasies from remembered fact. Did he kill his wife? Or was she just a prostitute? And who is this secret friend of his, this haunting *alter ego*? The first feature that Dennis Potter has directed from his own screenplay, *Secret Friends* is an intellectual mosaic of flashbacks, fantasy and reality that should drive the average viewer nuts. As usual, Potter attempts to get away

Dennis Potter directs Alan Bates in a scene from Secret Friends, *the former's brave offensive on conventional narrative – from Feature Film Co.*

from conventional narrative, but his pedestrian direction fails to animate his witty, thought-provoking script. [JC-W]

Cast: Alan Bates (John), Gina Bellman (Helen), Frances Barber (Angela), Tony Doyle (Martin), Joanna David (Kate), Colin Jeavons, Rowena Cooper, Ian McNeice, Davyd Harries, Niven Boyd, Martin Whiting.

Dir and Screenplay: Dennis Potter; 'suggested' by his novel *Ticket to Ride*. Pro: Rosemarie Whitman. Ex Pro: Robert Michael Geisler and John Roberdeau. Ph: Sue Gibson. Ed: Clare Douglas. Pro Des: Gary Williamson. M: Nick Russell-Pavier. Costumes: Sharon Lewis. Sound: John Midgley. (Film Four International/Whistling Gypsy–Feature Film Co.) Rel: 25 September 1992. 98 mins. Cert 15.

Shadows and Fog

This time Woody Allen, with his 21st movie as writer-director, pays homage to the cinema of Fritz Lang. Setting his story in an unnamed European city (in which the dollar is currency), Woody casts himself as 'an ink-stained nobody', a hapless clerk who becomes the catalyst for much confusion one dark, foggy night. Due to a chain of

The clown as tragedian: John Malkovich in Woody Allen's atmospheric comedy-thriller Shadows and Fog *(from Columbia Tri-Star)*

misunderstandings, he finds himself chased by a manic strangler, the police, his work colleagues and even a gun-toting old girlfriend (Julie Kavner), while he falls in with a sweet-natured sword-swallower (Mia Farrow) who has just left her boyfriend. This is very slight entertainment, but the atmospheric black-and-white photography is agreeable on the eyes and the one-liners are right up to scratch. It's also a relief to see Allen tackle something set outside Manhattan, even if the now-customary all-star cast is a little distracting. If this were on the menu, it'd be vichyssoise. [JC-W]

Cast: Woody Allen (Kleinman), John Cusack (student Jack), Mia Farrow (Irmy), Madonna (Marie), John Malkovich (clown), Kathy Bates, Jodie Foster, Fred Gwynne, Julie Kavner, Kenneth Mars, Kate Nelligan, Donald Pleasence, Lily Tomlin, Philip Bosco, Robert Joy, Wallace Shawn, Kurtwood Smith, Josef Sommer, David Ogden Stiers, Michael Kirby, James Rebhorn, Victor Argo, Anne Lange, Fred Melamed, John C. Reilly, W. H. Macy, Richard Riehle.

Dir and Screenplay: Woody Allen. Pro: Robert Greenhut. Ex Pro: Jack Rollins and Charles H. Joffe. Ph: Carlo Di Palma. Ed: Susan E. Morse. Pro Des: Santo Loquasto.

M: Kurt Weill. Costumes: Jeffrey Kurland. Sound: James Sabat. (Orion–Columbia Tri-Star.) Rel: 12 February 1993. 86 mins. Cert 15.

The Silent Touch

Copenhagen, Denmark; 1992. Riveting character study with Max Von Sydow on top form as a reclusive, unpredictable and often violent com-

poser driven into retirement by an inactive muse. When a saintly Polish student (Lothaire Bluteau) turns up on his doorstep at the behest of a dream, the drama begins. Unfortunately, this English version of an honourable Anglo-Polish-Danish co-production is confounded by a translation so banal that Von Sydow's tour-de-force is virtually undermined. [CB]

Cast: Max Von Sydow (Henry Kesdi), Lothaire Bluteau (Stefan Bugajski), Sarah Miles (Helena Kesdi), Sofie Grabol (Annette Berg), Aleksander Bardini (Prof. Jerzy Kern), Peter Hesse Overgaard, Lars Lunoe, Slawomira Lozinska, Trevor Cooper.

Dir: Krzysztof Zanussi. Pro: Mark Forstater. Co-Pro: Zanussi and Mads Egmont Christensen. Screenplay: Peter Morgan and Mark Wadlow; based on an original story by Zanussi and Edward Zebrowski. Ph: Jaroslaw Zamojda. Ed: Marek Denys. Pro Des: Ewa Braun. M: Wojciech Kilar. Costumes: Dorota Roqueplo. Sound: Wieslawa Dembinska. (Tor Film Group/Metronome Prods A/S/British Screen–Mayfair Entertainment.) Rel: 2 April 1993. 96 mins. Cert 15.

Simple Men

New York; 1992. Two brothers – one tough and self-sufficient, the other bookish and sensitive – set out for Long Island to find their father, a baseball legend, ex-con and radical activist. Along the way they encounter a variety of characters, each stranger than the last. Director/writer Hal Hartley is one of America's most idio-

Staged eccentricity: Holly Marie Combs is not the sort of convent girl you'd expect – in Hal Hartley's smugly strange Simple Men *(from Metro Tartan)*

syncratic filmmakers, but tends to do everything for effect. There *are* some memorable scenes here (the garage attendant picking up an electric guitar and jamming *Greensleeves*, a bizarre discussion about the merits of Madonna), but for the most part *Simple Men* is disjointed and aimless. An acquired taste. [JC-W]

Cast: Robert Burke (Bill McCabe), William Sage (Dennis McCabe), Karen Sillas (Kate), Elina Lowensohn (Elina), Martin Donovan (Martin), Jeffrey Howard (Ned Rifle), Holly Marie Combs (Kim), Damian Young (Sheriff), Mary McKenzie (Vera), Mark Chandler Bailey, Chris Cooke, Joe Stevens, Marietta Marich, John Alexander MacKay, Bethany Wright, Richard Reyes, Vivian Lanko.

Dir and Screenplay: Hal Hartley. Pro: Ted Hope and Hartley. Ex Pro: Jerome Brownstein and Bruce Weiss. Ph: Michael Spiller. Ed: Steve Hamilton. Pro Des: Dan Ouellette. M: Ned Rifle; numbers performed by Sonic Youth, and Yo La Tengo. Costumes: Alexandra Welker. Sound: Jeff Pullman. (Zenith/American Playhouse/Fine Line/Film Four Int/Bim Distribuzione/True Fiction–Metro Tartan.) Rel: 6 November 1992. 104 mins. Cert 15.

Singles

Seattle; 1992. Love isn't easy. Linda has just been jilted by a handsome, flagrant liar; Steve, also hurt and confused, is concentrating on his design to provide Seattle with its first traffic-defying supertrain; Janet thinks she is in love, and her dignity is suffering; Debbie believes she can find Mr Right with the aid of a flashy dating video; Bailey has begun to accept his fate as a single guy; while Cliff, a would-be rock star, *thinks* he's got it easy ('What can I say, man? She's crazy about me'). Cameron Crowe, who exposed teenage angst with a comic twist in *Fast Times at Ridgemont High*, turns his wry, affectionate gaze on the romantic lives of six yuppie twentysomethings who all love music. Beautifully played and skilfully crafted, *Singles* isn't going to change your life, but it's a gentle, eloquent, amusing, touching and observant comedy full of nice touches. N.B. The noteworthy soundtrack includes such on the up-and-up Seattle groups as Soundgarden, Pearl Jam and Alice in Chains. [JC-W]

Cast: Bridget Fonda (Janet Livermore), Campbell Scott (Steve Dunne), Kyra Sedgwick (Linda Powell), Sheila Kelley (Debbie

Love is in the air: Jim True, Bridget Fonda, Matt Dillon, Kyra Sedgwick and Campbell Scott in Cameron Crowe's exquisite Singles *(from Warner)*

Hunt), Jim True (David Bailey), Matt Dillon (Cliff Poncier), Bill Pullman (Dr Jamison), James Le Gros (Andy), Devon Raymond (Ruth), Camilo Gallardo, Ally Walker, Eric Stoltz, Jeremy Piven, Tom Skerritt, Peter Horton, Wayne Cody, Cameron Crowe, Jeff Ament, Chris Cornell, Alice Marie Crowe, Heather Hughes, Tim Burton.

Dir and Screenplay: Cameron Crowe. Pro: Crowe and Richard Hashimoto. Ex Pro: Art Linson. Co-Pro and Ed: Richard Chew. Ph: Ueli Steiger. Pro Des: Stephen Lineweaver. M: Paul Westerberg; numbers performed by Paul Westerberg, Soundgarden, Alice in Chains, Pearl Jam, Chris Cornell, Jimi Hendrix, Citizen Dick, Jane's Addiction, Muddy Waters, the Pixies, John Coltrane, REM, Sly & the Family Stone, etc. Costumes: Jane Ruhm. Sound: Art Rochester. (Atkinson/Knickerbocker Films-Warner.) Rel: 15 January 1993. 90 mins. Cert 12.

Single White Female

New York; today. When her boyfriend cheats on her, computer software maven Allison Jones advertises for a roommate to help pay the rent. The most friendly, natural and human applicant for the post is Hedra Carlson, a mousy, down-to-earth frump who works in a bookshop. The girls get on just fine, but Allison can't help snooping on her new friend. And Hedra just can't help tampering with Allison's life . . . A good-looking, skilfully scripted thriller that falls foul of

Persona non grata: Bridget Fonda and Jennifer Jason Leigh swap IDs in Barbet Schroeder's chilling Single White Female *(from Columbia)*

the old clichés and throws in a few new ones of its own, *SWF* wastes a bunch of psychological opportunities. Still, it's unnerving enough that it might keep you awake on a Saturday night. But *Persona* it ain't. [JC-W]

Cast: Bridget Fonda (Allison Jones), Jennifer Jason Leigh (Hedra Carlson), Steven Weber (Sam Rawson), Peter Friedman (Graham Knox), Stephen Tobolowsky (Mitchell Myerson), Frances Bay, Michelle Farr, Christiana Capetillo, Jessica Lundy, Rene Estevez, Amelia Campbell, Ken Tobey, Kim Sykes.
  Dir and Pro: Barbet Schroeder. Ex Pro: Jack Baran. Assoc Pro: Susan Hoffman. Screenplay: Don Roos; based on the novel *SWF Seeks Same* by John Lutz. Ph: Luciano Tovoli. Ed: Lee Percy. Pro Des: Milena Canonero. M: Howard Shore; Vivaldi. Sound: Gary Rydstrom. (Columbia TriStar.) Rel: 20 November 1992. 107 mins. Cert 18.

Sister Act

Reno/San Francisco. Lounge singer Deloris Van Cartier (Whoopi Goldberg) may be brash, loud and vulgar, but she's nobody's fool. Her one weakness is being the mistress of Mafia don Vince LaRocca, who puts a price on her head ($250,000) when she witnesses a mob killing. The police hide her out in a convent until she can testify, but until then Deloris has to come to terms with God – and the Mother Superior. Meanwhile, she turns the place inside out, attracting more attention than she'd anticipated . . . This is Whoopi at her broadest and most obvious, but once the story gets going there is plenty of heart, too, and the soundtrack is just divine. Although this is Whoopi's biggest solo hit to date, it's the nuns who steal the show. [JC-W]

Cast: Whoopi Goldberg (Deloris Wilson/Van Cartier/Sister Mary Clarence), Maggie Smith (Mother Superior), Harvey Keitel (Vince LaRocca), Bill Nunn (Eddie Souther), Kathy Najimy (Mary Patrick), Wendy Makkena (Mary Robert), Robert Miranda (Joey), Richard Portnow (Willy), Joseph Maher (Bishop O'Hara), Mary Wickes, Ellen Albertini Dow, Carmen Zapata, Pat Crawford Brown, Jim Beaver, Jenifer Lewis, Charlotte Crossley, A. J. Johnson, Toni Kalem, Kevin Bourland, David Boyce.
  Dir: Emile Ardolino. Pro: Teri Schwartz. Ex Pro: Scott Rudin. Screenplay: Joseph Howard. Ph: Adam Greenberg. Ed: Richard Halsey. Pro Des: Jackson DeGovia. M: Marc Shaiman; numbers performed by Fontella Bass, Etta James, Dee Dee Sharp, C&C Music Factory, Lady Soul, etc. Costumes: Molly Maginnis. Sound: Darin Knight. (Touchstone–Buena Vista.) Rel: 20 November 1992. 100 mins. Cert PG.

Slacker

Austin, Texas; 1989. Partly funded by credit card and partly by friends and relatives, *Slacker* is a low-budget ($175,000) film that defies everything Hollywood stands for. Devoid of structure, plot or even a leading character, it is a loosely connected series of vignettes observing unemployed, twentysomething dropouts (or neo-beatniks, per *The New York Times*) in conversation. Some scenes work (Teresa Taylor attempting to hawk a Madonna pap smear, an armed burglar offered coffee by a friendly target), but the film's aimless nature quickly numbs the bum. Not so much a movie, more a bus stop conversation you didn't want to overhear. [JC-W]

Cast: Richard Linklater, Mark James, Jerry Deloney, Scott Marcus, Stella Weir, Teresa Taylor, Don Stroud, Robert Pierson, Sarah Harmon, John Slate, Charles Gunning, and endless others.
  Dir, Pro and Screenplay: Richard Linklater. Ph: Lee Daniel. Ed: Scott Rhodes. Art: Debbie Pastor. Sound: D. Montgomery. (Feature Film Co.) Rel: 4 December 1992. 97 mins. Cert 15.

Sleepwalkers

See *Stephen King's Sleepwalkers*.

Holy unconvincing: Whoopi Goldberg as Sister Mary Clarence, a nun on the run, in Emile Ardolino's surprise hit of '92, Sister Act *(from Buena Vista)*

Sneakers

Super-slick, high-tec comedy-thriller about a crack surveillance team that stumbles on a revolutionary computer codebreaker. With this thing they can gain access to personal bank accounts, the Federal Reserve, air-traffic control, foreign governments ... As former CIA agent Sidney Poitier points out, 'There isn't a government on this planet that wouldn't kill us for that thing.' Ben Kingsley (wrestling with an American accent) is a case in point. He realises the importance of information as a weapon far greater than any firepower ... A starry cast of misfits try hard to pump humour and charisma into their lightweight roles, but it's the computer wizardry that wins the day. Scriptwriters Walter F. Parkes and Lawrence Lasker (*WarGames*) spent eleven years researching and refining their screenplay. [JC-W]

Cast: Robert Redford (Martin Bishop/ Brice), Dan Aykroyd (Mother), Ben Kingsley (Cosmo), Mary McDonnell (Liz), River Phoenix (Carl Arbogast), Sidney Poitier (Donald Crease), David Strathairn (Whistler), Timothy Busfield (Dick Gordon), George Hearn (Gregor), Eddie Jones (Buddy Wallace), Donal Logue (Dr Gunter Janek), Lee Garlington (Dr Elena Rhyzkov), Stephen Tobolowsky (Werner Brandes), James Earl Jones (Dr Bernard Abbott), Jojo Marr, Gary Hershberger, Amy Benedict.

Dir: Phil Alden Robinson. Pro: Walter F. Parkes and Lawrence Lasker. Ex Pro: Lindsley Parsons Jr. Screenplay: Robinson, Parkes and Lasker. Ph: John Lindley. Ed: Tom Rolf. Pro Des: Patrizia von Brandenstein. M: James Horner, Branford Marsalis; Chopin, Bach; numbers performed by Mike Bloomfield, Al Kooper and Steven Stills, Aretha Franklin, Bob Dylan, Miles Davis, Charlie Byrd, etc. Costumes: Bernie Pollack. Sound: Willie D. Burton. (Universal–UIP.) Rel: 13 November 1992. 126 mins. Cert 12.

Sniper

Panama; 1992. Richard Miller is a young, ambitious and highly trained government agent delegated to oversee veteran sniper Thomas Beckett. Beckett is a hardened, highly experienced Marine sergeant who is prepared to bend the rules if it means getting the job done. Together, they are assigned to 'put out' a drug lord leading a rebel coup against the government. Miller has also been ordered, if necessary, to

For their information only: Robert Redford, Dan Aykroyd and Sidney Poitier byte off more than they can chew – in Phil Alden Robinson's riveting Sneakers *(from UIP)*

'put out' Beckett who, in the eyes of Washington, has become something of a liability. But Washington has no idea what a courageous, brilliant and cunning soldier Beckett is ... *Sniper* is an action film which thinks it's a psychological thriller, and though it touches on some interesting points, they slow down the action in the process. Recurring 'assassinations' in slow motion and melodramatic tribal music don't help. Filmed entirely on location in Australia. [JC-W]

Cast: Tom Berenger (Thomas Beckett), Billy Zane (Richard Miller), J. T. Walsh (Chester Van Damme), Aden Young (Doug Papich), Ken Radley (El Cirujano), Rein-

A near-miss: Tom Berenger is tortured by Ken Radley in Luis Llosa's unsatisfactory psychological thriller Sniper *(from Entertainment)*

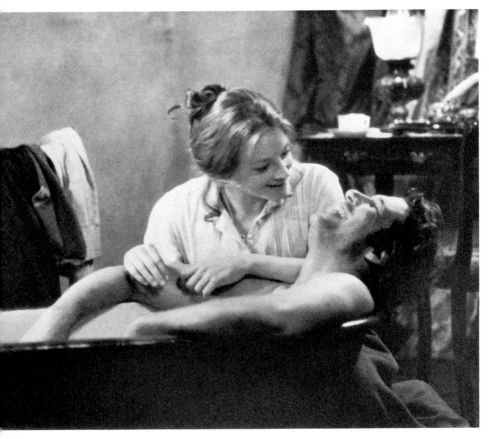

*The Return of Richard Gere: Gere and Jodie
Foster in* Sommersby, *Jon Amiel's handsome
remake of Daniel Vigne's* The Return of
Martin Guerre *(from Warner)*

*Road to ruin: Elaine Collins and Peter
Capaldi in Stefan Schwartz's quirky, funny,
charming* Soft Top, Hard Shoulder *(from
Feature Film Co.)*

aldo Arenas (Cacique), Carolos Alvarez
(Raul Ochoa), Roy Edmonds (Cabrera).

Dir: Luis Llosa. Pro: Robert L. Rosen.
Ex Pro: Mark Johnson, Walon Green and
Patrick Wachsberger. Screenplay: Michael
Frost Beckner and Crash Leyland. Ph: Bill
Butler. Ed: Scott Smith. Pro Des: Herbert
Pinter. M: Gary Chang. Costumes: Ray
Summers. (Baltimore Pictures–Enter-
tainment.) Rel: 26 February 1993. 97
mins. Cert 15.

Sofie

Picturesque drama marking Liv
Ullmann's directorial debut, the story
of a Jewish woman who loves a gentile
painter but is trapped in an arranged
marriage. While begging us to com-
miserate with the plight of Sofie
(beautifully played by Karen-Lise
Mynster), the film seems equally at
pains to paint a glowing and loving
portrait of Jewish life in 19th-century
Denmark. [CB]

Cast: Karen-Lise Mynster (Sofie), Ghita
Norby (Frederikke), Erland Josephson
(Semmy), Jesper Christensen (Hojby),
Torben Zeller, Henning Moritzen, Stig
Hoffmeyer, Kirsten Rolffes.

Dir: Liv Ullmann. Pro: Lars Kolvig.

Screenplay: Ullmann and Peter Poulsen.
Ph: Jorgen Persson. Ed: Grethe Moldrup.
Art: Peter Hoimark. Costumes: Jette Term-
ann. Sound: Michael Dela. (Nordisk
Film & TV A/S/Norsk Film A/S/AB Svensk
Filmindustri–Arrow.) Rel: 11 June 1993.
140 mins. Cert 15.

Soft Top, Hard Shoulder

London-Glasgow; 1992. Although the
product of misguided, bourgeois Scot-
tish-Italian stock, Gavin was meant for
greater things. An artist, he moves to
London to sell children's stories about
a marauding cannibal, but cannot
place his unconventional work. Desperate for cash, he is promised a cut
of the family's fortune if he can make
his father's 60th birthday in Glasgow
– *on time*. A most unusual British road
movie, this, scripted by and starring
Peter Capaldi who, encouraged to act
by Bill Forsyth, made his professional
debut in *Local Hero*. Here, he proves
he is an even better scriptwriter than
performer, swamping his screenplay
with fresh ideas, ingenious situations
and beautifully realised characters.
Charming, distinctive and very, very
funny. [JC-W]

Cast: Peter Capaldi (Gavin), Elaine Collins
(Yvonne), Simon Callow (Eddie Cher-
dowski), Richard Wilson (Uncle Sal),
Jeremy Northam (John), Frances Barber,
Phyllis Logan, Sophie Hall, Robert James,
Bill Gavin, Michael Nardone.

Dir: Stefan Schwartz. Pro: Richard
Holmes. Co-Pro: Georgia Masters. Screen-
play: Peter Capaldi. Ph: Henry Braham.
Ed: Derek Trigg. Pro Des: Sonja Klaus. M:
Chris Rea. Costumes: Christopher Woods.
Sound: Matthew Harmer. (Road Movies–
Feature Film Co.) Rel: 15 January 1993.
91 mins. Cert 15.

Sommersby

Virginia; c. 1865. When Laurel's husband, Jack Sommersby, returns home
from the American Civil War after an
absence of six years he is a changed
man. He is kinder, braver and now
reads Greek literature. Consequently,
Laurel falls in love with him all over
again. Except that she never loved her
old husband. But is Jack Sommersby
who he says he is? And does Laurel
care? A hard premise to swallow, but
a fascinating one, based on a true incident which was the basis for the 1982
French film *The Return of Martin
Guerre*. Here, the story has been

updated by three centuries, which makes the central conundrum even harder to believe, as Laurel even has a photograph of her husband as he was. Still, the film is handsomely presented, with stirring photography and a courtroom scene that will have you cheering. [JC-W]

Cast: Richard Gere (Jack Sommersby), Jodie Foster (Laurel Sommersby), Bill Pullman (Orin Meecham), James Earl Jones (Judge Issacs), Lanny Flaherty (Buck), William Windom (Rev. Powell), Frankie Faison (Joseph), Wendell Wellman, Clarice Taylor, Ronald Lee Ermey, Richard Hamilton, Karen Kirschenbauer, Carter McNeese, Paul Austin, Ray McKinnon, Maury Chaykin.

Dir: Jon Amiel. Pro: Arnon Milchan and Steven Reuther. Ex Pro: Richard Gere and Maggie Wilde. Co-Pro: Mary McLaglen. Screenplay: Nicholas Meyer and Sarah Kernochan; from a story by Meyer and Anthony Shaffer. Ph: Philippe Rousselot. Ed: Peter Boyle. Pro Des: Bruno Rubeo. M: Danny Elfman. Costumes: Marilyn Vance-Straker. Sound: Chris Newman. (Le Studio Canal Plus/Regency Enterprises/Alcor Films–Warner.) Rel: 23 April 1993. 114 mins. Cert 12.

South Central

Sentimental and poorly acted story about a member of an LA gang (the Deuces) who goes to prison for killing a drug dealer, leaving his young son to repeat his mistakes. Based on Donald Bakeer's book *Crips*, itself inspired by real events, the film carries about as much conviction (and entertainment value) as a TV movie with F words. Still, it's got its heart in the right place, which may explain Oliver Stone's involvement as executive producer. [JC-W]

Cast: Glenn Plummer (Bobby Johnson), Carl Lumbly (Ali), Christian Coleman (Jimmie Johnson), Byron Keith Minns (Ray Ray), LaRita Shelby (Carole), Kevin Best (Genie Lamp, the Smackman), Lexie D. Bigham (Bear), Vincent Craig Dupree (Loco), Tim DeZarn (Buddha), Ivory Ocean (Willie Manchester), Starletta Dupois (Nurse Shelly), 'Big Daddy' Wayne, Diane Manzo, Allen Michael Lerner, Vickilyn Reynolds, Donald Bakeer, Mark E. Anderson, Musa Bakeer.

Dir and Screenplay: Steve Anderson. Pro: Janet Yang and William B. Steakley. Line Pro: Lowell D. Blank. Ex Pro: Oliver Stone. Co-Ex Pro: Michael Spielberg and Brad Gilbert. Ph: Charlie Lieberman. Ed: Steve Nevius. Pro Des: David Brian Miller

Industrial strength: Anthony Hopkins in uncharacteristic mood in Mark Joffe's delightful Spotswood *(from Feature Film Co.)*

and Marina Kieser. M: Tim Truman; numbers performed by Vaughan Mason, Boo-Yaa T.R.I.B.E., Heatwave, Scarface, Cameo, Hi-C, Marvin Gaye, Lester Abrams, Vibe Squad, Lakeside, Slave, etc. Costumes: Mary Law Weir. Sound: Michael Florimbi. (Ixtlan/Monument Pictures/Enchantment Films–Warner.) Rel: 18 June 1993. 99 mins. Cert 15.

Splitting Heirs

Arguably one of the worst films of the year, in which we are expected to believe that Eric Idle is the ignorant heir to the dukedom of Bournemouth and that the sexually predatory Barbara Hershey is his mother (Hershey is in fact five years *younger* than Idle). Coincidentally, Idle's best friend, Rick Moranis, has inherited the Dorset title and is at the mercy of Idle's machinations. Idle himself scripted and executive produced this painful farce, so all complaints should be addressed to him personally. Formerly known as *Heirs and Graces*. [CB]

Cast: Rick Moranis (Henry), Eric Idle (Tommy), Barbara Hershey (Duchess Lucinda), Catherine Zeta Jones (Kitty), John Cleese (Shadgrind), Sadie Frost (Angela), Brenda Bruce, Bridget McConnel, Stratford Johns, Jeremy Clyde, William Franklyn, Richard Huw, Paul Brooke, Peggy Ann Wood, Eric Sykes, Madge Ryan.

Dir: Robert Young. Pro: Simon Bosanquet. Co-Pro: Redmond Morris. Ex Pro and Screenplay: Eric Idle. Ph: Tont Pierce-Roberts. Ed: John Jympson. Pro Des: John Beard. M: Michael Kamen. Costumes: Penny Rose. Sound: Peter Glossop. (Prominent Features–UIP.) Rel: 2 April 1993. 89 mins. Cert 12.

Spotswood

Melbourne; 1965. A hard, introverted economic consultant – 'a time and motion man' – is called in to assess the commercial viability of the 'Balls' Moccasin Company, which still manufactures 'the toughest-wearing moccasins in the Southern hemisphere'. Confronted by a friendly and easy-going regiment of eccentrics, Erroll Wallace is a little nonplussed at first, but soon his old ruthless streak returns. At least, for a while . . . An exquisitely judged social comedy, which is written, directed and played at just the right pitch, evoking fond memories of Ealing. A rare treat. [JC-W]

low figure for plumbing-supplies salesman Roy Knable, who has become so
addicted to TV that his wife is leaving
home. But, on her way out, he, she
and her suitcase are sucked into an
alternative medium which boasts 666
channels. Here the programmes are
different: *Three Men and Rosemary's
Baby, Meet the Mansons, Autopsies of
the Rich and Famous*... Roy and
Helen Knable have 24 hours to stay
alive in TV hell or face an eternity of
bad television. *Stay Tuned* is essentially
a series of gags played out at the
expense of popular American shows.
While some of these are quite funny,
others are downright moronic, and
none make sense in a movie. Ironically
enough, this satirical, episodic format
is perfect for late-night TV. [JC-W]

Cast: John Ritter (Roy Knable), Pam
Dawber (Helen Knable), Jeffrey Jones
(Spike), Eugene Levy (Crowley), David
Thom (Darryl Knable), Heather McComb
(Diane Knable), Erik King (Pierce), Bob
Dishy, Joyce Gordon, Don Calfa, Don
Pardo, Salt-N-Pepa.
  Dir and Ph: Peter Hyams. Pro: James G.
Robinson. Ex Pro: Gary Barber and David
Nicksay. Co-Pro: Arne L. Schmidt. Screen-
play: Tom S. Parker and Jim Jennewein;
from a story by Parker, Jennewein and
Richard Siegel. Ed: Peter E. Berger. Pro
Des: Philip Harrison. M: Bruce Brough-
ton; numbers performed by Salt-N-Pepa,
Auto & Cherokee, Kool Moe Dee, and Dr
Ice. Costumes: Joe I. Tompkins. (Morgan
Creek–Warner.) Rel: 12 February 1993. 89
mins. Cert PG.

Stephen King's Sleepwalkers
Travis, Indiana; the day before
tomorrow... Part-reptilian, part-
feline and part-human, the shape-
shifting Sleepwalkers need the lifeforce
of a virtuous young woman in order to
survive. Needless to say, food is
scarce... That makes Mary and
Charles Brady an endangered species,
a good-looking mother-and-son team
who aren't beyond a bit of nocturnal
nookie, while Charles goes virgin-
hunting in the day. If you enjoy
watching a mother tongue her son, a
number of cats meeting a messy end
and some rather impressive computer
effects, then *Sleepwalkers* is a lot of fun.
Amazingly, it is the first concoction
Stephen King has written directly for
the screen. [JC-W]

Cast: Brian Krause (Charles Brady), Madchen Amick (Tanya Robertson), Alice

*Dance with me: a heavily made-up Brian
Krause (actually, it's probably a stand-in)
escorts Madchen Amick round the dance floor,
in Columbia's joyfully unpleasant* Stephen
King's Sleepwalkers

Cast: Anthony Hopkins (Erroll Wallace),
Ben Mendelsohn (Carey), Toni Collette
(Wendy), Alwyn Kurts (Mr Ball), Rebecca
Rigg (Cheryl), Russell Crowe (Kim),
Angela Punch McGregor (Caroline
Wallace), Dan Wyllie, Bruno Lawrence,
John Walton, John Flaus, Jeff Truman,
Gary Adams, Leslie Baker, Jacob Kino,
Max Fairchild.

  Dir: Mark Joffe. Pro: Richard Brennan
and Timothy White. Screenplay: Max
Dann and Andrew Knight. Ph: Ellery
Ryan. Ed: Nick Beauman. Pro Des: Chris
Kennedy. M: Ricky Fataar. Costumes: Tess
Schofield. Sound: Lloyd Carrick.
(Meridian Films/Smiley Films/Australian
Film Finance Corp–Feature Film
Company.) Rel: 9 October 1992. 93 mins.
Cert PG.

Stay Tuned
Seattle; 1992. The average American
is said to watch seven and a half hours
of television a day. However, that's a

Krige (Mary Brady), Jim Haynie (Ira), Dan Martin (Andy Simpson), Glenn Shadix (Mr Fallows), Cindy Pickett, Ron Perlman, Lyman Ward, Cynthia Garris, Monty Bane, John Landis (lab technician), Joe Dante (lab assistant), Stephen King (cemetery caretaker), Clive Barker and Tobe Hooper (forensic techs), Frank Novak, Rusty Schwimmer, O. Nicholas Brown, Ernie Lively, Lucy Boryer, Judette Warren (Carrie), Stuart Charno.

Dir: Mick Garris. Pro: Mark Victor, Michael Grais and Nabeel Zahid. Ex Pro: Dimitri Logothetis and Joseph Medawar. Screenplay: Stephen King. Ph: Rodney Charters. Ed: O. Nicholas Brown. Pro Des: John DeCuir Jr. M: Nicholas Pike; numbers performed by Santo & Johnny, Enya, The Contours, and Extreme. Sound: Gary Krivacek and Tom McCarthy. (ION Pictures–Columbia.) Rel: 3 July 1992. 91 mins. Cert 18.

Stepkids

(US: *Big Girls Don't Cry . . . They Get Even*.) Each day, 1300 new stepfamilies are formed, and one in three American children live in such a stepfamily. So much for the facts. This sentimental atrocity, directed by the usually estimable Joan Micklin Silver (*Hester Street, Between the Lines, Crossing Delancey*), tramples over sensitive ground as it grapples for laughs, centring on the emotional neglect of a bright, funny 13-year-old stepkid (the excellent Hillary Wolf, last seen in *Waiting for the Light*). The film's sentiments are worthy enough, but its execution is so banal and trite that it trips up before it starts. An incessant and inappropriate rock soundtrack just adds to the damage. [JC-W]

Cast: Griffin Dunne (David Chartoff), Dan Futterman (Josh), Patricia Kalember (Barbara), Jenny Lewis (Corinne), Ben Savage (Sam), Adrienne Shelly (Stephanie), David Strathairn (Keith), Trenton Teigen (Kurt), Margaret Whitton (Melinda), Hillary Wolf (Laura Chartoff), Angelina Estrada (Rosario), Jessica Seely (Jessie), Sean Blackman, Joseph d'Angerio, Cory Danziger, Leslie Engelberg, Meagen Fay, Googy Gress, Jim Haynie, Denis Heames, Joann Passantino, Joey Sciacca.

Dir: Joan Micklin Silver. Pro: Laurie Perlman and Gerald T. Olson. Ex Pro: Peter Morgan and Melissa Goddard. Screenplay: Frank Mugavero; based on a story by Mark Goddard and Melissa Goddard. Ph: Theo Van de Sande. Ed: Janice Hampton. Pro Des: Victoria Paul. M: Patrick Williams; numbers performed by The Soup Dragons, The Escape Club, 1927, Todd Smallwood, etc. Costumes: Jane Ruhm. Sound:

Gong Li gives another startling performance in The Story of Qiu Ju, *the fifth film she has made with her 'partner' and director Zhang Yimou (from Electric)*

Susumu Tokunow. (New Line Cinema/MG Entertainment–Rank.) Rel: 10 July 1992. 104 mins. Cert PG.

The Story of Qiu Ju – Qiuju Da Guansi

A fascinating, almost documentary look at contemporary China and in particular the obsession of a pregnant peasant woman to see justice done. Her husband has been assaulted by the village chief, and she demands an explanation, first from the police, and then from higher authorities. Each new legal step necessitates the selling of her husband's precious chili crop to finance her trips to 'civilisation', but Qiu Ju is a stubborn woman. Zhang Yimou, the Chinese director known for his opulent period pieces (*Red Sorghum, Raise the Red Lantern*), changes his style here (under pressure from the Maoist hardliners), but still has produced a remarkable, moving work, rich in detail and metaphor and often very funny in the most unexpected ways. [JC-W]

Cast: Gong Li (Wan Qiuju), Lei Lao Sheng (Wang Shantang, the village chief), Liu Pei Qi (Wan Qinglai), Ge Zhi Jun (Officer Li Shunlin), Yang Liu Chun (Meizi), Zhu Wanqing, Cui Luowen, Yang Huiqin.

Dir: Zhang Yimou. Pro: Feng Yiting. Ex Pro: Ma Fung Kwok. Screenplay: Liu Heng; based on the novel *The Wan Family's Lawsuit* by Chen Yuan Bin. Ph: Chi Xiao Ning and Yu Xiao Qun. Ed: Du Yuan. Art: Cao Jiu Ping. M: Zhao Jiping. Costumes: Tong Huamiao. Sound: Li Han Hua. (Sil-Metropole Org. [HK]/Youth Film Studio [Beijing]–Electric.) Rel: 7 May 1993. 100 mins. Cert 12.

Straight Out of Brooklyn

The most remarkable thing about this grim, cut-price drama is that it marks the debut of teenage filmmaker Matty Rich (who started the production aged 17). Broaching such familiar territory as urban decay (the Red Hook housing project in New York), domestic friction and drug-related crime, the film nevertheless reveals a freshness that promises much for this young black director. As a movie, however, it's extremely amateur, hampered by endless establishing shots, tiresome shouting matches and aimless duologues. But what do you expect from a teenager? In other areas, it is a startlingly mature work, inspired by Rich's own

Dumb dancing: Tara Morice and Paul Mercurio trip the light slapstick in Baz Luhrmann's Strictly Ballroom *(from Rank)*

experiences, and was an enormous success at the 1991 Sundance Film Festival. [JC-W]

Cast: George T. Odom (Ray Brown), Ann D. Sanders (Dennis Brown), Lawrence Gilliard Jr (Dennis Brown), Barbara Sanon (Carolyn Brown), Reana E. Drummond (Shirley), Matty Rich (Larry), Mark Malone (Kevin), Ali Shahid Abdul Wahha, Joseph A. Thomas, James McFadden.

Dir, Pro and Screenplay: Matty Rich. Ex Pro: Lindsay Law and Ira Deutchman. Assoc Pro: Allen Black. Ph: John Rosnell. Ed: Jack Haigis. M: Harold Wheeler. Sound: Kevin Lee. (American Playhouse/PBS/Corporation for Public Broadcasting/National Endowment for the Arts/Chubb Group–Artificial Eye.) Rel: 4 September 1992. 83 mins. Cert 15.

A Stranger Among Us
See *Close to Eden*.

Strictly Ballroom
Touted as the 'hottest film at Cannes', this is, indeed, a surprising, spirited debut for director Baz Luhrmann. It is also a fatally flawed work. A high-octane farce about the crazy world of ballroom dancing, *Strictly Ballroom* wears its humour on its sleeve and mixes its styles with disconcerting abandon. A promising contender for the Pan Pacific Grand Prix Championships, Scott Hastings botches his chances and loses his partner when he starts making up his own steps. Enter bespectacled, ugly duckling Fran, who begs for just one chance to team up with the great, handsome, conceited Scott. The story is as predictable as the two-step, all the characters are pre-

posterous caricatures and even the choice of music is hackneyed. But the film's worst crime is fudging the line between reality and fantasy and sacrificing its emotions for cheap gags. [JC-W]

Cast: Paul Mercurio (Scott Hastings), Tara Morice (Fran), Bill Hunter (Barry Fife), Pat Thomson (Shirley Hastings), Gia Carides (Liz Holt), Peter Whitford (Les Kendall), Barry Otto (Doug Hastings), John Hannan (Ken Railings), Sonia Kruger-Tayler (Tina Sparkle), Kris McQuade (Charm Leachman), Pip Mushin (Wayne Burns), Antonio Vargas (Rico), Leonie Page, Armonia Benedito, Jack Webster, Lauren Hewett, Laura Mulcahy, Todd McKenney, Kerry Shrimpton.

Dir: Baz Luhrmann. Pro: Tristram Miall. Ex Pro: Antoinette Albert. Screenplay: Luhrmann, Andrew Bovell and Craig Pearce. Ph: Steve Mason. Ed: Jill Bilcock. Pro Des: Catherine Martin. M: David Hirschfelder. Costumes: Angus Strathie. Sound: Ben Osmo. (M&A Film Corp/AFFC–Rank.) Rel: 16 October 1992. 94 mins. Cert PG.

Sweet Emma, Dear Bobe – Edes Emma, Draga Bobe
Emma is a 28-year-old woman from the country who, for seven years, has been teaching Russian at a Budapest school. She shares a small room with a fellow teacher (Bobe) in a hostel, and cleans in her spare time. Life is hard, inflation is high and the old communist regime is crumbling. Western values are now flooding the country (punks haunt the buses), Russian has

Hard times: Eniko Borcsok and Johanna Ter Steege in Istvan Szabo's haunting Sweet Emma, Dear Bobe *(from Metro)*

been abolished in schools and English has been chosen to replace it. As Emma and Bobe scramble to learn the new language, Bobe dreams of a life of material gain, while Emma just wants to consummate her passion – for love. An intriguing character study, both of a woman and her country, *Sweet Emma* benefits from some commendably economic direction by Istvan Szabo (returning to his homeland after David Puttnam's *Meeting Venus*) and a luminescent performance from Johanna Ter Steege (*The Vanishing, Vincent & Theo*), fast becoming Europe's most interesting actress. A.k.a. *Sketches, Nudes – Vazlatok, Aktok*. [JC-W]

Cast: Johanna Ter Steege (Emma), Eniko Borcsak (Bobe), Peter Andorai (Stefanics), Zoltan Mucsi (Szilard, art teacher), Eva Kerekes, Erszi Gaal, Hedi Temessy.

Dir and Screenplay: Istvan Szabo. Pro: Lajos Ovari and Gabriella Grosz. Ph: Lajos Koltai. Ed: Eszter Kovacs. Pro Des: Attila Kovacs. M: Robert Schumann, Tibor Bornai, Fero Nagy and Mihaly Moricz. Costumes: Zsuzsa Stenger. Sound: Gyorgy Kovacs. (Metro.) Rel: 22 January 1993. 90 mins. Cert 18.

Swing Kids

As Nazism swept Germany in 1939 a small band of jazz-loving kids rebelled against the new order by growing their hair long, wearing British fashion and listening to the outlawed music of

Apparently, Kenneth Branagh was so disappointed by the end product of Swing Kids *(from Buena Vista), that he had his name removed from the credits. Other sources suggest that his American agent was unhappy with his billing*

Benny Goodman. Those are the facts, a little-known phenomenon brought vividly to the screen with this story of two 17-year-old boys forced to become a part of the Hitler Youth by day, but who still go nightclubbing at night. As much about the swing music of the late 1930s as the rise of Nazi Germany, *Swing Kids* also explores the shifting bond of friendship as the poisonous propaganda of Hitler clashes with the natural rebelliousness of youth. A fascinating, moving picture that addresses a familiar subject from a fresh perspective. Filmed in Prague. [JC-W]

Cast: Robert Sean Leonard (Peter Muller), Christian Bale (Thomas Berger), Frank Whaley (Arvid), Barbara Hershey (Frau Muller), Tushka Bergen (Evey), David Tom (Willi), Julia Stemberger (Frau Linge), Kenneth Branagh (Major Knopp), Jayce Bartok, Noah Wyle, Johan Leysen, Douglas Roberts, Martin Clunes, David Robb, Ciaran Madden, Neil Norman, Hana Cizkova, Jeremy Bulloch, Jochen Horst, Kate Buffery.

Dir: Thomas Carter. Pro: Mark Gordon and John Bard Manulis. Ex Pro: Frank Marshall and Christopher Meledandri. Co-Pro: Harry Benn. Screenplay: Jonathan Marc Feldman. Ph: Jerzy Zielinski. Ed: Michael R. Miller. Pro Des: Allan Cameron. M: James Horner; Harry James, Benny Goodman, Count Basie, Duke Ellington, Django Reinhardt, Louis Prima; Richard Wagner, Beethoven, etc. Choreographer: Otis Sallid. Costumes: Jenny Beavan. Sound: Ivan Sharrock. (Hollywood Pictures–Buena Vista.) Rel: 11 June 1993. 114 mins. Cert 12.

Following the Nietzsche dream: Daniel Schlachet and Craig Chester as the 'deranged perverts' Leopold and Loeb, in Tom Kalin's surreal Swoon *(from Metro)*

Swoon

Chicago; 1924. 'Revisionist' being the buzz word of the day, this is a 'revisionist' look at the Leopold and Loeb case, in which two homosexual Jewish intellectual 18-year-olds murdered the 14-year-old Bobby Franks 'to see what it felt like'. While the case was previously explored (fictitiously) in Alfred Hitchcock's *Rope* (1948) (from the play by Patrick Hamilton) and Richard Fleischer's *Compulsion* (1959), Tom Kalin's low-budget, black-and-white version sheds some fascinating new light on the facts, but fails to reveal the psychological motives. Here, the first-time director seems more obsessed with his filmmaking style (verging on the pretentious) than on character exploration. Art movie? Documentary? Or something more self-indulgent? Funded by America's National Endowment for the Arts. [JC-W]

Cast: Daniel Schlachet (Richard Loeb), Craig Chester (Nathan Leopold Jr), Ron Vawter (State's Attorney Crowe), Paul Connor (Bobby Franks), Michael Kirby, Michael Stumm, Valdaz Z. Drabla, Natalie Stanford, Mona Foot, Trash, Trasharama, Stanley Taub, Robert Austin, Barbara Bleier, Ed Altman, Todd Haynes.

Dir, Co-Pro, Screenplay and Ed: Tom Kalin. Pro: Christine Vachon. Ex Pro: Lauren Zalaznick and James Schamus. Ph:

Comedy tonight: Julie Kavner makes jokes at the expense of her children, in Nora Ephron's maudlin This Is My Life *(from Fox)*

Ellen Kuras. Pro Des: Therese Déprèz. M: James Bennett. Costumes: Jessica Haston. Sound: Susan Demskey. (Intolerance/American Playhouse–Metro.) Rel: 25 September 1992. 92 mins. Cert 18.

Tale of a Vampire

Dour, slow-moving vampire yarn set almost entirely in Deptford Library in South London. Julian Sands sleepwalks through his role as a sexually commanding bloodsucker, patrolling London's dingy backstreets in search of fog and veins. Mourning the death of his loved one last century, he spots her lookalike in the said library and moves in for the spill . . . A familiar tale, done cheaper. [JC-W]

Cast: Julian Sands (Alex), Suzanna Hamilton (Anne/Virginia), Kenneth Cranham (Edgar), Marian Diamond (Denise), Michael Kenton, Catherine Blake, Mark Kempner, Nik Myers.
　Dir: Shimako Sato. Pro: Simon Johnson. Co-Pro: Linda Kay. Ex Pro: Noriko Shishikura. Screenplay: Sato and Jane Corbett. Ph: Zubin Mistry. Ed: Chris Wright. Pro Des: Alice Normington. M: Julian Joseph. Sound: Robin Bailey. (State Screen Productions.) Rel: 20 November 1992. 96 mins. Cert 18.

Tetsuo II: Bodyhammer

Less a sequel to than a reworking of the same director's *Tetsuo – The Iron Man*, this version tones down its predecessor's graphic sexual content (with the terrorised salaryman protagonist now given a wife and soon-to-be-abducted infant), but more than makes up for it in extremely violent and explicit man/machine imagery. Not recommended for the fainthearted, this 90s update of *Blade Runner* and *Videodrome* is as close to the spirit of cyberpunk as the cinema is ever likely to get. [JC]

Cast: Tomoroh Taguchi (Taniguchi), Nobu Kanaoka (Kana), Shinya Tsukamoto (Yatsu – The Guy), Keinosuke Tomioka, Sujin Kim, Min Tanaja.
　Dir, Screenplay, Ed and Art: Shinya Tsukamoto. Pro: Fuminori Shishido and Fumio Kurokawa. Ex Pro: Tsukamoto and Hiroshi Koizumi. Ph: Tsukamoto, Fumikazu Oda and Katsunori Yokoyama. M: Chu Ishikawa; Tomoyasu Hotei. (ICA Projects.) Rel: 20 November 1992. 83 mins. No cert.

This Is My Life

New York/Las Vegas/Alberta; 1992. A 'heartwarming' story about a loud Jewish comedienne and her two kids may not be to everybody's taste. This one, directed and co-adapted by Nora Ephron from Meg Wolitzer's novel, *is* heavy on the syrup and one-liners, but is redeemed by the high calibre of the

Western promise: Dennis Dun and Rosalind Chao share a brief moment of happiness in racist Idaho, in Nancy Kelly's Thousand Pieces of Gold *(NFT)*

performances, particularly Samantha Mathis as the plain 16-year-old daughter used for comic material while coming to terms with her 'womanhood'. Dan Aykroyd, in a supporting role as the mother's agent, has very little to do. [JC-W]

Cast: Julie Kavner (Dottie Ingels), Samantha Mathis (Erica Ingels), Gaby Hoffmann (Opal Ingels), Carrie Fisher (Claudia Curtis), Dan Aykroyd (Arnold Moss), Marita Geraghty (Mia Jablon), Caroline Aaron (Martha Ingels), Danny Zorn (Jordan Strang), Estelle Harris (Aunt Harriet), Louis DiBianco (Norm Ingels), Bob Nelson, Welker White, Kathy Najimy, Renee Lippin, Joy Behar, Annie Golden, Tim Blake Nelson, Harvey Miller, Kate McGregor-Stewart, Valerie Bromfield, Diane Sokolow, Oly Obst.
　Dir: Nora Ephron. Pro: Lynda Obst. Ex Pro: Patricia K. Meyer and Carole Isenberg. Co-Pro: Michael R. Joyce. Screenplay: Nora and Delia Ephron (sisters). Ph: Bobby Byrne. Ed: Robert Reitano. Pro Des: David Chapman. M and songs: Carly Simon. Costumes: Jeffrey Kurland. Sound: Doug Ganton. (Fox.) Rel: 4 December 1992. 94 mins. Cert 12.

Thousand Pieces of Gold

In Northern China, a peasant girl is sold by her destitute father and shipped off to San Francisco. There, she is bought by proxy and taken to a frontier town in Idaho where she touches the lives of three men. Based on a true story, this surprisingly restrained, slow-moving film touches on some fertile dramatic territory but fails to mine it. Lacking a distinctive directorial style, and paying little attention to his-

torical detail, *Thousand Pieces of Gold* is a dull ride. Filmed in the Montana Rockies for under $2 million. [JC-W]

Cast: Rosalind Chao (Lalu), Chris Cooper (Charlie), Dennis Dun (Jim), Michael Paul Chan (Hong King).

Dir: Nancy Kelly. Pro: Kelly and Kenji Yamamoto. Co-Pro: Sarah Green. Ex Pro: Lyndsay Law, Sydney Kantor and John Sham. Screenplay: Anne Makepeace; from the novel by Ruthan Lum McCunn. Ph: Bobby Bukowski. Ed: Yamamoto. Pro Des: Dan Bishop. M: Gary Remal Malkin. Costumes: Lydia Tanji. (American Playhouse/Maverick Films Int./Film Four Int.–NFT.) Rel: 4 December 1992. 105 mins. No cert.

3 Ninja Kids

Home Alone meets *The Karate Kid* in this good-natured, surprisingly entertaining kids' picture about three young bros taken hostage by an army of Ninjas. However, thanks to the wise teaching of their grandfather, the kids prove more than a match for their captors. Hitting a tried and tested formula on the button, *3 Ninja Kids* turned out to be the second most profitable movie of the year (after *Sister Act*). [CB]

Cast: Victor Wong (Grandpa), Michael Treanor (Rocky), Max Elliott Slade (Colt), Chad Power (Tum Tum), Rand Kingsley (Snyder), Alan McRae, Margarita Franco, Kate Sargeant.

Dir: Jon Turteltaub. Pro: Martha Chang. Ex Pro: Shunji Hirano. Co-Ex Pro: James Kang. Line Pro: Susan Stremple. Co-Pro: Hiroshi Kusu and Akio Shimizu. Screenplay: Edward Emanuel; from a story by Kenny Kim. Ph: Richard Michalak. Ed: David Rennie. Pro Des: Kirk Petrucelli. M: Rick Marvin. Costumes: Mona May. Stunts: Rick Avery. Sound: Bill Robbins. (Global Venture Hollywood/Touchstone–Buena Vista.) Rel: 28 May 1993. 84 mins. Cert PG.

Thunderheart

Based on an amalgam of events that occurred on Indian reservations in the 1970s, this is a beautifully crafted, authoritative drama that suffers from an excess of self-importance. Val Kilmer, a lightweight casting choice, is Ray Levoi, a slick Fed from Washington DC improbably signed to a murder case on a reservation in South Dakota. A quarter Sioux himself, Levoi finds himself unaccountably drawn into a world of disturbing visions as he struggles to hang on to his urban sensibilities. Real-life Oneida Indian Graham Greene steals

Dancing with cops: Val Kilmer and Graham Greene investigate corruption and racism in Michael Apted's plodding Thunderheart *(from Columbia Tri-Star)*

the acting honours as a wry tribal cop, while the South Dakota scenery pinches everything else. Interestingly, the director Michael Apted explored the same material in his documentary *Incident at Oglaga*, produced by Robert Redford. Here, the producer is Robert De Niro. [JC-W]

Cast: Val Kilmer (Ray Levoi), Sam Shepard (Frank Coutelle), Graham Greene (Walter Crow Horse), Fred Ward (Jack Milton), Sheila Tousey (Maggie Eagle Bear), Chief Ted Thin Elk (Grandpa Sam Reaches), Fred Dalton Thompson, John Trudell, Julius Drum, Sarah Brave, Allan R. J.

Joseph, Patrick Massett, David Crosby.

Dir: Michael Apted. Pro: Robert De Niro, Jane Rosenthal and John Fusco. Ex Pro: Michael Nozik. Screenplay: Fusco. Ph: Roger Deakins. Ed: Ian Crafford. Pro Des: Dan Bishop. M: James Horner; numbers performed by Bruce Springsteen, Ali Olmo, and Exile. Costumes: Susan Lyall. Sound: Chris Newman. (Tribeca/Waterhorse/Tri-Star–Columbia Tri-Star.) Rel: 16 October 1992. 118 mins. Cert 15.

Tous les Matins du Monde

'Music,' says the great viol player and composer M. de Sainte Colombe,

Music makes my morning: Jean-Pierre Marielle and Gerard Depardieu discuss the intricacies of the viol, in Alain Coirneau's Tous les Matins du Monde *(from Electric)*

Toyland goes to war: Robin Williams and Michael Gambon in Barry Levinson's unique extravaganza Toys *(from Fox)*

'exists to say things that words cannot.' Frankly, you'd have to be a music enthusiast to fully appreciate this studied, slow-moving drama set in 17th-century France. Much as Jacques Rivette's *La Belle Noiseuse* illuminated the complexities of art through Michel Piccoli's reclusive painter, so this film explores the uncommon drive that creates real music for the stubborn, reclusive de Sainte Colombe. Gerard Depardieu, as the aged violist Marin Marais, recalls in flashback his days as pupil to the Master, who tells him, 'You make music. You are not a musician.' Part character study, part cultural thesis, *Tous les Matins du*

Monde is often absorbing, but hard work. It won seven Cesar awards, including a nod for best picture. [JC-W]

Cast: Jean-Pierre Marielle (M. de Sainte Colombe), Gerard Depardieu (Marin Marais), Anne Brochet (Madeleine de Sainte Colombe), Guillaume Depardieu (the young Marin Marais), Caroline Sihol (Madame de Sainte Colombe), Carole Richert (Toinette de Sainte Colombe), Jean-Claude Dreyfus (Abbe Mathieu), Michel Bouquet (Baugin).
Dir: Alain Corneau. Pro: Jean-Louis Livi. Screenplay: Corneau and Pascal Quignard; from the novel by Quignard. Ph: Yves Angelo. Ed: Marie-Josephe Yoyotte. Pro Des: Bernard Vezat. M: Jordi Savall. Costumes: Corinne Jorry. Sound: Pierre Gamet. (Film par Film/DD Prods/Sedif/FR3 Films/Paravision Int./CNC/Canal Plus–Electric.) Rel: 1 January 1993. 114 mins. Cert 12.

Toys

Following a string of hit movies (*Diner, Rain Man, Good Morning Vietnam, Bugsy*), director-writer Barry Levinson was finally in a position to realise his unique – and expensive – vision of *Toys*. Most of the critics gave it a drubbing (*Variety* called it 'a painful mess that makes *Hudson Hawk* look like a modest throwaway') and audiences stayed away in their droves. The problem with *Toys* is that it is neither one thing nor the other. It is not a truly innocent fairy tale like *Hook*, nor is it a darkly comic nightmare like *Gremlins*. And yet, it is *such* a unique movie that it is likely to gain a cult following in years to come. The story is simple: in his will, an eccentric toymaker leaves his fantastical factory to his brother, General Zevo (Michael Gambon). The latter, an egomaniacal military man, turns the place into an assembly line for the manufacture of deadly toys. Only Zevo's nephew, the timid and eccentric Leslie (Robin Williams), is qualified to challenge his uncle's terrifying plan. Set in a surreal Toyland of the imagination, the film suffers from Williams's contemporary improvisations regarding Michael Jackson, Mother Theresa and the royal family, but the mind-blowing production design, state-of-the-art special effects and the message that innocence must prevail over the forces of profit make for a daringly original and brilliantly realised film. Either go with it or bypass it entirely. [JC-W]

Cast: Robin Williams (Leslie Zevo), Michael Gambon (General Leland Zevo), Joan Cusack (Alsatia Zevo), Robin Wright (Gwen Tyler), LL Cool J (Patrick Zevo), Donald O'Connor (Kenneth Zevo), Arthur Malet (Owens Owens), Jack Warden (Zevo Sr), Debi Mazar, Wendy Melvoin, Julio Oscar Mechoso, Jamie Foxx, Shelly Desai, Blake Clark, Clinton Allmon, Art Metrano, Sam Levinson.
Dir: Barry Levinson. Pro: Levinson and Mark Johnson. Co-Pro: Charles Newirth and Peter Giuliano. Screenplay: Levinson and Valerie Curtin. Ph: Adam Greenberg. Ed: Stu Linder. Pro Des: Ferdinando Scarfiotti. M: Hans Zimmer and Trevor Horn. Choreography: Anthony Thomas. Costumes: Albert Wolsky. Sound: Richard Beggs. (Baltimore Pictures–Fox.) Rel: 5 March 1993. 121 mins. Cert PG.

Traces of Red

Palm Beach; 1992. Heard the one about *Basic Instinct*? A cop is obsessed with a beautiful, wealthy blonde (with black eyebrows) who may or may not be a serial killer. This time James Belushi is the cop whose libido is bigger than his gun, involved in a plot with more red herrings than Smithfield Market. Vastly entertaining trash, this, enhanced by a jazzy score, lush locations and a breezy voice-over narrative from Belushi. Lorraine Bracco, as the femme fatale, does a spot-on impersonation of Melanie Griffith. Take with a pinch of salt. [JC-W]

Cast: James Belushi (Jack Dobson), Lorraine Bracco (Ellen Schofield), Tony Goldwyn (Steve Frayn), William Russ (Michael Dobson), Faye Grant (Beth Frayn), Michelle Joyner (Morgan Cassidy), Joe Lisi (Lt J. C. Hooks), Victoria Bass (Susan Dobson), Melanie Tomlin (Amanda), Mario Ernesto Sanchez (Tony Garidi), Jim Piddock, Ed Amatrudo, Daniel Tucker Kamin, Joseph C. Hess, Will Knickerbocker.

Dir: Andy Wolk. Pro: David V. Picker and Mark Gordon. Screenplay: Jim Piddock. Ph: Tim Suhrstedt. Ed: Trudy Ship. Pro Des: Dan Bishop and Dianna Freas. M: Graeme Revell. Costumes: Hilary Rosenfeld. Sound: Steve C. Aaron. (Samuel Goldwyn–Entertainment.) Rel: 11 December 1992. 104 mins. Cert 15.

Trespass

Two firemen from rural Arkansas stumble on to a treasure map that leads them to a deserted warehouse in East St Louis, Illinois. There, they find themselves fighting for their lives as

Lipstick follies: James Belushi on the trail of a sick, imaginative, cunning serial killer. Aren't they all? A scene from Andy Wolk's Traces of Red *(from Entertainment)*

they become witnesses to a mob killing. Director Walter Hill, who bloated the testosterone quota in such actioners as *48 HRS*, *Extreme Prejudice* and *Red Heat*, is here defeated by a risible script (surprisingly from Bob Gale and Robert Zemeckis) and cardboard characters, a fatal combination that deprives this potentially exciting siege thriller of any suspense. As it stands, it's a poor man's *Treasure of the Sierra Madre* with rap stars. Previously known as *The Looters*, the title was changed after the LA riots of '92 – pre-

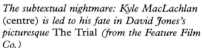

The subtextual nightmare: Kyle MacLachlan (centre) is led to his fate in David Jones's picturesque The Trial *(from the Feature Film Co.)*

sumably to deter firemen from looking for gold in deserted warehouses. [JC-W]

Cast: Bill Paxton (Vince), Ice T (King James), William Sadler (Don), Ice Cube (Savon), Art Evans (Bradlee), De'voreaux White (Lucky), Bruce A. Young (Raymond), Glenn Plummer (Luther), Stoney Jackson, T. E. Russell, Tiny Lister, John Toles-Bey, Byron Minns, Tico Wells, Hal Landon Jr, James Pickens Jr, L. Warren Young.

Dir: Walter Hill. Pro: Neil Canton. Ex Pro: Robert Zemeckis and Bob Gale. Screenplay: Gale and Zemeckis. Ph: Lloyd Ahern. Ed: Freeman Davies. Pro Des: Jon Hutman. M: Ry Cooder; numbers performed by Ice T, Ice Cube, Junior Brown, Public Enemy, Gang Starr, Black Sheep, etc. Costumes: Dan Moore. Pro: Charles M. Wilborn. (Universal–UIP.) Rel: 7 May 1993. 101 mins. Cert 18.

The Trial

Prague; 1912. One fine day, Josef K, senior clerk at a major bank, is arrested for an unknown crime. He is allowed to carry on his life as normal, but is frustrated in his attempts to find out

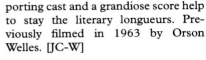

Sex, celluloid and supposition: Amos Poe's starkly original Triple Bogey on a Par Five Hole *(from ICA)*

In a film like this, no one is innocent: James Marshall and Sheryl Lee in David Lynch's smug exercise in weirdness, Twin Peaks: Fire Walk With Me *(from Guild)*

porting cast and a grandiose score help to stay the literary longueurs. Previously filmed in 1963 by Orson Welles. [JC-W]

Cast: Kyle MacLachlan (Josef K), Anthony Hopkins (priest), Jason Robards (Dr Huld), Juliet Stevenson (Fraulein Burstner), Polly Walker (Leni), Alfred Molina (Titorelli), Michael Kitchen (Block), David Thewlis, Tony Haygarth, Douglas Hodge, Paul Brooke, Harry Burton, Roger Lloyd Pack, Leon Lissek, Catherine Neilson, Trevor Peacock, Patrick Godfrey, Don Henderson, Robert Lang, John Woodvine. Dir: David Jones. Pro: Louis Marks. Ex Pro: Kobi Jaeger, Reniero Compostella and Mark Shivas. Assoc Pro: Carolyn Montagu. Screenplay: Harold Pinter. Ph: Phil Meheux. Ed: John Stothart. Pro Des: Don Taylor. M: Carl Davis. Costumes: Anushia Nieradzik. Sound: Helen Whitehead and Catherine Hodgson. (BBC Films/Europanda Entertainment–Feature Film Co.) Rel: 18 June 1993. 120 mins. Cert 12.

why he is being tried. Franz Kafka's classic, symbolic 1925 novel doesn't exactly cry out to be filmed, but this version, articulately (and amusingly) scripted by Harold Pinter and eloquently photographed by Phil Meheux, is as accessible a production as you're likely to find. A sterling sup-

Triple Bogey on a Par Five Hole

New York; 1991. A Franco-American scriptwriter is commissioned to write a screenplay about a hippy couple shot dead (on a golf course, hence the title) 14 years earlier. To augment his investigation he interviews the couple's three eccentric children, now grown up and living on a luxurious 120-foot yacht sailing round Manhattan. Shot in black-and-white, *Triple Bogey* contemplates life and film, and how the two can never meet. A quirky, playful and charming exercise, from the independent New York director Amos Poe (*The Blank Generation, Subway Riders*). [CB]

Cast: Eric Mitchell (Remy Gravelle), Daisy Hall (Amanda Levy), Angela Goethals (Bree Levy), Jesse McBride (Satch Levy), Alba Clemente (Nina Baccardi), Robbie Coltrane (Steffano Baccardi), Olga Bagnasco, Phil Hoffman, Tom Cohen, John Heys, Avital Dicker. Dir, Pro and Screenplay: Amos Poe. Co-Pro: Dolly Hall and Benjamin Gruberg. Ph: Joe DeSalvo. Ed: Dana Congdon. Pro Des: Jocelyne Beaudoin. M: Anna Domino, Michel Delory, Mader and Chic Streetman. Costumes: Ann R. Emo. Sound: Thomas Szabolcs. (ICA.) Rel: 29 January 1993. 88 mins. No cert.

Twin Peaks: Fire Walk With Me

You're either a *Twin Peaks* fan or you're not, but even devotees of the cult TV series hated this sordid mess. A cellu-

loid prequel, *Fire Walk With Me* begins one year one week previously, with the discovery of the corpse of Teresa Banks. Enter a couple of straightlaced 'J. Edgar' men (singer Chris Isaak and Kiefer Sutherland, both on perfect form), who find the remote Washington hamlet of Twin Peaks a damn strange place. And then they disappear. Changing direction radically, the film focuses on Laura Palmer herself, again played by Sheryl Lee, who overacts appallingly. All comedy is jettisoned in favour of horror, decadence, death, demons, dwarfs and angels. Being weird for the sake of being weird does not a movie make. P.S. The *Twin Peaks* regulars who do *not* appear include Richard Beymer, Joan Chen, Sherilyn Fenn, Piper Laurie, Michael Ontkean and Russ Tamblyn, while Donna Hayward is this time played by Moira Kelly. [JC-W]

Cast: Sheryl Lee (Laura Palmer), Ray Wise (Leland Palmer), Moira Kelly (Donna Hayward), David Bowie (Phillip Jeffries), Chris Isaak (Special Agent Chester Desmond), Harry Dean Stanton (Carl Rodd), Kyle MacLachlan (Special Agent Dale Cooper), Dana Ashbrook (Bobby Briggs), Pamela Gidley (Teresa Banks), David Lynch (Gordon Cole), James Marshall (James Hurley), Kiefer Sutherland (Sam Stanley), Grace Zabriskie (Sarah Palmer), Catherine E. Coulson (the Log Lady), Walter Olkewicz (Jacques Renault), Sandra Kinder (Irene at Hap's), Gary Bullock (Sheriff Cable), Julee Cruise (roadhouse singer), Lorna MacMillan (Angel in Red Room), Madchen Amick, Phoebe Augustine, Eric DaRe, Miguel Ferrer, Heather Graham, Peggy Lipton, Jurgen Prochnow, Lenny Von Dohlen, Frances Bay, Frank Silva, Al Strobel, Chris Pedersen, Victor Rivers, Rick Aiello, Kimberly Ann Cole, C. H. Evans, Calvin Lockhart.

Dir: David Lynch. Pro: Gregg Fienberg. Ex Pro: Lynch and Mark Frost. Screenplay: Lynch and Robert Engels. Ph: Ron Garcia. Ed: Mary Sweeney. Pro Des and Costumes: Patricia Norris. M: Angelo Badalamenti; Lynch. Sound: John Huck. (Francis Bouygues/Ciby Pictures–Guild.) Rel: 20 November 1992. 135 mins. Cert 18.

Under Siege

'My men are professionals. They can handle twenty marines – and a hundred cooks.' Thus says military terrorist William Strannix, an ambitious, clever and dangerous man who has kidnapped the USS *Missouri*

Under pressure: Rock 'n' roll villain Tommy Lee Jones cooks his goose when he provokes super-chef Steven Seagal, in Andrew Davis's rollicking Under Siege *(from Warner)*

(the US Navy's largest and most powerful battleship) on its final voyage. But Strannix hadn't bargained on chief cook Casey Ryback (played with a hint of humanity by Steven Seagal). While the ship's skeleton crew is locked in the hold, Ryback is in his kitchen cooking up a plan to rescue the *Missouri* single-handed . . . The pitch for this on-the-edge-of-your-seat thriller was '*Die Hard* at sea', and it's up to the challenge with explosive stunts, colourful villains and a cracking script with the obligatory roster of throwaway one-liners (Ryback rallying his reluctant crew: 'You're in the Navy, remember. It's not a job – it's an adventure!'). To date, *Under Siege* is Steven Seagal's biggest grossing movie

and broke American box-office records in October of 1992. Previously known as *Dreadnought* and *Last to Surrender*. [JC-W]

Cast: Steven Seagal (Casey Ryback), Tommy Lee Jones (William Strannix), Gary Busey (Commander Krill), Patrick O'Neal (Captain Adams), Glenn Morshower (Ensign Taylor), Duane Davis (Johnson), Erika Eleniak (Jordan Tate), Colm Meaney (Daumer), Richard Jones (Mr Pitt), Tom Wood (Private Nash), Nick Mancusco (Tom Breaker), Andy Romano (Admiral Bates), Dennis Lipscomb (Trenton), Dale A. Dye (Captain Garza), Damian Chapa, Troy Evans, John Rottger, Michael Welden, Bernie Casey, Raymond Cruz, Sandy Ward, Michael Des Barres, George Bush, Barbara Bush, Dick Cheney.

Dir: Andrew Davis. Pro: Arnon Milchan, Steven Seagal and Steven Reuther. Ex Pro: J. F. Lawton and Gary Goldstein. Co-Pro: Jack B. Bernstein and Peter MacGregor-Scott. Screenplay: J. F. Lawton. Ph: Frank Tidy. Ed: Robert A. Ferretti. Pro Des: Bill Kenney. M: Gary Chang; num-

Eastwood Ho!: Clint (seen here with Jaimz Woolvett) returns to the wide open spaces in his tenth and best western, Unforgiven *(from Warner)*

Peoples (*Blade Runner*) which was written in the mid-70s, *Unforgiven* is the perfect vehicle for Eastwood today, now 61. Grey-haired and balding, the actor is totally credible as the killer-gone-to-seed, his ravaged face revealing secrets of a violent past. Eastwood also directs (for the sixteenth time) and has created an atmospheric, realistic look at how the Wild West really was. As mythomaniacal gunmen brag about their apocryphal deeds (attended by star-struck biographers), the real killers keep their bodycount to themselves. A true masterpiece, one of the greatest westerns ever made and Clint's best film to date. Filmed predominantly in Alberta, Canada. [JC-W]

Cast: Clint Eastwood (William Munny), Gene Hackman (Little Bill Daggett), Morgan Freeman (Ned Logan), Richard Harris (English Bob), Jaimz Woolvett (the 'Schofield Kid'), Saul Rubinek (W. W. Beauchamp), Frances Fisher (Strawberry Alice), Anna Thomson (Delilah Fitzgerald), Anthony James (Skinny Dubois), David Mucci, Rob Campbell, Tara Dawn Frederick, Beverley Elliott, Josie Smith, Shane Meier, Cherrilene Cardinal, Robert Koons, Ron White, Mina E. Mina, Henry Kope, Jeremy Ratchford, Jefferson Mappin, Walter Marsh, Ben Cardinal.
Dir and Pro: Clint Eastwood. Ex Pro: David Valdes. Screenplay: David Webb Peoples. Ph: Jack N. Green. Ed: Joel Cox. Pro Des: Henry Bumstead. M: Lennie Niehaus. Sound: Rob Young. (Malpaso–Warner.) Rel: 18 September 1992. 131 mins. Cert 15.

bers performed by The Regulators, Snap, Jimi Hendrix, and Screams and Dreams. Costumes: Richard Bruno. Sound: Scott Smith. (Regency Enterprises/Le Studio Canal/Alcor Films–Warner.) Rel: 26 February 1993. 103 mins. Cert 15.

Unforgiven

1880; Wyoming. After a series of box-office bombs (*Pink Cadillac, White Hunter Black Heart, The Rookie*) Clint Eastwood, in desperation, returns to the terrain that made him a star – the western. Once again he is a killer of contemptible character (who has murdered women and children in his time), but one who has put down his guns to manage a small hog farm. A widower with two 'young-uns', William Munny lives in the memory of his beloved wife, who cured him of 'his drink and wickedness'. However, his farm is failing and Munny needs the $1000 offered by a brothel to kill two cowboys who disfigured a prostitute. But Munny is so unpractised at his craft that he can barely mount his horse or shoot a can off a post. Besides, other killers are riding into town to collect the bounty . . . Based on a screenplay by David Webb

Universal Soldier

Vietnam/ Nevada/ Arizona/ Utah/ Louisiana; 1969–94. Mario Kassar, producer of such big-budget action pictures as *Rambo III, Total Recall* and *Terminator 2*, pairs the Muscles from Brussels with the He-Man from Sweden in a better film than either has made before. Jean-Claude Van Damme and Dolph Lundgren play regenerated dead American soldiers, killed in Vietnam, but computerised to robotic life to go where even the SAS would fear to tread. But Dolph still holds a grudge against JC, and his human memory starts getting in the way. Enter feisty TV reporter Ally Walker to supply the acting and to escort JC on a rollercoaster ride across the US as they escape the vengeful

Swede, the police and other 'Unisols', all bent on total destruction. It isn't in *The Terminator* league, but *Universal Soldier* boasts enough thrills, spills and chills (and laughs) to make it a must-see for all action fans. [JC-W]

Cast: Jean-Claude Van Damme (Luc Devreux), Dolph Lundgren (Andrew Scott), Ally Walker (Veronica Roberts), Ed O'Ross (Col Perry), Leon Rippy (Woodward), Rance Howard (Mr Devreux), Lilyan Chauvin (Mrs Devreux), Jerry Orbach, Tico Wells, Ralph Moeller, Robert Trebor, Gene Davis, Drew Snyder, 'Tiny' Lister Jr, Simon Rhee, Eric Norris, Michael Winther, Joseph Malone, Monty Laird, Joanne Baron, Dona Hardy.

Dir: Roland Emmerich. Pro: Allen Shapiro, Craig Baumgarten and Joel B. Michaels. Ex Pro: Mario Kassar. Co-Pro: Oliver Eberle. Screenplay: Richard Rothstein, Christopher Leitch and Dean Devlin. Ph: Karl Walter Lindenlaub. Ed: Michael J. Duthie. Pro Des: Holger Gros. M: Christopher Franke; 'Body Count's In the House' performed by Body Count. Costumes: Joseph Porro. 2nd Unit Dir: Vic Armstrong. Sound: David Chornow. (Carolco–Guild.) Rel: 24 July 1992. 102 mins. Cert 18.

Unlawful Entry

On the outside, Michael and Karen Carr are your ideal yuppie couple. She's beautiful, he's rich. They share a beautiful home in a safe neighbourhood of Los Angeles. Then an intruder breaks into their house, holds a knife to Karen's throat and Michael looks on helplessly. So they call the police – and that's when their nightmare really begins. Police officer Pete Davis sees through the thin veneer of their happiness, and acts on it . . . Although dressed up as a routine thriller, and a pretty predictable one at that, *Unlawful Entry* nevertheless raises some disturbing questions – how far can the law go to uphold justice? How far do you go to protect your wife and home? How much sacrifice does a couple make to keep a marriage alive? Released during the aftermath of the Rodney King furore in LA, this was one helluva hot potato – and an extremely skilful one at that. [JC-W]

Cast: Kurt Russell (Michael Carr), Ray Liotta (Pete Davis), Madeleine Stowe (Karen Carr), Roger E. Mosley (Ray Cole), Ken Lerner (Roger Graham), Deborah Offner (Penny), Johnny Ray McGhee (Ernie Pike), Merv (Tiny, the cat), Carmen Argenziano, Andy Romano, Dino Anello,

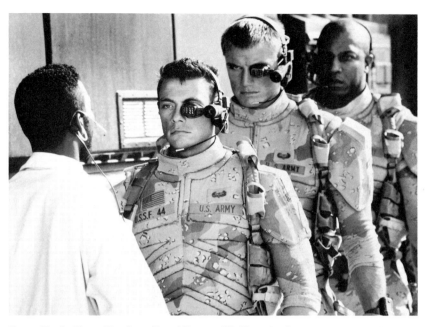

Sonny Davis, Harry Northup, Sherri Rose, Alicia Ramirez, Ruby Salazar, Dick Miller, Bob Minor.

Dir: Jonathan Kaplan. Pro: Charles Gordon. Line Pro: Gene Levy. Screenplay: Lewis Colick; from a story by Colick, George D. Putnam and John Katchmer. Ph: Jamie Anderson. Ed: Curtiss Clayton. Pro Des: Lawrence G. Paull. M: James Horner; numbers performed by Eddie Pal-

Would you let these men rescue your baby? Tico Wells (left) briefs Jean-Claude Van Damme and Dolph Lundgren in Roland Emmerich's adrenaline-pumping Universal Soldier *(from Guild)*

Defending his realm: Kurt Russell takes the law into his own hands in Jonathan Kaplan's provocative thriller, Unlawful Entry *(from Fox)*

Tender mercies: Christian Slater and Marisa Tomei in Tony Bill's unusual, touching Untamed Heart *(from UIP)*

Tomei (Caroline), Rosie Perez (Cindy), Kyle Secor (Howard), Willie Garson (Patsy), Charley Bartlett (young Adam), Joe Minjares (Jim), James Cada, Gary Groomes, Claudia Wilkens, Pat Clemons, Wendy Feder, Nancy Marvy, Paul Douglas Law, Josh Schaefer, Steve Cochran, Richard Grusin, Kay Bonner Nee.

Dir: Tony Bill. Pro: Bill and Helen Buck Bartlett. Ex Pro: J. Boyce Harman. Screenplay: Tom Sierchio. Ph: Jost Vacano. Ed: Mia Goldman. Pro Des: Steven Jordan. M: Cliff Eidelman; numbers performed by Brook Benton, LAPD, Los Lobos, DNA and Suzanne Vega, The Alarm, The Cowboy Junkies, Timbuk 3, Stacy Earl, Roger Williams, Holly Vincent, etc. Costumes: Lynn Bernay. Sound: Bill Phillips. (MGM–UIP.) Rel: 11 June 1993. 102 mins. Cert 15.

Used People

Queens, New York; 1969. When old Jack Berman shuffles off his mortal coil, his family find themselves at an emotional crossroads. His wife, Pearl, contemplates a life of mourning; his overweight daughter, Barbara, cannot escape the mocking clutches of her mother and sister; his other daughter, Norma, retreats into celluloid fantasy following the death of her husband and child; while Jack's mother-in-law, Freida, just waits for death to catch up with her. Then Joe Meledandri, an urbane, poetic Italian Lothario, enters their lives and changes them all for ever. On its own terms, *Used People* is an extremely funny, moving and truthful drama, brimming with hope, pain and artful observation. That it is scripted by the 33-year-old actor Todd Graff (*Five Corners, The Abyss*) and directed by the 31-year-old Englishwoman Beeban Kidron, puts it into the category of a small miracle. Graff based the material on his own grandmother's mourning, and he hasn't missed a trick. [JC-W]

Second-hand hearts: Jessica Tandy and Sylvia Sidney in Beeban Kidron's affectionate Used People *(from Fox)*

mieri, Sparks, Rozalla, and J. J. Cale. Costumes: April Ferry. Sound: Glenn Anderson. (Largo/JVC–Fox.) Rel: 30 October 1992. 111 mins. Cert 18.

Untamed Heart

Caroline is an attractive, spirited waitress at a Minneapolis diner and is having a terrible time with her boyfriends. God knows, she tries hard enough, but her efforts just seem to go unrewarded. Then one night she is assaulted in the park by two men and is saved by Adam, the odd, retiring bus boy from work. Adam seldom speaks, and when he does, he tells her he has the heart of a baboon. Against her better judgement she finds herself drawn to this strange man, an orphan who has no experience of love but who has the romantic devotion of a saint. An exemplary cast at the top of their form take this sweet, surprising story and turn it into cinematic gold. One of the year's most touching and unexpected delights. [JC-W]

Cast: Christian Slater (Adam), Marisa

Cast: Shirley MacLaine (Pearl Judith Berman), Kathy Bates (Barbara 'Bibby' Berman), Jessica Tandy (Freida), Marcello Mastroianni (Giuseppe 'Joe' Meledandri), Marcia Gay Harden (Norma), Sylvia Sydney (Becky), Joe Pantoliano (Frank), Matthew Branton (Swee' Pea), Bob Dishy (Jack Berman), Lee Wallace (Uncle Harry), Charles Cioffi (Paolo), Irving Metzman, Doris Roberts, Helen Hanft, Ida Bernardini.

Dir: Beeban Kidron. Pro: Peggy Rajski. Ex Pro: Lloyd Levin and Michael Barnathan. Screenplay: Todd Graff; based on material from his *The Grandma Plays*. Ph: David Watkin. Ed: John Tintori. Pro Des: Stuart Wurtzel. M: Rachel Portman; songs performed by Aaron Neville, The Mamas and The Papas, Marvin Gaye, Tom Jones, Simon & Garfunkel, Tommy Dorsey and Frank Sinatra, etc. Costumes: Marilyn Vance-Straker. Sound: Douglas Ganton. (JVC Entertainment–Fox.) Rel: 2 April 1993. 115 mins. Cert 12.

The Vanishing

Seattle; 1993. Following a lovers' tiff, Jeff and Diane make up and promise to be together for ever – and Diane disappears. Jeff then embarks on a massive manhunt, badgering the police, putting up flyposters, appearing on TV . . . Three years later his search has become his whole reason for being. He no longer cares if Diane is dead or alive, he just wants to know *what happened*. And then, just as Jeff gives up his quest, Barney Cousins decides to continue the experiment . . . By taking the chilling premise of his atmospheric Franco-Dutch film of the same name (1988) and tightening the emotional strings, director George Sluizer has produced an absorbing, superior Hollywood remake (although the tacked-on ending annoyed many critics). Nancy Travis, as Diane's loving and long-suffering successor, is particularly impressive. [JC-W]

Cast: Jeff Bridges (Barney Cousins), Kiefer Sutherland (Jeff Harriman), Nancy Travis (Rita Baker), Sandra Bullock (Diane Shaver), Park Overall (Lynn), Maggie Linderman (Denise Cousins), Lisa Eichhorn (Helene Cousins), George Hearn (Arthur Bernard), Lynn Hamilton, Garrett Bennett, George Catalano, Frank Girardeau, Stephen Wesley Bridgewater, Susan Barnes, Rich Hawkins.

Dir: George Sluizer. Pro: Larry Brezner and Paul Schiff. Ex Pro: Pieter Jan Brugge and Lauren Weissman. Co-Pro and Screenplay: Todd Graff; based on the novel

The Golden Egg by Tim Krabbe. Ph: Peter Suschitzky. Ed: Bruce Green. Pro Des: Jeannine C. Oppewall. M: Jerry Goldsmith. Costumes: Durinda Wood. Sound: Jeff Wexler. (Morra, Brezner, Steinberg/Tennenbaum–Fox.) Rel: 11 June 1993. 109 mins. Cert 15.

Waiting

Unusual, witty and pungent Australian comedy focusing on a surrogate mother and her gaggle of friends who

Experiment in evil: Nancy Travis and Kiefer Sutherland grapple with the unknown in George Sluizer's intriguing The Vanishing *(from Fox). Sixteen years ago Kiefer's father, Donald Sutherland, starred in* The Disappearance, *about a man whose wife mysteriously vanishes*

Four women and a foetus: Noni Hazlehurst, Deborra-Lee Furness, Helen Jones and Fiona Press in Jackie McKimmie's fresh and funny adult comedy Waiting *(from Contemporary)*

Dreams of normalcy: Elizabeth Pena and Eric Stoltz in Neil Jimenez's articulate, perceptive The Waterdance *(from Winstone)*

await the Big Day. The film starts with a picturesque shot of an isolated creek, its quiet waters broken by the sudden appearance of a swimmer surfacing. Our astonishment is compounded by the realisation that the swimmer, a woman, is naked, seconds later exposing her nine-month pregnant belly. *Waiting* is full of such surprises, not least within its sparkling dialogue and canny revelations of character. An effervescent, frank and moving exposé of human foibles, as hilarious as it is insightful. A minor classic. [JC-W]

Cast: Noni Hazlehurst (Clare), Deborra-Lee Furness (Diane), Frank Whitten (Michael), Helen Jones (Sandy), Denis Moore (Bill), Fiona Press (Therese), Ray Barrett (Frank), Noga Bernstein, Peter Tran, Brian Simpson, Matthew Fargher, Alan Glover.
Dir and Screenplay: Jackie McKimmie. Pro: Ross Matthews. Ex Pro: Penny Chapman. Ph: Steve Mason. Ed: Michael Honey. Pro Des: Murray Picknett. M: Martin Arminger; numbers performed by Doris Day, AC/DC, The Plunderers, The Beasts of Bourbon, Jean Stafford, etc. Sound: Nick Wood. (Filmside/Australian Broadcasting Corp./Film Four–Contemporary.) Rel: 14 August 1992. 95 mins. Cert 15.

The Waterdance

Neil Jimenez, who scripted the movies *River's Edge, For the Boys* and *The Dark Wind*, was paralysed when he broke his neck in a hiking accident. His new film, which he also co-directs (with Michael Steinberg), is about a writer who is confined to a wheelchair after such an accident. Eric Stoltz stars as Joel Garcia, a young novelist who not only has to come to terms with paraplegia, but the unlikely men he is forced to spend time with in rehab. While attempting to sidestep the sentimental pitfalls of a disease-of-the-week TV movie, *The Waterdance* does suffer from a certain 'tastefulness', complete with background classical music and close-ups of held hands. However, there are some unexpected moments of humour and some effective acting (particularly Wesley Snipes's optimistic loser), even if the emotions are never fully engaged. [JC-W]

Cast: Eric Stoltz (Joel Garcia), Wesley Snipes (Raymond Hill), William Forsythe (Bloss), Helen Hunt (Anna), Elizabeth Pena (Rosa), Grace Zabriskie (Pat), William Allen Young (Les), Tony Genaro (Victor), Fay Hauser (Rachel Hill), Tai Thai (Sang), Henry Harris, Kimberly Scott, Casey Stengal, Susan Gibney, Elizabeth Dennehy, Badja Djola, Thomas F. Duffy, Joey Ciccone, Ed Barkas, Barbara Alyn Woods.
Dir: Neil Jimenez and Michael Stein-

berg. Pro: Gale Anne Hurd and Marie Cantin. Ex Pro: Guy Riedel. Screenplay: Jimenez. Ph: Mark Plummer. Ed: Jeff Freeman. Pro Des: Robert Ziembicki. M: Michael Convertino. Costumes: Isis Mussenden. Sound: Steve Nelson. (Samuel Goldwyn–Winstone.) Rel: 27 November 1992. 106 mins. Cert 15.

Waterland

Pittsburgh; 1974. A sombre, extremely gaunt Jeremy Irons intones on the soundtrack, 'Once upon a time, children . . .' And so unfolds this extraordinary, double-edged tale of sexual awakening in the Fens and of the deterioration of the man telling it. Irons is a stuffy, somewhat disorientated history teacher whose career and marriage is in tatters, and who retreats into the past, regaling his students with details of his personal history instead of the French Revolution. The film's time-shifts are not only awkward but bizarre, as the American students *physically* wander through the East Anglia of 1911 – rather like *Fried Green Tomatoes* meets Lewis Carroll. [JC-W]

Cast includes: Jeremy Irons (Tom Crick), Ethan Hawke (Matthew Price), Sinead Cusack (Mary Crick), John Heard (Lewis Scott), Grant Warnock (young Tom), Lena Headey (young Mary), David Morrissey (Dick Crick), Pete Postlethwaite (Henry Crick), Cara Buono, Callum Dixon, Maggie Gyllenhaal, Gareth Thomas, Susannah Fellows, Tony Vogel, Alison Everns, Latoya Heard.
Dir: Stephen Gyllenhaal. Pro: Katy McGuinness and Patrick Cassavetti. Ex Pro: Nik Powell, Stephen Woolley and Ira Deutchman. Screenplay: Peter Prince; from the novel by Graham Swift. Ph: Robert Elswit. Ed: Lesley Walker. Pro Des: Hugo Luczyc-Wyhowski. M: Carter Burwell. Costumes: Lindy Hemming. (Palace/Fine Line/Pandora Cinema/Channel Four Films/British Screen–Mayfair Entertainment.) Rel: 21 August 1992. 95 mins. Cert 15.

White Men Can't Jump

Highly energised, fast-talking, muscular hit comedy from writer-director Ron Shelton, he who explored the world of amateur football (unsuccessfully) in *The Best of Times* and minor-league baseball (successfully) in *Bull Durham*. This time, exercising his uncanny ear for street dialogue, Shelton examines the tough, combative arena of pick-up basketball. Woody Harrelson, in his first cinema lead, is

Boyz N the Hoop: Woody Harrelson and Wesley Snipes make a leap for the big time in Ron Shelton's fiercely enjoyable White Men Can't Jump *(from Fox)*

a revelation as Billy Hoyle, the white hustler who listens to Jimi Hendrix, dates a Puerto Rican and plays basketball like a 'brother'. However, he meets his match when he teams up with all-round hustler Sidney Deane (Wesley Snipes), a big-league con man who can exploit Billy's colour to their advantage. Harrelson and Snipes work wonderfully together, and are sensational on the court as they perform *their own* stunts, both actors being basketball fanatics. The sport itself is excitingly choreographed, the characters well defined and the colourful dialogue rapid-fire. Shelton, shrewd filmmaker that he is, has managed to tap the energy and pertinence of the black cinema and harnessed it for cross-over audiences. The result is an entertaining, Saturday-night adrenaline rush. [JC-W]

Cast: Wesley Snipes (Sidney Deane), Woody Harrelson (Billy Hoyle), Rosie Perez (Gloria Clemente), Tyra Ferrell (Rhonda Deane), Cylk Cozart (Robert), Kadeem Hardison (Junior), Marques Johnson (Raymond), Ernest Harden Jr, David Roberson, Nigel Miguel, Freeman Williams, Louis Price, John Marshall Jones (a.k.a. J. J.), Kevin Benton, Duane Martin, Jon Hendricks, Bill Henderson, Sonny Craver, Eloy Casados, Frank Rossi, Alex Trebek.
    Dir and Screenplay: Ron Shelton. Pro: Don Miller and David Lester. Ex Pro: Michele Rappaport. Ph: Russell Boyd. Ed: Paul Seydor. Pro Des: Dennis Washington. M: Bennie Wallace; numbers performed by Riff, Boyz II Men, Jesse Johnson, College Boyz, James Brown, Jody Watley, Jimi Hendrix, Ray Charles, The O'Jays, Aretha Franklin, Go West, etc. Costumes: Francine Jamison-Tanchuck. Sound: Kirk Francis. (Fox.) Rel: 9 October 1992. 115 mins. Cert 15.

White Sands

Terribly complicated thriller set in New Mexico, with Willem Dafoe as a clean-cut, honest sheriff who finds half a million bucks next to a corpse in the

Mickey Rourke and Willem Dafoe walk the tenuous path between law and crime, in Roger Donaldson's laboured, long-winded White Sands *(from Warner)*

desert. Taking on the identity of the dead man, Dafoe teams up with gun-runner Mickey Rourke who has been hunted by the FBI for five years. The Feds and the CIA come and go like guest stars in an Oliver Stone movie and the layers of corruption start fur-ring up the plot like hard water. What might have been an intriguing look at the inside world of arms dealing turns into another knotty, meandering gun festival with the obligatory body-count. [JC-W]

Cast: Willem Dafoe (Ray Dolezal), Mary Elizabeth Mastrantonio (Lane Bodine), Mickey Rourke (Gorman Lennox), Samuel L. Jackson (Greg Meeker), M. Emmet Walsh (Bert Gibson), James Rebhorn (Flynn), Maura Tierney (Noreen), Mimi Rogers (Molly Dolezal), Beth Grant, Alex-ander Nicksay, Fredrick Lopez, Miguel Sandoval, John Lafayette, Ken Thorley, Jack Kehler, Steven Tyler, Meredith Mar-shall, John P. Ryan, Fred Dalton Thompson.
  Dir: Roger Donaldson. Pro: William Sackheim and Scott Rudin. Ex Pro: James G. Robinson, David Nicksay and Gary Barber. Screenplay: Daniel Pyne. Ph: Peter Menzies Jr. Ed: Nicholas Beauman. Pro Des: John Graysmark. M: Patrick O'Hearn; numbers performed by O'Hearn, Little Feat, Dwight Yoakam, and Jimmie Wood & The Immortals. Costumes: Deborah Ever-ton. Sound: Richard Goodman. (Morgan Creek–Warner.) Rel: 4 September 1992. 101 mins. Cert 15.

Wide Sargasso Sea

Jamaica; the 1840s. Who *was* the mad woman in the attic in *Jane Eyre*? This plodding and unconvincing melo-drama attempts to fill in her history, presenting her as an impassioned, beautiful sugar heiress deprived of love, who discovers lust in an arranged marriage with a stuffy Englishman – Edward Rochester. In spite of a prom-ising opening, the deadly pacing and stilted acting soon underwhelm the story, leading to terminal boredom. Based on Jean Rhys' final and most successful novel, *Wide Sargasso Sea* strives to be mysterious and erotic, but comes off like a neutered, compressed miniseries. [JC-W]

Cast: Karina Lombard (Antoinette Cosway), Nathaniel Parker (Edward Rochester), Martine Beswick (Aunt Cora), Claudia Robinson (Christophene), Michael York (Paul Mason), Rachel Ward (Annette Cosway), Huw Christie Williams (Richard Mason), Casey Berna (young

Antoinette), Rowena King (Amelie), Ben Thomas (Daniel Cosway), Ancile Gloudin (Nelson), Paul Campbell, Audbrey Pilatus, Dominic Needham.
  Dir: John Duigan. Pro: Jan Sharp. Line Pro: Karen Koch. Ex Pro: Sara Risher. Screenplay: Sharp, Duigan and Carole Angier. Ph: Geoff Burton. Ed: Anne Gour-saud and Jimmy Sandoval. Pro Des: Franckie D. M: Stewart Copeland. Cos-tumes: Norma Moriceau. Sound: Harry Cohen. (Laughing Kookaburra/ Polygram–Rank.) Rel: 4 June 1993. 98 mins. Cert 18.

Wild West

Perky low-budget comedy set in Lon-don's Southall district – 'Little India' – where three Pakistani brothers attempt to get a country & western band ('The Honky Tonk Cowboys') off the ground. Thanks to a roster of engaging performances from some lit-tle-known Asian actors, and fast-paced direction from TV director David Att-wood, *Wild West* is unusual, funny and endearing. [JC-W]

Cast: Naveen Andrews (Zaf Ayub), Sarita Choudhury (Rifat), Ronny Jhutti (Kay Ayub), Ravi Kapoor (Ali Ayub), Ameet Chana (Gurdeep), Bhasker (Jagdeep), Lalita Ahmed (Mrs Ayub), Shaun Scott (Tony), Neran Persaud, Nrinder Dhudwar, Parv Bancil, Paul Bhattacharjee, Rolf Saxon, Madhav Sharma.
  Dir: David Attwood. Pro: Eric Fellner. Screenplay: Harwant Bains. Ph: Nic Know-

The Honky Tonk Indians: country comes to town in David Attwood's fresh and breezy Wild West *(from First Independent)*

land. Ed: Martin Walsh. Pro Des: Caroline Hanania. M: Dominic Miller; numbers performed by Rebecca Price, Naveen Andrews, Dwight Yoakam, Steve Earle, etc. Costumes: Trisha Biggar. Sound: Chris Munro. (Initial Prods/Channel Four/Brit-ish Screen–First Independent.) Rel: 14 May 1993. 85 mins. Cert 15.

Wind

The important thing about competi-tive sailing, we are told, is finding your own wind. Unfortunately, this ambitious romantic adventure is winded as soon as the plot is tele-graphed in the first few scenes. Matthew Modine (with little material to act on) plays a promising skipper who loses his girlfriend *and* the Ameri-ca's Cup in one fell sloop. Inspired by the tenacity of real-life skipper Dennis Conner, who sailed against the Austra-lians in 1987, the film's sailing sequences are spectacular and cine-matic, but cannot compensate for the banalities of the story. Furthermore, a lot of the dialogue sounds better on the page than in the mouths of the actors ('Sometimes we pay too high a price for our dreams'). Still, it's prob-ably the best movie about yachting ever made. [JC-W]

Cast: Matthew Modine (Will Parker), Jen-nifer Grey (Kate Bass), Stellan Skargsard (Joe Heiser), Rebecca Miller (Abigail Weld), Cliff Robertson (Morgan Weld), Jack Thompson (Jack Neville), Ned Vaughn, Peter Montgomery, Elmer Ahlwardt, Saylor Creswell, James Rebhorn, Michael Higgins, Ron Colbin.

Dir: Carroll Ballard. Pro: Mata Yamamoto and Tom Luddy. Ex Pro: Francis Ford Coppola and Fred Fuchs. Assoc Pro: Betsy Pollack. Screenplay: Rudy Wurlitzer and Mac Gudgeon; from a study by Jeff Benjamin, Roger Vaughan and Kimball Livingston. Ph: John Toll. Ed: Michael Chandler. Pro Des: Laurence Eastwood. M: Basil Poledouris; Giacomo Puccini. Costumes: Marit Allen. Sound: Alan Splet. (Entertainment.) Rel: 26 March 1993. 125 mins. Cert PG.

A Winter's Tale – Conte d'Hiver

Paris; now. In spite of juggling two boyfriends, Felicie is still obsessed with the father of her 5-year-old daughter. Due to accidentally giving him a wrong address, Felicie has never heard from him since their idyllic summer together on the coast of Brittany – when she conceived his child. So she now has to choose between the intellectual lucidity of the good-looking, sensitive Loic, and the good-natured self-assurance of the more experienced Maxence, a down-to-earth hairdresser. Typical, tantalising Eric Rohmer comedy of indecision: very wordy, naturalistic and cerebral. The second episode in the director's 'Tales of the Four Seasons'. [JC-W]

Cast: Charlotte Very (Felicie), Frederic Van Den Driessche (Charles), Michel Voletti (Maxence), Herve Furic (Loic), Ava

Shock appeal: Sandra Bernhard in one of her many guises in the concert revue Without You I'm Nothing *(from Electric)*

Sailor beware: Matthew Modine and Jennifer Grey take a break in Carroll Ballard's long-winded Wind *(from Entertainment)*

Loraschi (Elise), Christiane Desbois (the mother), Rosette, Jean-Luc Revol, Haydee Caillot, Marie Riviere.
  Dir and Screenplay: Eric Rohmer. Pro: Margaret Menegoz. Ph: Luc Pages. Ed: Mary Stephen. M: Sebastien Erms. Costumes: Pierre-Jean Larroque. Sound: Pascal Ribier. (Les Films Du Losange CER/Soficas Investimage/Sofiarp/Canal Plus–Artificial Eye.) Rel: 1 January 1993. 114 mins. Cert 12.

Without *You* I'm Nothing

A cunning cinematic recreation of Sandra Bernhard's 'smash-hit one-woman show on Broadway' (her words), a collection of monologues, torch songs and provocative dance routines. Bernhard, the proctologist's daughter who had a much-publicised affair with Madonna, talks at length about her own (ambiguous) beauty, pays tribute to the likes of Warhol, Streisand and Prince, and otherwise contemplates her navel. Often witty, frequently amusing and seldom bland, the film's highlights include a 'safe sex' rendition of the Supremes' 'Stop! In the Name of Love' and an impromptu strip routine. A genuine, adult variety show – with plenty of visual surprises. [JC-W]

Cast: Sandra Bernhard, John Doe, Steve Antin, Lu Leonard, Ken Foree (Emcee), Cynthia Bailey, Paul Thorpe, Denise Vlasis (Madonna-lookalike stripper Shoshanna), Djimon Hounson.

Dir: John Boskovich, Pro: Jonathan D. Krane. Ex Pro: Nicolas Roeg. Screenplay: Sandra Bernhard and Boskovich. Ph: Joseph Yacoe. Ed: Pamela Malouf-Cundy. Pro Des: Kevin Rupnik. M: Patrice Rushen. Choreographer: Karole Armitage. Sound: Mark Sheret. (MCEG–Electric.) Rel: 14 August 1992. 90 mins. Cert 18.

Wittgenstein

Surprisingly accessible, witty and stylish film biography of the homosexual Austrian philosopher Ludwig Wittgenstein, who left Vienna (and his family's millions) to take up residence in Cambridge. Good performances, splendid costumes and sharp lighting help to steer this away from Derek Jarman's normally dour tracts on culture and homosexuality. Shot on a budget of under £300,000 in two weeks. [CB]

Cast: Karl Johnson (Ludwig Wittgenstein), Michael Gough (Bertrand Russell), Tilda Swinton (Lady Ottoline Morrell), John Quentin (Maynard Keynes), Clancy Chassay (young Wittgenstein), Lynn Seymour (Lydia Lopokova), Kevin Collins, Sally Dexter, Jan Latham-Koenig, David Radzinowicz, Howard Sooley, Jill Balcon.
  Dir: Derek Jarman. Pro: Tariq Ali. Ex Pro: Ben Gibson and Takashi Asai. Screenplay: Jarman, Terry Eagleton and Ken Butler. Ph: James Welland. Ed: Budge Tremlett. Art: Annie Lapaz. M: Jan Latham-Koenig. Costumes: Sandy Powell. Sound: George Richards, Toby Calder and Paul Carr. (Channel 4/BFI/Uplink (Japan)/Bandung–BFI.) Rel: 26 March 1993. 75 mins. Cert 15.

Wuthering Heights

See *Emily Brontë's Wuthering Heights.*

Letter from Hollywood

Anthony Slide

Nothing better illustrates the two sides to the city of Los Angeles than the riots that took place on 29 and 30 April 1992. The immediate impetus for the civil disorder was the brutal beating of a black motorist, Rodney King, by four police officers, while a dozen or more additional officers stood by and did nothing to halt the savage attack. To many in the Los Angeles Police Department, the beating was nothing more than a routine event – the police here and in other American cities are noted for the violence of their actions when the supposed perpetrator of a crime is non-white – but this time the attack was recorded on videotape by a member of the public. Thanks to that home video, Los Angeles and its police department will never be the same again.

The rioting was blamed on the 'not guilty' verdicts brought against the officers involved, but, in reality, what took place has more to do with the dividing line between the haves and the have-nots of Los Angeles. The haves are represented by those in the film community, the powerful studio executives and agents and the wealthy, reclusive stars. At a time when unemployment is at an all-time high, when budget cutting is the order of the day, when the homeless and the hungry are at every street corner, executives at Warner Bros and Walt Disney have taken home salaries in excess of $80 million a year. One disgruntled teacher pointed out that even if she

worked hard for the rest of her life, she would earn less than Jack Nicholson was paid for ten days' work in *A Few Good Men*.

The damage caused by the riots will be paid for by the middle class, not by the wealthy of the film community. The major studios brush off any threat of additional taxation with a threat of their own – they will leave the city. The response of Hollywood celebrities to the riots was pretty much as expected. Actor Edward James Olmos, who is actively considering a political career, led a volunteer group whose mission was to clean the streets of South Central Los Angeles, the heart of the riot district. Tom Petty recorded a song called 'Peace in LA'. Debbie Allen, Luke Petty, Anjelica Huston, Tim Matheson and a handful of other entertainers gathered on a Warner Bros sound stage to record public service announcements.

Of course, the threat by the rioters to the film industry was small. Los Angeles is such a large, spread-out community that those living elsewhere were perhaps unaware that the violence was limited to a small, predominantly black neighbourhood. Only two studios – ABC Television and Paramount, both located in East Hollywood – were close to the riot action, although there were reported threats to burn to the ground the Warner Bros facility in Burbank. Had the rioters targeted one or more of the studios, they might have more legitimately made their point, but instead they headed for liquor, clothing, appliance and grocery stores. Bookstores in the riot area came out relatively unscathed, although one chain reported that rioters stole videotapes of all the Walt Disney features.

One bookstore that was in imminent danger was Larry Edmunds, with its unique collection of film-related books, posters, lobby cards and still photographs. Heading down Hollywood Boulevard, rioters burned down shops less than six doors away from Larry Edmunds. A number of buildings on the Boulevard are owned by the controversial Church of Scientology (whose members include John Travolta and Kirstie Alley), and it was an amazing sight to see Church members forming human protective fences around Church property. Perhaps not surprisingly, the Church of Scientology was not willing to try and protect the infamous Frederick's of Hollywood and its Lingerie Museum on the opposite side of Hollywood Boulevard from the main Church building. Rioters smashed the windows of the store and stole most of its stock. Included in the theft were a bra belonging to actress Katey Sagal of television's *Married with Children*, the pantaloons of Ava Gardner and Madonna's bustier. The first two items were returned by a repentant rioter to the pastor at the Blessed Sacrament Catholic Church in Hollywood. Madonna's bustier remains missing.

Rioting and looting also took place within a couple of blocks of the Hollywood vaults of the UCLA Film and Television Archive. Had its 20 million feet of nitrate film been torched by the mob, the result would have been a catastrophe not only for film history but also for the city of Los Angeles.

Michael Jackson became embroiled in a Hollywood controversy in April 1992 when it was announced that an eighty-foot mural of the entertainer was to be painted on the side of the recently restored El Capitan Theater. Hollywood activists argued that a more appropriate mural for the building would be of Orson Welles, whose *Citizen Kane* received its premiere at the El Capitan in 1941.

Aside from the riots, the major news in Los Angeles, as elsewhere in the United States, has been the presidential campaign. The election of Bill Clinton led to a change in the Hollywood political scene. Arnold Schwarzenegger, Bob Hope, Tom Selleck, Phyllis Diller, Charlton Heston, Chuck Norris and Pat Boone, members of the conservative group that supported Presidents Bush and Reagan, are gone, replaced by Richard Dreyfuss, Chevy Chase, Warren Beatty, Mary Steenburgen and other Clinton fans.

In part because of a general disenchantment with the political system in the United States, many stars were unwilling to adopt a standard Democratic stance. When asked in the summer of 1992 if he would support Clinton, Jack Nicholson expressed doubts about the candidate's character. Sally Field admitted she was intrigued by independent candidate Ross Perot, who picked up endorsements from Katharine Hepburn, Willie Nelson and Kirstie Alley. At the Democratic convention in New York City, where Clinton was nominated, director Oliver Stone was present as a supporter and delegate of former California Governor Jerry Brown.

An unusual delegate at the Republican convention in Houston was Billy Barty, who has appeared in more than 200 films since his 1927 debut and is noted for his diminutive size. Barty, who founded the Little People of America in 1957, explained, 'I want to prove the Republican Party is for the little people,' and urged the return of the three Rs to our country: respect, responsibility and religion.

The Presidential Inauguration in Washington DC in January 1993 was a star-studded series of events, including an open-air concert in front of the Lincoln Memorial. Other entertainment at the Inauguration was produced by Harry Thomason and his wife Linda Bloodworth-Thomason (whose television series include *Evening Shade* and *Designing Women*). They are so close to Clinton and his wife that they are often referred to in the media as 'First Friends'. Ironically, the Thomasons produce their shows for MTM Entertainment, which shortly after the Inauguration was taken over by ultra-Conservative Pat Robertson and his International Family Entertainment company. It remains to be seen how the Thomasons and Robertson will work together, but apparently the bottom line is money (as it usually is with America's religious right) – so long as the Thomasons' series are profit-making, politics will not enter the picture.

Meanwhile back in Hollywood... In June 1992, in an effort to get people's minds off the riots, Mayor Tom Bradley declared Ginger Rogers Day, in honour of the lady's sixty years in show business. Miss Rogers was one of the guests of honour on 12 September 1992, which Mayor Bradley declared 'Hollywood's Chinese Theater Day'. The occasion was the publication of a new book, *Hollywood at Your Feet* by Stacey Endres and Robert Cushman, which documents the history of the prints of hands and feet in the forecourt of Grauman's Chinese Theater.

The event was hosted by Robert Dorian, who presents the films on the American cable network, American Movie Classics (AMC), and who managed to patronise an audience of Hollywood film buffs by offering comments on basic film history as if they were startling revelations. Ginger Rogers explained that the footprints in the cement were not hers: when she was invited to leave her mark in concrete, she felt her feet were too big and so borrowed her mother's shoes, one size smaller, for the occasion. Another invited guest, Jane Russell, said that when she and Marilyn Monroe came to put their hand and footprints in the cement, the latter suggested they might also offer their bust prints. Jane Russell told her colleague that there wasn't enough space for them.

Also on hand was Jane Withers, who positively sparkled with good health and humour, promising (or threatening) to return to acting next year. Just as prints of the feature films of Charlie Chaplin have been removed from distribution in order to build up a new audience for them, so it seems has Jane Withers been absent for quite a few years from the Hollywood events at which she was always a regular.

Observant readers will note that the event was billed as 'Hollywood's Chinese Theater Day' rather than 'Grauman's Chinese Theater Day'. Back in 1973, Ted Mann acquired the theatre, removed Sid Grauman's name and renamed the theatre Mann's Chinese Theater. In 1977, he had the audacity to put his footprints in the sacred Grauman cement, and in 1981

Audrey Hepburn with Sean Connery at the 1992 Moving Picture Ball

invited his wife, actress Rhonda Fleming, to do likewise. Now the theatre has been sold to Paramount, but Ted Mann insisted that the bill of sale require that his name, rather than Sid Grauman's, be kept on the theatre marquee!

Just down Hollywood Boulevard from the Chinese Theater is Grauman's Egyptian Theater, which opened in 1922 with the premiere of Douglas Fairbanks's *Robin Hood*. Long a part of the United Artists theatre chain, the marquee was in such poor shape that it could not even carry the names of the films playing the theatre and had been covered in cardboard. On 18 July 1992, the Egyptian finally closed. The city of Los Angeles has purchased the site and it is hoped the building will be taken over and reopened as a revival theatre by the American Cinematheque.

The latter had a difficult year in

1993 with the deaths from AIDS of its founder Gary Essert and his longtime companion and co-worker on the project, Gary Abrahams. The American Cinematheque's new executive director is Barbara Zicka Smith, and she is hopeful that the Egyptian can be acquired by her organisation. The American Cinematheque sponsors the annual Moving Picture Ball, and the 1992 event, held on 24 July, honoured British actor Sean Connery. More than 1,200 guests were present at the Beverly Hills Hotel to see the late Audrey Hepburn host the evening, which included tributes to Connery by Sidney Lumet, Neil Simon, F. Murray Abraham, Sidney Poitier, Faye Dunaway and Wesley Snipes. Taped messages of regard were delivered by Billy Connolly, Dame Edna Everage and Richard Harris.

While Hollywood has lost – albeit hopefully only temporarily – the Egyptian Theater, there has been a reprieve for another city landmark, the Max Factor Museum. One of the few original tourist attractions still open in

Hollywood, the Max Factor Museum is the only one for which admission is free. Housed in the old Max Factor Make-up Studio on Highland Avenue, the museum shows the facility as it looked in 1934, and offers a history of film make-up as well as such esoteric items as Frank Sinatra's and George Burns's toupees. Max Factor & Co was acquired by Procter & Gamble in July 1991, and the following summer the company announced that it would close the museum. In response to protests from community activists and a threatened boycott of Procter & Gamble's products, the company rescinded the closing, and agreed to keep the museum open for the foreseeable future in the hope that a plan can be worked out for its permanent upkeep.

Just as the Max Factor Museum was threatened with closure, another Hollywood relic, the famed Hollywood Sign, was the centre of a storm of controversy. In an attempt to publicise its latest release, *Cool World*, Paramount placed a cutout character from the film, Holli Would, on the 'D' of the sign. Residents of Hollywood were outraged by this blatant attempt to use the Hollywood Sign for a promotional stunt, particularly when it was revealed that Paramount had donated a mere $27,000 toward rebuilding Los Angeles after the riots. A plane flew over the sign with a banner proclaiming 'Paramount Not a Good Neighbor' and the Los Angeles Commission on the Status of Women expressed outrage that the caricature was of a scantily clad female.

The female in question was Kim Basinger, who was not present when the caricature was unveiled and had no comment on the protest. The attitude of many in Hollywood towards the film community was evident in March 1993, when Basinger was ordered to pay almost $9 million for breaching an oral agreement to appear in the film *Boxing Helena*. While the jury at the trial claimed it had no bias against the actress but was merely sending a message that Hollywood should do business like everybody else in America, the general feeling was that the average American and the average resident of Los Angeles is getting more and more tired of arrogant and overpaid Hollywood stars who care nothing for the community and for the values of society.

Kim Basinger represents the new breed of Hollywood star, but there was equal time in 1992–3 for the celebrities of the past. A massive crowd of 4,000 fans turned up at the Gene Autry Western Heritage Museum on 16 May 1992 for a tribute to the singing cowboys. On hand were host Dennis Weaver, Emmylou Harris, Dwight Yoakam and the Sons of the Pioneers, who presented a moving tribute to Roy Rogers and Dale Evans (unable to attend because she was confined to the couple's Apple Valley home following a heart attack a few days earlier).

Philip Dunne, one of the founders of the Writers Guild of America, was honoured with a lifetime award from that organisation on 27 May 1992. Dunne, whose films include *How Green Was My Valley, Pinky* and *Ten North Frederick*, was too ill to attend the ceremony (he died shortly thereafter), but present were Roddy McDowall and Dunne's fellow writer Norman Corwin, who called him 'a gentleman, a scholar, a citizen and an

artist – each on the highest plane'.

On 8 July 1992, a life-size bronze statue of Jack Benny by Ernest Shelton was unveiled in the plaza in front of the Academy of Television Arts and Sciences in North Hollywood. Present for the unveiling and subsequent film tribute were Benny's daughter Joan and the delightful Giselle McKenzie. The statue captures the quintessential Benny pose with three fingers on the cheek and the silent expression that could keep an audience laughing forever. It joins statues of Milton Berle, Sid Caesar, Carol Burnett, Mary Tyler Moore and other great names from American television. Somewhat off the beaten track, the plaza is well worth a visit by tourists, and the Academy also boasts a small library, open to the public, but in no way comparable to that of the Academy of Motion Picture Arts and Sciences.

One contemporary comedian who lacks the respect awarded Jack Benny is Woody Allen, whose tangled legal suits with Mia Farrow have so engrossed the American tabloid newspapers that Princess Di and Fergie are relatively forgotten. When a January 1993 tribute to Mike Medavoy, the head of Tri-Star, included a clip from a Woody Allen movie, the Hollywood audience began booing. For an American filmmaker to receive such an insult from his peers is unprecedented, but as one industry observer noted, Woody Allen is a New York rather than a Hollywood director.

The major Hollywood event for film buffs is the annual Cinecon convention held over the Labor Day weekend at the Hollywood Roosevelt Hotel. This year's guests included Sally Blane, Frances Dee, Alice Faye, William Bakewell and Jane Wyatt. Bob Gitt's restoration, for the UCLA Film and Television Archive, of the widescreen drama *The Bat Whispers* was screened for Cinecon attendees at Grauman's (or Mann's) Chinese Theater, and William Bakewell entertained the audience with his remembrances of the behaviour of the film's director Roland West, who would film only at night, rehearsing the actors in the scene and then turning his back as the sequence was being shot!

One of the most popular events at the Cinecon was a panel discussion on film preservation, chaired by myself, and attended by representatives from

George Eastman House, the Library of Congress, Turner Entertainment and the UCLA Film and Television Archive. Preservation is a much discussed if not much funded matter, and on the weekend of 12–14 March 1993, the cable network American Movie Classics hosted a weekend promoting film preservation and encouraging the public to provide money for the combined efforts of America's film archives. Examples of films recently restored or preserved were televised in their entirety and there were short presentations on the work of the various archives. The weekend was sponsored by Martin Scorsese's Film Foundation, and Scorsese sent out 75 letters to major names in the Hollywood film community asking for their financial support. Financial response from the public was somewhat disappointing, in that a mere $125,000 was raised. The response from the film industry was outrageous, however, with Scorsese receiving only $5000 from his colleagues.

This is evidence, if any is needed, that the film community has no interest in the preservation of its past. At the same time as American Movie Classics was presenting its Festival of Preservation, the Librarian of Congress was holding hearings on film preservation. A constant complaint from the public was that public money is utilised to preserve films the use of which is then restricted to the copyright owners, the film studios and producers, who pay nothing back to the taxpayer. A film such as *Hell's Angels* is restored by Bob Gitt at the UCLA Film and Television Archive utilising government (i.e. taxpayers') money from the National Endowment for the Arts. Once the restoration is completed, the copyright owner – in this case MCA/Universal – is able to release the restored version on home video without repayment of the funding provided by the taxpayer, and without any acknowledgement of the original source of funding or the party involved in the restoration.

The largest sum of money received by Martin Scorsese towards film preservation was $3000 from Jeffrey Katzenberg, chairman of the board of Walt Disney Studios. Katzenberg was recently appointed chairman of the newly organised Motion Picture and Television Fund Foundation, whose aim is to raise money for an industry charity which is facing hard times in these days of recession and unemployment. The heads of all the major studios are joining Katzenberg on the board of the foundation, along with Whoopi Goldberg, John Singleton and others.

The Motion Picture and Television Fund has always prided itself on the industry motto 'We take care of our own'. One of the major ways in which the industry has accomplished this is with the American Cinema Awards, held on an annual basis since 1983. The May 1992 awards honoured Milton Berle, Gene Kelly and Jimmy Stewart, all of whom had suites at the Motion Picture and Television Fund Hospital in Woodland Hills named in their honour.

Two major industry events of 1993 are worth noting. On 11 February, a tribute to the recently deceased head of Time Warner, Steve Ross, was held at New York's Carnegie Hall. A similar, if smaller, tribute was held at Warner Bros on the day following the Academy Awards.

On 29 January, Army Archerd celebrated his 40th year as *Daily Variety*'s 'Just for Variety' columnist with a charity event at the Beverly Hilton Hotel. The evening raised $700,000 for Archerd's favourite charities, and on hand to hear the columnist tell them 'Your lives have been my life' were Jack Nicholson, Warren Beatty, James Stewart, Shirley MacLaine, Anthony Hopkins, Gregory Peck, Kirk Douglas, Faye Dunaway and James Earl Jones.

Hollywood's biggest night of the year is the Academy Awards presentation, held this year on 29 March. The big question was not who would win but what Jaye Davidson, Best Supporting nominee for *The Crying Game*, would wear. Until the day of the show, there was even some doubt that Davidson would be there, but ninety minutes before the awards began, the focus of all the fuss came in through the stage door, avoiding reporters, and was barely seen by television cameras (despite subsequent visits by Vanessa Redgrave, Jane Fonda and other stars). For the record, Davidson wore a suitably androgynous costume consisting of a long black shirt with white stripes over trousers tucked into boots.

Arriving at the last minute, Jaye Davidson missed Saturday's Independent Spirit Awards, held under a tent on the beach at Santa Monica. Robert Altman's *The Player* was named the best independently produced film of 1992, while *Howards End* beat out *The Crying Game* as the best foreign-produced independent film of the year. On hand for the informal awards luncheon were Emma Thompson and mother Phyllida Law, Richard Harris, Forest Whitaker, James Ivory, Keanu Reeves, Jeff Goldblum, Mario Van Peebles, Neil Jordan, Buck Henry and Danny Glover. Celebrities had no alternative but to stand in line to use the portable toilets placed on the beach for the occasion, and while in line could hardly ignore fans demanding autographs.

If in the excitement nobody invited Jaye Davidson to an Oscar party, one choice might have been to pay $40.00 and go to Tatou's Restaurant in Beverly Hills, where Tony Curtis was hosting a three-course Oscar dinner. Once there, guests had the opportunity to preview some of the actor's paintings, on sale for prices of somewhat more than $40.00 each. Only in Hollywood can one pay to have dinner with a star of the past . . .

Movie Quotations of the Year

'It seems to me that apart from being mentally ill, Joon is pretty normal.'

> Johnny Depp talking to Aidan Quinn about his sister, in *Benny & Joon*

'Hey, I don't take credit. I'm a cash kinda guy.'

> Dustin Hoffman, refusing to accept the limelight for his valiant deed, in *Accidental Hero*

'She's pretending to be a person. She's actually a reporter.'

> Editor Chevy Chase on his star newswoman Geena Davis, in *Accidental Hero*

Dustin Hoffman, in Accidental Hero

'Some cultures are defined by their relationship to cheese.'

> Mary Stuart Masterson in *Benny & Joon*

Professor Van Helsing: 'I'll need a set of surgical knives before nightfall.' Jack Seward: 'Autopsy? On *Lucy*?' Van Helsing: 'No. Not exactly. I just want to cut off her head and cut out her heart.'

> Anthony Hopkins and Richard E. Grant making nocturnal preparations in *Bram Stoker's Dracula*

'Forgive me for not knowing about El Salvador – as if I'm going to Spain *anyhow.*'

> Airhead cheerleader Kristy Swanson in *Buffy the Vampire Slayer*

'All I want to do is graduate, go to Europe and marry Christian Slater.'

> Kristy Swanson explaining her true vocation to vampire hunter Donald Sutherland – in *Buffy the Vampire Slayer*

'If only I were black, I'd feel a lot better.'

> Timid, would-be blues singer Mary Steenburgen in *The Butcher's Wife*

'Kill a few people and they call you a murderer. Kill a million and they call you a conqueror. Go figure.'

> Conqueror wannabe John Lithgow in *Cliffhanger*

'I was so popular at high school that everybody hated me.'

> Matthew Modine in *Equinox*

Matthew Modine: 'Do you know the Andes?' Marisa Tomei: 'I know a couple of "Andy"s.'

> From *Equinox*

'Helen, I'm sorry, but this is a matter of national security. I'm going to have to tickle you.'

> A po-faced Mel Gibson to Isabel Glasser, in *Forever Young*

Bill Murray to head waitress: 'Do you ever have *déjà vu*, Mrs Lancaster?' Angela Paton: 'I don't know. I'll ask in the kitchen.'

> From *Groundhog Day*

Policeman: 'We've found your son, sir, and he's fifty feet tall.' Rick Moranis: 'That's impossible, my son's only fourteen foot!'

> From *Honey, I Blew Up the Kid*

'These men have been sworn to a vow of celibacy – like their fathers and their fathers before them.'

Part-time monk Charlie Sheen in *Hot Shots! Part Deux*

'Will you spend the night with me? You don't have to like it.'

Vondie Curtis-Hall making Alfre Woodard a proposition she can resist – in *Passion Fish*

Demi Moore to Robert Redford: 'I hate you!' Redford: 'No you don't. You *wish* you hated me.'

From *Indecent Proposal*

Charlie Sheen: 'I'm like putty in your hands.' Brenda Bakke: 'In my hands nothing turns to putty.'

From *Hot Shots! Part Deux*

Brenda Bakke, *in* Hot Shots! 2

'A woman is like a slingshot. The greater the resistance, the further you can go with her.'

Steve Martin – after Lolita Davidovich gives him the cold shoulder – in *Leap of Faith*

Jeff Goldblum: 'God creates dinosaurs. God destroys dinosaurs. God creates man. Man destroys God. Man creates dinosaurs.' Laura Dern: 'Dinosaurs eat man. Women inherit the earth.'

From *Jurassic Park*

Sam Neill to Jeff Goldblum: 'Are you married?' Goldblum: 'Occasionally.'

From *Jurassic Park*

'You know what's true? When something looks too good to be true, it's not true.'

Sean Connery in *Rising Sun*

'Fucking women. You can't live with 'em. You can't kill 'em.'

Gangster Bill Murray in *Mad Dog and Glory*

Bill Murray to Robert De Niro: 'Are you married?' De Niro: 'No. Not personally.'

From *Mad Dog and Glory*

'It is the nature of men to confuse genius with insanity.'

International terrorist Bruce Payne in *Passenger 57*

Wheelchair patient Mary McDonnell: 'Did they tell you I was a bitch?' Nurse Alfre Woodard: 'On wheels.'

From John Sayles's *Passion Fish*

'It's called a pot belly. We have them in England, along with culture.'

Stephen Fry defending his gut to a friend from Los Angeles – in *Peter's Friends*

Kenneth Branagh, *in* Peter's Friends

'Adults are just children who owe money.'

Kenneth Branagh in *Peter's Friends*

'It's not the mileage, honey, it's the make.'

John Lithgow debating the sexual superiority of older men, in *Raising Cain*

'To be fair to this dilemma, it is a beautiful spot.'

Survivor of a plane crash in the snowy Andes mountains, in *Alive*

Steve Buscemi: 'Kill anybody?' Harvey Keitel: 'Just a few cops.' Buscemi: 'No real people?'

A couple of homicidal jewel thieves in *Reservoir Dogs*

'You start out with a burning desire and you end up the next morning with a burning sensation.'

John Malkovich on the drawbacks of casual sex, from *Shadows and Fog*

'Incompetent? I don't know enough to be incompetent!'

Woody Allen in *Shadows and Fog*

Mia Farrow, in Shadows and Fog

'My father used to say, "We're all happy, if only we knew it." ,'
Mia Farrow in *Shadows and Fog*

Innocent waif: 'I slept with one person for money. Does that make me a whore?' Her new companion: 'No. Only by the dictionary definition.'
Mia Farrow and Woody Allen in *Shadows and Fog*

'The only love that lasts is unrequited love.'
Jodie Foster in *Shadows and Fog*

'Tomorrow, the first good-looking woman I see – I'm not going to fall in love with her. That'll show her.'
Robert Burke in Hal Hartley's *Simple Men*

'My dad left home and he told me, "Have fun. Stay single." I was eight.'
Campbell Scott recalling paternal advice – in Cameron Crowe's *Singles*

'I've got a kid, for chrissakes. I'm a person.'
Dustin Hoffman's grouchy loser, in *Accidental Hero*

On meeting his cousin Gavin's new friend: 'The pleasure's all mine – any friend of Gavin's is a bad judge of character.'
Richard Wilson in *Soft Top, Hard Shoulder*

'By the year 2000 it is estimated that one out of every three people will be members of my family.'
Hillary Wolf in *Stepkids*

'Do you eat?'
John Leguizamo attempting to ask Samantha Mathis for a date, in *Super Mario Bros*

'My life is like watching "The Three Stooges" in Spanish.'
A distraught Marisa Tomei in *Untamed Heart*

The year's most impassioned promise:
'Stay alive, no matter what occurs. I *will* find you. No matter how long it takes, no matter how far. I *will* find you.'
Daniel Day-Lewis to Madeleine Stowe under the waterfall, in *The Last of the Mohicans*

Daniel Day-Lewis, in The Last of the Mohicans

The year's most famous lines:
'Big mistake!'
Arnold Schwarzenegger as Jack Slater in *Last Action Hero*

'There's no crying in baseball!'
Exasperated coach Tom Hanks, spelling out the rules to a female player in *A League of Their Own*

Tom Hanks, in A League of Their Own

The year's most chilling riposte:
Flight attendant Alex Datcher resisting the sexual advances of terrorist Bruce Payne: 'You'll have to kill me first.' Payne: 'No, Marti. I'm going to kill you *during*.'
From *Passenger 57*

Understatements of the year:
'This man's a pain in the ass.'
Tommy Lee Jones observing Steven Seagal's one-man assault on the nuclear battleship USS *Missouri*, in *Under Siege*

'Carter isn't making any sense. He's not just looking after Amy, it's as if he's *studying* her.'
A perceptive Lolita Davidovich talking about her homicidal child psychologist husband (John Lithgow) taking an unhealthy interest in their daughter – in *Raising Cain*

TV Feature Films of the Year

F. Maurice Speed

In this section you will find listed all the made-for-television movies shown for the first time in the UK during the year 1 July 1992 to 30 June 1993. Films shown during the year which have been previously televised in the UK are not listed, but can be found in the edition of *Film Review* for the year when they were first shown. The date given in brackets after each title is the year when the movie was made or originally shown (often in the US).

In a few cases, despite being first shown on television, these films may have been made originally for the cinema.

When a film made for American TV receives its first UK showing in a cinema, it is of course reviewed in the 'Releases of the Year' section.

Amazone (1984). Daft TV feature film about a group of women planning to seize political power by any available means. With Madeleine Stowe. Dir: Paul Michael Glaser (of *Starsky and Hutch* fame). ITV, 21 December 1992.

Amityville Horror: The Evil Escapes (1989). The fourth in this silly series of haunted-house thrillers. With Patty Duke, Jane Wyatt, Norman Lloyd. Dir: Sandor Stern. ITV, 10 February 1993.

And I Alone Survived (1978). True story about the sole survivor of a mountain plane crash and her struggle back to civilisation. With Blair Brown. Dir: William A. Graham. BBC1, March 1993.

Angel of Death (1990). Familiar thriller about an escaped killer obsessed by a single mother. Mother obtuse; killer charming; script weak. With Jane Seymour, Gregory Harrison, Brian Bonsall. Dir: Bill L. Norton. ITV, 3 April 1993.

Assault on the Wayne (1971). Underwater skullduggery as spies among the crew of a nuclear submarine plan to steal the secret weapon. Joseph Cotten, Leonard Nimoy and Keenan Wynn do their best to keep this one afloat. Dir: Marvin J. Chomsky. ITV, 31 May 1993.

Bad Girl (1992). The British social services get a bashing in this 'based-on-fact' story of a niterie singer fighting to get her small son back after he is taken into care. Interesting and topical. With Jane Horrocks. Dir: George Case. BBC2, 15 July 1992.

Baywatch: Nightmare Bay (1991). Feature film introduction to the bimbo-littered series about life among the lifeguards of the Los Angeles beaches. Dir: David Hasselhoff. ITV, 13 September 1991.

Between Friends (1983). Elizabeth Taylor and Carol Burnett as a couple of divorcees – looking for very different kinds of men and lifestyle – who become friends. Fine performances make this worth seeing. Dir: Lou Antonio. BBC1, 25 March 1993.

Blind Witness (1989). Mediocre performances sink this routine thriller about a blind wife (Victoria Principal) who is the only witness of her husband's murder. Script by blind actor Tom Sullivan. Dir: Richard A. Colla. ITV, 17 April 1993.

Blue Lightning (1988). Routine private eye thriller with PE Sam Elliott in Australia trying to recover the jewel of the title, but finding it more hazardous than anticipated. With Robert Culp, Rebecca Gilling. Dir: Lee Philips. BBC1, 3 September 1992.

Breaking Point (1989). Routine remake of a 1964 war film about an Allied officer captured by the Nazis, who try to drug him into accepting their claim the war is over, in order to obtain invaluable knowledge from him. With Corbin Bernsen, Joanna Pacula. Dir: Peter Markle. BBC2, 9 November 1992.

Brink's: The Great Robbery (1976). Excellent reconstruction of the sensational 1950 Boston bank robbery. Well directed by Marvin Chomsky from an authentic script. Lively performances by Cliff Gorman, Darren McGavin etc. A good, convincing thriller. ITV, 25 December 1992.

Bye Bye Baby (1992). Writer Jack Rosenthal takes another glance back at his past; this time at National Service boys of the 1950s coming to the end of their two years in the Royal Navy. A clever mixture of comedy and sentiment set against a credible background. Entertaining. With Ben Chaplin, Nicholas Gleaves etc. Dir: Edward Bennett. Channel 4, 3 November 1992.

By Dawn's Early Light (1990). A nasty problem for two USAF pilots:

do they or don't they drop the atom bomb which would start World War Three? With Powers Boothe, James Earl Jones. Dir: Jack Sholder. BBC1, 4 August 1992.

Carly's Web (1987). Pilot feature for a series that never got the go-ahead: American lawyer (female) uncovers corruption in high places. With Daphne Ashbrook. Dir: Kevin Inch. ITV, 23 December 1992.

Changes (1991). Well-made, fast-moving, condensed but superficial telefilm adaptation of the Danielle Steel novel. About the romance of a glamorous TV newsreader and a doctor; and everyone is impossibly rich, beautiful and unreal. With Cheryl Ladd, Michael Nouri. Dir: Charles Jarrott. ITV, 28 September 1992.

Chips the War Dog (1990). Disney feature about a US Army-trained Alsatian dog and his increasingly admiring and loving handler. Dir: Ed Kaplan. ITV; in three parts, starting 24 April 1993.

Columbo: A Stitch in Time (1972). The sly sleuth in the decrepit raincoat once again makes villain-catching so easy, in this whodunnit feature film. BBC1, 13 December 1992.

A Connecticut Yankee in King Arthur's Court (1989). The *fourth* film version of the Mark Twain classic story about a modern youngster who wakes up in King Arthur's Camelot. With Kershia Knight Pulliam. Dir: Mel Damski. Channel 4, 23 December 1992.

The Countess Alice (1992). One of the magnificent BBC 'Screenplay' series. Lady Monroe married a Prussian count in 1935 but is now anxious to dissuade her daughter from visiting the ancestral home in East Germany – why? With Wendy Hiller, Zoë Wanamaker, Duncan Bell. Dir: Moira Armstrong. BBC2, 1 July 1992.

Cracked Up (1987). James Wilder as minister Ed Asner's athlete son who becomes hooked on 'crack'. A moving story of drug addiction. Dir: Karen Arthur. ITV, 5 May 1993.

Criminal Justice (1990). Uncompromising and highly critical look at a flaw in the American legal system; the way that defence and prosecution can strike a bargain to get a case finished quickly. Quite shocking. A superior production. With Forest Whitaker, Jennifer Grey. Dir: Andy Wolk. Channel 4, 22 October 1992.

Danielle Steel's Daddy (1991). Patrick Duffy gives a good performance in a best-seller adaptation, as a man suddenly faced with lots of pressing problems, including a runaway wife. Also with Lynda Carter. Dir: Michael Miller. ITV, 30 June 1993.

Danielle Steel's Kaleidoscope (1990). Routine private eye melo with PE Perry King trying to carry out his dying client's instructions to reunite three unwilling sisters. With Jaclyn Smith. Dir: Jud Taylor. ITV, 7 October 1992.

Dear America: Letters Home from Vietnam (1971). Just what it says . . . read by a rota of Hollywood stars, and all very emotional. Dir: Bill Couturie. BBC2, 31 January 1993.

Death Rides to Osaka (1983). White slavery in Japan; supposedly to be based on fact. Young American girls working in the night clubs are forced into prostitution by the Mobs. With Jennifer Jason Leigh. Dir: Jonathan Kaplan. ITV, 13 December 1992.

Diagnosis of Murder (1991). Good to see Dick Van Dyke back in action, playing a doctor who turns detective when his pal is framed on a murder charge. Unusual and amusing whodunnit. Also with Bill Bixby, Ken Kercheval. Dir: Christopher Hibler. BBC1 3 January 1993.

A Different Affair (1985). Routine story about a woman who adopts a son at long range but finds things get difficult when he turns up on her doorstep. With Anne Archer, Tony Roberts, Bobby Jacoby. Dir: Noel Nosseck. ITV, 3 April 1993.

Dinner at Eight (1989). A sadly misjudged effort to produce a modernised, telefilm remake of the classic, witty and biting comedy-drama by Edna Ferber and George Kaufman;

one of the great movies of the 1930s, here reduced to something very ordinary. With Lauren Bacall, Marsha Mason, Charles Durning. Dir: Ron Cagomarino. BBC1, 23 September 1992.

Don't Leave Me This Way (1993). Over-'arty' direction and eccentric editing make this an altogether infuriating whodunnit about two women who won't believe their friend's death was an accident and set out to investigate. But who cares? With Janet McTeer and Imelda Staunton. Dir: Stuart Orme. BBC1, 30 May 1993.

Dr Quinn: Medicine Woman (1992). Delightfully entertaining and old-fashioned feature introduction to a new series about a woman doctor who goes West in the 1860s and meets male – and female – prejudice. Jane Seymour gives an enjoyable performance as the determined medic. ITV, 28 May 1993.

Embassy (1983). Nick Mancuso sorting out some tricky problems at the US Embassy in Rome. With Eli Wallach, Sam Wanamaker, Kim Darby. Dir: Robert Michael Lewis. ITV, 16 December 1992.

Eric (1975). Real-life story of a young sportsman's fight against leukaemia. Inspiringly good. With Patricia Neal (splendid), John Savage. Dir: James Goldstone. Channel 4, 21 April 1993.

Face Value (1991). Small-town girl (Cheryl Pollak) comes to the big city hoping to become a model but instead becomes the victim of acute sexual harassment. Dir: John Gray. Channel 4, 29 June 1993.

The FBI Murders (1988). Reconstruction of what has been described as one of the most violent shoot-outs in FBI history, when the bureau apprehended a couple of ruthless killers. Once again, fact outdoes fiction; a remarkable film. With David Soul, Michael Gross. Dir: Dick Lowry. BBC1, 11 December 1992.

The FBI Story: Alvin Karpis (1974). Exciting documentary-style 1930s gangster piece: J. Edgar Hoover embarks on a war against the hoodlums and ends their reign of terror.

With Harris Yulin. Dir: Marvin Chomsky. BBC1, 6 March 1993.

Fighting Back (1980). Routine, sentimental, but true story of a baseball star badly injured in Vietnam and his subsequent struggle to win back his old place in the team. With Robert Urich, Art Carney (a fine performance), Bonnie Bedelia. Dir: Robert Lieberman. Channel 4, 9 June 1993.

Final Jeopardy (1985). A thriller that packs a fair number of thrills; good of its kind. With Richard Thomas, Mary Crosby. Dir: Michael Pressman. ITV, 30 December 1992.

Fool's Gold (1992). Rough-hewn story based on the headline-hitting Brink's-Mat robbery in which £26 million in gold bullion was stolen from Heathrow, never to be recovered. With Sean Bean, Trevor Byfield, Larry Lamb. Dir: Terry Winsor. ITV, 14 November 1992.

For Love of a Child (1990). A neighbourly relationship becomes soured when the son of one family drowns in next door's pool. Good performances, but somehow less than involving. With Michael Tucker, Kevin Dobson. Dir: James Dobson. BBC2, 13 July 1992.

Force of Duty (1992). Powerful, top-class drama about an RUC officer who becomes completely obsessed with finding the killer of one of his mates. With Donal McCann. Dir: Pat O'Connor. BBC2, 8 July 1992.

14 Going On 30 (1987). Disney family fun about a schoolboy who falls in love with his teacher and tries to prevent her wedding the horrid PE master. With Patrick Duffy, Steve Eckholdt, Loretta Swit. Dir: Paul Schneider. ITV, 15 August 1992.

Frankenstein – The Real Story (1992). The monster rides again – this time with some style. With Patrick Bergin. Dir: David Wickes. ITV, 29 December 1992.

Genesis 2 (1973). SF movie about a man buried for 150 years who wakes up to find the world divided into two opposing camps. Some good effects; not many exciting ideas. With Alex

Cord, Mariette Hartley. Dir: John Llewellyn Moxey. BBC2, 4 April 1993.

The Gladiator (1986). Pleasant young motor mechanic by day becomes ruthless vigilante by night, to avenge his brother, killed by a drunken driver. Similar to the *Death Wish* films. With Ken Wahl. Dir: Abel Ferrara. ITV, 31 May 1993.

The Golden Years (1992). Adaptation of one of Arthur Miller's lesser, and lesser-known, stage plays: about the bloody conquest of Mexico by Spain. With Ronald Pickup, Robert Powell, Cathy Tyson. Dir: Paul Bryers. Channel 4, 12 November 1992.

Goodnight Sweet Wife – A Murder in Boston (1990). Gripping story, based on fact: man rings police, claiming a burglar has just shot his wife and himself, thereby starting a massive search for the gunman. Above-average whodunnit. With Ken Olin, Margaret Colin. Dir: Gerald Freedman. ITV, 18 August 1992.

The Grass Arena (1991). A good performance by Mark Rylance makes this adaptation of John Healy's autobiography worth watching; an alcoholic vagrant fights his way back into society and becomes a chess player and writer. A true and uplifting story that nonetheless seems like familiar fiction. Dir: Gillies Mackinnon. BBC2, 4 January 1993.

The Great Escape II: The Untold Story (1988). Mediocre and daft TV sequel to the successful cinema film about POW thrills. Laughably cast with Christopher Reeve as the British officer and Donald Pleasence as the Nazi. A travesty of the original. Dir: Paul Wendkos. ITV, 13 March 1983.

The Guardian (1984). Above-average thriller about a man hired to protect a block of flats, the scene of a recent murder, who finds himself falling under suspicion. With Martin Sheen, Louis Gossett Jr. Dir: David Greene. BBC1, 9 December 1992.

Habitation of Dragons (1992). Not an animated cartoon, but a thoughtful and absorbing 1930s Texas family political drama. Based on the stage play by Horton Foote. With Brad Davis, Lucinda Jenney, Frederic Forrest. Dir: Michael Lindsay-Hogg. Channel 4, 8 October 1992.

Heart of Justice (1992). Superior, intelligent and engrossing TV feature based on a true story about a man who shoots a novelist when he thinks the writer is basing his work on the murderer's family story. With Eric Stoltz, Dennis Hopper, Vincent Price. Dir: Bruno Barreto. Channel 4, 15 October 1992.

Higher Ground (1988). Fighting the dope smugglers amid the Alaskan snows. Impressive scenery is about the film's greatest asset. With John Denver. Dir: Robert Day. ITV, 22 December 1992.

A Hobo's Christmas (1987). Tear-stained tale of a Christmas reconciliation between an old tramp and his son. With Barnard Hughes. Dir: William Mackenzie. ITV, 23 December 1992.

The Hunters (1974). Tony Lo-Bianco as the cop who becomes emotionally involved in his efforts to catch and bring to justice a particularly nasty criminal. Not bad at all. Dir: Richard Benedict. A Canadian TV feature. ITV, 18 January 1993.

The Image (1990). Albert Finney as an American TV newsreader who has to take stock of himself when faced with some difficult decisions. Also with Marsha Mason, John Mahoney etc. Dir: Peter Werner. BBC2, 22 February 1993.

Incident at Dark River (1989). Earnest and topical tale of industrial pollution of an American river. Star Mike Farrell also co-wrote and co-produced. Also with Tess Harper, Helen Hunt. Dir: Michael Pressman. BBC2, 23 November 1992.

The Incredible Hulk Returns (1988). The old Marvel Comics hero fights Thor the Viking. Fun for fans. With Bill Bisby, Lou Ferrigno. Dir: Nicholas Corea. ITV, 5 June 1993.

The Kansas City Massacre (1976). Highly entertaining gangster comedy set in the 1960s and featuring such notorious baddies as Pretty Boy Floyd, John Dillinger and Baby Face Nelson etc. With Dale Robertson, Scott Brady. Dir: Dan Curtis. ITV, 27 December 1992.

Kate's Secret (1986). Meredith Baxter Birney as a secret sufferer from the compulsive eating disorder bulimia, Compulsive the disorder may be – but this ain't. Dir: Arthur Allan Seidelman. BBC2, 5 September 1992.

Kenny Rogers as The Gambler: The Legend Continues (1987). Third of the series, with The Gambler proving the Indians are not guilty of a murder of which they are accused. A leisurely old-style boots-and-saddle movie. With Kenny Rogers, Bruce Boxleitner, Linda Gray. Dir: Dick Lowry. ITV, 9 April 1993.

King Crab (1980). Fraternal fighting between two brothers over the family crabbing business. With Barry Newman, Jeffrey DeMunn. BBC1, 17 December 1992.

The Lady and the Highwayman (1988). Hugh Grant as the heart-throb highwayman and Lysette Anthony as the loving lady. Penned by the pink-rinsed queen of romance, Barbara Cartland. Dir: John Hough. BBC1, 26 July 1992.

Larry (1974). True-life story about a man who though not mentally retarded spent the first 26 years of his life in a mental home. Intelligent treatment of a sad story. With Frederic Forrest, Tyne Daly. Dir: W. A. Graham. Channel 4, 2 June 1993.

The Last Best Year (1990). Twenty-tissue TV weepie with Mary Tyler Moore (bringing a touch of class to the proceedings) as a psychologist who becomes deeply involved with a patient dying of cancer. Also with Bernadette Peters. Dir: John Erman. BBC2, 21 September 1992.

Lawman Without a Gun (1978). Louis Gossett Jr as a black US civil rights worker who decides to risk running for Sheriff in a Southern town. Anti-racism movie based on truth. Dir: Jerrold Freedman. BBC1, 8 September 1992.

The Legend of Sleepy Hollow (1980). Reasonably entertaining children's film based on the Disney cartoon *The Adventures of Ichabod and Mr Toad*. With Jeff Goldblum. Dir: Henning Schellenup. ITV, 24 December 1992.

Lena: My Hundred Children (1987). Superior TV feature based on the true story of Lena Kuchler-Silberman (Linda Lavin, in a shiningly sincere performance), who brought a hundred Jewish children from Poland to Israel just after the end of World War II. Moving, tense and convincing. Dir: Ed Sherin. Channel 4, 13 August 1992.

The Long Summer of George Adams (1982). James Garner giving his usual easy and polished performance as an old-fashioned railwayman who feels threatened by the advent of the diesel engine. Set against an authentic small town background. Also with Joan Hackett, Anjanette Comer. Dir: Stuart Margolin. BBC1, 26 January 1993.

Lucky Day (1991). A retarded young woman wins a fortune, sparking off a struggle between her mother and sister as to who can get their hands on the loot. Nice performances from Olympia Dukakis, Amy Madigan, Chloe Webb. Channel 4, 6 August 1992.

Madigan: The London Beat (1971). Tough New York cop Madigan (Richard Widmark) is asked by Scotland Yard to help them smash an American-led gang of forgers. Run-of-the-mill but worth watching. With George Cole, Alun Armstrong. BBC1, 20 August 1992.

Mama's Going to Buy You a Mocking Bird (1988). Canadian TV film about a family coming to terms with the father's terminal illness. With Louise Tripp, Linda Griffiths, Geoff Bowes. Dir: Sandy Wilson. Channel 4, 4 January 1993.

Memories of Murder (1990). Amnesia victim Nancy Allen forgets who and what she is but recalls a murder . . . You won't believe a word of this ludicrous film. Also with Robin Thomas. Dir: Robert Lewis. BBC1, 9 January 1993.

Money, Power, Murder (1989). Routine, minor mystery thriller about a newshound trying to solve the mystery of a vanished radio star. With Kevin Dobson, Julianne Moore, Blythe Danner. Dir: Lee Philips. ITV, 5 June 1993.

Mr Inside Mr Outside (1973). Pilot for another projected series that didn't make it. A New York police thriller (not bad either) about undercover cops Tony LoBianco and Hal Linden smashing a formidable gang. Dir: William A. Graham. ITV, 24 May 1993.

Murder Takes All (1989). Stacy Keach (as Mike Hammer), in Vegas to solve a minor crime, finds himself framed for murder. Dir: John Nicolella. ITV, 31 December 1992.

Nairobi Affair (1984). Charlton Heston and John Savage tracking down illegal animal slayers in Africa. Routine safari stuff. Dir: Marvin Chomsky. ITV, 6 December 1992.

'Night Mother (1986). Fine performances by Anne Bancroft (as worried mum) and Sissy Spacek (as the suicidally inclined daughter) in good adaptation of Martha Norman's Pulitzer Prize-winning play. Dir: Tom Moore. BBC2, 5 September 1992.

The Night They Saved Christmas (1984). A family saves Father Christmas's polar toy factory from the oil-well diggers. A pleasant fantasy for the youngsters. With Jaclyn Smith. Dir: Jackie Cooper. ITV, 27 December 1992.

Norman Rockwell's Breaking Home Ties (1987). In spite of that cumbersome title, a very superior TV feature film about a farm boy who goes to the city to gain an education and learns his mother is dying. With Doug McKeon, Eva Marie Saint, Jason Robards, Claire Trevor. Dir: John Wilder. Channel 4, 3 March 1993.

One Magic Christmas (1985). Disney feature about the true meaning of Chistmas. With Mary Steenburgen. Dir: Phillip Borsos. ITV, 24 December 1992.

One Police Plaza (1986). Routine cops 'n' robbers and corruption in high places melo. With Robert Conrad, Anthony Zerbe. Dir: Jerry Jameson. ITV, 6 July 1992.

Only the Good Die Young (1990). Two friends die in an accident – or was it? Courtroom drama with a plushy background in the *Dallas* tradition. With Jaclyn Smith, Celeste Holm, Ralph Bellamy. ITV, 12 July 1992.

The Operation (1990). A doctor involved in a messy divorce case that becomes a murder investigation. Entertaining, even if it doesn't make a lot of sense. With Joe Penny, Lisa Hartman. Dir: Thomas J. Wright. Channel 4, 23 July 1992.

Panic at Lakewood Manor (1977). Routine thriller about killer ants on the rampage at a quiet holiday resort. With Suzanne Somers, Robert Foxworth, Myrna Loy. Dir: Robert Sheerer. ITV, 30 August 1992.

Passport to Terror (1989). Frightening but true: a holidaymaker buys some antiquities at an archaeological site, is arrested for smuggling and sent to a grim Turkish jail. Dir: Lou Antonio. BBC2, 5 October 1992.

The People Across the Bay (1988). Mildly entertaining murder mystery about a family expecting an idyllic rest cure in the country, but who keep finding bodies cropping up in their cellar! With Valerie Harper. Dir: Arthur Allen Seidelman. ITV, 28 December 1992.

Perry Mason: The Case of the Defiant Daughter. Third of the new series of four feature films starring Raymond Burr as the investigating lawman, defending a man accused of killing his blackmailer. Also with Barbara Hale, Robert Vaughn, Robert Culp. Dir: Christian I. Nyby II. BBC1, 20 June 1993.

Perry Mason: The Case of the Desperate Deception (1990). Hitherto unseen (in this country) Perry Mason feature about fugitive Nazis. Unfortunately well below the usual PM standard. With Raymond Burr, Barbara Hale. Dir: Christian I. Nyby II. BBC1, 6 December 1992.

Perry Mason: The Case of the Poisoned Pen. Perry, in the person of Raymond Burr, comes back into court in order to prove the cops have the wrong man accused of murder. The first of several feature-length Mason cases. Also with Barbara Hale. Dir: Christian I. Nyby II. BBC1, 6 June 1993.

Perry Mason: The Case of the Silenced Singer (1990). Second of the four new Mason feature movies; this time he proves that the killer of the warbler was *not* her husband. With Raymond Burr, Barbara Hale. Dir: Ron Satlof. BBC1, 13 June 1993.

The Price of Passion (1990). Mexican Mayor Victoria Principal finds the price is high when her night of love with a handsome stranger leads to blackmail – and worse. Dir: Richard A. Colla. ITV, 19 June 1993.

Prison for Children (1986). Moral story about a grim prison for young offenders, the caring but rule-bound superintendent, and the lad who brings things to a head. So-so. With John Ritter, Betty Thomas, Raphael Sharge etc. Dir: Larry Pearce. BBC1, 30 October 1992.

Prison Stories (1991). A good if grim trio of short films – all directed by women: *Parole Board*, with Lolita Davidovich etc. Dir: Joan Micklin Silver. *New Chicks*, with Rae Dawn Chong, Grace Zabriskie etc. Dir: Penelope Spheeris. *Esperanza*, with Rachel Ticotin, Talisa Soto etc. Dir: Donna Deitch. Commendable. Channel 4, 5 November 1992.

Promises to Keep (1985). Starring three generations of Mitchums (father Robert, son Christopher and grandson Bentley) – but otherwise not particularly interesting. Robert plays a dying rancher who decides to revisit his long-neglected family. Also with Claire Bloom. Dir: Noel Black. BBC1, 12 November 1992.

The Queen of Mean (1990). Apparently true story of a ruthlessly ambitious lady who earned herself this title during her rise to and fall from wealth and power. Very moral. With Suzanne Pleshette, Lloyd Bridges. BBC1 17 July 1992.

The Quick and the Dead (1987). Classic old-fashioned Western (with British star and director: Tom Conti and Robert Day) about the mysterious stranger who comes to the aid of bandit-plagued settlers. BBC2, 20 March 1993.

Quincy: A Star is Dead (1976). Jack Klugman (Quincy) suspects the actress who committed 'suicide' is actually a murder victim, and sorts out the suspects. Routine whodunnit. ITV, 30 August 1992.

Red River (1988). TV remake of the 1948 classic John Wayne Western, with James Arness in the big man's shoes and finding they almost fit. Quite good – but no real comparison. Dir: Richard Michaels. BBC2, 10 April 1993.

The Return of Maxwell Smart (1980). Incredibly bad feature spin-off from the TV series 'Get Smart'; shown in some cinemas under the title *The Nude Bomb*. Yes – it's about a new bomb which leaves everyone naked. With Don Adams, Sylvia Kristel (!). Dir: Clive Donner – Channel 4, 24 October 1992.

Rising Sun (1990). Family drama about the trauma suffered by a father when his job seems to be coming to an end and his son decides to give up his medical studies. Above average. With Brian Dennehy, Piper Laurie. Dir: John David Coles. BBC2, 12 October 1992.

Roxanne: The Prize Pulitzer (1988). True story of the high-profile divorce of the Pulitzers, the family who founded the famous literary prize. Presented without sympathy for anyone involved. With Chynna Philips, Perry King. Dir: Richard A. Colla. BBC2, 3 August 1992.

The Secret Garden (1987). Third screen version of Frances Hodgson Burnett's Victorian children's classic about an orphan, living with her uncle, who discovers a magical garden. Fascinating. With Michael Hordern, Billie Whitelaw, Derek Jacobi. Dir: Alan Grint. ITV, 20 July 1992.

Settle the Score (1989). Silly story about a city cop who returns to her home town where she was assaulted and raped twenty years before, grimly determined to settle the score. With Jaclyn Smith. Dir: Edwin Sherin. BBC1, 17 March 1993.

Sexpionage (1985). About a Russian Secret Service unit which teaches female beauties to become feminine Bonds. Amusingly daft. With Sally Kellerman, James Franciscus. Dir: Don Taylor. ITV, 14 April 1993.

Sexual Advances (1992). Outstanding drama about sexual harassment. In this case it nearly ruins a career and a marriage. Well acted; intelligently directed and written. Absorbing. With Stephanie Zimbalist, William Russ. Dir: Donna Deitch. Channel 4, 15 June 1993.

Shannon's Deal (1989). Excellent pilot for a regrettably short-lived series about a top-flight lawyer ruined by gambling and now clawing his way back up. Credible and consistently entertaining. With James Sheridan. Dir: Lewis Teague. BBC2, 8 February 1993.

Shattered Innocence (1988). Fictionalised story of porn star Shauna Grant, the out-of-town innocent who came to Hollywood with dreams of stardom but was sucked into a world of drugs, drink and pornography. Well made, but a bit lacking in punch. With Melinda Dillon, Jenna Lee, John Pleshette. Dir: Sandor Stern. BBC1, 6 November 1992.

Sins of the Mother (1991). Superior psychological thriller that leaves a vaguely unpleasant taste in the mouth. With Elizabeth Montgomery as the domineering mother of rapist son Dale Midkiff. Dir: John Patterson. BBC1, 13 November 1991.

Splash, Too (1988). A likely tail! The problems of a man and his mermaid wife living in New York: a sequel to the 1984 cinema film, which was much more fun. With Amy Yasbeck, Todd Waring. Dir: Greg Antonacci. ITV, 20 March 1993.

Stand By Your Man (1981). Biopic about country and western singer Tammy Wynette, based on her autobiography. With Annette O'Toole. Dir: Jerry Jameson. Channel 4, 20 August 1992.

Stones for Ibarra (1988). Glenn Close and Keith Carradine as the Americans who find some useful lessons about life are to be learned from the Mexican villagers among whom they live: polished, non-routine and superior TV feature. Dir: Jack Gold. BBC1, 11 December 1992.

Strange Voices (1987). Thoughtful TV feature about the problems faced by a caring mother (Valerie Harper) when her daughter (Nancy McKeon) is found to be a schizophrenic. Dir: Arthur Allan Seidelman. ITV, 19 April 1993.

Stranger on My Land (1988). Western in a modern setting: Vietnam veteran Tommy Lee Jones (excellent) fighting Uncle Sam's landgrabbing tactics. Dir: Larry Elkan. ITV, 10 March 1993.

Sunset Limousine (1983). Oddly titled American comedy with an English flavour (script and director) about an aspiring comic who accidentally becomes a gangster's target for tonight. Conventionally amusing. With John Ritter, Susan Dey. Dir: Terry W. Hughes. ITV, 17 October 1992.

Surviving. First-class acting from a first-class cast mitigates somewhat the grim story about teenage suicide and its effect on the parents. Compelling but depressing. With Ellen Burstyn, Paul Sorvino, Marsha Mason, River Phoenix. Dir: Waris Hussein. BBC1, 22 January 1993.

Sworn to Silence (1987). A topical and serious theme thoughtfully treated; should a lawyer stay silent if he finds some important evidence that puts his client in a new light? Well acted legal drama. With Peter Coyote. Dir: Peter Levin. BBC1, 17 June 1993.

Those She Left Behind (1989). Tear-jerking story about a husband having to bring up baby when the mother dies in childbirth. With Gary Cole, Joanne Kerns, Colleen Dewhurst. Dir: Waris Hussein. Channel 4, 3 February 1993.

Too Young To Die? (1990). Another 'based on fact' feature: an abused teenager kills her lover and then faces a legal struggle as to whether she should stand trial as an adult, with the consequent adult penalty. Only moderately interesting. With Juliette Lewis, Michael Tucker. Dir: Robert Markowitz. Channel 4, 24 September 1992.

The Trial of the Incredible Hulk (1989). Comic-strip stuff for the easily entertained. With Bill Bixby – who also directs. ITV, 12 June 1993.

Turbulence (1997). Telefilm about the topical and emotionally charged subject of child abuse. With Kelly Marcel. Dir: Adam Kossoff. Channel 4, 17 August 1992.

Turn Back the Clock (1989). Remake of the 1947 film *Repeat Performance*: about a wife who kills her husband and then explains what led up to the violence. With Connie Sellecca. Dir: Larry Ellikan. ITV, 28 December 1992.

The Undergrads (1983). A lovely performance by Art Carney gives an extra dimension to this Disney feature about a grandfather who goes back to college. Simple but delightful. Dir:

Steven Hilliard Stern. ITV, 14 December 1992.

The Water Engine (1992). When a man invents an engine that runs on water he doesn't realise what he's let himself in for, with sundry villains prepared to stop at nothing to get their hands on the secret. Excellent adaptation by David Mamet of his own hit stage play. With William Macy, Joe Mantegna, Charles Durning. Dir: Steven Schachter. Channel 4, 1 October 1992.

Weekend Reunion (1991). Mildly entertaining comedy about a US High School reunion. With Karin Kopins, Christopher Rich. Dir: Dick Lowry. BBC2, 20 July 1992.

When He's Not a Stranger (1989). Far-above-average TV feature about date-rape, with a good script, firm direction and an outstanding performance by Annabeth Gish (as the victim). This is one TV feature you'll never feel tempted to switch off. Dir: John Gray. BBC1, 9 October 1992.

Women and Men: Stories of Seduction (1990). Package of three short movies based on a trio of American writers' work about seduction and frustration. Casts include Beau

Bridges and Elizabeth McGovern (*The Man in the Brooks Brothers Suit*); Peter Weller and Molly Ringwald (*Dusk Before Fireworks*); and Melanie Griffith (*Hills Like White Elephants*). Dir: Frederic Raphael, Ken Russell and Tony Richardson respectively. Channel 4, 29 October 1992.

Women and Men 2: In Love There Are No Rules (1991). A three-story follow-up to the 1990 package, again variable in quality but well worth seeing. No. 1 is Irwin Shaw's story of a boxer forced into fighting by his wife; No. 2 is Carson McCullers's story of a drunken mother; No. 3 (by far the best of the trio) is based on a short story by Henry Miller about a love affair between a Parisian prostitute and an American writer. Cast includes (1) Matt Dillon as the fighter; (2) Andie MacDowell and Ray Liotta; and (3) Scott Glenn and Juliette Binoche. Good, adult watching. Dir: (1) Walter Bernstein, (2) Kristi Rea, (3) Mike Figgis. Channel 4, 22 June 1993.

Wonder Woman (1974). Feature spin-off from the popular series. Here she's helping the CIA to fight crime. Cartoonish but fun. With Cathy Lee Crosby. Dir: Vincent McEveety. ITV, 31 May 1993.

Video Releases

James Cameron-Wilson

(from July 1992 through to June 1993)

Afterburn Fact-based drama about a pilot's widow fighting to clear her husband's name. With Laura Dern (winner of the Golden Globe for her performance), Robert Loggia, Vincent Spano, Michael Rooker. Dir: Robert Markowitz. 15. November 1992 (New Age/Columbia Tri-Star).

After the Glory WW2 veterans fight racism and corruption back home in Texas. With Brad Johnson, Kathleen Quinlan, Josef Sommer, Tom Sizemore. Dir: John Gray. PG. October 1992 (Odyssey).

All-American Murder Pretentious, obvious shocker about a witty college student suspected of murder. With Christopher Walken, Charlie Schlatter, Josie Bissett, Joanna Cassidy. Dir: Anson Williams. 18. December 1992 (First Independent).

Ambition Lou Diamond Phillips wrote and stars in this dumb thriller about a hack novelist who befriends a serial killer in order to write about him. Also with Clancy Brown, Cecilia Peck, Richard Bradford. Dir: Scott D. Goldstein. 15. November 1992 (Columbia Tri-Star).

American Me Commanding, vivid and authentic look at three generations of a Mexican Mafia family. With Edward James Olmos, William Forsythe, Pepe Serna. Dir: Olmos. 18. January 1993 (CIC).

Another You Very thin comedy about a pathological liar and a street hustler. With Richard Pryor, Gene Wilder, Mercedes Ruehl, Stephen Lang, Vanessa Williams. Dir: Maurice Phillips. 15. August 1992 (20.20 Vision).

Are You Lonesome Tonight? A beautiful socialite teams up with a dumb detective to find out the tawdry truth about her vanished husband. With Jane Seymour, Parker Stevenson, Beth Broderick. Dir: E. W. Swackhamer. 15. August 1992 (CIC).

Article 99 Ray Liotta leads a team of renegade doctors to thwart government bureaucracy in this lightweight melodrama. With Kiefer Sutherland, Forest Whitaker, Lea Thompson, Kathy Baker, Eli Wallach. Dir: Howard Deutch. 15. April 1993 (20.20 Vision).

The Babe John Goodman stars as baseball legend George Herman 'Babe' Ruth in this agreeable biography. Also with Kelly McGillis, Trini Alvarado, Bruce Boxleitner. Dir: Arthur Hiller. PG. April 1993 (CIC Video).

Baby on Board Look who's talking to taxi driver Judge Reinhold, when a baby's left in the back seat of his New York cab. Also with Carol Kane. PG. February 1993 (First Independent).

No, No, Lolita: Drew Barrymore simmers in Beyond Control – The Amy Fisher Story

Baby Snatcher True story of a woman who fakes her pregnancy and then kidnaps a baby – to save her marriage. With Veronica Hamel, Nancy McKeon, Michael Madsen, David Duchovny. Dir: Joyce Chopra. PG. September 1992 (Odyssey).

Basic Deception When her husband disappears, Valerie turns sleuth to find out why. With Mark Harmon, Mimi Rogers, Paul Gleason, M. Emmet Walsh. Dir: Ivan Passer. 18. September 1992 (New Age Ent).

Becoming Colette Plodding period drama about the early life of novelist and socialite Sidonie Colette. With Klaus Maria Brandauer, Mathilda May, Virginia Madsen, Paul Rhys. Dir: Danny Huston. 18. October 1992 (Medusa).

The Berlin Conspiracy Missing the Cold War by a ton of bricks, this inept actioner cashes in on the collapse of the Berlin Wall to little effect. With Marc Singer, Mary Crosby, Stephen Davies, Dir: Terence H. Winkless. 18. August 1992 (Columbia Tri-Star).

Beyond Control – The Amy Fisher Story Taken from court records and reporters' notes, this small-screen document is just one of three indifferent films about the 17-year-old girl from Long Island who shot her 38-year-old lover's wife. With Drew Barrymore, Anthony John Denison, Harley Jane Kozak. Dir: Andy Tennant. 15. March 1993 (Odyssey).

Bingo Moronic 'family' adventure about a boy and the smart dog he can't keep. With Cindy Williams, David Rasche, Robert J. Steinmiller Jr. Dir: Matthew Robbins. PG. March 1993 (20.20 Vision).

Black Magic Routine supernatural comedy in which Judge Reinhold is bewitched by his late cousin's girlfriend. Also with Rachel Ward, Anthony LaPaglia. Dir: Daniel Taplitz. 15. March 1993 (CIC).

Blood and Sand Sexed-up version of the old Rudolph Valentino melo in which a bullfighter is torn between his love for his wife and femme fatale Sharon Stone. Also with Christopher Rydell, Ana Torrent. Dir: Javier Elorrieta. 18. May 1993 (Hi-Fliers).

Bonds of Love Protracted TV movie based on a real incident in which a twice-married woman seduced a retarded man from a protective Kansas family. Good acting. With Treat Williams, Kelly McGillis, Steve Railsback, Hal Holbrook, Grace Zabriskie. Dir: Larry Elikann. 15. March 1993 (Odyssey).

Bonnie & Clyde – The True Story Realistic look at real-life gangsters. With Dana Ashbrook, Tracey Needham. 15. October 1992 (Fox-Video).

Brain Donors Marx Bros-inspired farce about three idiots who try to cheat a wealthy widow. A.k.a. *Lame Ducks*. With John Turturro, Bob Nelson, Mel Smith, Nancy Marchand, George De La Pena. Dir: Dennis Dugan. PG. December 1992 (CIC).

The Burden of Proof Slow-moving legal drama based on Scott Turow's complex second novel. With Brian Dennehy, Hector Elizondo, Mel Harris, Adrienne Barbeau, Stefanie Powers, Victoria Principal. Dir: Mike Robe. 15. August 1992 (Odyssey).

Christmas in Connecticut Remake of the 1945 Barbara Stanwyck comedy, with Dyan Cannon a TV cook forced to fabricate a happy, domestic Christmas for the cameras. Also with Kris Kristofferson, Tony Curtis, Richard Roundtree. Dir: Arnold Schwarzenegger. U. December 1992 (First Independent).

Citizen Cohn James Woods at the top of his form as the lawyer and witch-hunter Roy Cohn in this distinguished, hard-edged TV movie. Also with Joe Don Baker, Lee Grant, Joseph Bologna, Ed Flanders, Frederic Forrest, Pat Hingle. Dir: Frank Pierson. 15. May 1993 (Warner).

Company Business Silly spy comedy with Gene Hackman and Mikhail Baryshnikov as outmoded CIA and KGB agents forced to run for cover. Also with Kurtwood Smith, Terry O'Quinn. Dir: Nicholas Meyer. 15. August 1992 (Warner).

The Comrades of Summer Joe Mantegna is hired to coach a Russian Olympic baseball team when he's fired from his own. Unfunny, routine and mechanical. Also with Natalya Negoda, Michael Lerner. Dir: Tommy Lee Wallace. 15. February 1993 (New Age Entertainment/Columbia Tri-Star).

Crash Landing: Flight 232 True-life drama about a crack rescue firefighting and medical team. With Charlton Heston, Richard Thomas, James Coburn, Leon Russom. Dir: Lamont Johnson. PG. August 1992 (Braveworld).

Crazy in Love Well-intentioned but somewhat precious look at three generations of women at odds with their menfolk. With Holly Hunter, Gena Rowlands, Frances McDormand, Bill Pullman, Julian Sands, Herta Ware. Dir: Martha Coolidge. PG. March 1993 (First Independent).

Criminal Behavior Fast-paced,

well-acted corkscrew thriller starring Farrah Fawcett as a tough defence attorney. Also with A. Martinez, Dakin Matthews. Dir: Michael Miller. PG. December 1992 (Braveworld).

Criss Cross Slow-moving melo about a waitress who turns stripper to support her 12-year-old son. With Goldie Hawn, Arliss Howard, James Gammon, Keith Carradine, Steve Buscemi. Dir: Chris Menges. 15. November 1992 (MGM/UA).

Crooked Hearts Tensions run deep in a dysfunctional American family. With Vincent D'Onofrio, Jennifer Jason Leigh, Peter Berg, Peter Coyote, Juliette Lewis. Dir: Michael Bortman. 15. July 1992 (MGM/UA).

A Day in October Engrossing portrayal of the 1943 evacuation of Danish Jews to Sweden. With D. B. Sweeney, Kelly Wolf, Tovah Feldshuh. Dir: Kenneth Madsen. 15. June 1993 (Hi-Fliers).

Defenseless Wildly improbable murder mystery about an attorney defending the wife of her murdered lover. With Barbara Hershey, Sam Shepard, Mary Beth Hurt, J. T. Walsh. Dir: Martin Campbell. 18. November 1992 (FoxVideo).

Delirious Achingly unfunny comedy about a soap writer who enters his own, poorly written world. With John Candy, Mariel Hemingway, Emma Samms, Raymond Burr. Dir: Tom Mankiewicz. PG. September 1992 (MGM/UA).

Desperate Choices: Save My Child See *Solomon's Choice*.

Devlin Tough, atmospheric conspiracy thriller set in New York. With Bryan Brown, Roma Downey, Lloyd Bridges, Lisa Eichhorn, Jan Rubes. Dir: Rick Rosenthal. 18. October 1992 (Columbia Tri-Star).

Dirty Tricks Well-acted but lukewarm comedy in which an outspoken children's author is courted by a presidential candidate. US title: *Running Mates*. With Diane Keaton, Ed Harris, Ed Begley Jr, Ben Masters, Russ Tamblyn. Dir: Michael Lindsay-Hogg. 15. May 1993 (Warner).

Doing Time on Maple Drive Gripping drama rattling a deep closet of family skeletons as a dysfunctional clan prepares for a wedding. With James B. Sikking, Bibi Besch, William McNamara, Lori Loughlin. Dir: Ken Olin. PG. September 1992 (Fox-Video).

Falling from Grace Absorbing look at life in midwestern America as a country singer returns to his roots. With John Mellencamp, Kay Lenz, Mariel Hemingway, Claude Akins. Dir: Mellencamp. 15. October 1992 (Columbia Tri-Star).

Fatal Love True-life drama of an upper-middle-class, heterosexual AIDS victim. US title: *Something to Live For – The Alison Gertz Story*. With Molly Ringwald, Lee Grant, Martin Landau, Perry King. Dir: Tom McLoughlin. 15. October 1992 (Odyssey).

Father and Son Louis Gossett Jr and Blair Underwood star as estranged father and son who must combine forces to fight a white supremacist group. Also with Rae Dawn Chong, Tony Plana, David Harris. Dir: Georg Stanford Brown. 18. December 1992 (Columbia Tri-Star/New Age Entertainment).

The Fear Inside Terrifying thriller in which an agoraphobic takes in two psycho lodgers. With Christine Lahti, Dylan McDermott, Jennifer Rubin. Dir: Leon Ichaso. 15. January 1993 (Medusa).

The Finest Hour At last: the first action-romance set during the Gulf War. With Rob Lowe, Tracy Griffith, Gale Hansen. Dir: Shimon Dotan. 15. January 1993 (20.20 Vision).

Fugitive Among Us Hard-hitting, believable drama about a Texas cop on the trail of a rapist. Music by Stewart Copeland. With Peter Strauss, Eric Roberts, Elizabeth Pena, Lauren Holly. Dir: Michael Toshiyuki Uno. 15. September 1992 (Odyssey).

The Great Diamond Robbery Released from prison, an infamous jewel thief is employed to test the security system protecting the world's biggest diamond. With Brian Den-

nehy, Ben Cross, Kate Nelligan. Dir: Al Waxman. 15. May 1993 (20.20 Vision).

Gun Crazy Violent, colourful thriller about two gun-toting young lovers on the run. With Drew Barrymore, James LeGros, Billy Drago, Michael Ironside, Ione Skye. Dir: Tamra Davis. 15. October 1992 (Medusa).

The Gun in Betty Lou's Handbag Wallflower Penelope Ann Miller shakes up her husband, friends and colleagues when she steals a gun and pretends to be a killer – much to the consternation of sadistic gangster William Forsythe. Also with Eric Thal, Alfre Woodard, Julianne Moore, Cathy Moriarty. Dir: Allan Moyle. 15. June 1993 (Touchstone Home Video).

Heaven Is a Playground Captivating look at the tough universe of ghetto basketball, well-pitched by a top-notch cast. With D. B. Sweeney, Michael Warren, Richard Jordan, Victor Love. Dir: Randall Fried. 15. June 1993 (20.20 Vision).

Immortal Sins Sex and spectres collide in a Spanish castle in this okay chiller. With Cliff De Young, Maryam D'Abo. 15. September 1992 (20.20 Vision).

In the Deep Woods Predictable chiller in which children's author Rosanna Arquette is terrorised by a serial killer. Also with Anthony Perkins, Will Patton, D. W. Moffett, Chris Rydell. Dir: Charles Correll. 15. June 1993 (Columbia Tri-Star).

Into the Badlands Three-part macabre western about a bounty hunter on the trail of a killer. With Bruce Dern, Mariel Hemingway, Dylan McDermott, Helen Hunt. Dir: Sam Pillsbury. 15. September 1992 (CIC).

Into the Sun Action-comedy about a method actor researching the role of a fighter pilot. With Anthony Michael Hall, Michael Paré, Deborah Maria Moore, Terry Kiser. Dir: Fritz Kiersch. 15. October 1992 (First Independent).

Intruders Richard Crenna stars as a psychiatrist whose patients claim

Desperately seeking Green Card: *Rosanna Arquette and David Bowie in* The Linguini Incident

they're the victims of UFO abductions in this suspenseful sci-fier. Also with Mare Winningham, Susan Blakely, Daphne Ashbrook, Ben Vereen, Steven Berkoff. Dir: Dan Curtis. 15. February 1993 (FoxVideo).

The Last of His Tribe Moving true story about a Yahi Indian who becomes a museum piece when he joins the civilised world in 1911. With Jon Voight, Graham Greene, Anne Archer. Dir: Harry Hook. 15. November 1992 (New Age/20.20 Vision).

Leaving Normal Two women take to the road in this poignant comedy enhanced by a sterling performance from Christine Lahti. Also with Meg Tilly, Lenny Von Dohlen, Maury Chaykin. Dir: Edward Zwick. PG. November 1992 (CIC).

Lies of the Twins Familiar drama about the good twin and his psychotic other, and this time they're zoning in on a top fashion model. With Aidan Quinn, Isabella Rossellini, Iman, Claudia Christian, Hurd Hatfield. Dir: Tim Hunter. 15. July 1992 (CIC).

The Linguini Incident Oh dear, another oddball comedy about eccentric New Yorkers falling in and out of love and crime. This one looks so concocted that you can see the cooking ingredients floating to the top. However, the dialogue *is* witty and Andre Gregory and Buck Henry are hilarious. Also with Rosanna Arquette, David Bowie, Marlee Matlin. Dir: Richard Shepard. 15. April 1993 (20.20 Vision).

Livewire Political thriller about a bomb expert up against a crazed terrorist. With Pierce Brosnan, Ben Cross, Ron Silver, Lisa Eilbacher, Brent Jennings. Dir: Christian Duguay. 15. November 1991 (Entertainment in Video).

Lonely Hearts Absorbing drama in which a con man meets his match when he zones in on a manic-obsessive loner. With Beverly D'Angelo, Eric Roberts, Joanna Cassidy, Herta Ware. Dir: Andrew Lane. 15. July 1992 (First Independent).

Miracle in the Wilderness God-awful preachy western about a frontier couple captured by Indians. With Kris Kristofferson, Kim Cattral, John Dennis Johnston. Dir: Kevin James Dobson. PG. September 1992 (First Independent).

Money Talks Monte Carlo-set Graham Greene comedy reduced to banality. A.k.a. *Loser Takes All* and *Strike It Rich*. With Robert Lindsay, Molly Ringwald, John Gielgud, Margi Clarke, Michel Blanc. Dir: James Scott. PG. September 1992 (20.20 Vision).

Mystery Date Surprising, darkly humorous teen romance in which a timid Ethan Hawke is mistaken for his ne'er-do-well older brother while on a dream date. Also with Teri Polo, Brian McNamara, Fisher Stevens, D. B. Wong. Dir: Jonathan Wacks. 15. February 1993 (20.20 Vision).

Nails A renegade cop avenges the death of his partner in this hackneyed thriller. With Dennis Hopper, Anne Archer, Tomas Milian, Keith David, Cliff DeYoung. Dir: John Flynn. 18. September 1992 (Medusa).

The Nutcracker Prince Stylish cartoon version of the Hoffman fairy tale *The Nutcracker and the Mouseking*, complete with Tchaikovsky score. Voices of: Kiefer Sutherland, Megan Follows, Peter O'Toole, Phyllis Diller. Dir: Paul Schibli. U. August 1992 (Entertainment in Video).

The Opposite Sex Standard and somewhat twee look at the battle of the sexes. With Arye Gross, Courtney Cox, Kevin Pollak, Julie Brown. Dir: Matthew Meshekoff. 15. February 1993 (Guild).

Over the Hill A 60-year-old American widow discovers a new life in Australia when she goes to visit her daughter in this whimsical, unremarkable comedy. With Olympia Dukakis,

Sigrid Thornton, Derek Fowlds, Bill Kerr. Dir: George Miller. PG. February 1993 (20.20 Vision).

Passed Away Lively, unexpected and well-acted black comedy centring on the funeral of the patriarch of an eccentric family. With Bob Hoskins, Jack Warden, William Petersen, Maureen Stapleton, Pamela Reed, Tim Curry, Blair Brown, Nancy Travis. Dir: Charlie Peters. 15. April 1993 (Buena Vista).

Past Midnight Rutger Hauer may or may not be a wrongly convicted psycho in this weak 'erotic thriller'. Also with Natasha Richardson, Clancy Brown, Guy Boyd. Dir: Jan Eliasberg. 15. August 1992 (Guild).

Paydirt Buried treasure in American suburbia sparks a finding frenzy in this daft comedy. With Jeff Daniels, Catherine O'Hara, Dabney Coleman, Rhea Perlman. Dir: Bill Phillips. 15. April 1993 (20.20 Vision).

Payoff Fast-moving revenge thriller involving an ex-cop and the Mafia. With Keith Carradine, Kim Greist, Harry Dean Stanton, John Saxon. Dir: Stuart Cooper. 15. October 1992 (Medusa).

Poison Ivy Deliciously tacky story of a precocious teenager who seduces her way through a wealthy Californian family. Drew Barrymore, Sara Gilbert, Tom Skerritt, Cheryl Ladd. Dir: Katt Shea Ruben. 18. March 1993 (Guild).

Power Play: The Jackie Presser Story More corruption in the unions as Brian Dennehy's Presser cheats and murders his way to the top in this inflated, unsurprising biopic. US title: *Teamster Boss: The Jackie Presser Story.* Also with Jeff Daniels, Maria Conchita Alonso, Eli Wallach, Robert Prosky, Tony LoBianco, Kate Reid. Dir: Alastair Reid. 15. May 1993 (Warner).

A Private Matter A mother of four contemplates abortion after taking thalidomide. An exceptionally astute, moving drama based on the real-life 1962 scandal. With Sissy Spacek, Aidan Quinn, Estelle Parsons, Sheila McCarthy. Dir: Joan Micklin Silver. PG. January 1993 (New Age Entertainment/Columbia Tri-Star).

Pure Luck Pleasant US remake of the French farce *La Chèvre* – about an accident-prone geek in Mexico. With Martin Short, Danny Glover, Sheila Kelley, Sam Wanamaker, Scott Wilson. Dir: Nadia Tass. PG. September 1992 (CIC).

Pyrates Designer-weird love-hate sex comedy in which a trendy photographer and a classical cellist start fires whenever they make love. The film frantically strives to be original, and does have some genuine comic moments, but lacks enough narrative momentum to keep our interest. With Kevin Bacon, Kyra Sedgwick, Bruce Payne. Dir: Noah Stern. 18. January 1993 (Columbia Tri-Star).

Queens Logic In this starry drama, old friends reunite for a wedding in Queens, New York. With Kevin Bacon, Linda Fiorentino, John Malkovich, Joe Mantegna, Ken Olin, Tom Waits, Jamie Lee Curtis. Dir: Steve Rash. 15. July 1992 (FoxVideo).

Quicksand: No Escape Plodding thriller about a blackmailed architect. With Donald Sutherland, Tim Matheson, Jay Acavone. Dir: Michael Pressman. PG. October 1992 (CIC).

Revenge of Billy the Kid Old MacDonald had a farm and on that farm he had a goat. Literally. And it is

Playing with fire: Kevin Bacon and Bruce Payne in Noah Stern's unusual Pyrates

this act of drunken bestiality that is his downfall. Reminiscent of a cheap, artless spoof of Monty Python, the film deserves a place in some record book for the number of obscenities it celebrates. With Michael Balfour, Samantha Perkins, Jackie D. Broad, Dean Williamson. Dir: Jim Groom. 18. July 1992 (Medusa).

Running Mates See *Dirty Tricks*.

Samantha Off-kilter comedy about a 21-year-old in search of her real parents – and herself. With Martha Plimpton, Dermot Mulroney, Hector Elizondo, Mary Kay Place, Ione Skye. Dir: Stephen La Rocque. 15. January 1993 (First Independent).

Secrets Danielle Steel melodrama set in the world of TV soap opera. With Christopher Plummer, Stephanie Beacham, Linda Purl, Gary Collins: Dir: Peter H. Hunt. 15. September 1992 (VPD).

Seduction Erotic thriller about a female serial killer. With Victoria Principal, John Terry, Andreas Katsulas. Dir: Michael Ray Rhodes. 18. October 1992 (New Age Entertainment/20.20 Vision).

Shout 1950s rock 'n' roll fantasy that failed to jump-start John Travolta's musical career. Also with Heather Graham, Richard Jordan, Linda Fiorentino. Dir: Jeffrey Hornaday. PG. August 1992 (CIC).

The Sinking of the Rainbow Warrior Finger-pointing reconstruction of the bombing of the Greenpeace ship in New Zealand. With Sam Neill, Jon Voight, Bruno Lawrence, Kerry Fox. Dir: Michael Tuchner. PG. April 1993 (20.20 Vision).

Solomon's Choice Capable heart-render about a daughter dying of leukaemia. US title: *Desperate Choices: Save My Child.* With Joanna Kerns, Bruce Davison, Reese Witherspoon, Joseph Mazzello, J. D. Hall. Dir: Andrew Tennant. PG. January 1993 (Odyssey).

Something to Live For – The Alison Gertz Story See *Fatal Love.*

Stalin Industrious but unconvincing and muddled portrait of the Russian leader spanning the years 1917 to 1973. With Robert Duvall, Julia Ormond, Maximilian Schell, Jeroen Krabbe, Joan Plowright, Frank Finlay, Roshan Seth, Daniel Massey. Dir: Ivan Passer. May 1993 (Warner).

The Super A ruthless slumlord is forced to live in one of his own decrepit apartment blocks in this OTT farce. With Joe Pesci, Vincent Gardenia, Madolyn Smith Osborne, Ruben Blades, Stacey Travis. Dir: Rod Daniel. 15. October 1922 (FoxVideo).

Sweet Talker Beguiling, old-fashioned Australian comedy from a story by Bryan Brown, who plays the conman of the title. Also with Karen Allen, Chris Haywood, Bill Kerr, Bruce Spence. Dir: Michael Jenkins. PG. August 1992 (FoxVideo).

Tales from the Crypt, Volume 3 Compilation of macabre stories featuring Demi Moore, William Hickey, Kelly Preston, Lance Henriksen and Kevin Tighe. 18. January 1993 (Warner).

A Taste for Killing Michael Biehn – on chilling form – terrorises wealthy students Henry Thomas and Jason Bateman in this diverting action-thriller. Dir: Lou Antonio. 15. April 1993 (CIC).

Teamster Boss: The Jackie Presser Story See *Power Play: The Jackie Presser Story.*

Triumph of the Heart: The True Story of Ricky Bell Workmanlike true-life tearjerker about a football star aiding the recovery of a disabled young boy. With Mario Van Peebles, Polly Holliday, Susan Ruttan, Lynn Whitfield, Lane Davis. Dir: Richard Michaels. U. December 1992 (Odyssey).

Trouble Bound Ex-con Michael Madsen (*Reservoir Dogs*) gives enigmatic Patricia Arquette a lift and finds himself on the run from the Mob. Good value. Also with Seymour Cassel. Dir: Jeffrey Reiner. 18. March 1993 (ITC).

Vendetta The New York and Sicilian Mafia battle for power while Carol Alt unwittingly marries her father's executioner. Also with Eric Roberts, Burt Young, Nick Mancuso, Eli Wallach. Dir: Stuart Margolin. 15. August 1992 (20.20 Vision).

Victimised Exploitative thriller about a serial killer knocking off the staple diet of America's porn industry. Previously known as *Calendar Girl Murders* and first shown on TV in 1984. With Sharon Stone, Tom Skerritt, Robert Morse, Robert Culp. Dir: William A. Graham. 18. January 1993 (Rio).

Whispers in the Dark Ridiculous psychological thriller in which shrink Annabella Sciorra finds herself turned on by the sexual revelations of a patient, leading to murder and endless talk. Also with Jamey Sheridan, Anthony LaPaglia, Jill Clayburgh, John Leguizamo, Deborah Unger, Alan Alda. Dir: Christopher Crowe. 18. June 1993 (Paramount/CIC).

White Lie Compelling race drama starring Gregory Hines as press secretary of NY Mayor David Dinkins, who goes south to discover the truth about his father's lynching. Also with Annette O'Toole, Bill Nunn, Gregg Henry. Dir: Bill Condon. 15. July 1992 (CIC).

Wild Hearts Can't Be Broken Charming, old-fashioned family tearjerker about a beautiful runaway who dreams of high-diving horses in a travelling carnival. With Gabrielle Anwar, Michael Schoeffling, Cliff Robertson. Dir: Steve Miner. U. April 1993 (Buena Vista).

Other Video Releases:

Alan and Naomi. With Lukas Haas, Vanessa Zaoui, Michael Gross. PG. April 1993 (Columbia Tri-Star).

Almost Pregnant. With Tanya Roberts, Joan Severence, Jeff Conaway, Dom DeLuise. 18. May 1993 (Columbia Tri-Star).

American Ninja 5. With David Bradley, Pat Morita. 18. June 1993 (Warner).

American Samurai. With David Bradley. 18. March 1993 (Warner).

Amityville 1992: It's About Time. With Stephen Macht. 18. October 1992 (FoxVideo).

And the Violins Stopped Playing. With Horst Buchholz. 15. May 1993 (Odyssey).

And You Thought Your Parents Were Weird. With Joshua Miller, Marcia Strassman. PG. July 1992 (First Independent).

Angel of Fury. With Cynthia Rothrock, Billy Drago, Sam Jones. 18. May 1993 (Columbia Tri-Star).

Angel Street. With Robin Givens, Pamela Gidley. March 1993 (Warner).

Animal Instincts. With Maxwell Caulfield, David Carradine. 18. November 1992 (20.20 Vision).

Animal Instincts 2. With Nick Cassavetes, Sandahl Bergman, Don Swayze, Richard Roundtree. 18. June 1993 (Columbia Tri-Star).

The Art of Dying. With Wings Hauser, Michael J. Pollard, Kathleen Kinmont, Sarah Douglas. 18. December 1992 (VPD).

Bad Channels. With Martha Quinn, Aaron Lustig, Charlie Spradling. November 1992 (CIC).

Basket Case 3: The Progeny. With Annie Ross. 18. October 1992 (Braveworld).

Beach Beverly Hills. With Glorio Pryor. 18. March 1993 (20.20 Vision/New Age Entertainment).

Bebe's Kids. Cartoon. May 1993 (CIC).

The Bikini Carwash Company. With Joe Dusic, Neriah Nepaul. 18. August 1992 (Medusa).

Bikini Island. With Hannon Styles. 18. September 1992 (Rio).

Black Death. With Kate Jackson, Al Waxman. 15. April 1993 (Imperial Entertainment).

Blind Man's Bluff. With Robert Urich, Lisa Eilbacher, Ron Perlman. 15. October 1992 (CIC).

Blood Love. With Dawn Wells, Paul Bartel, Griffin O'Neal. 18. June 1993 (Hi-Fliers).

Blood Ties. With Harley Newton, Patrick Bauchau, Bo Hopkins. 15. April 1993 (Braveworld).

Blown Away. With Corey Haim, Corey Feldman. 18. June 1993 (20.20 Vision).

Blue Tornado. With Dirk Benedict, Patsy Kensit, David Warner. 15. December 1992 (20.20 Vision).

Body Chemistry 2. With Lisa Pescia. 18. September 1992 (20.20 Vision).

Body Language. With Heather Locklear, Linda Purl. 15. February 1993 (CIC).

Broken Cord. With Jimmy Smits, Kim Delaney. PG. February 1993 (CIC).

Buford's Beach Bunnies. With Jim Hanks. 18. March 1993 (Imperial Entertainment).

Can It Be Love. With Charles Klausmeyer. 18. May 1993 (Hi-Fliers).

Child of Rage. With Mel Harris, Dwight Schultz, Mariette Hartley. 15. January 1993 (Odyssey).

Children of the Corn 2: The Final Sacrifice. With Terence Knox. 18. December 1992 (Hi-Fliers).

Child's Play 3. With Justin Whalin. 18. October 1992 (CIC).

Chopper Chicks in Zombie Town. With Don Calfa. 18. September 1992 (Troma).

Chrome Soldiers. With Gary Busey, Yaphet Kotto, William Atherton. 15. January 1993 (CIC).

Class Act. With Christopher Reid. 15. January 1993 (Warner Home Video).

Class Cruise. With Shelley Fabares, Billy Warlock. PG. September 1992 (Columbia Tri-Star).

Cool as Ice. With Vanilla Ice, Michael Gross, Candy Clark, Naomi Campbell. PG. December 1992 (CIC).

Sam Gifadi and Mel Harris in Larry Peerce's shocking true story, Child of Rage

Coopersmith: Sweet Scent of Murder. With Grant Show. 15. January 1993 (CIC).

Critters 3. With Don Opper. 15. September 1992 (Entertainment in Video).

Critters 4. With Don Opper. 15. January 1993 (Entertainment in Video).

Cyborg Cop. With David Bradley, John Rhys-Davies. 18. May 1993 (Medusa).

Dance of Death. With Barbara Alyn Woods, Maxwell Caulfield. 18. July 1992 (CIC).

Dangerous Game. With Carmen Di Pietro. 18. April 1993 (Rio).

Darkness Before Dawn. With Meredith Baxter, Stephen Lang. 15. June 1993 (Odyssey).

Dark Rider. With Joe Estevez. 15. August 1992 (20.20 Vision).

Da Vinci's War. With Michael Nouri, Joey Travolta, Vanity. 18. March 1993 (20.20 Vision/New Age Entertainment).

Dead Bolt. With Justine Bateman, Adam Baldwin, Chris Mulkey. 15. April 1993 (First Independent).

Dead in the Water. With Bryan Brown, Teri Hatcher. 15. July 1992 (CIC).

Deadly. 15. February 1993 (Hi-Fliers).

Deadly Relations. With Robert Urich, Shelley Fabares, Roxana Zal. 15. May 1993 (CIC).

Death Ring. With Billy Drago, Mike Norris, Don Swayze, Chad McQueen. 18. June 1993 (Hi-Fliers).

Deliver Us from Evil. With Nikki de Boer. 18. February 1993 (Hi-Fliers).

Delta Heat. With Anthony Edwards, Lance Henriksen. May 1993 (EV).

Devil in the Flesh. With Tracy Ray. 18. May 1993 (Rio).

Dirty Work. With Kevin Dobson, John Ashton. 15. February 1993 (CIC).

Doctor Mordrid. With Jeffrey Combs, Brian Thompson. 15. December 1992 (CIC).

Doppelganger. With Drew Barrymore, George Newbern. 18. February 1993 (ITC).

Double Vision. 18. February 1993 (20.20 Vision).

Dream Rider. With James Earl Jones, Leigh Taylor Young. U. April 1993 (First Independent).

Driving Me Crazy. With Billy Dee Williams, Dom DeLuise, Milton Berle. PG. November 1992 (Columbia Tri-Star).

Duplicates. With Gregory Harrison, Cicely Tyson, Lane Smith, William Lucking. 15. December 1992 (CIC).

Eerie, Indiana. With Omri Katz, Justin Shenkarow. PG. July 1992 (Braveworld).

Elvis & the Colonel: The Untold Story. With Beau Bridges, Rob Youngblood, Dan Shor. 15. April 1993 (Columbia Tri-Star).

The Erotic Adventures of the Three Musketeers. With Scott Callegos. 18. December 1992.

Excessive Force. With Thomas Ian Griffith, Lance Henriksen, James Earl Jones, Charlotte Lewis, Tony Todd, Burt Young. 18. January 1993 (Entertainment in Video).

Exiled. With Edward Albert, Maxwell Caulfield. 18. June 1993 (20.20 Vision).

Eyes of the Beholder. With Matt McCoy, Joanna Pacula, Charles Napier. 18. June 1993 (20.20 Vision).

Final Approach. With James B. Sikking, Hector Elizondo, Madolyn Smith, Kevin McCarthy. 15. April 1993 (Hi-Fliers).

Final Impact. With Lorenzo Lamas. 18. October 1992 (20.20 Vision).

Final Pulse. With Denis Arndt, Mark Blum. 15. April 1993 (Warner).

The Flash 3 – Deadly Nightshade. With Amanda Pays. PG. October 1992 (Warner).

Forgotten Prisoners. With Ron Silver, Roger Daltrey. 15. July 1992 (First Independent).

Frogs. With Scott Grimes, Paul Williams. U. July 1992 (Warner).

Hard Hunted. With Dona Speir. 15. June 1993 (20.20 Vision).

The Heart of the Lie. With Timothy Busfield, Lindsay Frost, Linda Blair, John Karlen. 15. December 1992 (Odyssey).

Highlander: The Gathering. With Christopher Lambert, Richard Moll. 15. March 1993 (Entertainment in Video).

Highlander: Freefall. May 1993 (EV).

Honour Thy Mother. With Sharon Gless, William McNamara, Brian Wimmer. 15. January 1993 (CIC).

Hot Laps. With Paul Green. 18. March 1993 (Rip Pictures).

A House of Secrets and Lies. With Connie Sellecca, Kevin Dobson. 15. June 1993 (Warner).

House Party II: The Pajama Jam. With Full Force, Tisha Campbell, Iman, Queen Latifah, Georg Stanford Brown. 15. December 1992 (First Independent).

Illusions. With Robert Carradine, Heather Locklear, Emma Samms, Ned Beatty. 15. April 1993 (CIC).

In the Arms of a Killer. With Jaclyn Smith, John Spencer, Michael Nouri. February 1993 (Warner).

In Excess. With Joanna Pacula, Julian Sands. 18. May 1993 (New Age Entertainment/20.20 Vision).

In the Heat of Passion. With Sally Kirkland, Nick Corri. 18. April 1993 (20.20 Vision).

In the Shadow of a Killer. With Scott Bakula, Lindsay Frost, Miguel Ferrer. PG. November 1992 (Odyssey).

Indecency. With Jennifer Beals, Barbara Williams, James Remar, Sammi Davis-Voss. 15. June 1993 (Universal/CIC).

Indio 2. With Marvellous Marvin, Jacqueline Carol. 15. August 1992 (FoxVideo).

Innocent Young Female. With Ray Sharkey, David Keith, Deborah May, Loretta Devine, Karen Black. 18. January 1993 (New Age Entertainment/20.20 Vision).

Inside Out. 18. December 1992 (20.20 Vision).

Intimate Obsession. 18. March 1993 (Columbia Tri-Star).

Invasion of Privacy. With Robby Benson, Jennifer O'Neill. 18. January 1993 (Hi-Fliers).

Keeping Secrets. With Suzanne Somers, Michael Learned, Ken Kercheval. PG. October 1992 (CIC).

Killer Image. With Michael Ironside, M. Emmet Walsh. 18. August 1992 (First Independent).

Killer Rules. With Jamey Sheridan, Sela Ward, Sam Wanamaker, Peter Dobson. 15. April 1993 (Warner).

The Killer's Edge. With Wings Hauser, Robert Z'Dar, Karen Black. 18. February 1993 (Imperial Entertainment).

The Killing Zone. With James Delasandro. 18. September 1992 (VPD).

Kung Fu – A Legend Reborn. With David Carradine. January 1993 (Warner).

Lady Boss. With Kim Delaney, Jack Scalia, Joe Cortese. 15. February 1993 (Odyssey).

Lady Dragon. With Cynthia Rothrock, Richard Norton, Robert Ginty. 18. August 1992 (20.20 Vision).

Lady Killer. With Mimi Rogers, John Shea. 15. June 1993 (Universal/CIC).

LA Goddess. With Kathy Shower, Jeff Conaway, Joe Estevez, David Heavener. 18. April 1993 (20.20 Vision).

The Land of Faraway. With Timothy Bottoms, Christopher Lee, Susannah York. U. August 1992 (Columbia Tri-Star).

Lapse of Memory. With John Hurt. PG. June 1993 (Columbia Tri-Star).

The Last Prostitute. With Sonia Braga, Wil Wheaton. 15. September 1992 (CIC).

Legacy of Lies. With Eli Wallach, Martin Landau, Michael Ontkean. 15. March 1993 (CIC).

Liar, Liar. With Kate Nelligan, Art Hindle. 15. June 1993 (Odyssey).

Liar's Edge. With Shannon Tweed, David Keith, Joseph Bottoms. 18. March 1993 (Hi-Fliers).

Liquid Dreams. With Richard Steinmetz, Mink Stole. 18. November 1992 (Hi-Fliers).

Lost in Time. With Bruce Campbell, Martin Kemp, Patrick Macnee. 15. August 1992 (Entertainment in Video).

Lower Level. With David Bradley. 15. October 1992 (CIC).

Maniac Cop 3: Badge of Silence. With Robert Davi, Robert Z'Dar. 18. February 1993 (Medusa).

A Message from Holly. With Shelley Long, Lindsay Wagner. PG. May 1993 (Odyssey).

Midnight Heat. With Michael Paré, Adam Ant, Dennis Hopper, Charlie Schlatter. 18. June 1993 (First Independent).

Midnight Ride. With Michael Dudikoff, Mark Hamill, Robert Mitchum. 18. November 1992 (Warner).

Mind, Body & Soul. With Ginger Lynn Allen, Wings Hauser. 18. November 1992 (Rio).

Miracle Beach. With Ami Dolenz, Alexis Arquette, Pat Morita. 15.

November 1992 (Columbia Tri-Star).

Mission of Justice. With Jeff Wincott, Brigitte Nielsen. 18. March 1993 (First Independent).

Naked Truth. With Bruce Thompson, Bubba Smith, Erik Estrada, Yvonne De Carlo, Zsa Zsa Gabor. 15. November 1992 (20.20 Vision).

Nasty Boy 3: Crack House. With Craig Hurley, Dennis Franz. 15. November 1992 (CIC).

Nickel and Dime. With C. Thomas Howell, Wallace Shawn, Lise Cutter. PG. June 1993 (20.20 Vision).

Night Hunt. With Stefanie Powers, Helen Shaver. 15. June 1993 (Medusa).

Night Rhythms. With Martin Hewitt, Sam Jones, Delia Sheppard, David Carradine. 18. January 1993 (Medusa).

Night Visions. With James Remar. March 1993 (MGM/UA).

Notorious. With John Shea, Jenny Robertson, Jean-Pierre Cassel, Marisa Berenson. 15. July 1992 (Guild).

Obsessed. With William Devane, Shannen Doherty. 15. March 1993 (Imperial Entertainment).

Oh, What a Night. With Corey Haim, Robbie Coltrane. 15. February 1993 (Columbia Tri-Star).

The Other Woman. With Adrian Zmed, Lee Anne Beaman, Sam Jones. 18. April 1993 (Imperial Entertainment).

Overkill: The Aileen Wuornos Story. With Jean Smart, Brion James, Park Overall. 15. February 1993 (Odyssey).

Overruled. With Donna Mills, John Getz, John Rubinstein. 15. November 1992 (Odyssey).

The Pamela Principal. With Frank Pesce, Troy Donahue. 18. February 1993 (Imperial Entertainment).

A Passion For Innocence. With Meredith Baxter, Judith Ivey. 15. March 1993 (Odyssey).

The Pistol: The Birth of a Legend. With Millie Perkins. PG. December 1992 (Hi-Fliers).

The President's Child. With Donna Mills, Trevor Eve, James Read, William Devane. PG. April 1993 (FoxVideo).

Prey of the Chameleon. With Daphne Zuniga, James Wilder, Alexandra Paul. 18. March 1993 (Imperial Entertainment).

Project Shadowchaser. With Martin Kove, Meg Foster, Joss Ackland, Paul Koslo. 15. January 1993 (First Independent).

Prototype. With Lane Lenhart. 18. February 1993 (20.20 Vision).

Psychic. With Michael Nouri, Zach Galligan, Catherine Mary Stewart. 18. September 1992 (Hi-Fliers).

Rage & Honour. With Cynthia Rothrock, Richard Norton. 18. November 1992 (20.20 Vision).

Rage & Honour II: Hostile Takeover. With Cynthia Rothrock, Richard Norton. 18. February 1993 (Medusa).

The Rape of Dr Willis. With Jaclyn Smith, Holland Taylor. 15. July 1992 (Odyssey).

Revenge of the Nerds III. With Robert Carradine, Ted McGinley, Curtis Armstrong. PG. December 1992 (FoxVideo).

Road to Ruin. With Peter Weller, Carey Lowell. 15. June 1993 (Medusa).

Another true story: Brian Dennehy as Sgt Jack Reed in John Korty's Shattered Promises

The Roller Blade Seven. With Scott Shaw, Frank Stallone, Joe Estevez, William Smith, Don Stroud, Karen Black. 18. March 1993 (First Independent).

Scanner Force. With Liliana Komorowska. 18. November 1992 (First Independent).

Secret Games. With Martin Hewitt, Billy Drago. 18. September 1992 (Medusa).

Secret Passion of Robert Clayton. With John Mahoney, Scott Valentine. 15. February 1993 (CIC).

Seed People. With Samm Hennings. 15. November 1992 (CIC).

Sexual Intent. With Gary Hudson. 18. April 1993 (Medusa).

Sexual Response. With Shannon Tweed, Catherine Oxenberg. 18. February 1993 (Columbia Tri-Star).

Shadowhunter. With Scott Glenn, Angela Alvarado. 18. March 1993 (Medusa).

Shadow of a Stranger. With Emma Samms, Parker Stevenson, Joan Chen. 15. June 1993 (Imperial Entertainment).

Shanghai Express. With Cynthia Rothrock. PG. January 1993 (VPD).

Shattered Promises. With Brian Dennehy, Treat Williams, Susan Ruttan. 15. April 1993 (Odyssey).

She Stood Alone. With Mare Winning-ham. April 1993 (Buena Vista).

Shootfighter. With Bolo Yeung, Maryam D'Abo. 18. June 1993 (New Age Entertainment/Columbia Tri-Star).

The Silencer. With Lynette Walden, Chris Mulkey, Morton Downey Jr. 18. April 1993 (Hi-Fliers).

Silent Thunder. With Stacy Keach, Lisa Banes, Sandahl Bergman. 15. May 1993 (Imperial Entertainment).

Silhouette. With Tracy Scoggins, Brion James. 18. July 1992 (New Age).

Sins of the Father. With Valerie Berti-nelli, George Dzundza. 15. July 1992 (Odyssey).

Slaughter PI. With Rob Stewart. 18. October 1992 (New Age Entertain-ment/Columbia Tri-Star).

Slowburn. With William Smith, Anthony James. 18. February 1993 (First Independent).

Somebody's Daughter. With Nicolette Sheridan, Nick Mancusso, Elliott Gould. 15. May 1993 (Hi-Fliers).

Steel Justice. With Robert Taylor, J. A. Preston. PG. March 1993 (CIC).

Stompin' at the Savoy. With Mario Van Peebles, Lynn Whitfield, Vanessa Williams. PG. March 1993 (CIC).

Stranded. With Deborah Wakeman. 15. May 1993 (Imperial Enter-tainment).

Strays. With Timothy Busfield, Kathleen Quinlan. 15. September 1992 (CIC).

Street Crimes. With Dennis Farina, Michael Worth. 18. August 1992 (VPD).

Street War. With Mario Van Peebles, Peter Boyle. 15. November 1992 (Braveworld).

Summer Vacation. With Corey Feld-man, Sarah Douglas, Jack Nance. 15. August 1992 (First Independ-ent).

Sunset Grill. With Peter Weller, Lori Singer, Stacy Keach, John Rhys-Davies. 18. April 1993 (EV).

Sunstroke. With Jane Seymour, Steve Railsback, Ray Wise, Don Ameche. 15. April 1993 (CIC).

Sweet Killing. With Michael Ironside, F. Murray Abraham. 15. May 1993 (Hi-Fliers).

Switching Parents. With Joseph Gor-don-Levitt, Bill Smitrovich, Kath-leen York, Robert Joy. PG. June 1993 (Odyssey).

The Swordsman. With Lorenzo Lamas. 15. December 1992 (Columbia Tri-Star).

Tales from the Crypt Volume II. With Amanda Plummer. 18. August 1992 (Warner).

Talons of the Eagle. With Billy Blanks, James Hong. 18. February 1993 (Braveworld).

Telling Secrets. With Cybill Shepherd, Ken Olin, Mary Kay Place. 15. April 1993 (Odyssey).

Those Bedroom Eyes. With Mimi Rogers, Tim Matheson. 18. May 1993 (Columbia Tri-Star).

Three Little Ninjas and the Lost Treasure. With Douglas Ivan. PG. December 1992 (20.20 Vision/New Age Entertainment).

Tiger Claws. With Cynthia Rothrock, Bolo Yeung, Jalal Merhi. 15. Octo-ber 1992 (Once Upon a Lifetime/20.20 Vision).

Time Trax. With Dale Midkiff, Peter Donat, Mia Sara. January 1993 (Warner).

To Kill For. With Michael Madsen, Laura Johnson. 18. November 1992 (Hi-Fliers).

To Protect and Serve. With C. Thomas Howell, Lezlie Deane, Richard Romanus, Joe Cortese. 18. April 1993 (EV).

The Tower. With Paul Reiser, Roger Rees. 15. February 1993 (Fox-Video).

A Town Torn Apart. With Michael Tucker, Jill Eikenberry. PG. May 1993 (Odyssey).

The Toy Maker. With William Thorne, Mickey Rooney. 18. January 1993 (Hi-Fliers).

Trancers III. With Tim Matheson, Helen Hunt, Stephen Macht. 15. May 1993 (CIC).

Treacherous Crossing. With Lindsay Wagner, Angie Dickinson, Joseph Bottoms. PG. January 1993 (CIC).

Twin Sisters. With Stephanie Kramer, Frederic Forrest, James Brolin. 15. February 1993 (First Independent).

Under Pressure. With Harry Hamlin, Teri Garr, Terry O'Quinn. 15. March 1993 (New Age Entertain-ment/20.20 Vision).

The Unnamable Returns. With John Rhys-Davies, David Warner. 18. October 1992 (New Age Entertain-ment/Columbia Tri-Star).

Vanished Without a Trace. With Karl Malden, Tim Ransom. PG. June 1993 (Braveworld).

Wild Card. With Powers Boothe, Cindy Pickett. PG. April 1993 (CIC).

Wild Orchid: The Red Shoe Diary. With David Duchovny, Brigitte Bako, Billy Wirth. 18. November 1992 (Entertainment in Video).

Wild Orchid: Red Shoe Diaries 2. With Steven Bauer, Joan Severence, Denise Crosby. 18. April 1993 (EV).

Witchcraft. With Christopher Lee, Jen-ilee Harrison. 18. September 1992 (Columbia Tri-Star).

With Savage Intent. With Elizabeth Montgomery, Robert Foxworth. 15. January 1993 (Imperial Entertain-ment).

A Woman Scorned. With Meredith Baxter, Stephen Collins. 15. July 1992 (Braveworld).

The Women of Windsor. With Sallyanne Law. PG. June 1992 (Imperial Entertainment).

Xtro II: The Second Encounter. With Jan-Michael Vincent, Paul Koslo. 18. September 1992 (First Inde-pendent).

The Ten Most Promising Faces of 1993

James Cameron-Wilson

Brendan Fraser

After making a Neanderthal ass of himself in *California Man* – one of the most painful films of 1992 – Brendan Fraser, aged 23, stunned his critics in his next picture, *School Ties*. Apart from displaying the mandatory hunk appeal of an up-and-coming star, Fraser demonstrated a surprising credibility, range and depth as David Greene, the product of a poor mining town who secures a football scholarship to an exclusive Ivy League school. At first winning friends and influen-

Brendan Fraser (second left), *with Sean Astin, Pauly Shore, Ronin Tunney and Megan Ward in* California Man

cing people with his athleticism on the playing field, his grace on the dance floor and his bonhomie in the dormitory, David soon finds his codes of honour tangled as he is forced to conceal the fact that he is Jewish while upholding his ethics as a human being. *School Ties*, a powerful, absorbing film, was one of the few genuine surprises to emerge from a major Hollywood studio in '92, and, properly nurtured, should have been a hit in the *Dead Poets Society* league. Alas, the embarrassing statistics reveal that *School Ties* grossed a measly $14 million, while *California Man* gambolled off with $40m.

The son of a Canadian tourism official, Fraser was born in Indianapo-

Jason Scott Lee as he appears in Dragon: The Bruce Lee Story

lis and raised in Holland, Switzerland and Canada. In Seattle, he attended the Actors' Conservatory at the Cornish College of the Arts and plodded the boards at the Intiman Theatre. He was also a member of the Laughing Horse Summer Theatre in Ellensburg, Washington, and clocked up a number of stage credits (*Waiting for Godot, Romeo and Juliet*) before moving to LA.

He made his film debut in Nancy Savoca's Seattle-set *Dogfight* with River Phoenix, appeared in the TV pilot *My Old School* and was in the TV movie *Guilty Until Proven Innocent*, starring Martin Sheen. In *California Man* (released as *Encino Man* in the States) he played Linkovitch Chomofsky, the hip caveman who is defrosted by two nerds and becomes a hit with the babes in high school. The film was designed as a vehicle for MTV comic

Pauly Shore, but it was Brendan who won any conciliatory reviews going.

Since then, he took a guest role in the ensemble piece *Twenty Bucks* (the story of a twenty-dollar note), played the son of Donald Sutherland and Lolita Davidovich in Percy Adlon's *Younger & Younger*, and starred opposite Joe Pesci and Moira Kelly in Alek Keshishian's *With Honors*. He then headed the cast of the rock 'n' roll comedy *Airheads* – co-starring Steve Buscemi and Adam Sandler – the story of three musicians who take a radio station hostage in order to air their demo.

Jason Scott Lee

Let's get one thing straight: Jason Scott Lee is not the son of the late Bruce Lee nor is he the brother of the late Brandon Lee. He is not a fan of martial arts, and is every inch an actor. He was, however, the star of *Dragon: The Bruce Lee Story*, the film that grossed almost $13 million in its opening week in the US. He also has a great

body, is of Chinese–Hawaiian parentage and is one of the hottest new actors in Hollywood. *That's* why he was cast in the role of the chop-socky legend. Rob Cohen, director of *Dragon*, praises the actor's 'magnetism', adding, 'besides the beautiful body there's some soulful level.' Linda Lee, Bruce's widow, was struck by his likeness to her late husband. 'It's not just the athletic moves,' she says, 'he has the expressions that remind me very much of Bruce.'

Born in Oahu, Hawaii, Jason studied acting under Sal Romeo while attending Fullerton College in Southern California. Eighteen months later, he was invited by Romeo to help set up The Friends & Artists Theatre Company in Los Angeles, where he performed in five productions. On film, he made his debut in 1986 with a small part in Cheech Marin's *Born in East LA*, played the hoverboarder 'Whitey' in *Back to the Future Part II* and had parts in *Ghoulies Go to College* and *Hubcap* as well as the TV movies *Vestige of Honor* and *American Eyes*. In the last-named he had the starring role, playing a Korean youth in search of his roots. He got his big screen break when cast as the half-caste Inuit, Avik, in Vincent Ward's photogenic epic *Map of the Human Heart*.

Following *Dragon*, Lee starred in the $20 million ecologically themed romantic epic *Rapa Nui*, directed by Kevin Reynolds and produced by Kevin Costner.

Robert Sean Leonard

made a memorable impact as the tragic student Neil Perry in *Dead Poets Society* (1989), and then all but vanished. In 1993 he came back with a bang, playing the yuppie husband of Mary Stuart Masterson in the ensemble comedy *Married to It*, starring in the Swing-era anti-war drama *Swing Kids* and playing Claudio, no less, in Kenneth Branagh's *Much Ado About Nothing*. Adept at portraying callow, sensitive young men in the Timothy Hutton mould, Leonard proved he could more than hold his own in *Swing Kids*, in which he played a member of the Hitler Youth by day and a rebellious hepcat by night. Plagued by guilt for selling out to the Nazi movement, Leonard's Peter Muller was a complex, multi-layered character which the young actor made movingly credible.

Born in Ridgewood, New Jersey, on 28 February 1969, the son of teachers, Leonard joined a local summer stock company at the age of ten. At fifteen he turned professional, performing in Joseph Papp's New York Shakespeare Festival, and made his Broadway debut acting opposite Derek Jacobi in *Breaking the Code*. At sixteen he had the lead in *Brighton Beach Memoirs* and repeated the role in a tour of the sequel, *Biloxi Blues*.

In 1986 Leonard made his film debut in the sci-fi fantasy *The Manhattan Project* and two years later starred in *My Best Friend Is a Vampire*, as the high-school bloodsucker in question. Then came Peter Weir's highly acclaimed *Dead Poets Society*, in which he was the student and would-be actor suffocated by his domineering father (Kurtwood Smith). The film was an enormous hit, and Leonard returned to the theatre to hone his craft. His other film credits include the TV movies *My Two Loves* (1986) and *Bluffing It* (1987), James Ivory's *Mr and Mrs Bridge* (as Paul Newman's son) and Martin Scorsese's *Age of Innocence*.

Mike Myers

is Wayne Campbell. At least, that is the public's perception. Party animal and metal head, Wayne was a unique comic invention. Constantly smiling and irrepressibly easygoing, he reinvented the American language by turning positive sentences into negatives with a resounding NOT! at the end of them. He also introduced the joyfully exuberant 'schwing!' into the national vocabulary, an expression which, combined with a thrusting of the hips, conveyed a sexual compliment of enormous vitality. Whatever else Wayne Campbell may have been, he was an original. And the world of Wayne was irresistible.

Myers himself, standing at '4 feet and 20 inches', was born in Toronto to (he swears) one mother and one father. Legend also has it that the very day he graduated from high school he auditioned for The Second City comedy troupe (birthing pool for Dan Aykroyd, John Candy, Rick Moranis, Martin Short and the late Gilda Radner), and was accepted. His audition piece? Wayne Campbell! Later, he joined The Second City in Chicago and fell in love with that town's nondescript suburb of Aurora (the setting for *Wayne's World*). In early 1989 Myers

became a featured performer and writer for the legendary TV revue *Saturday Night Live*, and received a shared Emmy award the same year.

On the show, his most memorable creations were Dieter, the avant-garde host of German TV's *Sprockets*; 'Mid-

Robert Sean Leonard as Claudio and Kate Beckinsale as Hero in Kenneth Branagh's Much Ado About Nothing

Mike Myers (left) *as the irrepressible Wayne Campbell, with Dana Carvey as Garth Algar, in the film version of* Wayne's World

Kathy Najimi as the irrepressible and saintly Sister Mary Patrick in Disney's Sister Act; *and as the necromantic companion of Bette Midler and Sarah Jessica Parker in* Hocus Pocus

dle-Aged Man', a character that understood mortgages; 'Lothar of the Hill People'; and 'Simon', 'a little boy in the bath'. But the big sensation was *Wayne's World*, a series of ten-minute sketches in which Myers played Wayne Campbell alongside Dana Carvey's Garth Algar, two excellent dudes who ran a public-access cable show from Wayne's Aurora basement. The slot became so popular that the likes of Madonna began begging for a guest appearance in the famous basement.

A film version followed, with an estimable supporting cast that included Rob Lowe, Lara Flynn Boyle, Meat Loaf, Ione Skye, Alice Cooper and Ed O'Neill. But nobody could have predicted the colossal popularity of the event. In its first seven days, *Wayne's World* grossed $21,701,780 at the US box office, and in ten weeks had accumulated more than $100m. It eventually took a whopping $132m – making it the second highest-grossing comedy of the year (after *Sister Act*).

Wayne's World 2 is already in the can and Myers's fee was not unsurprisingly in the seven-figure range. Meanwhile, the actor went on to star in his second film, *So I Married an Axe-Murderer*, in which he played a wannabe Beat poet who suspects his wife (Nancy Travis) of extracurricular practices. At various times the part had been envisaged as a vehicle for Woody Allen, Chevy Chase, Billy Crystal and Steve Martin, but when Myers came on board he turned the script around (in just eight days) to make the character hipper, younger and funnier. He also lost twenty pounds to fit his new image as leading man, and was permitted to make his own finishing touches to the completed film – an honour usually reserved for only the most powerful stars in Hollywood.

Kathy Najimy

Thanks to the phenomenal success of *Sister Act*, Whoopi Goldberg found herself in a position to demand $7 million for the sequel, making her the highest-paid actress of all time. Nobody denies that Whoopi is funny but, let's be honest, in *Sister Act* she had to fight for her laughs just to stay afloat. This was no reflection on Whoopi but on the scene-stealing antics of her wimpled supporting cast – the most memorable member of whom, without a doubt, was the generously proportioned Kathy Najimy, whose natural spirit and infectious laugh was a joy to share.

Kathy Najimy is not only a very funny comedienne, but an actress, writer, director and owner of a dog called Al Finney. She has had a one-woman show, *It's My Party*, has appeared in over a dozen musicals (including *Godspell* and *Grease*), and directed the award-winning *I Can Put My Fist in My Mouth* in Los Angeles. She was also resident director of the Emmy-winning New Image Teen Theatre, and won an Obie for her work on *The Kathy and Mo Show*, with Mo Gaffney. On TV, she and Mo repeated their act for HBO, and she hosted Comedy Central's *Short Attention Span Theatre*. As a writer, Najimy has worked for the *New York Times* and contributed to several national magazines, as well as penning the book *The Choices We Made*, published by Random House to coincide with the anniversary of the Roe v. Wade case. She also authored *The Kathy and Mo Book*.

Film-wise, Ms Najimy has been seen in *Topsy and Bunker*, *The Hard Way*, *Other People's Money*, *The Fisher King* and *This Is My Life*. In Michael Hoffman's hilarious *Soapdish* she appeared opposite Whoopi Goldberg, playing Tawny Miller, costume designer on the ill-fated TV serial *The Sun Also Sets*. The actress then donned her habit to portray the ebullient Sister Mary Patrick in *Sister Act*. On the strength of the last-named, she was signed up by Hollywood Pictures to write and star in two films for them, and was cast as the third witch in Disney's *Hocus Pocus* – opposite Bette Midler and Sarah Jessica Parker. She was then re-teamed with Whoopi and Maggie Smith for *Sister Act 2* and demanded a million for her services – whether or not she got it is not on record.

Chris O'Donnell

For a chap who turned down the chance of starring opposite Jessica Lange in his first movie in order to attend a Bruce Springsteen concert, Chris O'Donnell has the luck of the Irish. Offered a second opportunity to audition for the role of Ms Lange's eldest son in *Men Don't Leave*, O'Donnell opted for crew practice instead. Nevertheless, he turned up for a third interview, was called back, went to New York to read with Ms Lange (although, he says, 'I couldn't fit the face with the name'), read again in Chicago and was then flown to Los Angeles for a screen test. He got the movie, but admits, 'I still don't know what the hell I did to get the role.' Since then he's starred opposite Al Pacino in the Oscar-winning *Scent of a Woman* and played D'Artagnan in Disney's *The Three Musketeers*, co-starring Charlie Sheen and Kiefer Sutherland.

Now one of the most in-demand new faces in Hollywood, Chris O'Donnell is taking his acting more seriously. He was still 'goofing off and playing jokes' on the set of *School Ties*, but 'when *Scent of a Woman* came along, I stopped that cold and got more serious. I just wanted to get real focused and ready for the auditions.' His commitment to *Scent of a Woman* paid off, and even though his more experienced co-star hobbled off with the Oscar, it was O'Donnell who had the more difficult task of playing the young sidekick, juggling his character's conflicting naivety and wisdom to credible effect. Indeed, while we admired Pacino's larger-than-life performance, it was O'Donnell we believed in.

The youngest of seven children, O'Donnell grew up on the outskirts of Chicago in Winnetka, Illinois, and studied at the Loyola Academy. Following a few commercials (most memorably a McDonald's ad with basketball superstar Michael Jordan in 1983), he embarked on a four-year MBA course at Boston College. 'I planned a career in business,' he says, 'because it [acting] just seemed so

Chris O'Donnell as he appeared in Martin Brest's Scent of a Woman

unrealistic I didn't think it would ever really happen.'

It happened with a bang when he won the part (and good notices) in *Men Don't Leave*, and he hasn't looked backed since. He was re-teamed with Jessica Lange in Tony Richardson's last film, *Blue Sky*, and then played the ill-fated brother (Buddy) of Mary Stuart Masterson in the sleeper hit *Fried Green Tomatoes at the Whistle Stop Cafe*. He was Reece, the privileged gentile roommate of Brendan Fraser in the excellent ensemble drama *School Ties*, and then won the part of Charlie

Simms, another public school boy, in *Scent of a Woman*. He auditioned for the latter role along with several cast members of *School Ties*, but was the only one to be called back. It was his last audition.

'I was *offered* the role of D'Artagnan,' the actor, 23, says with some pride, adding: 'but I'm kind of worried – because it just seems like too much fun.'

Mary-Louise Parker

is thankfully not endowed with the sort of head-turning cosmetic sterotypicality that would get her cast opposite the likes of Jean-Claude Van Damme or Charlie Sheen. With a background in theatre, the actress steadily chipped

Mary-Louise Parker as Dee in Grand Canyon

her way into films with a string of laudable performances in some very good pictures. She was the sole female character in Norman Rene's highly acclaimed *Longtime Companion*, a sensitive look at a group of gay men confronting the monstrosity of AIDS. She was the diffident, conservative Ruth in *Fried Green Tomatoes at the Whistle Stop Cafe*, that irrepressible 'woman's' picture which confounded the Hollywood moneymen and went on to gross over $81 million in America alone. And then she played Dee, secretary and occasional lover of Kevin Kline, in Lawrence Kasdan's provocative, hard-edged satire of Los Angeles, *Grand Canyon*. If she keeps it up, Mary-Louise could become a regular at the Academy Awards over the next decade or so.

Initially considering a career in medicine, Mary-Louise Parker (born in 1966) opted for the North Carolina School of Arts instead, which she followed with a number of stage appearances in such plays as *Hay Fever* and *The Importance of Being Earnest*. On TV, she was a regular on the daytime soap *Ryan's Hope* and had a good role in the WW2 TV movie *Too Young the Hero*, starring Rick Schroder.

She made her big-screen debut in 1989 in the American Playhouse production *Signs of Life*, in which she was a stand-out (as a small-town waitress) in a cast that included Arthur Kennedy, Vincent D'Onofrio, Beau Bridges and Kathy Bates. However, the actress felt uncomfortable working in the cinema, revealing, 'I've never had much of a fascination for film. People in Hollywood can have cash registers where their hearts are.' She returned to the stage to play Rita Boyle in the original production of Craig Lucas's *Prelude to a Kiss*, opposite Alec Baldwin, and was nominated for a Tony, the Broadway equivalent of an Oscar. When Timothy Hutton took over the male lead she and Hutton became an item, but it was Baldwin and Meg Ryan who snared the movie version, a flop. Parker then re-teamed with Hutton in the play *Babylon Gardens* – at New York's Circle Rep.

Norman Rene, who had directed *Prelude*, cast her in *Longtime Com-*

Jeanne Tripplehorn with Michael Douglas in Basic Instinct

panion), also written by Lucas, and she was off. Following intelligent performances in *Fried Green Tomatoes* and *Grand Canyon*, she went on to star opposite Matt Dillon and William Hurt in *Mr Wonderful*, a bittersweet romantic comedy directed by the British playwright Anthony Minghella (*Truly, Madly, Deeply*). She then played a young Bostonian who dreams of becoming a photographer in the stellar *Naked in New York*, co-starring Eric Stoltz, Timothy Dalton, Kathleen Turner, Tony Curtis, Ralph Macchio and Whoopi Goldberg. Martin Scorsese produced the latter, which just shows the sort of positive direction in which Mary-Louise Parker is headed.

Jeanne Tripplehorn

Before she was manhandled by Michael Douglas in that *other* major sex scene in *Basic Instinct*, Jeanne Tripplehorn had just one film under her garter belt. And *that* was a TV movie. Then, overnight, the actress was reading for some of the biggest movies in Hollywood (*Sommersby*, *Groundhog Day*), before landing the female lead opposite Tom Cruise in *The Firm*.

A genuine head-turner, Ms Tripplehorn played police psychologist Dr Beth Garner in *Instinct*, the shrink who's more than a match for Sharon Stone in the brains department – and who gets roughed up by former lover Douglas in one of the film's steamiest sequences. But besides providing the movie with more good looks than it knew what to do with, Tripplehorn gave a performance of some complexity and vigour.

Born and raised in Tulsa, Oklahoma, she studied acting at Julliard in New York and, immediately after graduation, landed a good if underwritten part as an impromptu nurse in the Civil War TV movie *The Perfect Tribute*, co-starring Lukas Haas, Campbell Scott and Jason Robards. She followed this with a major role in the New York premiere of John Patrick Shanley's play *The Big Funk* before being snatched up for the key part of Beth in *Basic Instinct*. She was then signed on to play Abby, wife of hotshot lawyer Tom Cruise in *The Firm*, second-billed in an all-star cast.

She also starred alongside Matthew Broderick and Annabella Sciorra in the New York comedy *The Night We Never Met*, playing Broderick's former girlfriend, a performance artist.

Janine Turner

The daughter of a retired pilot, Janine Turner has made her name playing pilots on the big and small screen. On the hit CBS TV series *Northern Exposure* she starred as gamine bush pilot Maggie O'Connell, and then played the helicopter pilot in the vertiginous blockbuster *Cliffhanger*. Born in Lincoln, Nebraska, but raised in Fort Worth, Texas, Janine explains, 'My father flew at twice the speed of sound. We had a little old single-engine plane he would fly us in all around Texas. So I know a little about planes.'

Nominated for a Golden Globe award as best actress in *Northern Exposure*, Janine has yet to reveal her full potential in the movies (she had little to do but scream and frown in *Cliffhanger*), but definitely has the looks and mettle to make it big on the wide screen – in the very near future.

Born on 6 December 1962, Janine was not an obvious candidate to play mechanically minded windswept tomboys. At fifteen, an ex-child beauty queen, she moved to New York to embark on a modelling career and signed on as the youngest body at the Wilhelmina Agency. After two years of commercials (and a stint at the Professional Children's School), she returned to Texas to finish high school. Shortly afterwards she began her career in acting, playing Charlene Tilton's friend Susan in *Dallas* (1980). A year later she was the soap starlet Janie-Claire Willow in CBS's short-lived serial *Behind the Screen*, and then served time (as Laura Templeton) on the daytime soap *General Hospital* (1982–3), on which she befriended Demi Moore (who played her sister Jackie).

Janine's private life was equally busy.

Janine Turner playing another feisty pilot in Cliffhanger

Elijah Wood with Thora Birch in Disney's Paradise

In 1982, aged twenty, she was engaged to Alec Baldwin, and even bought her wedding dress, until she was unceremoniously dumped. In an attempt to make ends meet she tried to sell her engagement ring, and was later romantically linked to Mikhail Baryshnikov, Sylvester Stallone and a number of sports personalities.

Film-wise, she had a cameo (alongside Demi) in the soap spoof *Young Doctors in Love* (1982), spent ten weeks in China on the ill-fated *Tai Pan* ('86), had a bit in *Knights of the City*, took a supporting role in George A. Romero's *Monkey Shines: An Experiment in Fear* ('88), and played Olympia Dukakis's niece in *Steel Magnolias* ('89). In 1990 she was flat broke and considering a career change when she landed the audition for *Northern Exposure*.

Elijah Wood

We're not in the habit of highlighting child stars, but Elijah Wood's track record is so noteworthy and his future line-up of movies so impressive, that it would be an oversight not to include him here.

He was just seven when he landed the role of Barry Levinson's *alter ego* in that director's 1990 masterpiece *Avalon*, and then went on to play the central character in *Paradise* – as the boy who brings the estranged Melanie Griffith and Don Johnson together. Aged nine, he starred in Richard Donner's $30 million sci-fi fantasy *Radio Flyer*, playing an abused child who escapes reality by creating a flying machine out of a Radio Flyer wagon. More recently, he has starred opposite Mel Gibson in *Forever Young*, played the lead in *The Adventures of Huck Finn* and sparred with Macaulay Culkin in *The Good Son*, from an original script by Ian McEwan.

Although blessed with the mandatory doe-eyed good looks required by Hollywood, Elijah Wood also displays an uncanny, unaffected spontaneity, prompting Richard Donner to enthuse, 'You know, you look through his eyes and you see no harm, no pain – nothing but happiness.'

Born in the quaintly named Cedar Rapids in Iowa, Elijah attended the International Modelling and Talent Association convention in Los Angeles when he was spotted by a talent scout, who convinced his parents (who ran a deli back east) to up sticks and move to LA. Within a few months of settling in Burbank, the boy landed a Seven Seas salad-dressing commercial and appeared in the Paula Abdul video 'Forever Your Girl'. He then skewered parts in *Back to the Future Part II*, *Internal Affairs* (playing the son of William Baldwin) and the TV movie *Child in the Night*, with JoBeth Williams. *Avalon* followed, as did the other movies, in which more often than not young Elijah stole the notices from his older co-stars.

In *The Good Son*, a thriller, he plays an orphan who moves in with relatives and comes under the evil spell of cousin Macaulay. He'll then be seen in Rob Reiner's *North*, in which he stars as a child prodigy who divorces his parents, with no less a cast than Bruce Willis, Kathy Bates, John Ritter, Jon Lovitz and Kelly McGillis in support. Next, he was signed up to star in Universal Pictures' *The War*, in which Kevin Costner agreed to take a supporting role as Elijah's father. Now, those are *heavy* credits.

Still, Elijah Wood is not so sure he wants to remain in the business. He reflects that he may one day 'study sharks – or maybe be a secret agent'.

Film World Diary

James Cameron-Wilson

July 1992

Once again **Demi Moore** shocks Hollywood with her cover on *Vanity Fair*. Last August she appeared on the magazine naked and seven months pregnant. In the current issue she's also nude, but has a man's suit *painted* on her body ★ Sir **Andrew Lloyd Webber** threatens to take over artistic control of the animated film version of *Cats*. **Steven Spielberg** is working on a screenplay, but Lloyd Webber is no longer sure that the eternal Peter Pan shares his understanding of the **T. S. Eliot** original ★ *Batman Returns* breaks box-office records in the UK, grossing £2,774,796 in its opening weekend ★ *Hook* grosses $250 million worldwide ★ *Sister Act* grosses over $100 million in its first eight weeks in the US ★ **Tom Cruise** and his agent **Paula Wagner** start up their own production company, The Cruise–Wagner Co. ★ Production starts on **Wim Wenders**'s *Faraway, So Close!* in Berlin. His cast includes **Bruno Ganz, Nastassja Kinski, Peter Falk, Roberto Benigni, Mikhail Gorbachev** and **Lou Reed** ★ After much controversy, **Ice-T** removes his rap song *Cop Killer* from his latest album, Warner Records' *Body Count*. The title of his new film, *The Looters*, will also be changed (to *Trespass*). Meanwhile, American police have declared war on Ice-T, threatening companies who employ his services. One spokesman suggested that police 'could write parking tickets' for every Warner truck that stopped to make a delivery.

August 1992

It's official: **Woody Allen** and **Mia Farrow** split up. An acrimonious custody battle ensues over the couple's three children, two of whom are adopted. Mia hires **Alan Dershowitz** (played by Ron Silver in the 1990 film *Reversal of Fortune*) to fight her case. Over the last twelve years, Ms Farrow has starred in twelve of her husband's films ★ **Kit** and **Pat Culkin** start legal proceedings for custody of their children, in particular **Macaulay**, 11, who's just received $5 million for starring in *Home Alone 2* ★ It's out: **Woody Allen**, 56, admits to dating **Mia Farrow**'s adopted daughter, **Soon-Yi Previn**, 21 ★ *Basic Instinct* grosses $265 million worldwide ★ **Sting**, 40, marries **Trudie Styler**, 35, the mother of his three children and companion for over ten years ★ British filmmaker **Ken Russell**, 65, marries actress **Hetty Baynes**, 35, after working with her on a *South Bank Show* documentary. He will next cast her in his production of the BBC's *Lady Chatterley's Lover* ★ British newspapers announce that **Sharon Stone** will be getting $30 million for her role in the *Basic Instinct* sequel. And if you believe that . . . ★ It is official: **Julia Roberts** ditches boyfriend **Jason Patric** for 28-year-old actor **Russell Blake** ★ **Rebecca Broussard** ditches **Jack Nicholson**, father of her two children ★ **Michael York** and his wife, **Pat**, are attacked by six youths in Rio de Janeiro, where the actor is filming *Discretion Assured*. However, the couple are unhurt thanks to York chasing off his razor-wielding assailants with 'a theatrical yell'.

September 1992

Patsy Kensit gives birth to a little boy, James Kerr. The father is rock star **Jim Kerr**, singer with Simple Minds ★ **Harry Hamlin** sues his wife, the English-born **Nicolette Sheridan**, for fraud, claiming she only married him to obtain a green card ★ After a string of taxing auditions, **Richard Harris** beats out **Jack Nicholson**, **Kirk Douglas** and **Jack Lemmon** for a supporting role in **Randa Haines**'s *Wrestling with Ernest Hemingway*, starring **Robert Duvall** ★ **Joe Eszterhas**'s latest screenplay, *Layers of Skin* – the story of a lesbian cop – goes up for auction. You may recall that Eszterhas's script for *Basic Instinct* was bought for $3 million ★ According to the tabloids, **Emilio Estevez** fires supermodel **Kathy Ireland** from the cast of *National Lampoon's Loaded Weapon 1* – because she is five inches taller than he. Well, the papers were misinformed (surprise, surprise) ★ **Brigitte Bardot** hires bodyguards for her dogs following her anti-hunting campaign, when her mutts received

Emilio Estevez: trouble with Kathy Ireland, exchanging vows

death threats ★ **George Holliday** files a petition in the US District court in Los Angeles to stop **Spike Lee** using his video footage of **Rodney King**'s beating in *Malcolm X*. Holliday seeks $100,000 for 'wilful copyright infringement' ★ **Anthony Perkins**, 60, dies of AIDS ★ *A League of Their Own* grosses over $100 million in the US ★ **Nastassja Kinski**, 32, and **Quincy Jones**, 59, are expecting a little one ★ **Richard Dreyfuss** seeks divorce from his wife of nine years and mother of his three children ★ **Fisher Stevens**, 28, splits from his girlfriend of three years, **Michelle Pfeiffer**, 34. Stevens, who most recently co-starred in *Hero* and *Super Mario Bros.*, was 'seeing' a 17-year-old extra. Miaow ★ **Alec Baldwin** signs a first-look deal with 20th Century–Fox to develop projects for the studio ★ **Emilio Estevez** and **Paula Abdul** renew their conjugal vows at a glitzy ceremony – attended by 176 guests – in Thousand Oaks, California. Paula reportedly sported a $50,000 wedding gown, while best man **Tom Cruise** failed to turn up. Emilio's dad, **Martin Sheen**, stepped in to do the honours ★ **Jack Nicholson** blocks the release of *Blue Champagne*, a film he financed for his former girlfriend **Rebecca Broussard**, in which she stars ★ **Daryl Hannah** and long-time boyfriend **Jackson Browne** break up following a ferocious fight. Ms Hannah is left with a black eye and two fingers in plaster ★ Gossip queen **Liz Smith** reveals that **Ted Danson** is 'seeing' **Whoopi Goldberg**. The following day Danson's wife, Casey, moves out – taking their two children, Kate, 13, and Alexis, 8, with her ★ **Jean-Claude Van Damme** starts divorce proceedings against his wife.

October 1992

Legal permission for **Spike Lee** to use the amateur video of the **Rodney King** beating in *Malcolm X* is settled out of court ★ **Daniel Day-Lewis** turns down the title role in Universal's *Shakespeare in Love*, co-starring **Julia Roberts** ★ **Louis Malle**, 60, is rushed into open heart surgery at Los Angeles' Cedars-Sinai Medical Center ★ **Denholm Elliott** dies of AIDS ★ **Daryl Hannah** and **John F. Kennedy Jr** are videoed smooching outside a New York apartment building. The 16-minute video is subsequently screened on TV's *A Current Affair* and

a considerable media ruckus follows ★ An ailing **Rudolf Nureyev** denies having AIDS ★ **Julia Roberts** flies to London to select a new leading man for *Shakespeare in Love*. Hot choices include **Sean Bean** and **Ralph Fiennes** ★ **Brigitte Bardot** marries for the fourth time ★ *Under Siege* breaks box-office records in North America ★ It's official: **Whitney Houston** and **Bobby Brown** are expecting. The baby's due early next year ★ **Julia Roberts** turns down the female lead in *Shakespeare in Love*, after failing to find a suitable co-star ★ **Whoopi Goldberg** admits that she hated making *Sister Act*, and is subsequently offered $7 million to do the sequel – a record for a female star ★ **James Caan**, 52, pledges his Beverly Hills home to help meet the bail of underworld operator Ronald Lorenzo, who is indicted for cocaine trafficking, kidnap and robbery ★ **Julia Roberts** hits back at accusations that she caused 200 redundancies when she walked off the British film *Shakespeare in Love*. The actress claims she never signed any contract ★ **Bill Cosby** announces plans to buy the TV network NBC ★ Oscar-winning actress **Shirley Booth**, 94, dies of 'natural

Jack Nicholson: ditched by Broussard, blocking Champagne

causes'. She won the Academy Award for her performance as Lola Delaney in *Come Back, Little Sheba* ⋆ **Cleavon Little**, 53, who played the sheriff in Mel Brooks's *Blazing Saddles*, dies of colon cancer ⋆ **Britt Ekland**, 49, files for divorce from guitarist **Jim McDonnell**, 31, her husband of eight years.

November 1992

Hal Roach, the legendary comedy producer who launched the careers of Harold Lloyd, Laurel & Hardy, Will Rogers and the 'Our Gang' kids, dies in Bel-Air, aged 100 ⋆ **Tatum O'Neal**, 29, and **John McEnroe**, 33, split up after a row over Tatum's decision to return to acting. She moves out of their Malibu home and flies to New York to file for divorce ⋆ **Chuck Connors**, 71, the slit-eyed, 6ft 5in. star of TV's *The Rifleman*, dies of lung cancer. His films included *Old Yeller*, *The Big Country*, *The Deserter* and *Airplane II: The Sequel* ⋆ **Audrey Hepburn**, 63, is admitted to the Cedars-Sinai Hospital in Los Angeles to have a cancerous tumour removed from her colon ⋆ **Emily Lloyd** moves to New York, leaving her producer boyfriend **Brian Kestner** behind in Los Angeles. She assures us that the move is purely professional, albeit indefinite ⋆ **Eddie Murphy** and model **Nicole Mitchell** become the proud parents of a baby boy, Myles Murphy ⋆ Francis Coppola's *Bram Stoker's Dracula* grosses $30,521,679 in its first weekend in the States. This is not only the biggest opening in Columbia Pictures' history, but the biggest opening outside the lucrative summer season ⋆ The *National Enquirer* reveals that **Audrey Hepburn** has 'three months to live'. Her doctors dismiss the announcement as 'bogus' ⋆ **Tom Cruise** clinches a multi-picture deal with Paramount which will enable the actor to direct and produce future projects. The Cruise–Wagner Co. will now be based at the Paramount lot ⋆ The *National Enquirer* announces the engagement of **Whoopi Goldberg** and **Ted Danson** ⋆ After the instrument panel on his Gulfstream jet blacked out, **John Travolta** put out a Mayday call and safely landed the aircraft at Washington's National airport. His wife, the actress **Kelly Preston**, their baby daughter and five other passengers were aboard ⋆ **Grif-**

fin O'Neal, 28, hellraising son of the star of *Love Story*, is put on five years' probation for various drug-induced offences, including an attack on his girlfriend, **Lynn Oddo**, whose car he riddled with bullets. O'Neal is also to spend a year in drug and alcohol rehab ⋆ According to a New York newspaper, **Gerard Depardieu** assaulted a pianist at the Mayflower Hotel, allegedly for playing classical music in a restaurant. The story was that Depardieu hoisted the man off his stool, threw him to the ground and then punched him twice in the face. However, it was not made clear whether or not Depardieu, a former boxer, disliked classical music *per se* ⋆ *Home Alone 2: Lost in New York* breaks the box-office records just set by *Bram Stoker's Dracula*. In three days the **John Hughes** film amasses $31,126,882 at the US box office ⋆ After only two weeks, *Home Alone 2* has amassed over $78m in America. However, *Aladdin* is making even more money *per screen*, clocking up $27m in one week. *The Bodyguard* also reaches

Daryl Hannah: a black eye, public smooching, wedding bells?

that figure in seven days, but at 586 more cinemas. By all accounts, America has gone moviegoing mad – no previous November had it this good ⋆ In a TV interview, **Woody Allen** claims that his estranged lover, **Mia Farrow**, threatened to have him killed back in February. He admitted to becoming 'quite frightened' by her threats.

December 1992

Brigitte Nielsen reveals that she is to marry a third time, as soon as her divorce from video director **Sebastian Copeland** comes through. Mr Nielsen No. 4 will be **Raoul Meyer**, a Swiss fake fur tycoon. They are, the former Mrs Stallone informs us, 'very happy' ⋆ **Macaulay Culkin**, 12, dumps his first love, the actress model **Laura Bundy**, 11. 'I don't see Laura any more,' the young star candidly reveals. 'I've got lots of other girlfriends at the moment. Girlfriends aren't something I have a problem finding' ★ In the first leg of Woodygate, **Woody Allen** wins the right to send Christmas presents to his children and to view the videotape in which his adopted daughter allegedly says he sexually abused her ★ The multi-award-winning character actor **Vincent Gardenia**, 71, dies of a heart attack in Philadelphia. In a career spanning 66 years, he will be best remembered for his film roles in *Bang the Drum Slowly*, *Moonstruck*, *Little Shop of Horrors* and *The Super* ★ **Nancy Miracle**, 46, who claims she is the illegitimate daughter of **Marilyn Monroe**, is denied a share of the star's estate after a federal judge throws her claim out of court. She says she will continue her battle for recognition and will undergo DNA testing ★ **Guillaume Depardieu**, 22, son of **Gerard** and co-star of *Tous les Matins du Monde*, is arrested in Paris for importing, using and selling heroin ★ Actor **Dana Andrews**, 83, dies of pneumonia in California. He will be best remembered for the films *Laura*, *The Best Years of Our Lives* and *Zero Hour*, the last-named spoofed to hilarious effect by *Airplane!* ★ In Boris D'Acry prison, **Guillaume Depardieu** is set upon by fellow inmates and suffers a black eye, multiple bruises and a sprained wrist ★ **Tony Curtis**, 68, announces plans to marry a fourth time – to Hollywood lawyer Lisa Deutsch ★ **Harry Connick Jr** is arrested and jailed overnight in New York for illegally carrying a gun. He says it was a Christmas present from his sister and that he had forgotten to have it licensed ★ **John Cleese**, 53, secretly marries Alyce Faye Eichelberger, a psychoanalyst, in Barbados. British director/producer **Michael Winner** is best man. Ms Eichelberger is Cleese's third wife ★ **Halle Berry**, 24, marries baseball star **David Justice**, 26 (of the Atlanta Braves) – on New Year's Eve.

January 1993

Anthony Hopkins is knighted in the New Year's honours ★ *Aladdin* grosses $100 million in the US ★ **Emma Thompson** is voted best actress for *Howards End* by The Los Angeles Film Critics' Circle, The New York Film Critics' Circle, The National Board of

Review, The National Society of Film Critics, The Boston Critics and The Southeastern Film Critics' Association of America. The same bodies award their best actor prizes to, respectively, **Clint Eastwood** for *Unforgiven*, **Denzel Washington** for *Malcolm X*, **Jack Lemmon** for *Glengarry Glen Ross*, **Stephen Rea** for *The Crying Game*, **Denzel Washington** and **Denzel Washington** ★ *Basic Instinct* clocks up $353 million worldwide ★ *Home Alone 2: Lost in New York* passes the $150 million mark in the US ★ **Cher**, 46, announces her engagement to her 27-year-old boyfriend **Rob Camelletti** ★ *The Bodyguard* pockets $200 million worldwide – in seven weeks ★ Special ambassador for the United Nations Children's Fund **Audrey Hepburn**, 63, dies in Switzerland of colonic cancer ★ **Emma Thompson** is voted best actress and **Denzel Washington** best actor by the Dallas–Fort Worth film critics ★ After six weeks, *A Few Good Men* grosses $100 million in the US ★ **Emma Thompson** wins the Golden Globe for best actress ★ **Tom Cruise** and **Nicole Kidman** adopt a baby girl ★ *Bram Stoker's Dracula* breaks box-office records in Britain, taking £2,640,584 in just three days – at 315 cinemas.

February 1993

Universal Soldier clocks up $100 million worldwide ★ At The Evening Standard British Film Awards, **Emma Thompson** is voted best actress and **Daniel Day-Lewis** best actor, the latter for his performance in *The Last of the Mohicans* ★ **Rod Steiger**, 67, and his wife, **Paula**, 33, announce the birth of their first child, Michael Winston ★ **Demi Moore** reportedly visits a divorce lawyer to talk about her failing five-year marriage to **Bruce Willis** ★ *Aladdin* passes the $150 million mark in the US ★ The actor **Ray Sharkey**, stricken with AIDS, allegedly confesses to a close friend that he had 'unprotected sex with more than 200 women' – *after* he knew he was infected ★ In Italy, blood banks offer the public free tickets to *Bram Stoker's Dracula* in return for a pint of their plasma ★ **Dolly Parton**, 47, recovers at home after eleven and a half hours of cosmetic surgery, including liposuction and a face lift ★ The filmmaker **Joseph L. Mankiewicz**, 83, dies of heart failure in New York. He will be

best remembered for his pictures *A Letter To Three Wives*, *All About Eve*, *Guys and Dolls* and *Sleuth* ★ **Nastassja Kinski** and **Quincy Jones** are the proud parents of a baby girl, Kenya Julia Jones ★ *Home Alone 2* grosses $350 million worldwide ★ The Kansas City Film Critics' Circle vote **Emma Thompson** and **Denzel Washington** best thesps of '92 ★ Britain sweeps the Oscar nominations, with *Howards End* grabbing nine and *The Crying Game* skewering a surprising six ★ **Helena Bonham Carter** is granted a High Court injunction to stop a fan from pestering her. Andrew Farquharson, 27, is barred from entering a 'defined area' around the actress's London home, where she lives with her parents ★ **Woody Harrelson** becomes a proud father when his girlfriend Laura Louie gives birth to a seven-pound girl, Deni Montana ★ The Uruguayan picture *A Place in the World*, nominated as best foreign film in the 1992 Oscars, is disqualified for being Argentinian. The American Academy of Motion Picture Arts & Sciences also announces that there will be no replacement, leaving voters four films to choose from (instead of the usual five) ★ **Eddie Constantine**, 75, dies of a heart attack in Weisbaden, Germany. He will be best remembered for his starring role in Jean-Luc Godard's *Alphaville* ★ **Lillian Gish**, 99, dies in her sleep in New York ★ **Ruby Keeler**, 83, dies of cancer in Rancho Mirage, California.

March 1993

Last Action Hero becomes the first film to be advertised in space. Columbia Pictures pays £300,000 to paint the name of its new film on the side of an unmanned rocket to be launched in May ★ **Demi Moore** snaps back at rumours suggesting that she and **Bruce Willis** are heading for divorce, telling *Hello!* magazine that, 'our marriage continues to grow stronger and stronger' ★ **Kim Basinger**, braving bronchitis and a fever, attends the Los Angeles County Court to defend her departure from the Jennifer Lynch movie *Boxing Helena*. Main Line Pictures is suing her for reneging on a verbal contract to star in their picture. Ms Basinger says she withdrew from the project when she was refused permission to make script changes and because of 'gratuitous nudity' ★ **Glenn Ford**, 76, marries his fourth wife, his private nurse Jeanne Baus, 33 ★ **Michelle Pfeiffer**, 34, becomes a single mother after adopting a baby girl, Claudia Rose. The actress arranged the adoption privately through a lawyer, prompting much debate in the media ★ **Helen Hayes**, 92, dies ★ *Bram Stoker's Dracula* grosses $200 million worldwide ★ *A Few Good Men* grosses $200 million worldwide ★ **Eddie Murphy** finally ties the knot with his longtime girlfriend, model **Nicole Mitchell**. At the lavish wedding at New York's Plaza Hotel are **Arsenio Hall, Quincy Jones, Bill Murray, Robert Townsend, Donald Trump, Stevie Wonder** and the bride and groom's children – Bria, 3, and Myles, four months ★ **Woody Allen** says that he's been cleared of sexual abuse accusations hurled at him by his estranged lover, **Mia Farrow**, during their stormy battle for custody of their two adopted children and biological son, 5-year-old Satchel ★ **Fred Savage**, 16, is hit with a sexual harassment suit by the costume designer **Monique Long**, 31, who worked on the young star's TV series *The Wonder Years* ★ **Daniel Day-Lewis** goes to court to fight for his share of the profits of *My Left Foot*. He says he was promised $100,000 and ten per cent of the film's return, but to date has only received a total of $30,000. So far, the film has grossed $65 million worldwide ★ **Mia Farrow**, due to pressure from her court battle with **Woody Allen**, pulls out of Mike Nichols's *Wolf*, co-starring **Jack Nicholson** and **Michelle Pfeiffer**. Farrow was to have been paid $250,000 for her part ★ **Emma Thompson** wins the Oscar ★ A Los Angeles jury orders **Kim Basinger** to pay $8.9 million to Main Line Pictures for 'fraudulently and maliciously' reneging on her oral contract to star in their film *Boxing Helena* ★ **Richard Gere** starts work on **Mark Rydell**'s *Intersection*, opposite **Sharon Stone**. The film is an American 're-make' of Claude Sautet's 1969 drama *Les Choses de la Vie* (*The Things of Life*) which starred **Michel Piccoli** and **Romy Schneider**. This is the third time Gere will have starred in an American version of a French film, following his outings in *Breathless* and *Sommersby* ★ **Richard Gere, Susan Sarandon** and **Tim Robbins** are barred from future Oscar ceremonies for improvising on their written presentation speeches. Gere, a Buddhist, asked his billion viewers to help fight Chinese oppression in

Tibet, while Sarandon and Robbins called on the US Government to allow HIV-positive Haitians to emigrate. The Oscar show's producer, **Gilbert Cates**, called their political ad-libs 'rude and inappropriate and unacceptable behaviour' ★ **Daryl Hannah** is spotted buying a satin-and-lace wedding dress in California. She is currently linked with **John F. Kennedy Jr** ★ **Brandon Lee**, the 28-year-old star of *Rapid Fire* and *Showdown in Little Tokyo*, is shot dead by a 'blank' gun on the set of his new picture, *The Crow*. With one week's filming left, *The Crow* was in production in Wilmington, North Carolina. However, due to a series of disasters that had befallen the film (a carpenter was seriously burned by live power lines, a set sculptor crashed his car through the studio's plaster shop, a construction worker drove a screwdriver through his hand, a storm destroyed some of the sets, etc), the production had earned the title 'Curse of *The Crow*' – and that was *before* Lee was killed. Incidentally, the star's father, the martial arts legend **Bruce Lee**, died in mysterious circumstances in 1973 – aged 32.

April 1993

Rob Lowe and his wife of 22 months, **Sheryl Berkoff**, reveal that they are expecting their first child in September ★ Producer **Jon Peters** offers **Joe Eszterhas** a record $3.4 million to pen the screenplay about the downfall of **John Gotti**, Godfather of the Gambino crime family ★ **Kelly McGillis** gives birth to a baby girl, Sonora Tillman, the actress's second daughter ★ MGM coughs up $8 million to sign **Macaulay Culkin** to star opposite **Ted Danson** in their comedy *Getting Even with Dad*. Little Mac's father, **Kit Culkin**, had angled for $10m ★ Universal Pictures sues child star **Michael Oliver** for $190,000 for breaking his original contract to star in their *Problem Child II* for $80,000. Just days before the film was to start shooting, Oliver's mother held her son hostage to the tune of $500,000. Had Universal dumped their film at that stage, it would have cost the studio $4 million ★ With one month to go before filming, and with **Johnny Depp, Christian Slater, Bill Murray, Martin Landau** and **Jeffrey Jones** set to star, *Ed Wood* is beached. A film

Eddie Murphy: proud dad, proud husband

biography of the eccentric B-movie director **Edward D. Wood Jr** (*Glen or Glenda?, Plan 9 from Outer Space*), the film has been a pet project of **Tim Burton**'s for some time. However, because the director of *Batman* and *Beetlejuice* wanted to shoot *Ed Wood* in black-and-white, Columbia Pictures sank the project ★ **Kelly McGillis**'s husband, yacht broker **Fred Tillman**, is arrested by the Florida vice squad for offering $30 to an undercover police officer in exchange for sex ★ **Lisa Bonet** files for divorce from her husband of six years, singer **Lenny Kravitz**. The couple have been separated since 1990 ★ Paramount's big summer movie, *Sliver*, is in trouble. Test audiences disliked the ending and the studio has had its hand slapped by the ratings board. Thirty changes are implemented to satisfy the censor ★ *Aladdin* grosses $200 million in the US alone ★ Walt Disney Co. buys the fiercely independent art house distributor Miramax Film Corp., the company responsible for nurturing such pictures in the US as *My Left*

Foot, sex, lies and videotape and *The Crying Game.*

May 1993

Jane Seymour, 42, marries actor/director **James Keach**, 45, in California ★ *The Los Angeles Times* prints excerpts from the new book *Walt Disney: Hollywood's Dark Prince*, a hatchet job by **Marc Eliot** which reveals that the Mouse Man was an FBI informant and obsessed by his impotence ★ Actress/model **Paulina Porizkova** and her husband, rock star **Ric Ocasek**, announce the conception of their first child (due out mid-autumn) ★ **Mike Myers** marries his sweetheart in Toronto ★ *The New York Times* reveals that **Jennifer Grey** and White House spokesman **George Stephanopoulos** are an item ★ **Howard E. Rollins Jr**, who was nominated for an Oscar for *Ragtime*, is jailed for 70 days for traffic misdemeanours and violating parole ★ The British branch

Julia Roberts: ditching boyfriends, losing Daniel, gaining Lovett

of *Planet Hollywood* opens in London's Coventry Street. Besides the restaurant's partners – **Arnold Schwarzenegger**, **Sylvester Stallone** and **Bruce Willis** – the opening is attended by **James Belushi**, **Jacqueline Bisset**, **Michael J. Fox**, **Mel Gibson**, **Melanie Griffith**, **Don Johnson**, **Demi Moore**, **Christopher Reeve**, **Charlie Sheen**, **Patrick Swayze** and **Jean-Claude Van Damme**. Ten thousand fans turn up to watch ★ **Oliver Stone**'s wife of twelve years files for divorce ★ **Mike Leigh** is named best director and **David Thewlis** best actor – for *Naked* – at the 1993 Cannes Film Festival ★ **Kim Basinger**, worth only $5 million, files for bankruptcy.

June 1993

Clint Eastwood, 62, and his girlfriend, actress **Frances Fisher**, 40, are reportedly expecting their first baby ★ **Woody Allen** loses his court battle for custody of his children following a traumatic seven-week trial.

Judge **Elliott Wilk** denounces Allen as 'an inadequate, irresponsible and self-absorbed father', and gives custody to the filmmaker's former lover, **Mia Farrow** ★ After 38 weeks of release in the US, *Brother's Keeper* grosses $1,001,469, the first documentary to pass the million-dollar mark ★ **James Bridges**, 57, director of *The China Syndrome*, *Urban Cowboy*, *Perfect* and *Bright Lights, Big City*, dies of intestinal cancer in Los Angeles ★ **Burt Reynolds** files for divorce from **Loni Anderson**, his wife of five years and companion for twelve ★ **Ted Danson**, 45, agrees to pay his wife, Casey, 55, a divorce settlement of £26 million. The couple had been married for more than fifteen years, but separated in October when Danson became romantically involved with **Whoopi Goldberg** – on the set of *Made in America*. The former couple will, however, share custody of their two daughters: Katherine, 13, and Alexis, 8 ★ **Billy Dee Williams** files for divorce from his wife of twenty years ★ **Bernard Bresslaw**, 59, dies. His last film was *Leon the Pig Farmer* ★ *Jurassic Park* grosses $51,452,120 in its opening weekend in the States, an all-time record ★ Sir **Richard Attenborough**, star of *Jurassic Park*, is made a life peer in the Queen's Birthday Honours list. **Thora Hird**, whose numerous films include *2,000 Women*, *The Entertainer*, *A Kind of Loving* and *The Nightcomers*, is created a Dame ★ **Ray Sharkey**, 40, dies in Brooklyn of AIDS. He will be best remembered for the films *The Idolmaker* and *Willie and Phil*, and was most recently seen in *Zebrahead* and (his last picture) *Cop and a Half* ★ Rumours fly that **Madonna** is pregnant ★ After eleven weeks, *Indecent Proposal* becomes the first 1993 release to pass the $100 million mark in the US ★ *Jurassic Park* also clocks up $100m – *in nine days* (an all-time record) ★ *Unforgiven* follows with a $100m gross after 46 weeks ★ **Demi Moore** and **Bruce Willis** are expecting again ★ **Guillaume Depardieu** is sentenced to a three-year term in prison, with two years suspended, for peddling heroin ★ The wife of **Richard Thomas** files for divorce. The couple have been married for seventeen years ★ During a break from filming *The Pelican Brief*, **Julia Roberts**, 25, marries singer-actor **Lyle Lovett**, 35, in Washington. They met on the set of Robert Altman's *The Player*, in which they both appeared.

In Memoriam

F. Maurice Speed

Although not a great actor (in fact he turned in some pretty awful performances), **Dana Andrews**, who died aged 83 on 17 December 1992, was popular and capable of fine work in the right parts. Born in Missouri, the son of a Baptist minister, the family moved to Texas when Andrews was still a child. One of the jobs he took to support himself at college was in a cinema, and that gave him a taste for the medium. He made his way to California and studied acting at the Pasadena Playhouse. There he was seen and put under contract to Samuel Goldwyn who sold half of the agreement to Darryl Zanuck. In the early 1940s he was mainly cast in Westerns including the classic *The Ox-Bow Incident* (1943). He also did well in *Laura* (1944), *The Best Years of Our Lives* (1946) and *Boomerang* (1947). Others of his more than 70 films included: *Kit Carson* and *The Westerner* (1940), *Swamp Water* and *Tobacco Road* (1941), *Wing and a Prayer* (1941), *State Fair* (1945), *Daisy Kenyon* (1947), *Frogmen* (1951), *Elephant Walk* (1954), *Beyond a Reasonable Doubt* (1956), *Battle of the Bulge* (1965), *Airport* (1975), *The Last Tycoon* (1976) and *Prince Jack* (1984).

Arletty, one of the brightest stars of the vintage years of the French cinema, died aged 94 on 24 July 1992. Born Léonie Bathiat, Arletty began her working life as a factory worker and secretary but then became a

Dana Andrews

model and by 1918 was appearing in Paris in music hall, revues etc. It was not until 1931 that she made her film debut, in *Un Chien qui rapporte*. In 1938 she achieved stardom in Marcel Carne's *Hôtel du Nord* and established herself as one of France's foremost actresses, a status confirmed by her performance in the same director's outstanding 1945 film *Les Enfants du*

Arletty

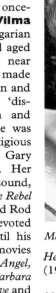

Showgirl (1957), *The Vikings* (1958), *Our Man in Havana* (1959), *The Trials of Oscar Wilde* (1960) and *The Looking Glass War* (1970).

News arrived this year that the once-famous Hungarian actress **Vilma Banky** – dubbed 'The Hungarian Rhapsody' by Hollywood – died aged 93 on 18 March 1991. Born near Budapest, as Vilma Lonchit, she made a number of Hungarian, German and Austrian films before being 'discovered' by Samuel Goldwyn and lured to Hollywood, where she was cast opposite a number of prestigious male stars such as Valentino, Gary Cooper and Ronald Colman. Her career ended with the advent of sound, her final appearance being in *The Rebel* in 1932. In 1927 she had married Rod La Rocque and remained a devoted wife for the next 42 years until his death. Among her American movies were *Son of the Sheik*, *The Dark Angel*, *The Eagle* and *The Winning of Barbara Worth* (all 1926), *The Night of Love* and *The Magic Flame* (1927), *Two Lovers* and *The Awakening* (1928), *This is*

Vilma Banky

Maxine Audley

Heaven (1929) and *A Lady to Love* (1930).

Although she made very few films, **Shirley Booth** (real name: Thelma Booth Ford), who died aged 94 on 16 October 1992, achieved the distinction of winning the 1952 Oscar with her

Paradis, one of the great landmarks in the French cinema. Thereafter Arletty divided her time between stage and screen. Although she refused to perform for the Germans during the Occupation she did take a German lover, a mistake that led to her spending two months in jail as a collaborator after the Liberation, followed by a period of unpopularity and lack of work. Some of her later films include *Le Grand Jeu* (1953), *Huis Clos* and *L'Air de Paris* (1954), *Maxime* and *Un Drôle de Dimanche* (1958) and *The Longest Day* (1962). Not beautiful in the conventional sense, her black hair, strong personality and intelligence made her a formidable presence. An accident in the late 1960s caused her to go blind and though an operation partially restored her sight it was never fully recovered. Her autobiography, *Je suis comme je suis*, was published in 1989.

Flame-haired **Maxine Audley**, who died at the age of 69 in July 1992, was primarily a stage actress who made only the occasional film, as a featured player. Making her debut in *A Midsummer Night's Dream* at the Open Air Theatre in Regent's Park in 1940, she was soon performing with the Old Vic company and at Stratford-upon-Avon as well as in the West End. Among her films were *The Sleeping Tiger* (1954 – her screen debut), *The Barretts of Wimpole Street* (1956), *The Prince and the*

Shirley Booth

Cantinflas

Chuck Connors

appeared in only a few films, including *A Study in Terror* (1965), *The Fixer* (1968), *Lock Up Your Daughters* (1969), *The Raging Moon* (1971), *Tales that Witness Madness* (1973), *Galileo* (1975), *The Seven Per Cent Solution* and *The Bawdy Adventures of Tom Jones* (1976).

Cantinflas (real name, Mario Moreno Reyes), who died in late May 1993 at the age of 81, was the clown beloved of the entire Spanish-speaking world. Originally a song-and-dance man of tented shows, Cantinflas switched to being a circus clown with enormous success. Lured to Hollywood to play Phileas Fogg's faithful companion in Mike Todd's spectacular success *Around the World in 80 Days*, Cantinflas achieved worldwide acclaim. But it was shortlived, for his next Hollywood spectacular, *Pepe*, was a dire failure with critics and moviegoers alike, and he returned to South America, where he continued to make movies for a more restricted audience.

Chuck Connors (born Kevin Joseph Connors), who died at the age of 71 on 10 November 1992, started his professional career as a baseball player, but after his four-year war service (mostly as a tank instructor) he turned to basketball instead, and it was as a member of a Los Angeles team that he began to pick up film parts. His first screen appearance was in *Pat and Mike* in 1952. Other early films included *Target Zero* (1955), *Walk the Dark Street* (1956) and *Tomahawk Trail* (1957). But it was as a result of his big success in the long-running TV series 'The Rifleman' that he was offered star roles. He went on to make some 30 movies in all, including *The Big Country* (1958), *Geronimo* (1958), *Captain Nemo and the Underwater City* (1970), *Support Your Local Gunfighter* (1971), *The Proud and the Damned* (1972), *Soylent Green* (1973), *Pancho Villa* (1975), *The Tourist Trap* (1979) and *Airplane II: The Sequel* (1982).

Craggy-faced **Eddie Constantine** was an American of Russian descent who found success in Europe, eventually becoming a citizen of France, and finding the popularity there that eluded him in his own country. He died in Wiesbaden on 25 February 1993 at the age of 75. Constantine originally studied singing at the Vienna Conservatoire, but without any success at the time, though later it was to pay off when he followed his ballet

debut movie – *Come Back Little Sheba*. Miss Booth began her long acting career at the age of 12 and won her first professional role in 1923. Her other films were *Main Street to Broadway* (1953), *About Mrs Leslie* (1954), *The Matchmaker* (1958) and *Hot Spell* (1958). But her greatest triumphs were achieved on stage, radio and TV, to which she devoted most of her time.

Georgia Brown (real name Georgia Klot), the singer/actress who died in July 1992 at the age of 58, will always be recalled for her magnetic performance as Nancy in *Oliver!* (oddly she was not asked to repeat the role when Carol Reed made the film). She

Eddie Constantine

dancer wife to Paris and became a popular night-club singer. Taken under Edith Piaf's wing, he began to get parts in French films and became something of a cult figure in a series of Lemmy Caution private-eye thrillers. After starring in Jean Luc Godard's *Alphaville* in 1965, Constantine's popularity waned until the late 1970s, when he starred in a series of German thrillers and television dramas. One's lasting impression of Constantine is as Peter Cheyney's tough character Caution, a cynical figure with a cigarette in his mouth, a glass of whisky in his hand and a pretty girl on his arm. He was the author of a novel, later published in the USA under the title *The Godplayer*.

His English-language films include *Passport to Shame* (1959), *SOS Pacific* (1959), *Lucky Joe* (1964), *It's Alive II* (1978), *The Long Good Friday* (1980), *Boxoffice* (1982) and *Helsinki Napoli All Night Long* (1988).

Florence Desmond (born Florence Dawson), who died aged 87 on 10 January 1993, was a child dancer who became the most famous impersonator of her period (her impression of Noel Coward was memorable) apart from earning accolades for her straight

acting performances. She appeared in a score or more movies including *The Road to Fortune* (her first, in 1930), *Sally in our Alley* (the following year), *Nine till Six* and *High Society* (two of the five she appeared in during 1932), *Long Live the King* (one of three she made in 1933), *No Limit* (1935), *Accused* (1936), *Kicking the Moon Around* (1938), *Charley Moon* (1950) and *Some Girls Do* (1968). Little known in recent years, she was a major star of her day.

One of Britain's most gifted actors, **Denholm Elliott** died, aged 70 on 6 October 1992 at his home in Ibiza, Spain. Although never a star, he was often the mainstay of the films in which he appeared, specialising in seedy, hard-drinking roles such as dubious reporters, small-time officials and others who never succeed in life. For his performance in *A Room with a View* he was nominated for an Oscar and he won three British Film Academy awards. Born in London, educated at Malvern College and trained at the Royal Academy of Dramatic Art, Elliott began by playing earnest young men, but it wasn't long before he began to specialise in shabbier parts, although he remained very versatile, playing in horror thrillers and comedy with equal ease. Being such a dependable actor he was constantly in demand and his output of films, plays and television work was prodigious. His films include: *Dear Mr Prohack* (his first in 1949), *The Holly and the Ivy*, *The Ringer* and *The Sound Barrier* (all three in 1952), *The Cruel Sea* and *The Heart of the Matter* (both in 1953), *They Who Dare* (1954), *The Night My Number Came Up* (1955), *Station Six Sahara* (1962), *King Rat* (1965), *Alfie* and *The Spy With a Cold Nose* (1966), *Maroc 7* (1967), *The Night They Raided Minsky's*, *Here We Go Round the Mulberry Bush* and *The Seagull* (1968), *The House That Dripped Blood* (one of four films made in 1970), *A Doll's House* and *The Vault of Horror* (1973), *The Apprenticeship of Duddy Kravitz* (1974), *To the Devil a Daughter* (1976), *A Bridge Too Far* (1977), *The Boys from Brazil* (1978), *Raiders of the Lost Ark* and *The Missionary* (1981), *The Razor's Edge* (1984), *Defence of the Realm* (1985), *A Room with a View* (1986), *Indiana Jones and the Last Cru-*

Denholm Elliott

sade (1989), *Maurice* (1988), *Toy Soldiers* (1991) – only a few of 70 or more which he made.

The son of a popular Naples actor, **Vincent Gardenia**, who died at the age of 71 on 9 December 1992, started his stage career when he was 5, three years after the family moved to Brooklyn, New York. Twice nominated for an Oscar, Gardenia – who once reckoned he had played more than 500 roles in film, stage and TV productions – won many awards. His films include *Murder Inc.* (1960), *A View from the Bridge* (1962), *Mission Impossible vs. the Mob* (1969), *The Front Page* (1974 – the year he appeared in the first of the several *Death Wish* films), *Heaven Can Wait* (1978) and *Skin Deep* (1989).

The last live link with the earliest days of the cinema was severed when **Lillian** (Diana) **Gish** died on 27 February 1993 at the age of 99. Lillian's long career began when she was 5, when, known as 'Baby Lillian', she toured with her even younger sister Dorothy in a series of stage melodramas. The Gish Sisters, as they were then billed, were introduced to David Wark Griffith and the cinema by another child actress Gladys Smith, later to become famous as Mary Pickford. Thus began a working relationship which persisted for many years. Beginning with one- and two-reelers, Lillian appeared in Griffith's first multi-reel drama *Judith of Bethulia* in 1913 and then was chosen as his star for *Birth of a Nation* in 1915. In the early 1920s, Lillian left Griffith (amicably, as her admiration and gratitude for him never waned) and made films for other companies including MGM and United Artists. By now she insisted that her contracts should include her approval of both story and director. She made one attempt at direction herself – *Remodelling Her Husband* with sister Dorothy in the leading role – but found it so complicated and arduous she never made a second attempt. She took the advent of the talkies in her stride, and her vast stage experience – despite all her films she never deserted the stage – made the transition easier for her. Lillian made her last film as a star in 1933 in *His Double Life*, thereafter appearing in feature roles almost until the time of her death. She aged with grace, retaining something of her former beauty right up to the end.

In 1946 Lillian was nominated for the Best Supporting Actress Oscar award for *Duel in the Sun*, and in 1970 was awarded a special Career Achievement award. She wrote her memoirs, *Life and Lillian Gish*, in the 1930s, later – in 1969 – expanding the work and republishing it as *The Movies, Mr Griffith and Me*.

Among her films are: *The Burglar's Dilemma* (1912), *The Musketeers of Pig Alley* (1912), *The Battle at Elderberry Gulch* (1913), *Just Gold* (1913), *The Stolen Bride* (1913), *The Angel of Contention* (1914), *The Battle of the Sexes* (1914), *The Lily and the Rose* (1915), *Intolerance* (1916), *Hearts of the World* (1917), *The Great Love* (1918), *Broken Blossoms* (1919), *Way Down East* (1920), *Orphans of the Storm* (1921), *The White Sister* (1923), *Romaloa* (1924), *The Scarlet Letter* and *La Boheme* (1926), *Annie Laurie* (1927), *The Enemy* and *The Wind* (1928), *His Double Life* (1933), *One Romantic Night* (1930), *Commandos Strike at Dawn* (1942), *Top Man* (1943), *Miss Susie Slagle's* (1945), *Duel in the Sun* (1947), *Portrait of Jennie* (1948), *The*

Lillian Gish

Cobweb (1955), *The Night of the Hunter* (1955), *Orders to Kill* (1958), *The Unforgiven* (1960), *Follow Me, Boys!* (1966), *The Comedians* (1967), *Warning Shot* (1967), *A Wedding* (1978), *Hambone and Hillie* (1984), *Sweet Liberty* (1986) and *The Whales of August* (1987).

It was not for nothing that they called **Helen Hayes** (born Helen Hayes Brown), who died on 17 March 1993 at the age of 92, 'The First Lady of the American Theatre', for it was the theatre that was her first and last love and it was on the stage that she made her greatest triumphs. Nevertheless she was to win two Oscars; the first for Best Actress in 1931 in *The Sin of Madelon Claudet*, and the second as

Best Supporting Actress in *Airport* in 1970. The daughter of a travelling salesman and a small-time actress, Miss Hayes made her professional stage debut at the age of five, and four years later appeared on Broadway in a production of *Old Dutch*, thereafter appearing constantly in touring shows. Eventually she returned to Broadway for her triumph in James Barrie's *What Every Woman Knows*, and from then on it was success after success for this tiny actress, on stage, television and screen. She published several books of memoirs, *A Gift of Joy* (1965), *On Reflection* (1969) and (with Anita Loos) *Twice Over Lightly* (1971).

Her films include: *The Weavers of Life* (1917), *Babs* (1920), *Arrowsmith* (1931), *A Farewell to Arms* and *The Son-Daughter* (1932), *The White Sister, Another Language* and *Night Flight* (1933), *What Every Woman Knows*

Helen Hayes

(1934), *My Son John* (1952), *Anastasia* (1956), *Portrait of an Actress*, a feature documentary in which she related her life story (1974), *Herbie Rides Again* (1974), *One of Our Dinosaurs Is Missing* (1975) and *Candleshoe* (1978).

'She's the only film star who looks and acts like a *real* lady,' a fellow critic once said to me of **Audrey Hepburn** (born Edda van Heemstra Hepburn Ruston), and that was a very sound judgement of an actress who, whatever role she took, remained a 'lady' – charming, elfin, beautiful, serene and gracious. Maybe her mother, Ella van Heemstra, a Dutch baroness, had something to do with Audrey's great charm and social grace. Tributes like this poured in at the news of her death, at the age of 63 on 20 January 1993. Born in Holland (her father was a banker of English-Irish lineage) she spent her war years – after school in England – in Holland, returning to Britain at the end of hostilities on a ballet scholarship, but became a fashion model, eventually getting small acting parts in films and plays. During the filming of *Monte Carlo Baby* Hepburn met the famous French writer Colette, who insisted she play the title role in the latter's stage adaptation of her novel *Gigi*, which opened on Broadway in 1951. Two years later Hepburn went to Hollywood to play the Princess in *Roman Holiday* and her

performance won her the 1953 Oscar. She was to be nominated for the award four more times, for *Sabrina* in 1954, *The Nun's Story* in 1959, *Breakfast at Tiffany's* in 1961 and *Wait Until Dark* in 1967. In the late 1960s, Hepburn more or less retired, although she subsequently did make the occasional film, including appearances as Maid

Audrey Hepburn

Marian in *Robin and Marian* (1976) and the threatened woman in the thriller *Sidney Sheldon's Bloodline* in 1979. In 1986 Audrey Hepburn became an unofficial goodwill ambassador for UNICEF and thereafter spent a great deal of her time travelling in Africa and trying to raise money for the cause.

Audrey Hepburn was married twice, initially to actor Mel Ferrer and subsequently to Andrea Dotti, an Italian psychiatrist. She had two sons. Apart from the films already mentioned, Audrey Hepburn appeared in *One Wild Oat*, *The Secret People* and *Young Wives' Tale* (all 1951), *The Lavender Hill Mob* (1952), *War and Peace* (1956), *Love in the Afternoon* (1957), *The Unforgiven* (1960), *The Children's Hour* (1961), *Charade* (1963), *Paris When It Sizzles* (1963), *My Fair Lady* (1964), *Two for the Road* (1967), *They All Laughed* (1981), and – her final film appearance – *Always* (1989). At the 1993 Oscar ceremony Audrey Hepburn was posthumously awarded the Jean Hersholt Humanitarian Award.

Mervyn (David) **Johns**, actor father of actress and film star Glynis Johns, died in September 1992 at the age of 93, after a long and distinguished

Mervyn Johns

career in plays, films and TV. Born in Pembrokeshire and a member of a mining family, he was always proud of his Welsh ancestry (naturally, he was a great rugby fan and was to be seen at most of the big games at Cardiff Arms Park). In the Royal Flying Corps during World War I, he enrolled at the Royal Academy of Dramatic Art upon demobilisation and won the academy's Gold Medal, their highest distinction. Making his professional stage debut in London at the Comedy Theatre in 1923 in *The Elopement*, he quickly attracted critical attention, including high praise from the most feared critic of his time, the legendary James Agate. Johns made his film debut in 1934 in

Allan Jones

Lady in Danger and quickly established himself as one of the most reliable and gifted feature players of his period, becoming a favourite with the Ealing Studios casting directors. Johns eventually decided after his wife's death to become a resident at the Actors' Trust Home, where he created a sensation by marrying widow Diana Churchill when he was approaching his 78th year! Johns was capable of outstanding performances and gave many during his long and busy career. His films include: *Jamaica Inn* (1939), *Convoy* (1940), *Next of Kin* and *Went the Day Well?* (1942), *The Halfway House* (1944), *Pink String and Sealing Wax* and *Dead of Night* (1945), *The Captive Heart* (1946), *Captain Boycott* (1947), *Quartet* and *Edward My Son* (1949), *Scrooge* and *The Magic Box* (1951), *Romeo and Juliet* (1954), *Moby Dick* (1956), *The Devil's Disciple* (1959), *Francis of Assisi* and *No Love for Johnny* (1961), *55 Days at Peking* and *The Old Dark House* (1964), *The Heroes of Telemark* (1965) and, his final screen appearance, *Kill and Kill Again* (1980).

Allan Jones, father of pop star Jack Jones, died aged 84 on 27 June 1992. Best known for his playing romantic leads in two of the Marx Brothers films, *A Day at the Races* and *A Night at the Opera*, it was in the 1937 film *The Firefly* that he first sang what was to become his signature tune, 'The Donkey Serenade'. Some of his other films were: *Show Boat* (1936), *The Great Victor Herbert* (1939), *The Boys from Syracuse* (1940), *Rhythm of the Islands* (1943), *The Singing Sheriff* (1944), *Honeymoon Ahead* (1945), *Stage to Thunder Rock* (1964) and *A Swingin' Summer* (1965). It was only a few months before his death that Jones (the son of a coal miner) had completed a singing tour of Australia.

Canadian-born **Ruby Keeler**, who died aged 83 on 28 February 1993, had a short but starry career on stage and screen, being especially remembered for her teaming with Dick Powell in a series of spectacular Busby Berkeley musicals. The glamour and glitz of Hollywood never in fact enthralled Miss Keeler, who eventually walked out on the movies and quite happily devoted herself to dom-

Ruby Keeler

esticity, first as the wife of Al Jolson and then of businessman John Lowe Jr. Ruby Keeler was not particularly beautiful, but she had an endearing lively zest and two happy dancing feet. Modest to a fault, she didn't think highly of her 'awful' (her own words) voice – nor even of her dancing. In 1969, 40 years after leaving Broadway, she returned there and appeared in a revival of *No, No, Nanette*. She also had small roles in several films.

Her films included: *42nd Street, Gold Diggers of 1933* and *Footlight Parade* (1933), *Dames* and *Flirtation Walk* (1934), *Go Into Your Dance* and *Shipmates Forever* (1935), *Colleen* (1936), *Ready, Willing and Able* (1937), *Mother Carey's Chickens* (1938), *Sweetheart of the Campus* (1941) and *The Phynx* (1970).

Among the most literate, civilised and commercially successful of writer-directors and producers, **Joseph L. (for Leo) Mankiewicz** died, aged 83, on 5 February 1993. The son of German immigrants, Mankiewicz graduated from Columbia University at the age of 19 and worked briefly as a news reporter in Berlin but moved to Hollywood in 1928, encouraged by his scenarist brother Herman (who among other things was co-writer with Orson Welles of *Citizen Kane*), who helped him obtain a post as general writer with Paramount. As such Mankiewicz won his first Oscar nomination, for co-writing the script of *Skippy*. At this time he wrote scripts for W. C. Fields, Jack Oakie and Wheeler and Woolsey comedies. Louis B. Mayer persuaded him to become a producer, despite Mankiewicz's persistent ambition to direct, an idea that Mayer refused to do anything about. So when the opportunity suddenly occurred at Fox to write and direct *Dragonwyck*, Mankiewicz jumped at the chance, and helmed the 1943 success. Three other successes followed: *The Late George Apley* (1947), *The Ghost and Mrs Muir* (also in 1947) and the British production *Escape* in 1948. *A Letter to Three Wives* (1949) brought two Oscars (for Best Direction and Best Screenplay) and a third nomination (for Best Film). From then on it was one success after another, including the multi-Oscar winner *All About Eve* (1950). Mankiewicz's final feature film was *Sleuth* in 1972, although he subsequently contributed in various ways to several documentaries in the 1980s, and remained full of exciting plans right up to his death. Mankiewicz proved that moviegoers appreciate superior, intelligent movies when offered them, and he never underrated his audience.

Other productions that Mankiewicz wrote and directed include: *House of Strangers* (1949), *No Way Out* (1950), *People Will Talk* (1951), *Five Fingers*

Anthony Perkins

(1952), *Julius Caesar* (1953), *The Barefoot Contessa* (1954), *Guys and Dolls* (1955), *The Quiet American* (1958), *Cleopatra* (1963), *The Honey Pot* (1967) and *There Was a Crooked Man* (1970).

Anthony Perkins, who died in Hollywood at the age of 60 on 12 September 1992, will always be recalled for his performance as Norman Bates in the Hitchcock classic thriller *Psycho*, a role he was to repeat – with considerably less success – some twenty years later in *Psycho II*, *Psycho III* (which he also directed) and *Psycho IV*. The son of stage and screen actor Osgood Perkins, he made his stage debut as a teenager in summer stock, making his film debut in 1953 in *The Actress*. He was seldom idle and he continued working up to his death. Perkins also did a great deal of TV work, both features and series. His films included *The Tin Star* (1957), *Desire Under the Elms* (1957), *On the Beach* (1959), *The Trial* (1962), *Pretty Poison* (1968), *Catch–22* (1970), *The Life and Times of Judge Roy Bean* (1972), *Murder on the Orient Express* (1974), *Remember My Name* (1978), *The Black Hole* (1979), *Crimes of Passion* (1984) and *Edge of Sanity* (1989).

Mary Philbin, who died aged 89 on 7 May 1993, was a popular silent screen star of the twenties who failed to survive the advent of sound. She will be best remembered for her highly praised performance in the 1925 movie *The Phantom of the Opera*. It was this film that caused a major uproar when the importers into Britain managed to persuade the powers that be to give the film a full military escort, with band, on its journey from Southampton docks to London's Wardour Street! Miss Philbin was originally discovered by Carl Laemmle when she was sixteen: noticing her as the runner-up in a beauty contest which he was judging, he gave her a role in his next film *Blazing Trail* in 1921. This brought her to the attention of Erich von Stroheim, who gave her a role the following year in his *Foolish Wives*. In all Miss Philbin appeared in some twenty-five films, including *Temple of Venus* (1923), *The Rose of Paris* (1924), *Stella Maris* (1925), *The Man Who Laughs* (1927), *Love Me and the World Is Mine* (1928), *The Last Per-*

Mary Philbin

formance, *Girl Overboard*, *After the Fog* and *The Shannons of Broadway* (all in 1929), her final year in front of the cameras).

The world in general and moviegoers in particular owe a great deal to **Hal Roach**, who died at the age of 100 on 2 November 1992. For Roach had the rare gift of being able to create universal laughter through his slapstick, essentially visual film comedies. With Harold Lloyd, Charlie Chase, Laurel and Hardy etc as his players, writer, director and producer Roach made a series of slapstick comedies which are as funny today as when they were made. Born in New York, Roach began his working life with a series of diverse jobs, including a spell as a gold prospector in Alaska. When he eventually drifted into Hollywood he got a job as an extra and a stunt man. But it was typical of the man that when he inherited some $3000 he set up his own production company with Harold Lloyd (another extra) and began making the 'Willie Work' comedies starring Lloyd. By the late 1920s Roach had established the Laurel and Hardy team and had become a big success, embracing sound when it arrived in the 1930s. During the war the Roach Studios turned out a string of training films for the Army as well as numerous propaganda movies. But at the end of the war Roach seemed to have lost his touch and no longer found it as easy to turn out the successful comedies of the past. It was left to his son to keep the studios occupied with TV series. In 1984 Roach was awarded an honorary Oscar. At a time when many films are concerned with cruelty and violence it is refreshing to look back at Roach's simple slapstick comedies which stand the test of time so well.

Cardew Robinson (real name, Douglas Robinson), who died aged 75 on 27 December 1992, was a British comedian who gained popularity with his creation of the broadly comic character 'Cardew the Cad', a farcical overgrown schoolboy. He also appeared in plays, in vaudeville and the occasional film – the last of which was *Shirley Valentine*. He also contributed comic material for Peter Sellers and Dick Emery.

Cool Canadian beauty **Alexis Smith** (real name Gladys Smith), who died in Los Angeles at the age of 72 in June 1993, was a popular screen star of the 1940s and 1950s. Usually cast as a scheming woman, it is generally acknowledged she gave her best performance in Joseph Losey's British film *The Sleeping Tiger* in 1954. And her versatility was proved with her per-

Alexis Smith

formance in the musicals *Night and Day* (1946) and *Rhapsody in Blue* (1945), and the Jack Benny comedy *The Horn Blows at Midnight* (1945). She retired in 1959 but returned to the stage in 1971 to score a triumph – and win a Tony award – in Stephen Sondheim's *Follies*, leading to her making a few more films (she made some fifty movies in all).

Apart from those already mentioned her films include: *Dive Bomber* (1941), *Gentleman Jim* (1942), *The Constant Nymph* (1943), *The Adventures of Mark Twain* (1944), *Of Human Bondage* (1946), *The Woman in White* (1948), *Whiplash* and *Any Number Can Play* (1949), *Undercover Girl* (1950), *Here Comes the Groom* (1951), *The Eternal Sea* (1955), *Beau James* (1957), *Once Is Not Enough* (1975), *The Little Girl Who Lives Down the Lane* (1977), *Casey's Shadow* (1978), *La Truite* (1982) and *Tough Guys* (1986).

It is to **John Sturges** (born John Carne) that we owe some of the finest classical Westerns, many of them with unexpected depths, such as the racial prejudice that motivates *Bad Day at Black Rock* (1954). The director/producer, who died on 18 August 1992 at the age of 82, entered the film business in 1932 with the help of his brother Sturges Carne, who was already an established art director. After periods as assistant production designer and editor, Sturges enlisted in the USAAF, where he made nearly 50 documentaries and training films. When the war ended he joined Columbia, where he directed B movies, making the Randolph Scott Western *The Walking Hills* in 1949. He won acclaim with *Escape from Fort Bravo* in 1953, followed by the classic *Bad Day at Black Rock*. Other outstanding Sturges Westerns included *Gunfight at the OK Corral* (1957), *The Law and Jake Wade* (1958), *Last Train from Gun Hill* (1959) and, of course, his remarkably successful re-filming of the Japanese *The Seven Samurai* as *The Magnificent Seven* (1960), the first film in which he doubled as producer and director. Some of his non-Westerns included the thrilling POW drama *The Great Escape* (1963), *The Magnificent Yankee* (1956), *The Old Man and the Sea* (1958), *Ice Station Zebra* (1968), *Marooned* (1969) and *McQ*, with John Wayne (1974). His last film, made in

Ann Todd

1976, was the British war thriller *The Eagle Has Landed*. In all, Sturges contributed – as screenwriter, editor, producer or director – to more than fifty movies.

Cool, calm and collected are terms that spring to mind when writing about **Ann Todd** (full name Ann Todd Mayfield), the actress and film director who died on 6 May 1993 at the age of 84. A product of the Central School of Speech and Drama, Ann Todd's career began when picked by playwright Ian Hay to appear in one of his West End stage comedies. He was so satisfied with her performance that he employed her, despite her serious appearance, in his next two comedies, after which she was seldom without work. However, she never got over her natural reluctance to appear in public, and is on record as saying that any applause she got always embarrassed her! Her film career took off when she gave a memorable performance as the pianist in *The Seventh Veil* (1945), in which she suffered at the hands of her sadistic guardian (James Mason). After this, Hitchcock chose her for his *The Paradine Case* (1947). Her busy schedule of plays, films and TV was halted when she was robbed and seriously assaulted by an intruder, leaving her face seriously scarred. The result was a determination to start a new career as film writer, director and producer, resulting in a series of noteworthy documentaries which included *Thunder in Heaven* (1964), *Thunder of the Gods* (made in Greece, 1966), *Thunder of the Kings* (made in Egypt, 1967), *Thunder of Silence* (in Jordan) and *Thunder of Light* (in Scotland). Although she was subsequently lured back to the stage on a couple of occasions, she remained in seclusion for her last years. She was the author of two novels and an autobiography, *The Eighth Veil*.

Other films include *The Ghost Train* (1931), *The Water Gypsies* (1932), *The Return of Bulldog Drummond* (1934), *Things to Come* (1936), *Action for Slander* (1937), *Poison Pen* (1939), *All This and Heaven Too* (1940), *Blood and Sand* (1941), *The Passionate Friends* (1948), *Madeleine* (1949), *The Sound Barrier* (1952), *The Green Scarf* (1954), *Time Without Pity* (1957), *Taste of Fear* (1961), *The Fiend* (1971) and *The Human Factor* (1979).

Bill Williams (real name William H. Kate Sr.), who died at the age of 77 on 21 September 1992, was a veteran film and TV actor who was often to be seen in Westerns. For 46 years the husband of Barbara Hale ('secretary' to Raymond Burr's Perry Mason during a long series of features), Williams started his career in vaudeville and repertory and it was only after World War II (in which he served with the USAAF) that he started his film career as a contract player at RKO Radio. Some of his films were *Thirty Seconds Over Tokyo* (1944), *Son of Paleface* (1952), *Deadline at Dawn* (1946), and *Rio Lobo* (1970). Other films include two co-starring with his wife – *A Likely Story* (1947) and *The Clay Pigeon* (1949) – and *Till the End of Time* (1946), *Oklahoma Territory* (1960) and *The Hallelujah Trail* (1965). His final film was *69 Minutes* in 1977. He was the father of the actor William Katt.

Ted Willis (or Lord Willis), who died at the age of 74 on 22 December 1992, earned lasting fame as the creator of Dixon, the good-hearted bobby of Dock Green police station, who built and retained a devoted TV audience for 21 years. Dixon, perfectly portrayed by Jack Warner, was everyone's idea of the stolid and dependable British copper. Willis was a prolific writer of film and TV scripts, stage plays, and novels – an output including 39 feature films, 37 plays, 41 TV series and 12 novels. He was awarded his life peerage in 1963.

Others who have died during the year include:

Bernard Bresslaw, who died on 10 June 1993 at the age of 59, was a comedian of stature – he was 6ft 5in tall – who occasionally played straight roles in plays. He was performing in *The Taming of the Shrew* at Regent's Park Theatre when he was taken ill. He was best known, however, for his many appearances in the 'Carry On' films.

Mary Duncan, who died in late May 1993, was a well-known Broadway actress before being lured to Hollywood to play a series of vamp roles. She retired from the screen in 1933 and married into the international social set. Films include *Very Confidential* (1927), *The River* (1929), *Kismet* (1930), *The Age for Love* (1931), *Thirteen Women* (1932) and *Morning Glory* (1933).

Sterling Holloway, the American character actor who will be remembered as the voice of the honey-loving bear in several films of A. A. Milne's Winnie-the-Pooh stories. He also gave the voice to the Cheshire Cat in Disney's *Alice in Wonderland*, and was the snake in Disney's *Jungle Book*. He died in January 1993 at the age of 87.

Victor Maddern, the cockney character actor, who died in late June 1993 at the age of 65, appeared in some 200 films including the comedies *I'm All Right Jack* and *Private's Progress*, as well as more serious efforts such as the war epic *Cockleshell Heroes*.

Leslie Norman, who died aged 81 on 18 February 1993, started his film career sweeping the floor at the old Ealing Studios, where he ended up as one of their most dependable director/producers. As producer his films include *The Overlanders* (1946), for which he created Australia in Kew Gardens, *Eureka Stockade* (1948), *A Run for Your Money* (1949), *Where No Vultures Fly* (1951) and *Mandy* (1952). As director he made *X – the Unknown* (1956), *The Shiralee* (1957), *Dunkirk* (1958), *The Summer of the Seventeenth Doll* (1959) and *Mix Me a Person* (1962). He retired in 1977 owing to illness but returned later to direct segments of the TV series 'The Saint' and 'The Persuaders'. Film critic Barry Norman is his son.

Vivienne Segal, in January 1993 at the age of 95. Primarily a stage star, notably in *Pal Joey*, she made the occasional film, including *Golden Dawn* (1930), *Bride of the Regiment* (1930) and *The Cat and the Fiddle* (1933).

John Sharp, in January 1993 at the age of 72. Heavily built character actor who appeared in numerous plays and films; among the latter were: *The Dresser* (1983) and *The Fiendish Plot of Dr Fu Manchu* (1980). In spite of all his stage and film work he will be best recalled in the UK as the owner of the corner shop in TV's *Coronation Street*.

Vladek Sheybal, the brilliant Polish actor/director who made his home in Britain. He was 69 when he died in January 1993. Apart from his considerable stage work and TV appearances, he made quite a number of films including *From Russia With Love* (1963), *Puppet on a Chain* (1970), *Scorpio* (1973), *The Exorcist II* (1977), *The Lady Vanishes* (1979), *Avalanche Express* (1983) and *Red Dawn* (1984).

Ben Warriss, who died on 14 January 1993 aged 83, was the 'straight man' of the long-time top-billing music hall act of Jewel and Warriss (Jimmy Jewel was Warriss's cousin). The partnership began in 1934 and was dissolved in 1967, after which Warriss made occasional solo forays into pantomime, revue and repertory – in 1991 he appeared in John Osborne's *The Entertainer*. Warriss made only a couple of screen appearances, in *What a Carry On* in 1949 and *Let's Have a Murder* in 1950.

Bookshelf

Ivan Butler

A selection of the year's books on cinema

From a list that contains a number of notable film books I have selected the following personal choice:

Among biographies: James Harding's excellent, enthusiastic biography of *Emlyn Williams*; Alexander Walker's hard-hitting but balanced portrait of Rex Harrison, *Fatal Charm*; and Charles Higham's splendidly detailed story of MGM's super-Mogul L. B. Mayer, *Merchant of Dreams*.

Among reference and semi-reference books: Doug McClelland's wholly delightful collection of interviews and comments, *Forties Film Talk*; Jerry Vermilye's *The Complete Films of Laurence Olivier*, among the very best of the long-running Virgin Film Library series; and the massively splendid third volume of the *International Dictionary of Films and Filmmakers – Actors and Actresses*.

Mention should also be made of the updated and revised version of *Enser's Filmed Books and Plays* (compiled by Ellen Baskin and Mandy Hicken), an original and indispensable work of reference despite a calamitously inaccurate final short section.

Details of all the above will be found in the following pages.

Academy Award Winners, Ronald Bergan, Graham Fuller and David Malcolm; Prion, £18.95

Yet another book of Oscars? This handsomely produced coffee-table album scores over many of the others in its lavish illustrations (in monochrome and colour), and in being far more than a 'list of lists'. Lengthy commentaries from three leading film historians provide information, criticism and anecdotal amusement. Full details of nominations would have been welcome, if only for the sake of completeness, but this is a welcome and (for today) reasonably priced survey, which extends up to 1991.

The book, it is stated with considerable emphasis, is neither authorised nor endorsed by the Academy of Motion Arts and Sciences.

Albert Finney in Character, Quentin Falk; Robson Books, £16.95

Considering his fame and achievements, Albert Finney has not had very much written about him – though, judging by his remarks to the author in the book's Acknowledgements, this does not particularly worry him. However, despite failing to obtain Finney's involvement, Quentin Falk has written a satisfyingly full (and enthusiastic) account of his life and career, paying equal attention to the stage, screen and television performances, and providing credit lists for all three. In the final pages are interesting comparisons between Finney's work and that of Laurence Olivier. An eminently useful survey of the story so far.

Alfred Hitchcock – The Hollywood Years, Joel Finler; Batsford, £12.99

No book on Hitchcock nowadays can avoid being to a certain extent repetitious, but Joel Finler approaches the director's work from a fresh angle, with much emphasis on the commercial side (budgets, box-office receipts, etc.) including useful tables setting this out. The films themselves receive adequate critical attention, set against Hitchcock's working methods and personal relationships.

Al Jolson – a Bio-Discography, Larry F. Kiner and Philip R. Evans; Scarecrow Press, dist. Shelwing, £79.50

Following a short biographical introduction this massive volume lists all Jolson's recordings, songs, videos, radio programmes and other similar activities. The large-size pages are beautifully set out on a day-by-day chronological basis and form a complete definitive record. Fully illustrated with production photographs, portraits, record labels, album covers, etc.

Anjelica Huston – The Lady and Her Legacy, Martha Harris; Robson Books, £14.95

Comparatively short but interesting biography of the daughter of John (and granddaughter of Walter) Huston, tracing the career of an actress who fought her way from a disastrous and tragic start (her first film was a failure, and its bad reviews arrived at the moment of her mother's death in a car crash) to wide recognition and respect. She won an Oscar for *Prizzi's Honor*, but her most memorable performance was in *The Dead* – her father's last and most moving film, which he directed from a wheelchair. Her purely accidental connection with the scandal that drove director Roman Polanski out of America is briefly recounted. Sympathetically and well written, but – particularly regrettable in a biography – unindexed.

Autopsy, Carl Richardson; Scarecrow, dist. Shelwing, £22.15
Assault on Society, Donald W. McCaffrey; Scarecrow, dist. Shelwing, £26.26

Two more intriguing explorations into the byways of film analysis – *film noir*, and satire.

Film noir, in Carl Richardson's study, is a corpse in a movie morgue, and the author is performing an autopsy on it. He traces its life and decline through three significant films – *The Maltese Falcon*, *The Naked City* and *Touch of Evil*. His main theme is the growing influence of the practice of location work as it takes over from the enclosed studio, and he mentions many other films on the way.

Donald W. McCaffrey, well known for his books on movie comedy, here studies various types of satirical films – black comedy, parody, fantasy – as far apart as *Dr Strangelove*, *A Day in the Death of Joe Egg*, *Little Big Man* and the cartoon *Fritz the Cat*.

In both books a fresh point of view is clearly and forcefully presented.

Baseball in the Movies, Hal Erickson; McFarland, dist. Shelwing, £30.00

It was inevitable that eventually a book would appear devoted solely to what many regard as THE American sport. This is a good solid reference work, covering films from 1915 to 1991, with synopses, commentaries, technical and other details, and cast lists that contain many well-known names of stars and supporting players. Short subjects and films in which baseball is only incidental are also included.

Bram Stoker's Dracula – the Film and the Legend, Francis Ford Coppola and James V. Hart; Pan Books, £7.99

This richly produced large-format paperback contains the full script of Coppola's new film (in which he claims, not unjustifiably, to have stayed closer to the original than has any other yet made). It also includes extracts from the book, informative notes on the production, and quotes from the director and players, set out in attractive panels. The text is embellished with a very large number of

photographs and stills, in colour and black-and-white.

Casablanca – As Time Goes By..., Frank Miller; Virgin, £12.99

This richly produced and lavishly illustrated paperback first appeared (in hardback) as a celebration of the film's fiftieth anniversary in 1992, and is a complete survey of this astonishingly long-lasting cult movie. A detailed and informative history is embellished with a magnificent collection of production photographs, portraits, stills, posters, press cuttings, reviews, etc. A useful chronology and a bibliography are provided, but, oddly, no cast list or credits. Perhaps it is taken for granted that the film's devotees will know them by heart.

Casablanca, Script and Legend, Howard Koch; Aurum Press, £12.95

This quality paperback consists of the full script of the movie, attractively set out and illustrated. A number of commentaries follow, two of which (especially that by a professor of semiotics at the University of Bologna) get bogged down in strained efforts to dig out 'hidden meanings' in this workmanlike and perennially popular romantic thriller. One is reminded of Hitchcock's crisp remark to Ingrid Bergman when she became agitated over questions of interpretation and significance – 'It's only a movie, Ingrid!' It is a relief finally to reach a couple of down-to-earth reports from critics of the period.

Originally published in 1973, the book has been reissued to tie in with the film's fiftieth anniversary.

Celluloid Power, edited by David Platt; Scarecrow Press, dist. Shelwing, £72.50

A scholarly and important collection of essays on social criticism in films, from '1896 and Lumière' (by Maxim Gorky) to 'Judgement at Nuremberg'. The films discussed vary from *The Grapes of Wrath* to *The Great Dictator* and *Dr Strangelove*, and the subjects from the Hollywood Blacklist to 'The Screen and the Holocaust' and 'Who Killed Marilyn Monroe?'. Many well-known names are among the contributors, such as Anthony Slide, Bela Balasz, Lewis Milestone, Kevin Brownlow, Roger Manvell and Jean Renoir.

Children in the Movies, Neil Sinyard; Batsford, £17.99

In this literate and original study, the author investigates in detail the treatment of childhood in, and the influence of children on, some fifty films arranged under such headings as 'Dreams of Adventure', 'Wargames', 'Arrested Development' and 'Brat Packs'. Titles range from *The Kid* (1925) – the only silent film included – to *A World Apart* (1988), with many others briefly mentioned. A number of British productions are included (*Kes, Mandy* and *The Go-Between*, for instance) together with foreign-language films such as Bergman's *Fanny and Alexander*, Buñuel's *Los Olvidados*, and Truffaut's strange and fascinating *L'Enfant Sauvage*.

The large-page format and good-quality paper allow for excellent reproduction of a number of interesting stills.

Cinematic Vampires, John L. Flynn; McFarland, dist. Shelwing, £34.00

This must surely be the fullest list of films on the subject yet published, ranging from 1896 to 1992, and from all over the world, with credits, casts and commentaries. Many of the latter are brief, but most are informative essays. The films are arranged chronologically and the book can be read as a consecutive history of the *genre* and its many sidelines. Television films are also included. Appendices list projects for 1993; best and worst examples (purely personal opinions, of course); and a brief note on Hamilton Deane's 1924 stage production. An excellent handbook for all fang-fans.

The Complete Films of Laurence Olivier, Jerry Vermilye; Virgin Film Library, £12.99

It is fitting that the leading actor of the age should be celebrated in one of the very best of the Virgin Film Library (familiar in the past as the prestigious, long-running Citadel series). Jerry Vermilye, author of two similarly excellent volumes (*The Great*

British Films and *The Films of the Twenties*), has not only compiled a first-class survey of all Olivier's films, on both large and small screen, but has also provided, in a lengthy biographical foreword, an account of his work in the theatre with a number of fascinating photographs. The arrangement of the main section follows the usual form: cast and credits, plot and commentary (including interesting notes from Olivier himself) and a selection of reviews, together with ample stills. Anthony Holden's biography, though written before Olivier's death, is the best and fullest to date; this compilation is an essential companion to it – or indeed to any future biography that may appear.

Directory of African Filmmakers and Films, ed. Keith Shiri; Flicks Books, £33.00
Directory of Eastern European Filmmakers and Films 1945–1991, ed. Grzegorz Balski; Flicks Books, £40.00

These volumes form the second and third in a new series (the first of which, on Jewish films, was reviewed in last year's *Film Review*). One covers the work of some 300 filmmakers from 29 countries, giving brief biographical notes and full filmographies. The other, more than twice the size, deals similarly with Eastern Europe, including selected shorts as well as features.

Both books have three comprehensive indexes – Country, Title and General – and in each case British translations of foreign titles are cross-referenced. These are volumes of specialist interest perhaps, but excellent in this respect. They may not find a place on every private bookshelf but, well set out and stoutly bound, they should certainly be available in all large-scale film libraries and institutes.

Emlyn Williams, James Harding; Weidenfeld & Nicolson, £20.00

The appearance of a misprint in the three-line paragraph on the illustrations at the beginning of the book may cause anyone familiar with Dr Harding's usual strict regard for accuracy to raise an eyebrow, but his latest biography is well up to the fine standard of its predecessors such as those on Cochran, Ivor Novello, Jacques

Tati and Gerald du Maurier, and is written with his usual warmth, candour and enthusiasm. He gives a full and vivid account of the brilliance of Williams's career, and of the pleasure he gave to his many friends and wide public as writer, actor and reader of Dickens, Saki and Dylan Thomas. As usual with Dr Harding's work, the pages sparkle with good stories, with numerous examples of Williams's often acerbic wit, and with many side glances at people with whom he was associated. Full attention is given to the two main people in his life, his loyal and delightful wife, Molly, who died so suddenly and tragically while he was touring in America (an event from which he never fully recovered), and Sarah Grace Cooke, the original Miss Moffat of *The Corn Is Green*, who had an incalculable influence on his career.

Regarding Williams' known bisexuality, the author emphasises it to the extent that it formed an integral part of his personality, and no further. As Dr Harding writes: 'In his time he loved both women and men. Women, indeed, played a very important part in his existence . . . For Molly, his wife, he had a deep and passionate love which endured in spite of the disagreements that characterise any lengthy relationship . . . He was frank on the subject of his bisexuality. She was no less frank in her acceptance of it, for she realised, as the heroine of *Accolade* puts it, that: "It's no use pretending I don't wish he were – otherwise . . . But if he were, how do we know he'd still have talent? And he might not even be human . . ." '

With a full list of Williams's works, good illustrations and an excellent index, this is one of the star biographies of the year.

'The End', R. Donna Chesher; McFarland, dist. Shelwing, £22.50

Despite the inclusion of a number of impressive speeches and famous single lines (e.g. 'Louis, I think this is the beginning of a beautiful friendship,' from *Casablanca*), this collection of the final words spoken in over three thousand movies inevitably results in a certain amount of bathos and monotony, especially as many are unfamiliar. Examples: 'No, no, no, no!' (*The Loves of Carmen*); 'Yes, yes, yes!' (*Lucky*

Stiff); 'Yes,' (*The Outlaw*); 'No,' (*The Poseidon Adventure*); 'Swell!' (*Flying Tigers*); 'Stop!' (*The Outing*); 'Encore!' (audience member in *Reckless*); 'Look, the west wing!' (spectator at fire, in *Rebecca* – after which the west wing is duly shown to us). Much may be forgiven, however, for the inclusion of Oscar Wilde's request in the 1959 film of that name: 'Will you play something gay?'

Enser's Filmed Books and Plays 1928–1991, compiled by Ellen Baskin and Mandy Hicken; Ashgate, £45.00

From its inception in 1968, through several editions to 1987, this unique reference book has been of great use to researchers, historians and serious film enthusiasts alike. This latest 950-page edition has been so enlarged, updated and revised as to justify being regarded almost as a new version. While hundreds of new entries have been included, numerous former ones have been omitted (e.g. films which were announced in advance but never actually made), enabling the vast amount of material to be spaciously and attractively laid out. Apart from the three main subjects (author; film title; change of original title) there are sections on musicals, films made for television, mini-series and serials, and animated films. A couple of errors (possibly repeated from earlier editions) may be spotted in the main text: Patrick Hamilton's famous play was originally entitled *Gaslight*, not the feeble and pointless *Angel Street* foisted on it later; and the title of Hugh Walpole's fourth book in the 'Herries Saga' is simply *Vanessa*, without the cloyingly sentimental addition, 'Her Love Story'.

Despite the general approbation due to the body of the book, however, the final section, on production and distribution companies, must be approached with caution. The address of the British Film Institute (suggested as a source 'for further information') is given as 127 Charing Cross Road – they left there five years ago; a second company (also 'for further information'), The British Film and Television Producers Association, merged with another concern two years ago and is no longer at the address given; 'Zeotrope' (Zoetrope?)

appears out of order in the list and the address is unavailable by telephone; Zenith left the address given, ten years ago; Regent, three years ago. Goldcrest said they had no knowledge of the address given them. At least two other companies with London addresses are not listed in the telephone directory. After this, I gave up. Despite the disclaimer at the opening of the section, this is a sadly disappointing conclusion to an otherwise useful reference book.

Fantastic Cinema Subject Guide, Bryan Senn and John Johnson; McFarland, dist. Shelwing, £38.25

After many years of comparative neglect this branch of cinema must now be the most fully covered of all. In this comprehensive volume (almost 650 packed pages dealing with 2,500 films) the contents are arranged under a large number of subject headings, fully cross-referenced. To name but a few: Aliens, Androids, Computers, Jekyll, Dr & Family, Dolls, Elizabeth Bathory the Bloody Countess, Bats, Bears, Birds, Blobs, Brains (disembodied, living heads, suckers and transplants), Rats, and Reincarnation.

Most of the entries, inevitably, are brief and the cast lists skeletal, but adequate space is given to major films. A full index is coupled with a critical rating scale ranging from 10 (top) to 1 (bottom), plus a zero for those with no redeeming qualities whatever.

Note: Like other writers, the compilers have missed the brief shot at the end of *Dead of Night* (1945) which reveals that *this* time it is *not* a recurring dream.

Fatal Charm – The Life of Rex Harrison, Alexander Walker; Weidenfeld & Nicolson, £18.99

Alexander Walker heads the main sections of his superb biography with the names of Harrison's six wives, which seems as good a method as any. This is a long book, packed with incident and unfailingly interesting. Walker firmly draws the distinction between the man and the artist, giving full credit to Harrison's skilful and conscientious (though frequently monumentally selfish) work on stage and screen. On the personal side, Walker's approach is equally forceful, conceal-

ing nothing of his subject's arrogance, ruthless disregard of others to suit his own ends, or lack of generosity. Throughout, however, the author maintains a fair balance, dealing sympathetically with such traumatic events as the suicide of Carole Landis or the long-drawn-out troubles over Rachel Roberts. But he is unable to avoid the picture of someone who, under all the outward charm, was an unpleasant and at times a petty man. Only over the tragic illness and death of the beautiful Kay Kendall does Harrison seem to have been genuinely heartbroken, showing a side that was only too seldom in evidence.

The index is excellently full and very well set out.

The Films of Reginald LeBorg, Wheeler Winston Dixon; Scarecrow, dist. Shelwing, £21.25

In any discussion on film history the name of Reginald LeBorg is unlikely to come readily to mind. Yet from the thirties on he had an extremely busy and varied career, directing everything from musicals to Westerns and light comedies, though he is probably best known for his horror films, often made with Lon Chaney Jr. In this collection of essays and interviews, and in a lengthy opening appreciation, he is revealed as a man of great imagination and charm. Though his name is more likely to be found in books on B-picture directors rather than those with better-known names, he had a steady and finally appreciated career. A glance through the very full filmography bears this out. LeBorg died in 1989, at the age of 87, after suffering a heart attack on his way to receive a lifetime achievement award in recognition of his large body of work.

This study is no. 31 in the Filmmakers Series edited by Anthony Slide.

Forties Film Talk, Oral Histories of Hollywood, Doug McClelland; McFarland, dist. Shelwing, £42.50.

The first half of Doug McClelland's enormously entertaining book consists of about 170 personal interviews with people who worked in the cinema during the 1940s in various capacities: actors and actresses, directors, writers, producers, designers, composers, photographers and others. The interviews (one is glad to see) are not simply questions and answers, and have been skilfully condensed by the author. Many famous names appear, but he has sought out many others who are less often quoted, and their often uninhibited opinions, favourable and otherwise, make a refreshing addition to the usual roll-call. What a pleasure, for instance, to read Ruth Warrick's curt dismissal of critic Pauline Kael's monotonous denigration of Orson Welles and *Citizen Kane* – 'She's like an old maid stooping in an asparagus patch.'

The second half of this 400-page book is a vast collection of brief comments and stories culled from various sources, in which 'forties' people from all fields and degrees of eminence vigorously voice their opinions on colleagues and other subjects. The book is illustrated with lobby-cards – the small colour section brilliant, but the rest fairly variable in quality. Altogether an original, amusing (and at times even touching) record of a great Hollywood period.

Frank Capra – The Catastrophe of Success, Joseph McBride; Faber & Faber, £25.00

This monumental book of over 700 crowded pages will surely rank as the definitive biography of the director known – from many of his films – as the 'champion of the common man'. Born in Sicily in 1897, Capra died in America at the respectable age of 94, living through all the great years of Hollywood, but doing his best work as a comparatively young man in the thirties and forties, in films such as *American Madness, It Happened One Night, Mr Deeds Goes to Town, Lost Horizon* and *Mr Smith Goes to Washington*. In relating the story of Capra's eventful life, the author also paints a vivid picture of the world in which he lived for so long. Highlights in the book are his professional relationship with Harry Langdon, the severance of which was so fatal for the little comedian ('he died,' said Capra, 'of a broken heart'); and the detailed account of his own involvement with the infamous HUAC inquisition – a period that had a devastating effect on both himself and his career.

Despite its weight and bulk, this tome holds the attention throughout.

Fully documented, it should be read beside Capra's own autobiography, *The Name Above the Title* – if only to set various matters straight.

The Great Hollywood Musical Pictures, James Robert Parish and Michael R. Pitts; Scarecrow Press, dist. Shelwing, £79.50

This 800-page reference book in the 'Great' series by the indefatigable Parish/Pitts partnership is fully up to standard in its coverage of almost 350 American film musicals. Arranged in alphabetical order (but with a useful chronology at the end) each film is given credit and comprehensive cast lists, all song titles, and a critical and historical commentary. A handsome volume, with a reasonable though not lavish number of illustrations.

H. G. Wells – Six Scientific Romances adapted for Film, Thomas C. Renzi; Scarecrow Press, dist. Shelwing, £29.50

The six 'scientific romances' (a term invented by Wells himself) are subjected to critical analysis in this comparatively brief but interesting book. They are: *The Time Machine, The Island of Dr Moreau, The Invisible Man, The War of the Worlds, The First Men in the Moon* and *The Food of the Gods and How It Came to Earth*. The differences between story and film – both in form and content – are discussed in detail, and open new windows on Wells's work and ideas. Appendices deal with two later films: *Things to Come* and *The Man Who Could Work Miracles*.

Hitchcock and Homosexuality, Theodore Price; Scarecrow Press, dist. Shelwing, £37.15

Despite its conveniently alliterative title this is not solely concerned with the suggested homosexuality in Hitchcock's films; in fact, as the author states, the Jack-the-Ripper and the Superbitch-Prostitute themes may be regarded as of at least equal importance. The homosexuality component was first pointed out by the French writers Eric Rohmer and Claude Chabrol. Mr Price follows these authors but delves far deeper in his more than 380 pages, leaving no stone unturned in order to reveal a homo-

sexual or quasi-homosexual ingredient in every film made by the Master of Suspense. No plot, and scarcely a person, is allowed to escape his relentless pursuit. Even a (very interesting) survey of German silent films is brought in to enlarge the field. So much enthusiasm, emphasis (italics and exclamation marks a-plenty) and single-mindedness may sound rather formidable, but in fact the author writes entertainingly and accessibly. And one has to admit that he knows his subjects, all of them.

Hollywood Holyland, Ken Darby; Scarecrow Press, dist. Shelwing, £35.00

The Greatest Story Ever Told is among the better of the 'Life of Christ' films, so maybe it deserves a 270-page book devoted solely to its making. With a cast that seemed to include most Hollywood personalities in bit parts (including John Wayne's famous portrayal of a Roman centurion), and lasting originally four hours (the critics responded so badly that thirty minutes had to be lopped off), it could certainly be described – if only for sheer size – as an epic. Ken Darby has collected together a vast amount of firsthand information, and dispenses it with an engagingly light touch.

Hollywood 1930–1990 – Sixty Great Years; Prion, £24.95

This large, weighty and lavishly illustrated book is a collection of lengthy surveys (over 600 pages in all) by six leading film historians – Jack Lodge, John Russell Taylor, Adrian Turner, Douglas Jarvis, David Castell, Mark Kermode – each of whom covers a decade. With so much space given to illustrations and so wide a field to cover, it is inevitable that many films, including some important ones, receive somewhat cursory mention, but all the writers are experts at significant encapsulation. Summaries of the work of Hitchcock and Brian De Palma, for example, are excellently compressed analyses. Some unexpected judgements are made: for example, it is surprising to find a film writer of standing actually *praising* the alteration of the ending of so fine a play as Maxwell Anderson's *Winterset* from a tragic to a 'happy' one, resulting in a travesty perpetrated for the sake of 'box-office'. Among the hundreds of illustrations are many rare stills, a welcome change from the tired old shots so often encountered. On the whole they are well reproduced, though one could do without the unnecessary tinting of those originally in black-and-white.

Horror, Mark Jancovich; Batsford, £9.99

The inclusion of this title in the new series of Batsford Cultural Studies is surely another indication of the increasing academic recognition of the once-despised horror film. Though dealing also with literature, a large part of the book is concerned with the films, and once having ploughed through the somewhat dense opening pages, the reader will find that the author has many fresh and stimulating points to make on master figures such as Dracula, Frankenstein and Messrs. Jekyll & Hyde; on individual movies such as *Rosemary's Baby*, *Psycho*, *The Fly*, *The Omen*, *The Night of the Living Dead*; and on writers such as Nathaniel Hawthorne, Richard Matheson, Edgar Allan Poe and (in particular) Stephen King.

The text and index have been rather carelessly proofread. Garbo's first American film, for instance, was *The Torrent*, not *The Temptress* (which was her second).

International Dictionary of Films and Filmmakers – Volume 3, Actors and Actresses, ed. Nicholas Thomas; St James Press, £75.00

This mighty (and weighty) tome matches its predecessors in magnificence and like them has been greatly enlarged and updated, with well over 600 entries – an increase of 85. Each entry consists of a brief biographical note, full filmography (including in some cases hundreds of shorts), detailed bibliography and critical appraisal. The range stretches back to very early days, with old-time players generously represented. In view of the title more attention might have been given to the minor and character actresses and actors who often afford more pleasure than the stars and big names, details of whom are already

available elsewhere; but otherwise this is a full and handsome reference work, embellished with a large number of superb full-page photographs.

Volume 4, dealing with Writers and Production Artists, is in preparation, to be followed by a final volume comprising a full index of titles.

Judy Garland, David Shipman; Fourth Estate, £17.99

Among the mass of material available on Judy Garland this major biography stands out as probably the fullest and most deeply researched we are likely to see. David Shipman follows the tragicomedy of her life with both sympathy and frankness, concealing nothing of her apparently self-destructive behaviour – the tantrums, the drugs, the unreliability, the suicide attempts, the alcohol – and on the other hand recognising her unparalleled skill as a performer. Whether she was indeed 'the greatest of this century' (a fairly tall order) may well be open to question, but undoubtedly she was one of the most famous: yet we learn that when she asked for a copy of *Meet Me in St Louis* to be screened at the National Film Theatre in the last year of her life it turned out that, astonishingly, no one on the present staff of MGM had ever heard of her. *Sic transit . . .*

There are some good illustrations, but the index is dauntingly full of solid blocks of page numbers, and (surprising in so thorough and authoritative a book) there are no reference sections such as a filmography or chronology of her career.

Maggie – A Bright Particular Star, Michael Coveney; Victor Gollancz, £16.99

This delightful biography of Maggie Smith is written with obvious affection and admiration, yet with full recognition of the sometimes sharp and indeed formidable side of an enchanting and witty actress. It is full of amusing, even hilarious, anecdotes and paints vivid pictures, first of her somewhat lonely and Spartan but by no means deprived upbringing in 'sleepy' Ilford and Cowley; followed by her brilliant and almost ceaseless career both in Britain and in Stratford, Ontario. Four 'Entr'actes' in which the

author steps aside from the course of his story to consider such matters as 'Maggie among her peers' and as 'the soul of wit' add to the pleasures of the book.

An opening reference section, 'Career at a Glance', is useful in keeping the reader on track when the chronology jumps about a little.

Marilyn Monroe, Donald Spoto; Chatto and Windus, £17.99

As a fitting climax to the flood of books, articles and other material over the years, this weighty volume is boldly announced as *The* biography, with 680 pages of text plus over 50 more of reference, mainly copious notes. At last, most of the notorious scandals repeated *ad nauseam* are refuted – the Kennedy connection, the drugs, the alcoholism, the unprofessionalism, the empty-headedness are all firmly slammed down. In particular, records of the events leading up to those traumatic last hours are ruthlessly laid open to question. In a final chapter the author exposes the errors and calumnies of his predecessors. His account is certainly convincing (but then, each earlier story also seemed to be as it appeared). The closing pages are probably the ones that will be most eagerly turned to, but they should not overshadow the rest of the book, which is authoritative and unfailingly interesting. At the very least, it is refreshing to read a showbiz biography which approaches its subject sympathetically, rather than seeking to destroy it.

Just as it was beginning to seem as if the Marilyn Marathon was reaching its end, the literary floodgates will probably be opened anew. It looks as if there's life in the old girl (she'd be 67 this year) yet.

Memoirs of a Professional Cad, George Sanders; Scarecrow, dist. Shelwing, £29.75

Taken by itself, George Sanders's book (published in 1960) is an often amusing but unsatisfyingly incomplete record, valuable mainly as a collection of witty reflections and caustic comments. In this edition, the well-known film writer Tony Thomas fills in the details of his early life in an introduction, and of his later life in an epilogue.

He also provides a very useful, fully annotated filmography. This could be a useful companion to the biography by Richard Vanderbeets, reviewed in *Film Review 1992–3*.

Men, Women and Chainsaws – Gender in the Modern Horror Film, Carol J. Clover; BFI, £15.95

The boundaries between horror, fantasy and science-fiction films have always been shadowy, 'horror' frequently being used to cover all three. Carol J. Clover here concentrates mainly on the darker and more violent varieties – the slasher, splatter, rape-revenge and Satanic possession type of movies. Taking a number of key films as a basis (*Peeping Tom, Psycho, The Exorcist, Deliverance, Poltergeist* and the notorious *I Spit on Your Grave*), she examines in particular the relation between them and their audience, challenging – and indeed reversing – the theory that it is generally a matter of the male finding sadistic satisfaction in the sufferings of the female, and suggesting that nowadays it is often what she terms the Final Girl, the 'victim/hero', who ends, as it were, on top. It is a detailed and complex book (and not, perhaps, for the very squeamish), but she guides us through the murky waters with comparative ease, and the result is an original and compellingly readable study.

Merchant of Dreams – Louis B. Mayer, Charles Higham; Sidgwick & Jackson, £20.00

In this lively and authoritative unauthorised biography (subtitled 'MGM and the secret Hollywood') the author is concerned to set straight the legend of L. B. Mayer as a scheming, devious, hypocritical and vengeful tyrant (which at one time or another he admittedly was), and to show that he often revealed the exact opposite of all these traits. The result is a vivid and rounded portrait of the super-Mogul who ruled over the super-studio during the great Hollywood period. Charles Higham threads his way clearly through the labyrinthine wheelings and dealings, and through the scandals, gossip, studio battles and temperamental outbursts involving the 'galaxy of stars' who worked with Mayer during those colourful years. It

is a compelling and often witty account, by a writer with a neat gift of summing up a character in a short, sharp adjectival phrase – from Mary Miles Minter ('willful, temperamental and spoiled') to Michael Balcon ('a difficult, tense man, fussy and irritable').

Louis B. Mayer may well have deserved at least some of the unpleasant things said about him, but seeing what he often had to put up with it is difficult – particularly after reading this book – not to feel that he may have had some excuse.

Million-Dollar Movie, Michael Powell; Heinemann-Mandarin, £20.00

Sequels often fail to come up to the standard of their predecessors, but Powell's second volume of memoirs is a triumphant exception. Together with *A Life in Movies* (see *Film Review 1987–8*) it completes well over 1,000 pages of sparkling humour, charm, frankness and often sharp comment. The first book concluded with *The Red Shoes*, and this one opens with *The Small Back Room* and includes such major productions as *The Tales of Hoffman, The Battle of the River Plate* (a.k.a. *The Pursuit of the Graf Spee*) and the film that caused such a furore in 1960 and lived on to become a classic, *Peeping Tom*, the vituperative reviews of which Powell fearlessly quotes while vigorously defending it against the critics' onslaughts.

Michael Powell sadly died in 1990, two years before this book was published.

Missing Believed Lost, Allen Eyles and David Meeker; BFI, £14.95

One of the saddest (and, indeed, most shameful) tragedies of the early cinema has been the loss of many hundreds of films through indifference, carelessness, ignorance (of the fatal effects of nitrate cellulose) or deliberate destruction. With this attractively produced book the British Film Institute is launching a voyage of discovery that just *might* uncover, in some hidden corner of the world, some – or even one – of the films at present listed as missing. The humblest and least intrinsically valuable movie can present a fascinating record

of the past; and the horrific sight of a print disintegrating in a dusty can is heartrending and infuriating for any true lover of the cinema.

Around one hundred vanished films, from 1914 to as late as 1943, are presented here with credits and stills. The latter may revive pleasant memories in those of us fortunate enough to have seen them in their time, but this is no mere exercise in nostalgia; it is a clarion call to rescue before it is too late.

Note: the 'unknown performer' on p. 63 is Leon Quartermaine.

The Motion Picture Guide – 1992 Annual, James Monaco; Baseline Cinebooks, dist. Bowker-Saur, £99.00

In writing about the 1991 edition of this mammoth annual last year I regretted the omission of the excellent obituaries and illustrations, and the reduction of the print size to microscopic proportions, in favour of an immense and not particularly useful master list of films contained in former volumes. This year, I am delighted to report, readable print size and the obituaries have been restored – the latter covering two years to make up for the loss. The already huge and excellently compiled review section has been considerably increased, and the massive indexes (22 sections, from 'Actors' to 'Stunts') are as invaluable as ever. Even if the price is daunting for home use the book should have its place on the shelves of every self-respecting library.

The Motion Picture Serial, Wayne Schutz; Scarecrow, dist. Shelwing, £31.90

The stalwart old 'to be continued next week' serial has disappeared (the last film date in the book is 1956), to be replaced by the ubiquitous television soap opera and sitcom. This excellent and all-encompassing annotated bibliography is divided into two main sections, 'Silent' and 'Sound' (a general history of each), followed by chapters on production personnel and players. It may be aimed primarily at historians, but the last section in particular – which takes up half the book – contains quite a few names still familiar today, from Jean Arthur to John Wayne.

The Movie Book of Film Noir,
ed. Ian Cameron; Studio Vista, £16.99

This collection of some twenty essays, by various writers connected formerly with the prestigious *Movie* magazine, is probably the most detailed examination of *film noir* that has yet appeared; so detailed, in fact, that it seems occasionally to delve more deeply than this important but nevertheless limited and vaguely defined genre warrants. However, the articles are varied and informed, and offer numerous fresh insights. Some of the most famous films (*The Woman in the Window, Double Indemnity, The Big Sleep, Criss Cross, Phantom Lady*) are given close analysis. The extension of the genre to include later productions such as Polanski's *Chinatown* seems to be forcing it beyond its true boundaries, however, as I would contend that black-and-white, rather than colour, is essential for true *film noir*.

My Name Is Michael Caine, Anne
Billson; Muller, £10.99

When one opens a film-star biography in which the author spends most of the first page denigrating every other British actor in favour of her chosen subject, one fears the worst. However, this is quite an entertaining account of Michael Caine's films, demonstrating his acclaimed skill and versatility. Even so, what can one make of sentences such as 'Michael Caine in underpants is about as real as you can get – he could be anyone's husband or father, he could be *you*'?

Nelson Eddy – a Bio-Discography, Larry F. Kiner; Scarecrow
Press, dist. Shelwing, £79.50

Following a short biographical introduction this massive volume lists all Eddy's recordings, songs, videos, radio programmes and other similar activities. The large-size pages are beautifully set out on a day-by-day chronological basis and form a complete definitive record. Fully illustrated with production photographs, portraits, record labels, album covers, etc.

The Oscars, Anthony Holden;
Little, Brown, £20.00

This hefty 700-page volume neatly mixes entertainment with information.

It is indeed, as its subtitle declares, 'A Secret History' by a witty and lucid writer. All the scandals and upheavals are here (Fonda, Brando, Scott, Redgrave), as well as the undeserved rewards, the unjustified omissions, the generosities, the meannesses, the wheeling and dealing, the rightly honoured and the unjustly neglected; all set against a serious history of an annual event which might be said to present a picture of Hollywood in miniature.

The huge appendices of award lists and comparative tables are rather clumsily arranged, the awards and nominations being set out in categories rather than complete years, with no page headings to indicate to the researcher where each section may be found, and no detailed contents list at the beginning of the book. Only main categories are included, which is reasonable; however it is extraordinary to find that, though writers and composers are entered (the latter even extending to individual songs and best scoring awards) there is no mention of those all-important creative filmmakers – the cinematographers.

Peter Cushing, Deborah del Vec-
chio and Tom Johnson; McFarland, dist. Shelwing, £38.25

Compiled on the lines of 'The Films of . . .' series, this will be warmly welcomed by the countless admirers and friends of Cushing 'The Gentle Man of Horror and his 91 Films', as the subtitle has it. Written with obvious affection and esteem, but without any attempt to play down the few failures he experienced, this is a full and satisfying account of his life and work. In the lengthy commentary sections there are many interesting side glances at, and brief biographical notes on, people with whom he was associated, such as Terence Fisher. Cushing's autobiographies somewhat disappointed a number of readers who would have preferred more in them about the films themselves; this book adequately fills the gaps. Many excellent stills and portraits.

Poverty Row Horrors, Tom
Weaver; McFarland, dist. Shelwing, £27.40

The undoubted star of this account of small-company horror films of the

forties is Bela Lugosi (his index entries alone outnumber all others at least twentyfold), and to anyone interested in the original – or almost original – Dracula, this is a treasury of little-known facts and photographs. This is not to say that other horror players are neglected, and a useful bonus at the end of the book is a *complete* filmography of 35 of them. Illustrated with stills, portraits and lobby cards.

Prostitution in Hollywood
Films, James Robert Parish; McFarland, dist. Shelwing, £42.50

Reading the name J. R. Parish on the cover of a film book, one can rest comfortably assured that, whatever the subject, it will be thoroughly researched and fully documented. In the present case, in addition to the usual reference material, he has added commentaries of sufficient length to justify the description 'miniature essays'. The book's 650 pages cover no fewer than 389 films, both silent and sound, including made-for-television productions. An opening chapter relates a short history of the regulatory codes in the American film industry; an appendix lists the films in chronological order, from *The Inside of the White Slave Traffic* (1913) to the short and simple *Whore* (1991). A massive index includes all the names and titles even remotely connected with the subject.

Quinlan's Illustrated Directory
of Film Comedy Stars, David Quinlan; Batsford, £19.99

A very welcome addition to the invaluable Quinlan reference book family. With fewer people to cover in this category, it has been possible to give much longer paragraphs to each – many of them, in fact, can be fairly described as miniature biographies. The period ranges from the early 1900s to now, and the great silent comics (John Bunny, Snub Pollard, Mabel Normand, Mack Swain, Ben Turpin, etc.) are generously represented. The listing of the countless short films in these cases is almost a life's work in itself. Apart from a personal photograph in each instance, there are also many more stills than in the previous volumes of the series.

The Republic Chapterplays, R. M. Hayes; McFarland, dist. Shelwing, £27.65

This is a useful handbook on a neglected cinematic sideline. Space is not wasted on unnecessary and often boring synopses, but is devoted entirely to a list of chapter titles, technical and other credits, and an excellently full cast list in each case. There are numerous stills and lobby cards, and the book warrants its subtitle as a complete filmography of the Republic serials released between 1934 and 1955.

The Saint, Burl Barer; McFarland, dist. Shelwing, £55.00

The complete story of the famous character of novel, film, radio and television is presented in extremely full detail. Following the history itself, almost half this 400-page book is devoted to seven appendices, including full synopses of 114 radio scripts, an episode guide and complete list of players in the Roger Moore series, credits and synopses of all episodes of 'Return of the Saint', and a long list of the French 'Saint' books. Together with plenty of illustrations, enough is here, surely, to satisfy the most avid devotee.

Scandinavian Cinema, Peter Cowie; Tantivy Press, £14.95

First published in French to celebrate a retrospective season, this finely produced and illustrated history/reference book may be regarded as the most comprehensive and important study of its subject that has yet appeared in English. The first section consists of a long chronology setting out the progress of the cinema of Denmark, Finland, Iceland, Norway and Sweden against the political and cultural events of the time. This is followed by a full film history of each country, with filmographies from 1910 to 1991 and a biographical dictionary of leading directors with photographs and lists of films. An added attraction is the collection of some three hundred magnificent and often rare stills. Peter Cowie, long regarded as the leading writer in English on the Swedish cinema, together with his three expert collaborators Françoise Bouquet, Risto-Mikael Pitkänen and Godfried

Talboom, has compiled an invaluable record, unlikely to be superseded in the foreseeable future.

Screening History, Gore Vidal; André Deutsch, £12.99

In this entertaining and sometimes provocative short book the author divides his attention between the favourite films of his youth and the exposition of his theory that what we see on the screen (in particular the television screen) can affect or even replace our visions of history and the world about us. Two main chapters, one on the British film *Fire Over England* and the other on *Abraham Lincoln*, are used as a sort of framework for his thesis. In a pertinent paragraph Vidal states, 'The first time that the screening of history became truly fabulous was after we lost our long and pointless war in Vietnam. This defeat, screened daily on television, was then metamorphosed into a total victory with the *Rambo* movies, films which not only convinced everyone that we had, thanks to Mr Stallone, won that war but which made almost as much money at the world box-office as was wasted on the war itself.

'In the end, he who screens the history makes the history.'

An original and stimulating essay.

Sean Connery – The Untouchable Hero, Michael Feeney Callan; Virgin, £5.99

This is the paperback issue, extensively revised and updated, of the biography that was first published by W. H. Allen in 1983 under the title *Sean Connery and his Films* and reviewed in *Film Review 1983–4*. During the intervening years the author has managed to gather a good deal of further information about a man noted for his personal reticence, and to add further interest to what has already been described as a rounded, frank and sympathetic portrait. Its reappearance is thus doubly welcome. The cast lists are of exemplary fullness.

Shooting Stars, Ricky Spears; Stewart, Tabori & Chang, £20.00

The subtitle of this collection is 'Contemporary Glamour Photography'. Although 'glamour' is described in my dictionary as 'alluring or exciting

beauty or charm' the general purpose here (with a few notable exceptions) seems to be to startle rather than attract. The book is apparently a tribute to the modern cult of the grotesque, bizarre or even plain ugly. As such, it succeeds admirably, being handsomely produced, with sharply defined photographs. A useful feature is a section of filmographies of all those appearing in it; some of these are so up to date that they include films dated 1993.

Showman – The Life of David O. Selznick, David Thomson; Andre Deutsch, £20.00

David Puttnam has already described this vast biography as 'definitive', but unlike some of the overblown tomes thus labelled, this is extremely well written, packed with information lightly imparted, and eminently readable. In 700 pages of text, plus 50 of reference material, the author, with the advantage of access to hitherto unpublished papers, has painted a brilliant canvas of Hollywood life in its most golden years, centred on one of its most colourful, many-faceted, intelligent, maddening, memo-showering and (when he wanted to be) wholly charming figures. *Gone With the Wind* is, inevitably, given a good deal of space, but is by no means allowed to overshadow Selznick's other notable films – *Rebecca, Duel in the Sun, Dinner at Eight, David Copperfield, The Prisoner of Zenda, A Star is Born* (1937), to name but a handful. Fully documented, adequately (if not lavishly) illustrated and handsomely produced, this deserves a prominent place on any film bookshelf.

Simone Signoret, Catherine David; Bloomsbury, £17.99

This fairly short but excellent biography must rank high among the year's best. Catherine David knew Simone Signoret for only a brief period towards the end of the actress's life, but has written a sympathetic, frank, perceptive and often amusing account. The films, such as the unforgettable *Casque d'Or* and the very different but equally memorable *Les Diaboliques*, are discussed briefly but adequately. Of almost more interest is the account of her life as the great 'espouser of causes' during the tempestuous, euphoric but ultimately disillusioning political and social events of the 1950s and 1960s; together with that of her 36-year relationship with her husband Yves Montand, including the latter's brief but widely publicised affair with Marilyn Monroe.

In her final years Simone Signoret achieved new success, despite failing health, in writing memoirs and a best-selling novel. Here Catherine David examines in fascinating detail the whole mystique of authorship, whether of fact or fiction – a fitting conclusion to her beautifully written book, flowingly translated by Sally Sampson.

Included are illustrations and filmography but not – regrettably – an index.

Slightly Mad and Full of Dangers, Forsyth Hardy; The Ramsay Head Press, £14.99

This tells the story of the Edinburgh Film Festival, founded in 1947 (and thus about two years younger than *Film Review*), though the author says it could be considered to have begun in 1925, as its formation indirectly developed from the pioneering Film Society and the Edinburgh Film Guild. It was a bold undertaking that has fully deserved its lasting and solid success. The Festival's programmes have covered the widest range of films, British and foreign, from Terence Fisher's *Dracula* to von Stroheim's *Greed*, from Norman McLaren's eight-minute *Neighbours* to Abel Gance's five-hour *Napoléon*. The book contains a large number of interesting stills and other photographs. A short reference section would however have been welcome, or at least an index of film titles.

Sound Films – 1927–1939, Alan G. Fetrow; McFarland & Co., dist, Shelwing, £48.75

For some reason, really full and reliable records of the early sound and thirties periods of American films have been harder to come by than those of other years. Here, in another of the invaluable large-scale specialist reference books from McFarland, the omission has been handsomely remedied. The 950 pages contain details of 5,418 films, together with a list of awards and an enormous index of

names. Additional facts, such as song titles in musicals, are included in certain cases – *Gone With the Wind*, for instance, has three columns all to itself. The result will be a boon to researchers and historians alike, and the sight of a long-forgotten title may awaken a touch of nostalgia in many an older filmgoer.

The Spaghetti Westerns – The Good, the Bad and the Violent, Thomas Weisser; McFarland, dist. Shelwing, £38.25

This encyclopedic book on one of the odder sub-genres of the cinema must be the most complete record available. It covers 558 Euro-Westerns, arranged in alphabetical order, with casts, credits and commentary together with full (and very necessary) cross-references. In addition it gives lengthy filmographies of performers, directors, composers, scriptwriters and cinematographers, with appendices on two serial characters (Django and Sartana), American-made counterparts, and a list (surprisingly short to anyone who has had to sit through numbers of these films) of the Worst Spaghetti Westerns. Illustrations are sparse, but there is a good index.

The Stars Appear, Richard Dyer MacCann; Scarecrow, dist. Shelwing, £16.90

An interesting seventeen-page introduction on the early lives of a number of major silent film stars is followed by a compilation of essays and extracts from books by well-known film writers, based largely on an examination of the particular qualities they possessed, showing how these brought them fame and fortune, and how these famous figures both influenced and were influenced by the spirit of the times in which they flourished. Numerous other subjects are touched on (such as the art of silent film acting) in this unique and excellent anthology. Illustrations are thin on the ground, but useful appendices include brief biographical paragraphs on over 170 stars, a chronology of film careers and a very large bibliography.

Steven Spielberg, Philip M. Taylor; Batsford, £12.99

Steven Spielberg, the innovative and amazingly successful master of the fan-

tastic and original, is given the full treatment in this detailed and perceptive analysis of his work and personality. Opinions on the quality of some of his films vary widely, but the success is undeniable. The fans, as the author states, may have loved *Hook*, based somewhat insecurely on Barrie's *Peter Pan*, despite critical condemnation; however, the final line of the book – Spielberg's remark that he 'really likes being a children's storyteller' – sits oddly with the recent report of the father who took his schoolgirl daughter to see the film and was shaken (but in full agreement with her) when she turned to him and exclaimed, 'But Daddy, this is *disgusting*!'

Sweethearts of the Sage, Buck Rainey; McFarland & Co., dist. Shelwing, £71.25

At last the heroines of the Western (258 of them) come into their own with this huge (630 large-page) collection of biographies and filmographies. The biographies are in many cases lengthy, and the filmographies at times enormous, covering not merely the Westerns but every film in which the actress appeared including TV series and shows. The first three parts are divided into 'The Pathfinders' (pre-1920), 'The Trailblazers' (the 1920s) and 'The Pioneers' (1930s and 1940s). A fourth part, entitled 'The Homesteaders', lists those heroines who distinguished themselves in 'non-programmer Westerns'. There are many excellent photographs, both portraits and stills. A reference book for every Western devotee to gloat over.

Thank Heaven for Little Girls, Edward Behr; Hutchinson, £18.99

In this 'true story of Maurice Chevalier's life and times' the author paints a vivid portrait of the great entertainer, set against equally vivid backgrounds of world events. Of particular interest are the detailed account of the Parisian music hall years before World War I, in which he grew up and developed his unique public personality; and by contrast the appalling Petain period in World War II during which he faced fearsome problems and often unjust obloquy. What is finally revealed is a far more interesting, if more tragic, figure than the straw-hat-waving, lower-lip-jutting entertainer who charmed the millions for so many years.

It is a pity the book is at times so carelessly edited, with misprints, hideously ugly end-of-line word breaks ('un – ctuously'!), and even (pp. 317 and 319) an entire paragraph repeated, in slightly different words, within a couple of pages. And the famous, tragically shortlived 'Blackbirds' singer of the 1920s was of course Florence Mills, not (as twice misnamed here, and dutifully repeated in the index) Florence Moore.

The 247 Best Movie Scenes in Film History, Sandford Levine; McFarland, dist. Shelwing, £18.75

Even with a less grandiose claim, a 'best' list is inevitably restricted to the preferences of the selector or selectors – in this case a sort of club of speciality filmgoers who apparently frequently watch a film for the odd purpose of re-seeing only one (often very brief) scene, before leaving the cinema, or switching off the set. Even odder are the subjects listed – ranging (among about forty) from Accountant Scenes to Brain Tumour, Button, Clock, Haircut, Neck Braces, Sagging Shoulders and Fluttering Drapes. An amusingly written piece of film trivia.

They Still Call Me Junior, Frank 'Junior' Coghlan; McFarland, dist. Shelwing, £22.45

A rather long, but interesting and pleasantly written autobiography by an actor who made his first film appearance at the age of three (in *Mid-Channel*, 1920) and his last as an unfeatured player 71 years later in an American television special on Shirley Temple. In between he was to be seen in almost every type of filmed or recorded product – from feature films to commercials. During a twenty-year break, from 1943 to 1965, he first served in the US Navy and later was in charge of the Navy Office – but even then was connected in one way or another with the world of film.

This Is Orson Welles, Orson Welles and Peter Bogdanovich; HarperCollins, £20.00

In this long series of interviews, conducted over a number of years, and expertly edited by Jonathan Rosenbaum, Peter Bogdanovich draws from Welles his views, stories, opinions, working methods, aims and other matters in a book as large and fascinating as its subject. In over three hundred pages, written in what in inexpert hands can be the most tiresome of literary forms – the question-and-answer routine – much of Orson Welles's life, work and personality is revealed. Even here, however, a question remains – with this most elusive of subjects under scrutiny can one really feel that the title's assertion is completely justified? Probably (and perhaps happily) the question will never be answered. What can be admired and accepted *without* question, however, is the magnificently detailed chronology of his career – over two hundred pages in length and often following events on an almost day-to-day basis.

Variety International Film Guide 1993, ed. Peter Cowie; André Deutsch, £11.50

This bumper edition celebrates the 30th anniversary of the Guide, and is a tribute to the stamina and skill of what must seem at times to be a Herculean task of reviewing annually the films of no fewer than 69 countries (from Argentina to Zimbabwe) and in addition providing information on a dozen or more cinematic subjects such as film schools, books and bookshops, awards, festivals, and special articles. This year's 'dossier' concerns Iranian productions – an adventurous choice. A number of countries have compiled their own list of the year's ten top-grossing films – interesting but slightly depressing reading. Stoutly bound and attractively presented, and very fully illustrated, the Guide looks set fair for another few decades at least.

Variety Movie Guide, ed. Derek Ellery; Hamlyn, £12.99
The Virgin Film Guide, James Monaco and editors of Baseline; Virgin, £12.99

The *Variety Movie Guide* (an update of last year's volume) in 820 pages contains fairly brief reviews of about 6,000 films written at the time of their first appearance; *The Virgin Film Guide* in over 1,000 pages contains fuller reviews of over 3,000 written around the present day. Some readers of the *Variety* guide may be repelled by the relentless slanginess of some of the writing which actually requires a glossary to make it intelligible – others may enjoy it as jargon.

Virgin dates its entries from the 1930s; *Variety* goes back to the silent days, but these are fairly cursorily treated. *Variety* has a useful index of directors; Virgin a conveniently arranged list of alternative titles. Other features are pretty evenly matched.

Both books tend to concentrate on better-known films, which may disappoint film enthusiasts who are interested in those on which information is less readily available. Both are attractively set out, and both are exceedingly good value for (the same) money. Together they can be regarded as companions rather than rivals.

Other Titles Include:

Celluloid Wars, F. J. Wetta and S. J. Curley; Greenwood Press, £35.95
Cher in Her Own Words, ed. Nigel Goodall; Omnibus Press, £6.95
Cinema and Fiction, New Modes of Adapting, 1950–90, Colin Nicholson and John Orr (eds); Edinburgh University Press, £30.00
Cinema and Spectatorship, Judith Mayne; Routledge, £35.00 hb/ £11.99 pb
Cinema in France – After the New Wave, Jill Forbes; BFI, £40.00
Clark Gable in His Own Words, ed. Neil Grant; Hamlyn £7.99
Clark Gable – Portrait of a Misfit, Jane Ellen Wayne; Robson, £16.95
Clint Eastwood – Sexual Cowboy, Douglas Thompson; Smith-Gryphon, £15.99
Complete Films of Bela Lugosi, Richard Borarski; Virgin Film Library, £12.99
Deadline at Dawn: Film Writings 1980–90, Judith Williamson; Marion Boyars, £17.95
Films of Nicolas Roeg, John Izod; Macmillan, £45.00
Hispanic Image on the Silver Screen, A. C. Richard; Greenwood Press, £52.50
Hitchcock: The First Forty-four Films, Eric Rohmer and Claude Chabrol; Roundhouse Publishing, £10.95
The Hollywood Connection, Michael Munn; Robson, £14.95

100 Best Films of the Century, Barry Norman; Chapman Publishers, £16.99

The Illustrated Vampire Movie Guide, Stephen Jones; Titan Books, £7.99

The Incredible World of 007, Philip Lisa and Lee Pfeiffer; Boxtree, £15.99

Inner Views – Filmmakers in Conversation, David Breskin; Faber & Faber, £9.99

Jean Renoir – Projections of Paradise, Ronald Bergan; Bloomsbury, £25.00

Judy Garland, John Fricke; Little, Brown, £19.99

Like a Film – Ideological Fantasy on Screen, Camera and Canvas, Timothy Murray; Routledge, £35.00 hb/£11.99 pb

Loitering with Intent, Peter O'Toole; Macmillan, £14.99

Marilyn and Me, Susan Strasberg; Doubleday, £14.90

Marilyn – The Last Take, Peter Brown and Patte Barham; Heinemann, £17.50

Marilyn's Men, Jane Ellen Wayne; Robson Books, £16.95

Marlene Dietrich – Her Life and Legend, Steven Bach; HarperCollins, £18.00

Master Space – Film Images of Capra, Lubitsch, Sternberg and Wilder, Barbara Bowman; Greenwood Press, £34.50

New Australian Cinema, Brian McFarlane and Geoff Mayer; Cambridge University Press, £35.00 hb/£11.95 pb

Platinum Girl – Life and Legends of Jean Harlow; Eve Golden; Abbeville, Grantham Book Services, £11.95

Poverty Row Horrors, Tom Weaver; McFarland, dist. Shelwing, £27.40

Richard Burton, David Jenkins; Century, £15.99

Richard Burton – a Bio-bibliography, Tyrone Stepherson; Greenwood Press, £35.50

Rita Hayworth in Her Own Words, ed. Neil Grant; Hamlyn, £7.99

The Road to Romance and Ruin, Jon Lewis; Routledge, £35.00 hb/£9.99 pb

Robert Altman's America, Helene Keyssar; Oxford University Press, £14.95

Screening the Male – Exploring Masculinities in Hollywood Cinema, ed. Stephen Cohan and Ina Rae Hark; Routledge, £35.00 hb/£10.99 pb

Screen Memories – Hollywood Cinema on the Psychoanalytic Couch, Harvey R. Greenberg; Columbia University Press, £20.00

Set Pieces – Being about Film Stills, Mostly, Daniel Meadows; BFI, £29.95 hb/£12.95 pb

What's It All About?, Michael Caine; Century, £17.99

Women and the New German Cinema, Julia Knight; Verso, £32.95

Awards and Festivals

We have always concentrated principally on the major established festivals and award ceremonies around the world. There are of course several hundred others which space does not allow us to include here; some are highly specialised events appealing principally to a small minority, while we have also – some may say unfairly – excluded many Middle and Far East festivals. Full details of most of these are published periodically in *Variety*.

Nationality is stated only where films originate from a country other than that in which the award is given – though when this information would be unnecessary or repetitive, we have not included it.

The 65th American Academy of Motion Picture Arts and Sciences Awards ('The Oscars') and Nominations for 1992, 29 March 1993

Best Film: *Unforgiven*. Nominations: *The Crying Game*; *A Few Good Men*; *Howards End*; *Scent of a Woman*.

Best Director: Clint Eastwood, for *Unforgiven*. Nominations: Robert Altman, for *The Player*; Martin Brest, for *Scent of a Woman*; James Ivory, for *Howards End*; Neil Jordan, for *The Crying Game*.

Best Actor: Al Pacino, in *Scent of a Woman*. Nominations: Robert Downey Jr, in *Chaplin*; Clint Eastwood, in *Unforgiven*; Stephen Rea, in *The Crying Game*; Denzel Washington, in *Malcolm X*.

Best Actress: Emma Thompson, in *Howards End*. Nominations: Catherine Deneuve, in *Indochine*; Mary McDonnell, in *Passion Fish*; Michelle Pfeiffer, in *Love Field*; Susan Sarandon, in *Lorenzo's Oil*.

Best Supporting Actor: Gene Hackman, in *Unforgiven*. Nominations: Jaye Davidson, in *The Crying Game*; Jack Nicholson, in *A Few Good Men*; Al Pacino, in *Glengarry Glen Ross*; David Paymer, in *Mr Saturday Night*.

Best Supporting Actress: Marisa Tomei, in *My Cousin Vinny*. Nominations: Judy Davis, in *Husbands and Wives*; Joan Plowright, in *Enchanted April*; Vanessa Redgrave, in *Howards End*; Miranda Richardson, in *Damage*.

Best Original Screenplay: Neil Jordan, for *The Crying Game*. Nominations: Woody Allen, for *Husbands and Wives*; George Miller and Nick Enright, for *Lorenzo's Oil*; John Sayles, for *Passion Fish*; David Webb Peoples, for *Unforgiven*.

Best Screenplay Adaptation: Ruth Prawer Jhabvala, for *Howards End*. Nominations: Peter Barnes, for *Enchanted April*; Michael Tolkin, for *The Player*; Richard Friedenberg, for *A River Runs Through It*;

Director/producer/actor Clint Eastwood is comforted by Anna Thomson in a scene from his Oscar-winning Unforgiven

Bo Goldman, for *Scent of a Woman*.

Best Cinematography: Philippe Rousselot, for *A River Runs Through It*. Nominations: Stephen H. Burum, for *Hoffa*; Tony Pierce-Roberts, for *Howards End*; Robert Fraisse, for *The Lover*; Jack N. Green, for *Unforgiven*.

Best Editing: Joel Cox, for *Unforgiven*. Nominations: Frank J. Urioste, for *Basic Instinct*; Kant Pan, for *The Crying Game*; Robert Leighton, for *A Few Good Men*; Geraldine Peroni, for *The Player*.

Best Original Score: Alan Menken, for *Aladdin*. Nominations: Jerry Goldsmith, for *Basic Instinct*; John Barry, for *Chaplin*; Richard Robbins, for *Howards End*; Mark Isham, for *A River Runs Through It*.

Best Original Song: 'A Whole New World', from *Aladdin*, music by Alan Menken, lyrics by Tim Rice. Nominations: 'Beautiful Maria of My Soul', from *The Mambo Kings*, music by Robert Kraft, lyrics by Arne Glimcher; 'Friend Like Me', from *Aladdin*, music by Menken, lyrics by Howard Ashman; 'I Have Nothing', from *The Bodyguard*, music by David Foster, lyrics by Linda Thompson; 'Run To You', from *The Bodyguard*, music by Jud Friedman, lyrics by Allan Rich.

Best Art Direction: Luciana Arrighi (art direction) and Ian Whitaker (set decoration), for *Howards End*. Nominations: Thomas Sanders (art) and Garrett Lewis (set), for *Bram Stoker's Dracula*; Stuart Craig (art) and Chris A. Butler (set), for *Chaplin*; Ferdinando Scarfiotti (art) and Linda DeScenna (set), for *Toys*; Henry Bumstead (art) and Janice Blackie-Goodine (set), for *Unforgiven*.

Best Costume Design: Eiko Ishioka, for *Bram Stoker's Dracula*. Nominations: Sheena Napier, for *Enchanted April*; Jenny Beavan and John Bright, for *Howards End*; Ruth Carter, for *Malcolm X*; Albert Wolsky, for *Toys*.

Best Sound: Chris Jenkins, Doug Hemphill, Mark Smith and Simon Kaye, for *The Last of the Mohicans*. Nominations: Terry Porter, Mel Metcalfe, David J. Hudson and Doc Kane, for *Aladdin*; Kevin O'Connell, Rick Kline and Bob Eber, for *A Few Good Men*; Don Mitchell, Frank A. Montano, Rick Hart and Scott Smith, for *Under Siege*; Les Fresholtz, Vern Poore, Dick Alexander and Rob Young, for *Unforgiven*.

Best Sound Effects Editing: Tom C. McCarthy and David E. Stone, for *Bram Stoker's Dracula*. Nominations: Mark Mangini, for *Aladdin*; John Leveque and Bruce Stambler, for *Under Siege*.

Best Make-up: Greg Cannom, Michele Burke and Matthew W. Mungle, for *Bram Stoker's Dracula*. Nominations: Ve Neill, Ronnie Specter and Stan Winston, for *Batman Returns*; Ve Neill, Greg Cannom and John Blake, for *Hoffa*.

Best Visual Effects: Ken Ralston, Doug Chiang, Doug Smythe and Tom Woodruff, for *Death Becomes Her*. Nominations: Richard Edlund, Alec Gillis, Tom Woodruff Jr and George Gibbs, for *Alien 3*; Michael Fink, Craig Barron, John Bruno and Dennis Skotak, for *Batman Returns*.

Best Animated Short Film: *Mona Lisa Descending a Staircase*. Nominations: *Adam*; *Reci, Reci, Reci . . .*; *The Sandman*; *Screen Play*.

Best Live Action Short Film: *Omnibus*.

Nominations: *Contact*; *Cruise Control*; *The Lady in Waiting*; *Swan Song*.

Best Documentary Feature: *The Panama Deception*. Nominations: *Changing Our Minds: The Story of Dr Evelyn Hooker*; *Fires of Kuwait*; *Liberators: Fighting on Two Fronts in World War II*; *Music For the Movies: Bernard Herrmann*.

Best Documentary Short: *Educating Peter*. Nominations: *At the Edge of Conquest: The Journey of Chief Wai-Wai*; *Beyond Imagining: Margaret Anderson and the 'Little Review'*; *The Colours of My Father: A Portrait of Sam Borenstein*; *When Abortion was Illegal: Untold Stories*.

Best Foreign Language Film: *Indochine* (France). Nominations: *Close to Eden* (Russia); *Daens* (Belgium); *Schtonk!* (Germany).

Honorary Oscar: Federico Fellini.

Jean Hersholt Humanitarian Award: Elizabeth Taylor, Audrey Hepburn.

The Australian Film Critics' Circle Awards, 26 March 1993

Best Film: *Strictly Ballroom*.

Best Actor: Russell Crowe, in *Romper Stomper*.

Best Actress: Lisa Harrow, in *The Last Days of Chez Nous*.

Best Supporting Actor: Barry Otto, in *Strictly Ballroom*; tying with Bill Hunter, in *Strictly Ballroom* and *The Last Days of Chez Nous*.

Best Supporting Actress: the late Pat Thomson, in *Strictly Ballroom*.

Best Director: Baz Lurhmann, for *Strictly Ballroom*.

Best Screenplay Adaptation: Lurhmann and Craig Pearce, for *Strictly Ballroom*.

Best Original Screenplay: Helen Garner, for *The Last Days of Chez Nous*.

Best Photography: Peter James, for *Black Robe*.

Best Music: The late Georges Delerue, for *Black Robe*.

Best Documentary: *Black Harvest*.

Best Foreign Film: *Raise the Red Lantern*, by Zhang Yimou (China).

Best English Language Foreign Film: *The Player*, by Robert Altman (USA).

The Australian Film Institute Awards, 16 October 1992

Best Film: *Strictly Ballroom*.

Best Actor: Russell Crowe, for *Romper Stomper*.

Best Actress, Lisa Harrow, for *The Last Days of Chez Nous*.

Best Supporting Actor: Barry Otto, for *Strictly Ballroom*.

Best Supporting Actress: the late Pat Thomson, for *Strictly Ballroom*.

Best Director: Baz Luhrmann, for *Strictly Ballroom*.

Best Screenplay: Luhrmann and Craig Pearce, for *Strictly Ballroom*.

Best Cinematography: Peter James, for *Black Robe*.

Best Editing: Jill Bilcock, for *Strictly Ballroom*.

Best Production Design: Catherine Martin, for *Strictly Ballroom*.

Best Costumes: Angus Strathie, for *Strictly Ballroom*.

Best Documentary: *Black Harvest*.

Best Foreign Film: *Truly, Madly, Deeply*, by Anthony Minghella (UK).

The 43rd Berlin International Film Festival, February 1993

Golden Bear for Best Film: *The Woman From the Lake of Scented Souls*, by Xie Fei (China); tying with *The Wedding Banquet*, by Ang Lee (Taiwan–USA).

Silver Bear, Special Jury Prize: *Arizona Dream*, by Emir Kusturica (USA).

Best Director: Andrew Birkin, for *The Cement Garden* (Germany–UK–France).

Best Actor: Denzel Washington, in *Malcolm X* (USA).

Best Actress: Michelle Pfeiffer, in *Love Field* (USA).

Special Silver Bears: *The Sun of the Wakeful* (Georgia); *Samba Traore* (Burkina Faso).

The Blue Angel (new prize for European features): *Young Werther*, by Jacques Doillon (France).

Children's Jury (Children's Festival), First Prize: *Jasper's Ghost*, by Brita Wielopolska (Denmark).

Wolfgang Staudte Film Prize: *Laws of Gravity*, by Nick Gomez (USA).

The 1992 British Academy of Film and Television Arts Awards, 21 March 1993

Best Film: *Howards End*, by James Ivory.

David Lean Award for Best Direction: Robert Altman, for *The Player*.

Best Original Screenplay: Woody Allen, for *Husbands and Wives*.

Best Adapted Screenplay: Michael Tolkin, for *The Player*.

Best Actor: Robert Downey Jr, for *Chaplin*.

Best Actress: Emma Thompson, for *Howards End*.

Best Supporting Actor: Gene Hackman, for *Unforgiven*.

Best Supporting Actress: Miranda Richardson, for *Damage*.

Best Score: David Hirschfelder, for *Strictly Ballroom*.

Best Foreign Film: *Raise the Red Lantern*, by Zhang Yimou (China–Hong Kong).

Best Short Film: *Omnibus*.

Best Animated Short: *Daumier's Law*.

Best British Film: *The Crying Game*.

Best TV Film: *An Ungentlemanly Act* (BBC).

Special Award: Dame Maggie Smith.

The 1992 Canadian Film Awards ('Genies') 22 November 1992

Best Film: *Naked Lunch*.

Best Director: David Cronenberg, for *Naked Lunch*.

Best Actor: Tony Nardi, in *La Sarrasine*.

Best Actress: Janet Wright, in *Bordertown Cafe*.

Best Supporting Actor: Michael Hogan, in *Solitaire*.

Best Supporting Actress: Monique Mercure, in *Naked Lunch*.

Best Original Screenplay: Jean-Claude Lauzon, for *Léolo*.

Best Adapted Screenplay: Cronenberg, for *Naked Lunch*.

Best Cinematography: Peter Suschitzky, for *Naked Lunch*.

Best Editing: Michel Arcand, for *Léolo*.

Best Art Direction/Production Design: Carol Spier, for *Naked Lunch*.

Best Costumes: Francois Barbeau, for *Léolo*.

Best Overall Sound: Bryan Day, Peter Maxwell, David Appleby and Don White, for *Naked Lunch*.

Best Sound Editing: David Evans, Wayne Griffin, Janet Tattersall, Tony Currie, Andy Malcolm and Rick Cadger, for *Naked Lunch*.

Air Canada Award: Michael Spencer, president of Film Finances Canada.

Holly Hunter and Anna Paquin in Jane Campion's The Piano, *winner of the Palme d'Or at Cannes*

The 46th Cannes Film Festival Awards, 24 May 1993

Palme d'Or for Best Film shared by: *The Piano*, by Jane Campion (New Zealand); and *Farewell to My Concubine*, by Chen Kaige (China).

Grand Prix du Jury: *Faraway, So Close!*, by Wim Wenders (Germany).

Best Actor: David Thewlis, in *Naked* (UK).

Best Actress: Holly Hunter, in *The Piano*.

Best Director: Mike Leigh, for *Naked*.

Prix du Jury shared by: *The Puppetmaster*, by Hou Hsiao-hsien (Taiwan); and *Raining Stones*, by Ken Loach (UK).

Palme d'Or for Best Short: *Coffee and Cigarettes*, by Jim Jarmusch (USA).

Camera d'Or: *The Scent of Green Papaya*, by Tran Anh Hung (France).

Camera d'Or (special mention): *Friends*, by Elaine Proctor (UK–France).

Grand Prix Technique: *Mazeppa*, by Jean Gargonne and Vincent Arnardi (France).

Grand Prix Technique (special mention): *The Singing Trophy*, by Grant Lahood (New Zealand; short).

The International Critics' Prizes:

Best Film (in competition): *Farewell to My Concubine*.

Best Short: *The Debt*, by Bruno de Almeida (USA).

Best Film (other sections): *Child Murders*, by Ildiko Szabo (Hungary).

Jury: Louis Malle, Claudia Cardinale, Judy Davis, Emir Kusturica, Tom Luddy, Gary Oldman, etc.

The 33rd Cartagena, Colombia, International Film Festival, March 1993

Best Film: *Mascaró, El Cazador, Americano* (Chile).

Best Director: Eliseo Subiela, for *El Lado Oscuro del Corezón* (Argentina).

Special Jury Prize: *Like Water for Chocolate* (Mexico).

Best First Film: *La Frontera*, directed by Ricardo Larraín (Chile).

Best Screenplay: *You Only Live Once – La Vida Esuna Sola* (Peru).

Best Actor: Patricio Contreras, in *La Frontera*.

Best Actress: Gloria Lazo, in *La Frontera*.

The David di Donatello Awards ('Davids'), Rome, June 1993

Best Film: *The Great Pumpkin*, by Francesca Archibugi.

Best Foreign Film: *Un Coeur en Hiver*, by Claude Sautet (France).

Best Director: Roberto Faenza, for *Jonah Who Lived in the Whale*; and Ricky Tognazzi, for *La Scorta*.

Best Actor: Sergio Castellitto, for *The Great Pumpkin*.

Best Actress: Antonella Ponziani, for *Verso Sud*.

Best Supporting Actor: Claudio Amendola, for *La Scorta*.

Best Supporting Actress: Marina Confalone, for *Arriva la Bufera*.

Best New Director: Mario Martone, for *Death of a Neapolitan Mathematician*.

Best Producer: Claudio Bonivento, for *La Scorta*.

Best Screenplay: Francesca Archibugi, for *The Great Pumpkin*.

Special Jury Prize: Carlo Cecchi.

Luchino Visconti Award: Edgar Reitz.

Franco Cristaldi Prize: Carlo Ludovico Bragaglia.

The 46th Edinburgh Film Festival, 15–30 August 1992

The Chaplin Award for Best First Feature film: shared by Bill Anderson's *Creatures of Light* and Vadim Jean and Gary Sinyor's *Leon the Pig Farmer*.

The Michael Powell Award for Best British Feature: Richard Spence's *You, Me and Marley*.

The Pressburger Award for Best First European Screenplay: Clas Lindberg's *Subterranean Secrets* (Sweden).

FIRRESCI Jury Award: Zhang Yuan's *Mama* (China).

Post Office McLaren Animation Award: Piotr Dumala's *A is for Autumn*.

Channel Four Young Filmmakers' Award: Stuart Robertson's *Road to Alice* (Australia).

The 'Evening Standard' 1992 Film Awards, London, 31 January 1993

Best Film: *Howards End*.

Best Actor: Daniel Day-Lewis, for *The Last of the Mohicans*.

Best Actress: Emma Thompson, for *Howards End* and *Peter's Friends*.

Best Screenplay: Terence Davies, for *The Long Day Closes*.

Best Technical Achievement: Sue Gibson, for *Hear My Song*.

Most Promising Newcomer: Peter Chelsom, for *Hear My Song*.

The Peter Sellers Comedy Award: Kenneth Branagh, for *Peter's Friends*.

The 1993 Fantasporto International Film Festival, Oporto, Portugal, February 1993

Best Film: *Braindead*, by Peter Jackson (New Zealand).

Best Director: Jean-Claude Lauzon, for *Léolo* (Canada).

Best Actress: Evangelina Sosa, in *Angel de Fuego* (Mexico).

Best Actor: Harvey Keitel, in *Bad Lieutenant* (USA).

Best Screenplay: Billy Bob Thornton and Tom Epperson, for *One False Move* (USA).

New Director's Award: Tom Kalin, for *Swoon* (USA).

The 18th French Academy (César) Awards, March 1993

Best Film: *Savage Nights*, by the late Cyril Collard.

Best Director: Claude Sautet, for *Un Coeur en Hiver*.

Best Actor: Claude Rich, in *Le Souper*.

Best Actress: Catherine Deneuve, in *Indochine*.

Best Supporting Actor: Andre Dussolier, in *Un Coeur en Hiver*.

Best Supporting Actress: Dominique Blanc, in *Indochine*.

Best New Actor: Emmanuel Salinger, in *La Sentinelle*.

Best New Actress: Romane Bohringer, in *Savage Nights*.

Best First Film: *Savage Nights*.

Best Screenplay: Coline Serreau, for *La Crise*.

Best Photography: Robert Fraisse, for *The Lover*.

Best Editing: Lise Beaulieu, for *Savage Nights*.

Best Music: Gabriel Yared, for *The Lover*.

Best Costumes: Sylvie de Segonzac, for *Le Souper*.

The late director/writer/actor Cyril Collard in Savage Nights, *recipient of the Best Film award at the French Césars*

Best Set Design: Jacques Bufnoir, for *Indochine*.

Best Foreign Film: *High Heels*, by Pedro Almodovar (Spain).

The 7th Goya Awards by the Spanish Academy of Arts and Sciences, March 1993

Best Director and Best Film: Fernando Trueba, for *Belle Epoque*.

Best Actor: Alfredo Landa, in *La Marrana*.

Best Actress: Ariadna Gil, in *Belle Epoque*.

New Director: Julio Medem, for *Vacas*.

Best Original Screenplay: Fernando

Trueba, Rafael Azcona and Jose Luis Garcia, for *Belle Epoque*.

Best Cinematography: Jose Luis Garcia, for *Belle Epoque*.

Best European Film: *Indochine* (France).

The 50th Hollywood Foreign Press Association (Golden Globe) Awards, January 1993

Best Film – Drama: *Scent of a Woman*.

Best Film – Comedy or Musical: *The Player*.

Best Actor – Drama: Al Pacino, in *Scent of a Woman*.

Best Actress – Drama: Emma Thompson, in *Howards End*.

Best Actor – Comedy or Musical: Tim Robbins, in *The Player*.

Best Actress – Comedy or Musical: Miranda Richardson, in *Enchanted April*.

Best Supporting Actor: Gene Hackman, in *Unforgiven*.

Best Supporting Actress: Joan Plowright, in *Enchanted April*.

Best Director: Clint Eastwood, for *Unforgiven*.

Best Screenplay: Bo Goldman, for *Scent of a Woman*.

Best Original Score: Alan Menken, for *Aladdin*.

Best Original Song: 'A Whole New World', by Alan Menken and Tim Rice, for *Aladdin*.

Best Foreign Language Film: *Indochine*, by Regis Wargnier (France).

The 28th Karlovy Film Festival, Czechoslovakia, 9–18 July 1992

Crystal Globe for Best Film: *Krapatchouk*, by Enrique Gabriel Lipchutz (Belgium–France–Spain).

Best Actress: Yevdokiya Germanova, in *Crecked* (Russia).

Best Actor: Guy Pion, in *Krapatchouk*.

Special Jury Prize: Moses Makhmalbaf's *Once Upon a Time, the Movies* (Iran).

International Critics Award: shared by *Krapatchouk* and *Once Upon a Time, the Movies*.

City of Karlovy Prize: Hussein Erkenov's *The Cold* (Russia).

The 45th Locarno Film Festival, Switzerland, 5–15 August 1992

Golden Leopard, Premier Prize: Clara Law's *Autumn Moon – Qiuyue* (Hong Kong–Japan).

Silver Leopard: Darezhahn Omirbaev's *Kairat* (Kazakhstan).

Bronze Leopard: Philip Groning's *Terrorists – Die Terroristen!* (Germany).

Fourth Prize: Gidi Dar's *Eddie King* (Israel).

Special Jury Prize: Heinz Butler and Manfred Eicher's *Holocene – Holozaen* (Switzerland–Germany).

Critics' Prize: shared by Reni Mertens's *Kairat* and Walter Mari's *Requiem* (both Switzerland).

Swissair Special Prize: Jean Pierre Bekolo's *Quartier Mozart* (Cameroons–France).

The 14th London Film Critics' Circle Awards ('The Alfs'), 22 February 1993

Best Film: *Unforgiven*, by Clint Eastwood.

Best Actor: Robert Downey Jr, in *Chaplin*.

Best Actress: Judy Davis, in *Husbands and Wives*, *Barton Fink* and *Naked Lunch*.

Best Director: Robert Altman, for *The Player*.

Best Screenwriter: Michael Tolkin, for *The Player*.

Non-British Newcomer of the Year: Baz Luhrmann, director and screenwriter of *Strictly Ballroom*.

Best British Film: *Howards End*.

British Producer of the Year: Stephen Woolley, for *The Crying Game*.

British Director of the Year: Neil Jordan, for *The Crying Game*.

British Screenwriter of the Year: Neil Jordan, for *The Crying Game*.

British Actor of the Year: Daniel Day-Lewis, for *The Last of the Mohicans*.

British Actress of the Year: Emma Thompson, for *Howards End*.

British Newcomer of the Year: Peter Chelsom, director and co-screenwriter of *Hear My Song*.

British Technical Achievement of the Year: Roger Deakins, cinematographer of *Barton Fink*.

Best Foreign Language Film: *Raise the Red Lantern* (China–Hong Kong).

Dilys Powell Award: Freddie Young, cinematographer and director.

Special Award: Freddie Francis, cinematographer, director and producer.

The Los Angeles Film Critics' Association Awards, December 1992

Best Film: *Unforgiven*.

Best Actor: Clint Eastwood, in *Unforgiven*.

Best Actress: Emma Thompson, in *Howards End*.

Best Supporting Actor: Gene Hackman, in *Unforgiven*.

Best Supporting Actress: Judy Davis, in *Husbands and Wives*.

Best Director: Clint Eastwood, for *Unforgiven*.

Best Screenplay: David Webb Peoples, for *Unforgiven*.

Best Foreign Film: *The Crying Game* (UK).

The National Board of Review, December 1992

Best Film: *Howards End*.

Best Actor: Jack Lemmon, in *Glengarry Glen Ross*.

Best Actress: Emma Thompson, in *Howards End*.

Best Supporting Actress: Judy Davis, in *Husbands and Wives*.

Best Director: James Ivory, for *Howards End*.

Best Foreign Film: *Indochine* (France).

The 58th New York Film Critics' Circle Awards, December 1992

Best Film: *The Player*.

Best Actor: Denzel Washington, in *Malcolm X*.

Best Actress: Emma Thompson, in *Howards End*.

Best Supporting Actor: Gene Hackman, in *Unforgiven*.

Best Supporting Actress: Miranda Richardson, in *The Crying Game*, *Damage* and *Enchanted April*.

Best Director: Robert Altman, for *The Player*.

Best Screenplay: Neil Jordan, for *The Crying Game*.

Best Cinematography: Jean Lepine, for *The Player*.

Best New Director: Allison Anders, for *Gas Food Lodging*.

Best Foreign Film: *Raise the Red Lantern* (China–Hong Kong).

The San Sebastian Film Festival, 17–26 September 1992

Golden Shell for Best Film: *A Place in the World – Un Lugar en el Mundo*, by Adolpho Aristaraine (Argentina).
Silver Shell for Best Director: Goran Markovic, for *Tito and I – Tito I Ya* (Serbia).
Special Jury Prize: *Passing Farewell – Zwoiniena Z Zycia*, by Waldemar Krzystek (Poland–France).
Silver Shell for Best Actor: Roberto Sosa, in Alex Cox's *Highway Patrolman* (Mexico).
Special Silver Shell prize to child actor Dimitri Vonjov in *Tito I Ya*.
Best Creative Documentary: *JFK Assassination*, by John Barbour (USA).
FIPRESCI International Critics' Prize: *Zwoiniena Z Zycia*.
Donostia Prize (for career): Lauren Bacall.

The 38th Taormina International Film Festival, Italy, July 1992

Best Film: *Once Upon a Time, the Movies*, by Moses Makhmalbaf (Iran).
Best Director: Ryu Murakami, for *Tokyo Decadence Topaz* (Japan).
Best Actor: Juanjo Puigcorbe, in *Un Paraguas Para Tres* (Spain).
Best Actress: Marie Trintignant, in *Betty* (France).
Special Mentions by the Jury: Claude Chabrol's *Betty* (France) and Geoffrey Wright's *Romper Stomper* (Australia).

The 5th Tokyo International Film Festival, 25 September – 4 October 1992

Gold 'Young Cinema' Prize: *Vacas*, by Julio Medem (Spain).
Silver Prize: *The Peach Blossom Land*, by Stan Lai (Taiwan).
Bronze Prize: *Bob Roberts*, by Tim Robbins (USA).
Tokyo Grand Prize: *White Badge*, by Chung Yi-Young (Korea).
Special Jury Prize: *Ai Ni Tsuite Tokyo*, by Mitsuo Yaganimachi (Japan).
Best Director: Chung Yi-Young.
Best Actor: Max von Sydow, in *The Silent Touch*.

Best Actress: Lumi Cavazos, in *Como Agua Para Chocolate* (Mexico).

The 27th US National Society of Film Critics Awards, January 1993

Best Film: *Unforgiven*.
Best Actor: Stephen Rea, in *The Crying Game*.
Best Actress: Emma Thompson, in *Howards End*.
Best Supporting Actor: Gene Hackman, in *Unforgiven*.
Best Supporting Actress: Judy Davis, in *Husbands and Wives*.
Best Director: Clint Eastwood, in *Unforgiven*.
Best Screenplay: David Webb Peoples, for *Unforgiven*.

The Valencia Film Festival, Spain, 15–23 October 1992

Golden Palm for Best Film: *Virginia*, by Srdjan Karanovic (Yugoslavia).
Silver Palm: *Amazing Grace*, by Amos Gutman (Israel).
Bronze Palm: *Verbal Letters*, by Latif Abdel Hanid (Syria).
Best Acting Awards: Arnon Zadock and Muhamad Bari, in *Amazing Grace*.

The 37th Valladolid Film Festival Awards, Spain, 23–31 October 1992

Golden Spike for Best Film: shared between *Léolo*, by Jean-Claude Lauzon (Canada–France), and *The Long Day Closes*, by Terence Davies (UK).
Silver Spike: *Daens*, by Stijn Coninx (Belgium).
Special Jury Award: *Whistle Stop – Estacion de Paso*, by Gracia Qurejeta (Spain).
Best Actress: Brigitte Rouan, in *Olivier, Olivier* (France).
Best Actor: shared between Al Pacino, Jack Lemmon, Alec Baldwin, Ed Harris, Jonathan Pryce, Alan Arkin and Kevin Spacey, in *Glengarry Glen Ross* (USA).
Best New Director: Sussanne Bier, for *Freud Flyttar Hemifran* (Switzerland).

Best Cinematography: Renato Berta, for *Swisschaison* (Switzerland).

The 49th Venice International Film Festival Awards, 12 September 1992

Golden Lion for Best Film: *The Story of Qiu Ju*, by Zhang Yimou (China).
Special Jury Prize: *Death of a Neapolitan Mathematician*, by Mario Martone (Italy).
Silver Lions: *Jamon Jamon*, by Bigas Luna (Spain); *Un Coeur en Hiver*, by Claude Sautet (France); *Hotel de Lux*, by Dan Pita (Romania).
Best Actor: Jack Lemmon, in *Glengarry Glen Ross* (USA).
Best Actress: Gong Li, in *The Story of Qiu Ju*.
Senate Medal: *Guelwaar*, by Ousmane Sembene (France–UK).
FIPRESCI International Critics' Jury Prize: *Un Coeur en Hiver*; and *Leon the Pig Farmer*, by Vadim Jean and Gary Sinyor (UK).
Golden Lions for career achievement: Francis Ford Coppola, Jeanne Moreau and Paolo Villaggio.
Jury: Dennis Hopper, Peter Bogdanovich, Anne Brochet, Neil Jordan, Hanif Kureishi, Ennio Morricone, Sheila Whitaker etc.

The 12th Vevey International Comedy Film Festival, Switzerland, 24–9 July 1992

The Golden Cane Grand Prize: *Curse the Day I Met You* (Italy).
Best Actress: Margherita Buy, in *Curse the Day I Met You*.
Best Actor: James Le Gros, in Stacy Cochran's *My New Gun* (USA).
Special Jury Prize: *Menialy – The Big Exchange*, by Georgei Shengelia (Russia).
Prix du Public: *La Postiere*, by Gilles Carle (Canada).

The 2nd Viareggio 'Noir in Festival', Italy, June 1992

Best Film: *Happy Birthday Detective*, by Doris Dorrie (Germany).
Best Actor: Jeremy Irons, in *Kafka*.
Best Actress: Theresa Russell, in *Cold Heaven*.
The Noir 92 Sipra Prize: *Afraid of the Dark*, by Mark Peploe (UK).

Index